Recent American Opera

A PRODUCTION GUIDE

OTHER COLUMBIA UNIVERSITY PRESS REFERENCE BOOKS

The Columbia Granger's Index to Poetry, Ninth Edition
Edith P. Hazen and Deborah J. Fryer, eds.

The Concise Columbia Book of Poetry
William Harmon, ed.

The Concise Columbia Dictionary of Quotations
Robert Andrews, ed.

The Concise Columbia Encyclopedia

The Columbia Granger's Guide to Poetry Anthologies
William Katz and Linda Sternberg Katz, eds.

Recent American Opera

A PRODUCTION GUIDE

Rebecca Hodell Kornick

COLUMBIA UNIVERSITY PRESS
NEW YORK

Columbia University Press
New York Oxford

Library of Congress Cataloging-in-Publication Data

Kornick, Rebecca Hodell.
Recent American opera : a production guide / Rebecca Hodell Kornick.
p. cm.
Includes bibliographical references and index.
ISBN 0-231-06920-0
1. Opera—United States—20th century—Production and direction.
I. Title.
MT955.K82 1990
792.5′0232′0973—dc20 90-2576
CIP
MN

Casebound editions of Columbia University Press books are Smyth-sewn and printed on permanent and durable acid-free paper

Book design by Cathryn S. Aison

Printed in the United States of America
c 10 9 8 7 6 5 4 3 2 1

To Joe, Adria and Adam

CONTENTS

PREFACE

There have been several hundred operas written by American composers just in the past twenty years. *The Central Opera Service Directory of American and Foreign Contemporary Operas* lists 455 American operas written between 1975 and 1980 alone. The number of American opera companies has also continued to grow. Most operas written in America today, however, if performed at all, are performed once, even though audience response and reviews may be favorable. Nevertheless, Maria Rich's 1989 *Opera News* survey shows that 400 different American contemporary operas and 279 different musicals were performed by the 1,285 opera organizations in this country in the 1989 season. Clearly, the demand for contemporary works exists. And yet, one-time premieres or the repetition of a few safe works from the standard repertoire will not insure the future of American opera as a living art. The goal of this book is to stimulate the production, development, and repertory reworking of contemporary American works, so that more of these works can win places in the standard opera repertoire.

This production guide is designed to make discovery of new works a simpler process for opera producers, coaches, performers, and opera historians. It provides ready access to vital information on 213 American opera/music theatre works. Having spent several years researching these works, I can fully understand why every opera company cannot afford to take the time to find them. The sheer logistics of locating the scores alone would be prohibitive since very few are available through music libraries or stores. Most scores are available only directly from the composer or from publishers for rental only.

(Once located, however, all are more than willing to offer them for perusal).

The first task on beginning this book was to find a criterion for selecting works that would be included. The reference books *Opera Production I* and *Opera Production II,* by Quaintance Eaton, well-used tools of the business, provided one point of departure for the selection of American works. Of the 213 works cited in the following pages, most were premiered after 1972 (when research ended on *Opera Production II*) or are earlier works not included in the *Opera Production* books. In addition, each of the works included has received at least a premiere performance, and all but a handful have been subsequently reviewed by major publications. The recent trend toward inclusion of musical theater works in the seasons of opera organizations also prompted me to include many of those works deemed suitable for the resources of opera companies.

The reader will find 180 complete entries on the pages that follow. A full explanation of the format for those entries is provided in the Introduction. I have also included incomplete entries for 33 additional operas. These were works that have been premiered for which reviews were found, but which for a number of reasons we were not able to include in this volume—I may have traced the information on the work too late for inclusion or in some cases may not have found the score, etc. My apologies to the composers involved, but I did want to give the interested reader the opportunity to pursue this information on his own. One of the best ways to learn more about a work would be to call the performing companies, which are usually very helpful.

With regard to works not included in this volume, I welcome any information on operas which have received premiere performances. In light of the constantly growing repertory, information which could be included in a revised edition or a volume 2 is welcome. Please contact me through Columbia University Press.

ACKNOWLEDGMENTS

Compiling the operas in *RECENT AMERICAN OPERA* was certainly not a one-woman job. From its inception as my doctoral dissertation, I owe my thanks to two professors from Northwestern University: Dr. Judith Schwartz, for careful editing and astute criticism, and Elizabeth Fischer for moral support. Alan Stone at the Chicago Opera Theatre, Ardis Krainik at the Lyric Opera of Chicago, Robert Gay, Professor Emeritus from Northwestern University, and Charles MacKay at the Opera Theatre of Saint Louis, provided words of encouragement and letters of support that helped me obtain two research grants from the Opera–Musical Theater program of the National Endowment for the Arts. Because of these grants, I was able to enlist the aid of several researchers. Thanks especially go to Michael Nealon and Jenny Doctor, who, through many months of work, shared my enthusiasm for viewing each score. Claudia Lasareff-Mironoff, Helen Hudgens, and Jeffrey Stirling also contributed wholeheartedly to keeping the project moving.

Since so much of our work revolved around obtaining the 180 scores, I must thank some of the people who helped make those scores available. Don Roberts, Head Music Librarian at Northwestern University, was able to obtain several of the published scores for Northwestern's collection, while librarians Ruth Young and Jim Hobbs fielded numerous questions. Eero Richmond at the American Music Center was extremely helpful—the center certainly proved to be a great resource. Richard Barrios at Boosey & Hawkes, Arthur Cohn at Carl Fischer, Gary Williams at Dunvagen, Eugene Moon at Galaxy Music, George Sturm at Music Associates of America, Marc

Alexander Katz at Music Theatre International, Wayne Alan Blood at The Rodgers and Hammerstein Theatre Library, Leslie Brooks and Ella Winfield at G. Schirmer, Sargeant Aborn at Tams-Witmark Music Library, and Maria Iannacone at Theodore Presser were all generous about lending scores, as well as in answering numerous questions.

Several individual composers also provided information, scores, tapes, etc.: Seymour Barab, Paul Dresher, Philip Hageman, Lee Hoiby, Ulysses Kay, Frederick Koch, Tod Machover, William Neil, Robert Xavier Rodriguez, Eric Salzman (for both his own works and the American Music Theatre Festival). Peter Schickele, Judith Anne Still Headlee (for the estate of her father, William Grant Still), Richard Wargo, Hugo Weisgall, Dan Welcher, and Jack Eric Williams. In fact, very few of my letters of query went unanswered. I only wish I had had the time to pursue those composers whose entries I was not able to complete.

Opera companies lent their support as well: Jim Chambers at the Houston Grand Opera, Chris Stollery at the Lyric Opera Center for American Artists, Russell Patterson at the Lyric Opera of Kansas City, Kathy Davis Graves at the Minnesota Opera, and Jeff Thurston at the Opera Theatre of Saint Louis.

Suggestions and words of encouragement came from John Ludwig at the National Institute for Music Theater, Ann Smith at the Opera for the Eighties and Beyond program of Opera America, and Ted Chapin at the Rodgers & Hammerstein Foundation. A special note of thanks goes to Quaintance Eaton, who was my original inspiration and whom I've had the pleasure of knowing better.

In addition, I must thank Dr. Thomas Bennett at Loyola University of Chicago for making copying services available. My thanks also goes to James Raimes of Columbia University Press for his patience, as the process of locating the more obscure works, as well the birth of my daughter, Adria, made things move a bit more slowly than we anticipated.

INTRODUCTION

An explanation of the format of the entries herein should clarify any questions the reader may have. Entries are listed alphabetically by composer, with each work carefully described in the format that follows.

Introductory Paragraph. Genre classification of the drama; number of acts, scenes, number of sets (where designated), and length of work in minutes; style and structure of the music; unique orchestral requirements, description of vocal writing; unusual performance requirements.

Dramatic classifications include such categories as tragedy, comedy, historical drama, pageant, etc.

The timings in minutes are given early in the entry, so that a producer can quickly determine whether he is dealing with an opera that will fill a whole program or one that must be combined with others. To aid in the programming of shorter operas, see the "Index by Duration" that includes the exact timings of shorter operas (those of less than 90 minutes duration).

The wide diversity of styles represented here was one of the most exciting aspects of perusing each of these scores. Yet this fact and the eclecticism often found within a single work made brief descriptions of the music a difficult task. A number of harmonic styles are represented: tonal; dissonant, yet largely tonal; atonal; serial; aleatoric; microtonal; those with elements of minimalism; those that use vernacular elements such as jazz, blues, folk, religious, rap, rock, funk; and those that use electronic and computer music. The comments in the opening section were drawn from perusal of vocal-piano scores, generally without the aid of recordings. For this reason, a great attempt was made to include additional descriptions of the music in the "Reviews" section of each entry, quotations by those who actually heard the music performed.

Structural descriptions designate those operas that are through-composed or those that include set numbers. Orchestral requirements attempt to give the reader of sense of the demands on the orchestra—whether there is a great deal of purely orchestral music or whether it merely doubles the singers. Descriptions of the vocal writing classify the vocal lines as melodious, disjunct, etc., and also give an idea of special demands on the singers. Unusual requirements such as quarter-tone tunings, large choral forces, etc., alert the reader immediately to other unique aspects of a work, whatever they may be.

Second Paragraph. Author and source of the libretto; the commission, if any; the company, place, and date of the premiere; place and date of other performances with versions or adaptations noted; recordings.

The names of performing companies provide the reader with the opportunity to contact producers for additional information, tapes of performances, etc. Available professional recordings are listed, where available, with record company and label numbers given. Interested readers may want to request performance tapes from composers or performing companies.

Plot. Setting of the action; act and scene divisions (optional); synopsis of plot.

Scene divisions are given only for long works where the composer or librettist specifies traditional scene changes. Most of the other works suggest more abstract stagings.

Plot synopses for unfamiliar works convey the story, as well as the relationships of major characters. These are not, however, act-by-act descriptions.

Production requirements. Subcategories include Major Roles, Supporting Roles, Minor Roles, Bit Roles, Speaking Roles, and Mute Roles. The following information is listed after each character's name: his relationship to other characters, where clarification is required; voice type for all roles; for major and supporting roles, the extremes of range with optional notes or any unique requirements of the role given in parentheses. The following abbreviations are used:

s: soprano	buf: buffo
m-s: mezzo-soprano	col: coloratura

a: alto

c: contralto

t: tenor

bar-t: bari-tenor

bar: baritone

bs-bar: bass-baritone

bs: bass

dram: dramatic

fals: falsetto

lyr: lyric

opt: optional note

spin: spinto

tess: tessitura

tr: treble

Extremes of range are delineated by numbering notes falling within each octave, with the octave above low C labeled "1," etc., as shown below.

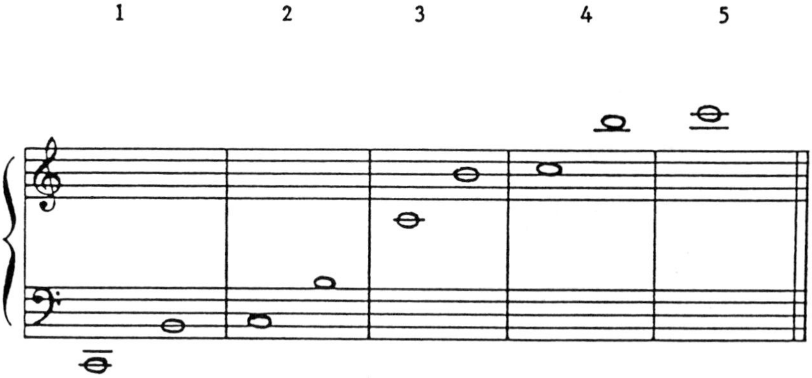

Under the category of Speaking Roles, the reader will note that the musical theater entries differ in one respect: they do not include a complete listing of all speaking roles but focus on the musical resources required to mount a production.

In addition to vocal roles, the following categories are listed where they apply to the work.

Chorus. SATB (soprano, alto, tenor, bass), the abbreviations representing the minimum number of chorus divisions shown in the score. Additional divisi and exact numbers required are provided when the composer specifies them.

Ballet. The type and number of dancers required is provided when designated in the score.

Orchestra. The number of each type of instrument required is given. An instrument in parentheses after another one means that the instrumentalist plays both. For example, 2 fls (picc) indicates that the production requires two flutists, with the second doubling on piccolo.

Abbreviations used are shown below.

fl: flute	bs drum: bass drum
picc: piccolo	sn drum: snare drum
rec: recorder	perc: percussion
ob: oboe	accord: accordian
Eng hrn: English horn	cel: celeste
cl: clarinet	glock: glockenspiel
bs cl: bass clarinet	harm: harmonium
bsn: bassoon	harpsi: harpsichord
cont bsn: contra bassoon	synth: synthesizer
hrn: horn	vib: vibraphone
trp: trumpet	xyl: xylophone
trb: trombone	vln: violin
cor: cornet	vla: viola
sax: saxophone	vcl: violoncello
timp: timpani	cb: string bass
	mand: mandolin

Material. FS–P (full score–parts), VS (vocal score). This section names the publisher from which the full score, the vocal score, or the orchestral parts may be rented or obtained. Full addresses for publishers can be found in the back of the book under "Publishers and Other Sources." For most operas, vocal scores and full scores are usually rented. In addition, indicated here are scores that are available for perusal from the American Music Center. This resource enables interested parties to view the scores (for only the cost of return mail) without having to purchase or rent before a production decision has been reached.

Reviews. Full publication information is given about these articles. Reviews are included to offer interested producers, directors, singers, and opera buffs first-hand quotations about new and unusual works. The reader will note, therefore, that musicals that had substantial Broadway runs and for which recordings and scores are more readily available do not include quotations from reviews. The selected quotations are not offered as judgments but rather to give a feeling of the ambiance or for the specific highlights in these new works.

A word of caution to those who may draw definitive conclusions from reviews of premieres: Nicolas Slonimsky stated that his purpose in collecting his *Lexicon of Musical Invective* was "to demonstrate that music is an art in progress, and that objections leveled at every musical innovator are all derived from the same psychological inhibition, which may be described as nonacceptance of the unfamiliar." The reviewers cited in this *Guide,* much like the historic ones in Slonimsky's volume, are undoubtedly "men of great culture . . . who . . . excel in the art of imaginative vituperation. . . . Their only failing [may be at times] . . . that they confuse their ingrained listening habits with the unalterable ideal of beauty and perfection."

One need only be reminded of this contrast in the following examples that refer to the same work. The day following the premiere of Alban Berg's *Wozzeck* in Berlin on December 14, 1925, Paul Zschorlick of the *Deutsche Zeitung* wrote: "In Berg's music there is not a trace of melody. There are only scraps, shreds, spasms and burps. Harmonically, the work is beyond discussion, for everything sounds wrong."[1]

This work might have been buried as a disaster after the first hearing, in which case it never would have received the status conferred upon it in a 1985 article in *Opera News:* "It seems safe to assume that Berg's operas (*Wozzeck* and *Lulu*) have found their place in the standard repertory."[2]

These comments are not intended to reflect negatively on the reviews in this volume but are cited to remind the reader to keep an open mind — to enjoy reading about these new works.

---

1. Nicolas Slonimsky, *Lexicon of Musical Invective* (2d ed., New York: Coleman-Ross, 1965), p. 3.
2. George Perle, "Martyr to His Profession," *Opera News* (January 19, 1985), p. 12.

Recent American Opera

A PRODUCTION GUIDE

THE PRODUCTION GUIDE

Alphabetical Listing by Composer

John Adams (1947–   )

NIXON IN CHINA

A historical, heroic drama. Two acts, six scenes (180 minutes with intermission). Some minimalist characteristics within a more quickly changing formal structure. Orchestration and style includes references to American popular music, jazz, and swing. Linear vocal lines contrast rhythmic patterns in orchestra.

Libretto by Alice Goodman. Co-commissioned by Houston Grand Opera, the Brooklyn Academy, Kennedy Center, and the Netherlands Opera. Premiere: Houston 10.22.87. Performances: Brooklyn 12.4.87; Washington, D.C. 4.88; Netherlands 6.88; Los Angeles 89. Recordings: De Waart/ Orchestra of St. Luke's. Complete: NONESUCH 79177–2. Excerpts: NONESUCH 79193.

PLOT

Setting: Peking, China, February 1972.

Act I, scene i: The Capital Airport near Peking; ii: The Imperial City; iii: The Great Hall of the People. Act II, i: Mrs. Nixon's sightseeing; ii: The Peking Opera; iii: The last night in Peking.

A large Chinese military honor-guard, Premier Chou En-lai and a group of officials wait as the "Spirit of '76" descends. As Nixon greets the officials, he expresses his thoughts, excitement and fears.

Chou, Mao, Nixon, Kissinger and Mao's secretaries meet, all expressing their contrasting philosophies at once. The crowded banquet which follows provides a colorful exchange of toasts by Chou and Nixon.

Pat Nixon is ushered to various sights, developing a sympatico with the guides, as she shares her philosophy of life and her vision of America.

The Nixons attend a performance of the ballet "The Red Detachment of Women." The action becomes surreal, when the Nixons rush in to defend virtue against a villanous warlord (played by Kissinger, in disguise). But Madame Chiang Ch'ing interrupts the chaos with her showpiece soliloquoy.

Finally, Nixon, Chou, and Mao appear in their respective bedrooms, revealing their past glories and human foibles.

PRODUCTION REQUIREMENTS

Major Roles. CHOU EN-LAI (bar): A♭1 to G3. NIXON (bar): A1 to A♭3. KISSINGER (bs): E1 to E3. MAO TSE-TUNG (helden t): C2 to B3. PAT NIXON (s): A2 to C5. CHIANG CH'ING (col s): C3 to D5 (high tessitura).

Supporting Roles. MAYO'S SECRETARIES: FIRST (m-s): B2 to G4, SECOND (c): G2 to D4, THIRD (c): E2 to C♯4.

Chorus. SATB.

Ballet. 8 required.

Orchestra. 2 fls, 2 obs, 3 cls, 4 saxs (s,a,t,bar), 3 trps, 3 trbs, 2 electric pianos, HX-1 synthesizer, strings (2–2–3–3–2), perc.

Material. FS–P and VS: Boosey & Hawkes.

REVIEWS

Stephanie von Buchau "Not Just an Entertainment," *Opera News* (October 1987), pp. 24–26

> "there is no sense of gimmicky, jarring, postmodernist juxtaposition. Adam's score [is] . . . very rich in its ability to express emotion."

> "Chiang Ch'ing launches [a] tremendous showpiece, . . . which . . . displays all the . . . fervor of China's demonic first lady."

> "Poetic, quiet, nonclimatic, the last scene . . . dies away like Debussy's *Pelleas et Melisande,* full of mature wisdom."

Peter G. Davis "Nixon—The Opera," *New York* (November 9, 1987), pp. 102–104

> "Madame Mao's devilish coloratura aria that climaxes the ballet is . . . a theatrical coup that should stop the show but doesn't. The last scene is even more musically uneventful and prosaic, as the intended visionary apotheosis meanders aimlessly."

> "*Nixon in China* looks terrific . . . from the spectacular landing of the presidential aircraft . . . to the dazzling poster art that decorates Madame Mao's ballet."

Manuela Hoelterhoff " 'Nixon' in Texas Sings for his (Chinese) Supper," *Wall Street Journal* (October 29, 1987), p. 20

> " . . . (Adam's) repetitive patterns are cut from a finer quality bolt than Philip Glass's. . . . Mr. Adam's field of arpeggios does not bloom with a thousand melodies, but 'Nixon' has many catchy moments."

> "The opera's one brilliant entertainment is a ballet scene . . . that finally cuts away from the tedious history lesson into a surrealist fantasy."

John von Rhein "Cowtown culture," *Chicago Tribune* (November 1, 1987), pp. 6–7

> "That 'Nixon' draws on the rich mother lode of American vernacular music — a fox trot here, funky Motown there — helps to explain its immediacy as well as its charm."

Michael Walsh "Stagecraft as Soulcraft," *Time* (November 9, 1987), p. 110

> "Progressing from the impersonal panoply of statecraft to an almost hallucinatory intimacy of soulcraft, the libretto, . . . written in couplets, . . . may sometimes be elliptical, but [is] . . . psychologically observant and very singable."

> "The banquet scene in the Great Hall of the People that concludes the first act becomes a brilliantly calibrated choral scene . . . punctuated by popping flashbulbs and delirious, crashing chords."

Bruce Adolphe (1955–   )

THE FALSE MESSIAH

Drama based on history and legend. Two acts, ten scenes (150 minutes). Harmonically conservative work. No overture, brief orchestral interludes between scenes, recitatives, arias, and conversational sections. Many Hebrew words used.

Libretto by Mel Gordon, based on the life of Shabtai Zvi, the Turkish Jew, who was hailed by his followers as "The Son of God." Premiere: Jewish Opera at the Y. New York City 4.9.83.

PLOT

Setting: 1663–1667.

Act I, scene i: A Polish monastery, changing to the old Jewish cemetery; ii: An old room in Gaza, Palestine, 1663; iii: Outside of merchant's house in the Jewish quarter of Smyrna, 1664; iv: A merchant's house in Amsterdam, 1664; v: By the Wailing Wall in Jerusalem, 1665. Act II, i: The port of Amsterdam, 1666; ii: The shore of Gallipoli, 1666; iii: Shabtai is lead by Turkish guards to the Grand Vizier's Council Room in Adrianople; iv: In a Moslem Castle at Dulcigno, Albania, 1667; v: De Souza's house in Amsterdam, 1667.

It was prophesied that a Jewish Messiah would emerge in 1666. Various events foreshadow the prophecy's fulfillment: in Poland, Sarah envisions that she will be the Messiah's bride; in Palestine, the three Marys visit Natan and announce that the Messiah will be Shabtai Svi of Smyrna; in Smyrna, strange happenings cause some to believe that Shabtai is allied with Satan, but the Badchen defends his holiness; in Amsterdam, Sarah visits a merchant's house on her way to Palestine and mesmerizes Miriam with the idea of a Jewish redeemer on earth; finally, in Jerusalem, Natan, Cardoza, and Sarah recognize Shabtai as the new Messiah. Although Shabtai initially refuses the title, he is persuaded to accept the role by Sarah, who offers herself as his bride.

The next year in Amsterdam, the merchant and Rabbi Sasportas condemn Miriam and the growing number of Jews who support Shabtai. At the shore of Gallipoli, Shabtai is confronted by Nehemia Ha-Cohen, who claims to be the Messiah and calls for proof of Shabtai's powers. Shabtai and the Badchen are taken by Turkish soldiers to the Grand Visier. When accused of heresy, Shabtai is unable to admit that he is the Jewish king. Given the choice of proving his powers or becoming an Islam guard, Shabtai accepts the Islam robe. The Visier's mother secretly acknowledges her belief in his holiness: her son's illness disappeared when Shabtai spoke to the court.

The next year in Albania, Natan visits Shabtai and the Badchen, and expresses his disappointment in Shabtai. When he tells them of the current devastation of the Jews, Shabtai claims that the Lord took back his power. In Amsterdam, Miriam and Sasportas are to marry the next day. Although the Rabbi is burning all materials related to the false Messiah, Miriam still believes in the force that moved the Jewish people to take responsibility for themselves.

PRODUCTION REQUIREMENTS

Major Roles. SHABTAI ZVI, The False Messiah (bs): D1 to F3 (includes improvisational, cantor-like passages). NATAN OF GAZA, the prophet of Shabtai (bar): B1 to G♯3. SARAH, bride of Shabtai Zvi (col s): D3 to C♯5.

Supporting Roles. BADCHEN, Shabtai's friend (t): D2 to A3. ABRAHAM DE SOUZA, a wealthy Jewish merchant (bs): A1 to E3. MIRIAM, De Souza's blind daughter (s): D♭3 to B♭4. GRETA, De Souza's Dutch maid (s): D3 to A4. RABBI JACOB SASPORTAS (bar): C♭2 to G3. CARDOZA, a Marrano (t): E2 to G♯3.

Minor Roles. Supporting role which could double some of the minor roles appears in brackets. A minimum of eleven singers are required. KARA MUSTAPHA, PRIEST, [SASPORTAS] (bar). NEHEMIA, GHOST, [DE SOUZA] (bs). VAN EFFENDI, YOSEF, [CARDOZA] (t). MOURNER #1, [BADCHEN] (t). AARON, MAYATI ZEDA, MOURNER #2 (bs-bar). MARY THE RIGHTEOUS. [GRETA] (s). MARY THE VIRGIN, [MIRIAM] (s). LATIFE, MARY MAGDELENE (m-s).

Chorus. Chorus of Women, Chorus of Men, and Mixed Chorus.

Orchestra. 1 fl, 1 ob, 1 cl, 1 bsn, 1 hrn, 1 trp, 1 trb, harp, perc, piano, strings (2–1–1–1), harpsichord (on stage).

Material. FS–P: the composer (address available through AMC). VS: American Music Center.

REVIEWS

Bernard Holland "Opera: 'False Messiah' by Bruce Adolphe at Y," *New York Times* (April 11, 1983), section 3, p. 21

> "Mr. Adolphe's music is colored by its religious and ethnic allusions to characters and settings. When these rhythms, modal flavors and melodies are allowed to dominate, then his music has a real lyric attraction."

> "Mr. Adolphe and his librettist . . . seem very much to want us to share the wideness of Shabtai Zvi's impact, yet. . . . [the] dispersal of dramatic energy among so many people in so many parts of the world . . . tends to disrupt our concentration."

MIKHOELS THE WISE

Historical drama. Two acts, seven scenes, three or four sets (150 minutes). No overture. Highly chromatic, disjunct vocal lines in conversational passages contrasted with melismatic, florid, linear passages and simple melodies. Overall, vocal roles very demanding with some singers playing two or three smaller roles.

Libretto by Mel Gordon, based on the life of Solomon Mikhailovich Mikhoels, a great Russian-Jewish actor. Premiere: Jewish Opera at the Y, New York 5.8.82.

PLOT

Setting: Russia from revolutionary times through becoming the Soviet Union, about 1917 to shortly after World War II.

Trying to find work in the new Soviet Republic, Mikhoels' clever audition earns him a position as a revolutionary Yiddish actor, and he soon becomes the star Jewish entertainer. He meets and falls in love with his future wife, Nina, after a performance. At the Bureau of Jewish Records, a worker describes the better life that awaits them in Biro Bidzhan, the Jewish settlement that Stalin is establishing in Siberia. When Mikhoels alights at the Biro Bidzhan train station, he is greeted by a Korean girl Sin-cha. Sin-cha foresees danger for the Jewish people, but serves as their protector, hoping that the Jewish people can free her nation in the future.

In a radio appeal, Mikhoels asks American Jews to support the Red Army's defense of the Jews against Hitler's forces. During an evening of political entertainment, his cause is supported by Charlie Chaplin and Paul Robeson. Back in Moscow, the actor's friendship with Stalin encourages the Jews to appeal to him to improve their living conditions and lessen their misery. However, Mikhoels' attempted intervention leads to his death. Der Nister metaphorically explains to Nina about her husband's rise to fame, his association with Stalin, his subsequent loss of favor, and his destruction by his former mentor. In a final lament, the people mourn the loss of their homes and families, as well as their cultural heritage and freedom.

PRODUCTION REQUIREMENTS

Major Roles. SOLOMON MIKHOELS (bar): A1 to G#3 (fals). BEN GOLD, BOLSHEVIK OFFICER, and GRANOVSKY (bs): A1 to E3. NINA (m-s): A2 to A4. DER NISTER (bs): F#1 to F#3 [also sang offstage voice of PAUL ROBESON (bar) at premiere]. SIN-CHA (s): D3 to B4.

Supporting Roles. YOUNG MOTHER, PROTESTER, and BUREAUCRAT (s): B2 to G♯4. SERGEI and WORKER (t): C2 to B♭3. SARAH (s): E3 to A4. ENNOCH and WILLIE (t): D2 to A3. AARON and JOE (bar): A1 to F3. INFORMANT and CHARLIE CHAPLIN (t): F2 to B♭3.

Minor Roles. There are ensembles throughout the opera with identifiable characters (Hassid, Old Soldier, Businessman, etc.) These parts may also be played by characters listed above.

Orchestra. 1 fl (picc), 1 ob, 1 cl in B♭, 1 bsn, 1 trp in B♭, 1 hrn in F, 1 trb, perc, harp, strings (1–1–2–1–1).

Material. FS: American Music Center. FS–P: Galaxy Music Corp.

REVIEWS

Leighton Kerner "Obopies III and Last," *Village Voice* (June 15, 1982), p. 86

"their biography of Solomon Mikhailovich Mikhoels . . . dwells hardly at all on the man as hero of his own and his country's tragedy as it hops the globe with him."

"the music, while genuinely interesting in its manner of weaving an orchestral latticework of arpeggiated phrases into a supple, emotionally suggestive background, needs a more incisive profile in the foreground."

Theodore W. Libbey Jr. "92nd St. Y Offers Jewish Opera 'Mikhoels,' " *New York Times* (May 11, 1982), section 3, p. 17

"The approach—weaving a tapestry around the life of a central figure instead of adhering to a narrative—is not new . . . and it works satisfactorily in 'Mikhoels' as well."

"Numerous political and cultural issues are aired along the way through the opera's loosely connected tableaux; fortunately, the piece does not leave a lopsided impression of the protagonist or the issues."

THE TELL-TALE HEART

Horror story. One act, five scenes (60 minutes). Varies from chromatic, dissonant to lyrical. Vocal style mainly declamatory with ensembles more conservative than solos. Orchestra provides musical atmosphere.

Libretto by the composer, based on the short story and additional poems by Edgar Allan Poe. Premiere: Boston and New England Conservatories, Mass. 82. Performances: Marymount Manhattan College, N.Y. 11.11.88.

PLOT

Setting: New York City, early twentieth century.

Andrew List, a young poet, is a boarder at blind old Mason's house. Although he gets along quite well with Mason, he becomes obsessed with Mason's blind eye, and decides that he must kill him. Helen, Andrew's girl friend, comes often to read to Mason. She senses that something is wrong with Andrew, but to no avail. Later that night, Andrew does, indeed, murder the old man in his bedroom, hiding his dismembered body under the floor boards.

Convinced that he has committed the perfect crime, Andrew is quite at ease entertaining Helen the next day. When two policemen arrive to investigate a report of shrieking that neighbors had heard during the night, Andrew explains that Mason is away in the country. Feeling cocky, Andrew even offers to show the policemen Mason's room. The police search as Andrew sits above the floor boards. Andrew becomes more and more agitated, believing that he can hear a beating heart below him. Finally, he tears up the floor, revealing his act and confessing his guilt.

PRODUCTION REQUIREMENTS

Major Roles. ANDREW LIST, a poet (t): C2 to C4 (sprechstimme in final scene).

Supporting Roles. HELEN, Andrew's friend (s): C3 to B4. MASON, Andrew's landlord (bar): A1 to E3. POLICEMAN I (bar): $B^{b}1$ to $G^{b}3$. POLICEMAN II (bs): $F^{\#}1$ to D3 (G3 falsetto).

Orchestra. fl, ob, cl, bsn, hrn, trp, trb, piano, perc, string quintet.

Material. FS–P and VS: Galaxy Music. VS: American Music Center.

REVIEWS

Will Crutchfield "Wrestling With Guilt, in Adaptation of Poe Tale," *New York Times* (November 13, 1988), p. 76

> "Mr. Adolphe's score contains several admirable passages . . . He sets English well. The opening bit of narrative is convincing and avoids several pitfalls. The musical idiom is dissonant-lyrical, and is handled with skill."

"But the only satisfying extended musical movement . . . comes with the scherzo-like arrival of the investigators, who sing in an out-of-sync duet style that calls to mind the rustics from Britten's 'Midsummer Night's Dream.' "

Noa Ain (1941–)

TRIO

Psychological drama. One act (60–70 minutes). Jazz/gospel chamber opera. Arias, duets, trios joined by rapid declamation and a recurring refrain to create a through-composed feeling.

Libretto by the composer. Premiere: American Music Theatre Festival, Philadelphia 7.84.

PLOT

Setting: the present.

Looking forward to experiencing motherhood motivates Dahlia to reevaluate and improve her relationship with her own mother, Francine. In the course of the stream of consciousness discussion of their stormy relationship, basic issues of mother/daughter affiliations are explored, including the expectations that a child has of her mother as well as the difficulties of motherhood. Francine's mother, Mary, joins the others, opening the discussion to yet another generation of memories and expectations. With the addition of the grandparent viewpoint, new issues surface, including growing old and remembering daughters when they were children. Dahlia's pregnancy frees her from the unpleasant ties and disappointments that predominated in her relationship with her mother. When her daughter is born at last, the baby fulfills a basic need in all three women, each passing on a bit of themselves to yet another generation.

PRODUCTION REQUIREMENTS

Major Roles. DAHLIA (m-s): G2 to B4. FRANCINE (m-s): G2 to G4. MARY (c): F2 to F♯4. (Low tessitura for all roles.)

Orchestra. vln, bs, guitar (acoustic and electric), piano.

Material. FS–P: The composer (contact AMC for address) and American Music Center.

REVIEWS

Harry Harris "Philly Fest Has Its Moments, But Overall It's A Bit Sluggish," *Variety,* 315 (July 25, 1984), pp. 83, 85

"The festival's most enthusiastic kudos went to the least costly enterprise, 'Trio,'. . . . one of three black-oriented festival entries."

Robert Massa "Philly Harmonics," *Village Voice,* 29 (July 17, 1984), pp. 83–84

"Noa Ain's *Trio* . . . is nearly as bland as the title suggests, despite the solid subject and a few patches of sharp writing."

"The music is stronger than the lyrics in this 'inner opera,' embracing, if not pulling together, a wide variety of styles, though the long recitatives do make you wish the characters were more vibrant and quirky."

Daniel Webster "American Music Theatre Festival No. 1," *Musical America,* 34 (December 1984), pp. 22, 39

"it turned out to be seventy minutes of lyrical singing rooted in gospel style. It lacked a dramatic turning point to bring grandmother, mother, and daughter into understanding, but it featured a potent performance by Karla Burns as the grandmother."

"A combo of piano, violin, guitar, and bass . . . provide a gentle score for a gentle, stylized piece."

Hugh Aitken (1924–)

FABLES

Ten short Aesop's fables. Two acts, twelve scenes, one set (90 minutes). Emulates many styles from Rameau to chromatic contemporary. Orchestra generally provides accompaniment only. Each fable forms independent movement with spoken narration between. Frequent meter changes to accommodate word accents.

Libretto by the composer, based on *Fables* by Jean de La Fontaine. Commissioned by Elizabeth Sprague Coolidge Foundation. Premiere: New York Chamber Soloists, Library of Congress 11.1.75. Performances: Caramoor Festival, Katonah, NY 6.25.76.

PLOT

The opera is presented as a courtly entertainment: the four soloists don various costumes and roles in acting out the following short fables, which teach the evils of flattery, jealousy, pride, sloth, and misplaced trust:

The Cicada and the Ant
The Oak and the Reed
The Wolf and the Lamb
The Pilgrims and the Oyster
The Companions of Odysseus
The Raven and the Fox
The Meeting Held by the Rats
The Cat and the Two Sparrows
The Animals Sick with the Plague
Death and the Woodcutter

PRODUCTION REQUIREMENTS

Major Roles. SOPRANO: THE ANT, THE LAMB, CIRCE, THE CAT RODILANDA, THE DONKEY, DEATH: G♯2 to C♯5 (D5 required as a short toss-off note). TENOR I: THE REED, PILGRIM I, THE WOLF, THE FOX, A RAT, SPARROW I: B♭1 to B3. TENOR II: THE CICADA, PILGRIM II, THE LION, A RAT, THE WOLF, THE WOODCUTTER: A♭1 to B3. BASS: THE OAK, THE WOLF, A LAWYER, ODYSSEUS, THE RAVEN, A RAT, SPARROW II, THE LION: D1 to G3.

Orchestra. fl, 2 obs, bsn, string quintet.

Material. FS–P: Theodore Presser. VS: American Music Center.

REVIEWS

Robert Parris "A Celebration of Chamber Music," *Musical America* (March 1976), pp. 29+

"Aitken's unpretentiousness is admirable; he knows very well that apparent frivolity can cut deeper in exposing the deadly, the vicious, in human nature than grandiloquent moralizing. But here he went too far. The stage business was too arch to be funny."

"I can't help wondering . . . whether Aitken hoped that innumerable cliches, spiced and mixed well, would somehow amalgamate to make a workable set of materials. For my part, it's carrying nostalgia pretty far. The audience ate it up; clearly, down this road lies popular success."

Stephen Wadsworth "Katonah, N.Y.," *Opera News* (September 1976), p. 69

"*Fables* is a sophisticated cartoon. . . . The scoring . . . refers parenthetically to many operatic models from Rameau to Strauss, Aitken's allusive pen always responsive to the dramatic gestures and moods in his text and situations."

Garland Anderson (1933–   )

SOYAZHE

Supernatural tale. One act, one scene, one set (70 minutes). Conservative modern idiom, chromatic at times, but generally tonal. Importance given to speech accent and delivery. Recitative, arioso style with spoken dialogue as well.

Libretto by Jamie Lee Cooper. Premiere: Central City Opera, Denver 7.28.79.

PLOT

Setting: within a Navajo lodge.

Witch Slayer, the tribe's seer and magician, lies slowly dying, attended by Ruins, Bitter Water (Ruin's wife), and the young brave Stands Alone. Witch Slayer is believed to be plagued by witches' spirits, though Witch Slayer claims that all the witches have been driven from the tribe by his own magic — Stands Alone had killed the last one with his own hands. The spirit of Soyazhe enters, clad in the glittering jewels the Indians bury along with their dead. She is the daughter of Ruins and Bitter Water, and is Stands Alone's young wife, who was slain as the last witch.

Writhing in pain, Witch Slayer curses Stands Alone for not killing Soyazhe the first time. Stands Alone had been appointed to lead Soyazhe to the Place of the Old Dead People, and to murder her according to Witch Slayer's demands. Stands Alone confesses that his love for Soyazhe made it impossible for him to kill her, but that a single shot from an unseen marksman killed her. Soyazhe cannot believe her husband, believing that she saw him from her grave as he dug for buried jewels in the Place of the Old Dead People. Believing that he is the only remaining witch, Soyazhe has returned from the dead to take Stands Alone back with her.

Though Stands Alone denies these accusations, Soyazhe pulls a knife from her belt and stabs him. As Stands Alone falls dead, Ruins admits that it was he who followed them to the place where Soyazhe was to be slain. Seeing that Stands Alone could not murder his own wife, it was Ruins who fired the shot. Soyazhe reels in disbelief, now guilty of her loving husband's murder. Soyazhe sings to the Holy Ones for guidance, but as she chants, Witch Slayer writhes in pain. It is he whom the gods accuse of ransacking the holy graves. He had condemned Soyazhe to death because he thought she had seen him digging in the hallowed earth. As Witch Slayer's evil is brought to light, Stands Alone rises from the dead, free once more to embrace his wife.

PRODUCTION REQUIREMENTS

Major Roles. SOYAZHE (m-s): B2 to A♯4. RUINS, Soyazhe's father (t): C♯2 to B♭3.

Supporting Roles. STANDS ALONE, Soyazhe's husband (t): D2 to B♭3. WITCH SLAYER, witch doctor (bar): G1 to E3.

Minor Roles. BITTER WATER, Soyazhe's mother (s): E3 to B♭4. CRIER (t) (chorus member).

Chorus. SATB (singing and speaking, small role).

Orchestra. 2 fls, 2 obs, cl, 3 bsns, 2 hrns, timp, harp, strings.

Material. FS–P and VS: Central City Opera Association, 1615 California, No. 614, Denver, CO 80202. VS: American Music Center.

REVIEWS

Emmy Brady Rogers "Denver," *Music Journal* (November/December 1979), p. 53–54

"[*Soyazhe*] left this writer somewhat numb, especially after listening to Soyazhe's incantation bringing her husband . . . back to life. It was a monotonous repetition of one note for page after page against a subdued instrumental background."

"Some good choral writing here and there highlighted the talents of the excellent chorus that made a colorful background visually and aurally."

Bill Zakariasen "Central City—Anderson's 'Soyazhe,'" *Musical America* (December 1979), pp. 18–19

"this muddled tale of necromancy among the Navajos only turned our understanding of these people back to wigwam one. Anderson's music, however, despite its lack of racial atmosphere . . . proved well-orchestrated, smoothly developed, and firmly attuned to the dramatic action, whatever it was. It might be rewarding to hear another Anderson opera saddled with less obtuse prosody."

Theodore Antoniou (1938–)

PERIANDER

"Scenes from the life of a tyrant." Prologue, two acts, ten episodes, one set (100 minutes). Modified 12-tone writing for instruments and voices, repeated "sound blocks," unconventional notation employed. Many vocal styles required: declamatory speaking, sprechstimme, approximation of pitches, disjunct lines, lyricism. Combination of live and taped music. Chorus and dancers produce various percussive sounds on stage.

Libretto by George Christodoulakis, based on the historic figure Periander. Commissioned for the Theatre am Gartnerplatz, Munich. Premiere: Munich 2.6.83.

PLOT

Setting: the ancient Greek city of Korinth.

Through episodes in the past, present and future, we learn of Periander's manical abuse of power, his paranoia, and delight in cruelty. The drama takes place simultaneously on different planes of meaning and action. Each role is portrayed by a singer, a dancer and an actor. Past, present and future may be seen simultaneously. The audience can also witness the action while another "Periander" expresses what is going on in Periander's mind.

Haunted by the beauty and love of Melissa, his wife, Periander stabs her to death. Incensed at the murder of their mother, Periander's two sons, Lykophron and Kypselos, plan their father's destruction. They enter into an alliance with Prokles, Melissa's father, and king of the neighboring Epidaurus. Periander hears of the plot against him, kills Kypselos, and traps Prokles, who is burned alive in his own throne room. Lykophron is banished and Periander proclaims death to any who would offer him aid. Lykophron's lover, Myrto, is the first to meet this fate. Even the Narrator of the drama, acting the part of the Chorus in this Greek tragedy, is strangled by Periander.

Periander finally goes mad, haunted by images and ghostly apparitions of those that he has slain. Lykophron seizes the opportunity, returning with an army to kill Periander. As Lykophron's soldiers descend upon Periander, so do the ghosts of Melissa, Kypselos, Prokles, and Myrto.

PRODUCTION REQUIREMENTS

Major Roles. PERIANDER, tyrant of Korinth (bar): E1 to G3. MELISSA, his wife (m-s or dram s): B2 to B4.

Supporting Roles. LYKOPHRON, Periander's older son (t): B1 to $B^{\flat}3$. PROKLES, Periander's father-in-law (bs): F1 to F3. KYPSELOS, Periander's younger son (t): D2 to $A^{\sharp}3$. MYRTO, Lykophron's fiancee (s): $B^{\flat}2$ to $B^{\flat}4$.

Speaking Roles. NARRATOR (bs) (suggested by composer, though character does not sing.) ACTORS (double major and supporting listed above.)

Minor Roles. OFFICER (bar). MESSENGER (bar).

Chorus. SATB.

Ballet. Six dancers to pantomime six major and supporting roles listed above.

Orchestra. 2 fls (picc, 2 alt fls), 2 obs, 2 cls, bs cl, 2 bsns (2 cont bsns), 4 hrns, 2 trps, 3 trbs, tuba, 3 perc, harp, piano (amplified), cel (amplified), strings (10–8–5–5–3), tape.

Material. FS–P and VS: the composer (address available through AMC). VS: American Music Center.

REVIEWS

Beate Kayser "Munich," *Opera* (May 1983), 34:534–536

"The way in which George Christodoulakis's libretto piles horror upon horror causes the opera to lose its effect and, in particular, to lose tension. In addition, the action becomes very confused as a result of scenes taking place simultaneously and of changes in time sequence."

"Antoniou is technically competent, understands choral effects, knows how to create large-scale melodic phrases and deftly combines taped music with live scenes. But he never manages to define clearly a character, or a situation that can be dramatically portrayed."

Herbert E. Reed "Munich," *Opera News* (May 1983), pp. 34–36

"Grisly episodes document the disintegration of a personality, but they abound in flashback projections, alter egos and hallucinations to the point of total diffuseness and non-communication."

"The intermittently effective musical structure is a mixture of live and taped, orchestral and electronic sequences, of arioso, choral chants, stone-clapping, declamation and what have you. The dramatic and musical strands acquire compelling focus only in the closing scenes as Periander's doom approaches."

Dominick Argento (1927–   )

THE ASPERN PAPERS

Melodrama. Two acts, two prologues, nine scenes (116 minutes). Writing includes theme based on a tone row, atonal and tonal. Vocal lines lyrical to rhythmically and intervallically difficult. Ensembles contrapuntally conceived. Orchestra plays important role, especially in long pantomime, narrated by the lodger.

Libretto by the composer, based on concept of the novella by Henry James with several additions and adaptations. Premiere: Dallas Opera 11.19.88. PBS telecast: 6.9.89.

PLOT

Setting: a villa on Lake Como, Italy, the summer of 1895, flashing back to the summer of 1835.

Juliana Bordereau, a famed opera diva and her lover, John Aspern, are spending a blissful summer at their favorite retreat. Aspern, who has grown famous writing operas for the diva, completes his masterwork (the opera *Medea*), which will co-star her talented pupil, Sonia, the mistress of Aspern's friend and Juliana's manager, Barelli.

Sixty years later, Juliana, a wheelchair-bound recluse, still inhabits the villa, cared for by her spinster niece, Tina. Because money is tight, Juliana agrees to take on a lodger who, unknown to her, has designs on gaining information about Aspern's life and works. The lodger, a writer and biographer, will go to any lengths to obtain such information, especially any sketches of the never-performed opera, *Medea.* He hires a gardener and transforms the crumbling villa to the lovely haven it had once been. He sends flowers to the ladies daily, his advances toward Tina being part of his plan to gain access to the hidden treasures. When the lodger discovers that Juliana has Aspern's portrait in her possession, he becomes convinced that she must also have the opera. As the lodger contemplates its history, we see the opera, *Medea,* in pantomime, with Juliana, Aspern, Barelli, and Sonia assuming the roles.

Returning to the summer of 1835, Aspern and Juliana rejoice at the completion of his opera. But Juliana also realizes that Aspern and her pupil, Sonia, are having an affair. She lets afloat her own boat so that Aspern might not be tempted to keep a late night rendezvous with Sonia. Finding the boat missing, Aspern decides to swim across the lake. He never reaches his destination, and his body is never found. Grief-stricken, Juliana seizes the manuscript and locks it away, claiming that the composer burned it, thus killing it as Medea had killed her "child" in Aspern's opera. From that moment, the stricken woman abandons her own career.

The old Juliana catches the lodger searching for the opera score. His treachery sends her into a fit from which she never recovers. Finally returning after the old woman's funeral, the lodger still hopes that Tina might share Aspern's opera with him. Tina, however, intimates that she would gladly share the papers with a member of the family. But the lodger recoils, thus admitting that marriage is too high a price to pay. Tina realizes that he never really loved her, but used her to get the opera just as the aging diva, Juliana, was used years before by Aspern. Alone, Tina feeds the opera, page by page, into the fireplace, as the four characters from *Medea* appear for a fleeting moment behind her.

PRODUCTION REQUIREMENTS

Major Roles. Juliana Bordereau, an opera singer, now an elderly recluse (s): B^b2 to B^b4 [C5 ossia]. Tina, her niece (m-s): B2 to B^b4. The Lodger, a critic and biographer (bar): A^b1 to G3.

Supporting Roles. Aspern, a composer (t): C2 to B^b3. Barelli, an impressario (bs-bar): G1 to $F^\#3$. Sonia, his mistress, a singer (m-s): A2 to G4.

Minor Roles. Pasquale, the Lodger's servant and gardener (also The Painter) (bs). Olimpia, Juliana's maid (also the offstage voice of Juliana in Prologue I) (s).

Chorus. SATB (offstage only).

Orchestra. 2 fls (picc), 2 obs (Eng hrn), 2 cls (bs cl), 2 bsns (cont bsn), 3 hrns, 2 trps, 2 trbs, tuba, timp, 2 perc, piano (cel), harp, strings.

Material. FS–P and VS: Boosey & Hawkes.

REVIEWS

Katrine Ames "Argento's Treasure," *Newsweek* (November 28, 1988), p. 91

> "Argento has fashioned a brilliant libretto from the 1888 novella, faithful to its spirit and outlines. He retains much of James's dialogue and narrative but fleshes out characters and actions James only alluded to."

Harold Blumenfeld "The Henry James—Dominick Argento *Aspern Papers*," *The Opera Journal* (March 1989), 22(1):34–37

> "the contained and subtly suspenseful Jamesian tones are lost. Standing in its place is an overt and thoroughly operatic work of music theater in which intimation has been fleshed out into actuality, and in which the foreground action is complemented in a dual set of flashbacks—one historical in nature, the other mythic-metaphoric."

> "the second act prologue provides a remarkable 'coup de theatre.' The Lodger emerges from darkness to read a synopsis he has found of Aspern's opera. As he reads, the ancient and blood-curdling epic of abandonment, murder and infanticide is enacted in pantomime. . . . Closing the metaphor and the opera, as Tina

prepares to burn the manuscript, Medea-Juliana makes a final ghostly appearance, cradling a slain child just as Juliana herself had once clutched to her breast the score of the opera."

Bernard Holland "In Dallas, a Turn on James's 'Aspern Papers,' *New York Times* November 21, 1988), section C, p. 15

"His orchestrations have a fragile glow to them that lets the sound of singers soar out freely. There are some good theatrical ideas. Snippets of the lost 'Medea' are evoked from time to time, and made to murmur indistinctly. We share the lodger's tantalization."

Andrew Porter "From Page to Stage," *New Yorker* (December 12, 1988), pp. 69–71

" 'The Aspern Papers' is indeed an ambitious attempt at a new romantic opera. It contains some imaginative, and not merely well-made, music. But it defers rather too readily and rather too often to a contemporary audience's conventional expectations."

Willard Spiegelman "Opera: Dominick Argento's 'Aspern Papers,' " *Wall Street Journal* (November 22, 1988), p. A12

"Mr. Argento has not found a musical language to match the literary density and structural sophistication of his libretto. . . . [he] self-consciously unites two layers of past time in his opera, and embeds within them references to operas by Bellini, Donizetti and Strauss. Yet in this opera he employs only a single musical idiom. The music glistens. And glistens. And still is never artificial enough for a work that is an elegant, deliberate pastiche."

Patsy Swank "Dallas," *Opera News* (February 18, 1989), p. 38

"Argento's libretto is written tautly and, in Mark Lamos' direction, could almost be played as spoken theater. The dark, sparkling score, however, reveals the depth and fullness of the drama. The music, while melodic and made to be sung, is far from simple. This opera keeps a sense of the traditions of its period, but always in the context of the present."

CASANOVA'S HOMECOMING

Opera buffa. Three acts, nine scenes. (134 minutes). Conservative, contemporary idiom with allusions to the atmosphere of eighteenth-century Venice. Through-composed. Vocal lines are melodic, chromatic, and disjunct, with metric alternations. Vocal roles generally demanding.

Libretto by the composer based on facts, events, and people drawn from Casanova's own memoirs as well as fictional episodes. Commissioned by Minnesota Opera Association. Premiere: The Minnesota Opera 4.12.85. Performances: New York City Opera 11.2.85; New York City Opera 9.20.87.

PLOT

Setting: Venice, Carnival Season, 1774.

Act I, scene i: In the Piazza San Marco; ii: At the Opera; iii: At the Ridotto. Act II, i: In Madame d'Urfe's laboratory; ii: In Signora Croce's kitchen; iii: On the lagoon. Act III, i: In Casanova's bedroom; ii: In the Inquisitor's Chambers; iii: In the Piazza San Marco.

After years in exile, Casanova returns to Venice, having agreed with the authorities to reform his ways. When an old friend pleads for a dowry for his goddaughter, he begins his old scheming. This time, he decides to swindle a rich old widow, who believes he has the power to perform a supernatural "Great Work."

The widow's nephew, the Marquis, also plans a scheme to discredit the great lover by soliciting an operatic castrato to seduce Casanova at a post-opera party. After the public humiliation, Casanova's luck returns, when he insists in private that the castrato is really a woman. Thus, the door is open for another evening of Casanova style romance.

The plot to swindle the widow ensues. Casanova convinces Madame that he can accomplish the "Great Work." The scheme involves a box of her jewels (which he replaces with lead) which must be ceremoniously offered into the lagoon at midnight. The stormy weather causes Casanova and Madame's gondola to sink as well. The old woman dies the next day, raving about Casanova and the "Great Work." Charged by her nephew with murder, Casanova explains to the Inquisitors that there is a "Great Work" which he has performed for many women. Amused, they are convinced that Casanova was Madame's gigolo. Thus, Casanova's reputation is saved, the jewels become the dowry for the happy ingenues, and all ends well.

PRODUCTION REQUIREMENTS

Major Roles CASANOVA (bar): $G^{\sharp}1$ to A3. LORENZO, abbe and friend of Casanova (bar): $A^{\flat}1$ to G3 [$G^{\sharp}3$ parlando]. MARQUIS DE LISLE (t): $D^{\flat}2$ to C4. BELLINO/TERESA (m-s): $A^{\flat}2$ to A4. MADAME D'URFE (c): $G^{\sharp}2$ to A4. GIULIETTA, Barbara's mother (c): $A^{\sharp}2$ to $B^{\flat}4$. MARCONTONIO, serving boy to Casanova (treble or s): B2 to G4.

Supporting Roles. GABRIELLE, Barbara's fiance, and GONDOLIER (lyr t): B1 to $B^{\flat}3$. BARBARA, Casanova's god-daughter (lyr s): C3 to C5. BUSINELLO, friend of Marquis (bs-bar): B1 to F3.

Minor Roles. FIRST, SECOND, AND THIRD INQUISITORS (t, bar, bar) (chorus members).

Chorus. 24 minimum (6 each SATB). Each of these has a small solo role, as carnival revelers, party guests, inquisitors, etc.

Orchestra. 2 fls (picc), 2 obs (Eng hrn), 2 cls (bs cl), 2 bsns, 2 hrns, 2 trps, 1 trb (t-bs), tuba, timp, 2 perc, harp, harpsichord (cel), strings.

Material. FS–P and VS: Boosey & Hawkes, Inc.

REVIEWS

Roy M. Close " 'Casanova's Homecoming' is triumphal," *St. Paul Pioneer Press and Dispatch* (April 14, 1985), pp. 17A–18A

"Argento's new comic opera . . . is at once sophisticated, witty, colorful, urbane, sexy and enormously entertaining."

Peter G. Davis "Casanova's Latest Conquest," *New York* (November 18, 1985), pp. 92–93

"Argento never seems to run out of fresh, creative ways to ring changes on familiar tonal patterns and use them to illuminate the action and the characters."

"Not since Virgil Thomson has an opera composer set the English language with such grace and elegance."

Shirley Fleming "Minnesota Opera: Argento 'Casanova's Homecoming,' " *Musical America* (August 1985), pp. 19–20

"Argento contrives a splendid array of scenes and situations: a carnival in the Piazza San Marco; a deft opera-within-an-opera. . . . an irresistible scene in the Inquisitors' Chambers."

Donal Henahan "Opera: New Production of Argento's 'Casanova,' " *New York Times* (November 3, 1985), p. 87

"Mr. Argento . . . has written a libretto that sings consistently, even at those not infrequent moments when his music . . . fails to do so."

Robert Jacobson "St. Paul," *Opera News* (July 1985), p. 34

"Exposition is swift and crafty, quickly setting the scene for the main action. . . . Argento conceives this opera in cinematic terms, so that one scene melts instantly into the next."

MISS HAVISHAM'S FIRE

Tragedy. Prologue, two acts and an epilogue (180 minutes). Music is chromatic, atonal, yet conservative. Through-composed in mostly dialogue fashion with several arias and occasional brief trios or quartets. No overture. Prologue is sung a capella with orchestra tacet for first six minutes.

Libretto by John Olon-Scrymgeour, in the form of an investigation with present-day testimony and flashbacks. Uses characters from Dickens' *Great Expectations,* "Being an Investigation into the Unusual and Violent Death of Aurelia Havisham on the Seventeenth of April, in the Year Eighteen Hundred and Sixty." Commissioned by the New York City Opera. Premiere: New York City Opera 3.22.79.

PLOT

Setting: Satis House, Essex, England, 1860.

Prologue: The Garden of the Satis House (1860); Act I, scene i: The Library of Satis House (1860); ii: Miss Havisham's dressing room (1810); iii: The Library (1860); iv: The room of Mirror's (1860); v: The Library (1860); vi: Miss Havisham's Reception Room (1847); vii: The Library (1860); viii: The Garden (1846). Act II, i: The Garden (1860); ii: The Library (1860); iii: A brilliantly lighted Ballroom and Terrace (1859); iv: The Library (1860); v: The Garden (1860); vi: The Library (1860); Epilogue: The Dressing Room.

The inquest of Miss Havisham's death by fire reveals the tragic life that led to her unhappy death. Testimony begins with Miss Havisham's wedding day of fifty years before, on which she was jilted by her fiance. This experience caused her to avoid contact with all except Estella, her adopted daughter. The inquest reveals that as Estella grew up, her benefactress promised her jewels, causing jealous relatives to accuse Estella of greedily speeding Miss Havisham's death. In addition, Miss Havisham encouraged her ward to hate men by being cruel to Pip, in spite of his faithful love for Estella. Even after the old woman's death, Pip loves Estella and she is incapable of returning that love. Further testimony reveals that Estella and Bentley Drummle married because her upbringing would not allow her to love and he would not suffer the indignity of being loved. The day before the fire, Estella, abandoned by her husband, had a violent argument with Miss Havisham. Instead of destroying her husband, Estella had been hurt and blamed Miss Havisham's influence. Estella further disclosed that she was pregnant, causing the old woman to lose control. The following day, Miss Havisham bemoaned her loss of Estella and mourned her cruelty to Estella and Pip. She invited Pip to her house to beg his forgiveness before she went along into the house. Witnesses recall hearing screams and seeing window curtains pulled down to reveal a woman enveloped in flames, before Pip wrapped the curtains around her. The examiner concludes that all were the victims of Miss Havisham's sick illusions.

PRODUCTION REQUIREMENTS

Major Roles. AURELIA HAVISHAM (col): A2 to C4 (D4 opt). ESTELLA DRUMMLE, nee Havisham, adopted daughter of Miss Havisham (m-s): B2 to A♭4 (B♭4 opt). PIP (bar): C2 to A3.

Supporting Roles. NANNY (s): C3 to A♯4. JAGGERS, legal counsel to Miss Havisham (bs): B♭1 to F3. EXAMINER, officiating at the Inquest (bs-bar): B1 to F♯3. BENTLEY DRUMMLE, man-about-town (t): E♭2 to B3. ORLICK, drunken and demented caretaker of Satis (bs): A♭1 to G♭3.

Minor Roles. Relatives of Miss Havisham: SARAH POCKET (c). CAMILLA POCKET (s). GEORGIANA POCKET (m-s). RAYMOND POCKET (t). PUMBLECHOOK, Uncle to Pip (unseen, spoken). YOUNG ESTELLA (tr). YOUNG PIP (tr).

Chorus. SSAATTBB

Orchestra. 1 fl (picc), 1 fl (alto), 2 obs (Eng hrn), 1 cl in B♭ (s sax in C), 1 cl in B♭ (bs cl), 2 bsns (cont bsn), 3 hrns in F, 2 trps in B♭, 2 trbs, tuba, 2 perc, timp, harp, piano (cel), harmonium, strings.

Material. FS–P: Boosey & Hawkes, Inc. FS: American Music Center.

REVIEWS

Manuela Hoelterhoff "A New Opera to Delight the Imagination and Ear," *Wall Street Journal* (March 30, 1979), p. 15

"On the whole a musically absorbing, seamlessly crafted work. . . . Though the fourteen scenes plus a prologue and epilogue pass before us, they do so smoothly, fading into each other like sequences in a dream."

Highlights "lunatic" wedding day scene: describing it as an "operetta-like ballroom scene."

Robert Jacobson "New York," *Opera News* (June 1979), pp. 39–40

"The climactic event of Miss Havisham's decaying wedding gown set afire at the beginning of the work, and the subsequent rehashing of the event . . . in an inquest with flashbacks, are not the stuff of which theatre is made."

Robert T. Jones "Miss Havisham's Fire," *Musical America* (August 1979), p. 28

"A drastic revision of the scenario might salvage the overcomplicated structure. (There is) a good deal of interesting music."

Argento is "quite persuasive with his flowing, melismatic vocal writing and a rich orchestra."

Andrew Porter "Fire in April," *New Yorker* (April 9, 1979), pp. 125–9

The music was "easy and attractive to listen to . . . skillfully composed. (The) dramatic structure of the whole . . . seems contrived and even flimsy."

"Highlights the aria 'A Looking Glass' as the finest passage in the score."

The half-hour monologue at the end "originally had an independent existence as a monologue entitled 'Miss Havisham's Wedding Night' . . . written as a companion piece to 'A Water Bird Talk' in 1974." [This is a] "striking and effective piece that might well be performed with success on its own — even as a work of concert hall musical theatre."

Alan Rich "Expectations Unfulfilled," *New York* (April 16, 1979), pp. 91–93

> The "work is a mess dramatically, . . . a hoked-up investigation into how and why Miss Havisham died . . . overshadows the marvelous wealth of character portrayal that the opera now and then does bring forth."
>
> "Purely on the strength of the music, *Miss Havisham's Fire* was worth doing . . . If this work fails — meaning if he isn't given the encouragement to do a major overhaul . . . that will be sad news."

Harold C. Schoenberg "City Opera: 'Miss Havisham,' " *New York Times* (March 23, 1979), section 3, p. 3, column 4

> It is "hard to work up much interest in Mr. Argento's music. It is rather conservative . . . featureless, with a vocal style that . . . breaks up vowel sounds and expands them into quasi-vocalises."

MISS HAVISHAM'S WEDDING NIGHT

Dramatic monologue. One act (30 minutes). Through-composed in a conservative, tonal style. A "tour de force" work for soprano, with trills, glissandi, parlando, cackling and cadenzas.

Libretto by John Olon-Scrymgeour, based on the character from "Great Expectations" by Charles Dickens. Premiere: The Minnesota Opera, Minneapolis 5.1.81. Performances: New York Lyric Opera 4.7.83.

PLOT

Setting: Satis House, Essex, England, 1850.

On the morning of her wedding day, Miss Havisham is dressing for the ceremony when a note arrives from the groom-to-be, jilting her; she smashes the clocks, blocks out the light and vows never to leave her rooms or remove her wedding attire. In this monodrama Miss Havisham deals with the consequences of her impetuous decision, as she has over a period of decades, spending solitary nights vascillating between boredom, despair, madness and self-pity. She relives that traumatic moment, receives imaginary visitors, and delivers tirades or appeals to her faithless lover.

PRODUCTION REQUIREMENTS

Major Roles. AURELIA HAVISHAM, an elderly recluse (s): A2 to C5 ($D^{\flat}5$ opt).

Mute Roles. ESTELLA, a beautiful young girl. A CHAMBERMAID.

Orchestra. fl, ob, cl in $B^{\flat}$, bsn, hrn in F, trp in $B^{\flat}$, tuba, perc, harp, piano (cel), organ (harmonium), strings (1–1–1–1–1).

Material. FS–P: Boosey & Hawkes (rent). VS: Boosey & Hawkes.

REVIEWS

Bernard Holland "Opera: American Pair at the New York Lyric," *New York Times* (April 2, 1983), p. 7, column 3

> "It is an extended mad scene in the bel canto tradition, but really, its principal attractions derive not from the vocal part . . . but from the pit. It is Mr. Argento's delicate ear for orchestral sound . . . that holds our attention, and its clean, light sense of texture manages to support and filter the voice while never competing with it."

Kurt Saffir "New Argento and Owen Operas Premiered in New York," *Opera Journal* (1983), 16(2):25–27

> "just right for sopranos who are comfortable with Strauss's Sophie and Zdenka. With so much of the vocal writing above the staff, words are frequently [un]intelligible, but since the dramatic situation is clear throughout, this is not an important drawback."

THE VOYAGE OF EDGAR ALLAN POE

Psychological fantasy. Two acts (125 minutes). Each scene through-composed mainly in dialogue form, with occasional arias, duets, trios. Thick ensemble writing in nearly all scenes with solo lines continuing over chorus. No overture. Tonal, melodious vocal line.

Libretto by Charles Nolte, using Poe's words as part of text. Commissioned by the University of Minnesota in commemoration of the American Bicentennial. Premiere: Minnesota Opera, St. Paul 4.24.76.

PLOT

Setting: a dock by the sea, a ship's lounge, various fantasy environments.

Act I Prologue: Darkness; scene i: The Dock; ii: The Ship's Lounge; iii: A small boat gliding over the water; iv: A make-shift stage; v: The Ship's Lounge. Act II, i: The Ship's Lounge; ii: Poe's cottage; iii: An auction; iv: A crypt; v: The Ship's Lounge; Epilogue: The Dock.

Feverish and ill, Poe plans to sail to Baltimore, having been told by Griswold, his literary executor, about a ship departing that evening. Although Poe's doctor informs him that no ship is scheduled to leave and warns him against Griswold, Poe boards a ghostly vessel which materializes out of the darkness, captained by Griswold. Poe hallucinates about events that have occurred during his life: his mother's death, arguments with his stepfather, and happy memories with Virginia, his wife. He is tried for madness by his fictional detective, Dupin, who forces Poe to confess that he longed for his wife's death and needed her suffering to inspire his art. In a crypt, his embrace gives life to his wife's body, but she dies when he insists that she tell him about the land beyond the grave. When the trial resumes, Griswold, as the judge, becomes Poe's soul. Poe flogs his own image in a mirror. At dawn, the doctor finds Griswold on the dock, standing over Poe's body. The doctor remembers that Poe wished to leave on a ship the previous night, but Griswold assures him that no vessel departed.

PRODUCTION REQUIREMENTS

Major Roles. DOCTOR (t): D2 to A3. EDGAR ALLAN POE (t): B♭1 to B3. GRISWOLD (bar): A♭1 to G♯3. Poe's mother, MRS. POE (s): E3 to C5. MRS. CLEMM (m-s): G♯2 to A♭4. MRS. ALLAN (a): G2 to A4. THEATRE DIRECTOR (bs-bar): F♯1 to F3. Poe's wife, VIRGINIA POE (lyr s): C3 to B4.

Minor Roles. ROSY (s). WILLIE (bar).

Chorus. SSAATTBB (minimum of 24)

Orchestra. 2 fls (picc), 2 obs (Eng hrn), 2 cls (bs cl), 2 bsns, 3 hrns, 2 trps (bs trp), 2 trbs (bs trb), tuba, timp, perc, harp, piano (cel), strings (min:6–5–5–4–3).

Material. FS–P and VS: Boosey and Hawkes. VS: American Music Center.

REVIEWS

William Bender "Last Voyage," *Time* (May 10, 1976), p. 80

"In essence, Argento and Nolte have written an opera for the music lover who also enjoys the dreamscapes of Fellini and early Bergman."

"The music is a mix of serialism and tonality . . . as gruff as Strauss at one moment, as ethereal as Debussy the next."

"Most important, Argento can write for the voice."

Raymond Ericson "Argento's 'Poe,' a Rich Opera, Is Staged in St. Paul," *New York Times* (April 26, 1976), p. 38

Argento "knows how to vary the texture and dramatic impact of successive scenes . . . This listener found the opera absorbing and admirably made without being gripped by it . . . but this can be the mark of a work which has no great surface flash on first hearing but has a depth that reveals itself only on repetition."

"The opera is seldom free from ensemble singing . . . [making] the text frequently difficult to understand."

John H. Harvey "Minn. Op.: 'Edgar Allan Poe,' " *Musical America* (August 1976), 26:19–20

The score matches the libretto "in levels and density of events and in dramatic impact." The music is "a fully integrated dodecaphonic idiom of freedom and flexibility."

Andrew Porter "By a Route Obscure," *New Yorker* (May 17, 1976), pp. 159–161

"The work is indeed less fantastic, less strange than a Poe opera should be. The music is lyrical, rich, imaginative and interesting; however, it is not so extraordinary that it seizes the listener's mind . . . Not everything works out precisely or clearly, but in the theatre it proves gripping enough."

Porter highlights "touching lyrical passages, . . . the use of choruses onstage and offstage, the colors drawn from the orchestra, the variety of textures, the control of pace . . ."

Hubert Saal "Hell's Bells," *Newsweek* (May 10, 1976), pp. 121–122

> "Argento succeeds . . . [at] writing music that reflects the insistent nightmare of Poe's mind and still provides a diversity of emotionally charged sounds . . . Though he makes use of a variety of musical idioms, Argento is a conservative composer who makes his points melodically."

> "What marred the evening was the word, not the deed, a libretto that turned on itself like smoke. Although Poe scholars have established Griswold's defamation of the poet's character, the libretto seemed to reinforce the defamation by presenting a hapless Poe victimized by a misspent life."

A WATERBIRD TALK

Monodrama. One act (45 minutes). Theme and six variations with coda. The theme is a lyrical twelve-tone melody.

Libretto freely adapted by the composer from "On the Harmfulness of Tobacco" by Anton Chekov and "The Birds of America" by J. J. Audubon. Premiere: Brooklyn Academy of Music, N.Y. 5.19.77.

PLOT

Setting: a nineteenth-century provincial club in Maryland or Virginia.

A lecturer addresses a ladies' club on the subject of water birds. As he delivers his talk and accompanying slide show, it becomes clear that he is revealing not only the bird's habits, but his own idiosyncracies as well. Each of his bird descriptions in some way becomes a comment about his wife (who is reacting in the wings, coughing, clearing her throat, etc.)

PRODUCTION REQUIREMENTS

Major Roles. The Lecturer (bar or t): $B^{\flat}1$ to G3 ($D^{\flat}4$).

Orchestra. fl, ob, cl in $B^{\flat}$, hrn in F, vln I & II, vla, vcl, bs, harp, piano (cel), 1 perc.

Material. FS–P and VS: Boosey and Hawkes. VS: American Music Center.

REVIEWS

Andrew Porter "A Lecture and 'a Parable.' " *New Yorker* (June 6, 1977), pp. 108–111

"The work is at once a tragicomedy, a scena that provides a tour de force for its singer, and a shapely, attractive suite. *A Water Bird Talk* should have a future on the concert platform as well as in the theatre."

"Chekhov's paragraphs are punctuated by snatches of bird lore, also derived from Audubon, which provide a poignant, poetic, entertaining commentary upon them . . . As the lecturer (describes each bird), he tells of himself."

Alan Rich "Fame and Misfortune," *New York* (June 6, 1977), p. 98

"It is always dangerous to set Chekhov to music, since the writer supplied so much of his own words, but Argento's slight, elegant piece is an excellent try. The vocal line is fluent and intricate; the dramatic sense, as in all of Argento's music, is pure."

John Rockwell "New Opera Offering Work of Argento and Ullman," *New York Times* (May 21, 1977), p. 11

"Although the conception has its clever moments, Mr. Argento's words seem hung rather awkwardly between surface farce and disorienting tragedy. The main character was never really funny . . . he just seemed peculiar."

"Mr. Argento's music was long on ingenious structural devices . . . and coloristic ones, but . . . offered mostly uninteresting, flatly declamatory singing."

Dennis Arlan (1945–)

THE BALLAD OF THE BREMEN BAND

"A Little Opera for Children." One act (45 minutes). Light opera/musical theater/pop style with spoken dialogue. Generally tonal with occasional jazzy dissonances. Refrains, reprises and short numbers. Orchestral overture and reprises.

Libretto by James Billings, based on "The Brementown Musicians" by Grimm Brothers. Premiere: Caramoor Festival, Katonah, N.Y. 77.

PLOT

Setting: make-believe, on the road to Bremen town.

Dobbin (a donkey), Herefred (a dog), Melissa Mew (a cat), and Sir Reginald (a rooster), having run away from their respective masters, have joined ranks, hoping to travel to the village of Bremen to join its famous town band. However, they learn that Bremen has been marauded by thieves (Bomb, Slick and Scary). Even the town's musical instruments have been stolen! In searching for a resting place for the night, the barnyard quartet happens upon the robber's hideout. Sir Reginald is caught and nearly served up as the bandit's supper, but his friends frighten the robbers away by disguising themselves as a two-headed monster.

The animals finally arrive in Bremen town the next day, bringing with them the instruments which they had recovered. The Mayor himself greets them, declaring them the official Band of Bremen as a reward for their bravery.

PRODUCTION REQUIREMENTS

Major Roles. (Arlan indicates that the roles of the animals may be sung by children or adults. For this reason, the composer refrains from assigning vocal qualities. Ranges are written in the treble clef.) DOBBIN, a donkey: C3 to F♯4. HEREFRED, a dog: A♯2 to E4. MELISSA MEW, a cat: G2 to A4. SIR REGINALD, a rooster: B2 to F4.

Supporting Roles. Three robbers: BOMB (bs), SLICK (bar), SCARY (t).

Minor Roles. CLAUDE HOPPER, BRUNO BROAST, MAYOR OF BREMEN (bar). CLAUDIA HOPPER, MOLLY MISTRESS, THE MAYOR'S WIFE (m-s). (The above roles may be doubled or played by separate people.)

Orchestra. fl, cl, bsn, hrn, piano, perc, vln, bs.

Material. FS–P and VS: European American Music. VS: American Music Center.

REVIEWS

Christopher Pavlakis "New York," *Music Journal* (September 1977), p. 42

"A work such as this can be judged by other factors besides the quality of the score and the singing, and these aspects were nicely served. There were solos, duets, trios, etc. . . . 'We're on the

Road to Bremen Town,' [is] a modified 6/8–3/4 meter number reminiscent of 'America' from *West Side Story*. . . . The robbers have their moment with 'Oh, Sing Me a Song of the Drumstick,' in a kind of music-hall 3/4 time."

Stephen Wadsworth "Katonah, N.Y.," *Opera News* (November 1977), pp. 77–78

"The dramaturgy was fruity enough to cause the little people quantities of fear, shock and relief and the big people considerable amusement."

MEANWHILE, BACK AT CINDERELLA'S

Comic opera. Four scenes (64 minutes). Modern musical theatre/operatic idiom. A short overture and intermezzos precede each of the four scenes. Arias and duets are set pieces with melodic lines often doubled by the orchestra.

Libretto by James Billings—a new slant on the Cinderella story. Premiere: New York Lyric Opera 5.5.76.

PLOT

Setting: Kingdom of Quagmire.

In this inversion of the Cinderella story, Cinderella is disgusting, ugly and wicked. She refuses to go to the ball until her Godfather threatens to turn her into a toad if she stays home. At the ball, all enjoy themselves except the clumsy, crude Prince. Cinderella enters in her normal, filthy attire, and meets the Prince when she asks him for directions to the bathroom. They discover that they hate the same things about parties. Before departing, Cinderella leaves her shoes, which hurt her feet. Her sisters also go home shoeless, hoping that their suitors will return their shoes to them. No one is disappointed; both sisters are claimed by their lovers, and just as all give up hope for Cinderella, the Prince enters, apologizing for being late. Cinderella accepts the Prince's marriage proposal and all join the celebration.

PRODUCTION REQUIREMENTS

Major Roles. NARRATOR (m-s): G2 to E4. CINDERELLA NABGRATZ (m-s): $B^{b}2$ (E2 optional) to E4. HAROLD, THE HERALD (dram t): D2 to $A^{b}3$ (B3 optional). PRINCE DIMMLY (t): $D^{b}2$ to $A^{b}3$.

Supporting Roles. FILBERT NABGRATZ, Cinderella's father (bs): $A^{b}1$ to $E^{b}3$. Cinderella's stepsisters ARIADNE NABGRATZ (s): $E^{b}3$ to C5, and DAPHNE NABGRATZ (s): $E^{b}3$ to $A^{b}4$. FAIRY GODFATHER (bar): C2 to $E^{b}3$.

Non-singing Roles. ALMONDINE NABGRATZ, Cinderella's stepmother (offstage voice).

Orchestra. fl (picc), ob, cl, bsn, 2 hrns, 2 trps, trb, timp, perc, harp, piano, strings.

Material. FS–P and VS: Jerona Music Corporation.

REVIEWS

June Carson "*Meanwhile, Back at Cinderella's,* A Baby Grand Opera," *NATS Bulletin* (September/October 1984), p. 50 (A review based on perusal of the piano, vocal score.)

> "The balance of the work is full of arias and ensembles, delightful music that heightens the humor of the libretto. Along the way we find many of the traditional dance forms such as a corrente, a gavotte, an allemande, and a sarabande."

> "Dennis Arlan's music may be classified as moderately easy for both voice and instruments, and is filled with rhythmic vitality and variety. It should be great fun for college singers and intermediate adult students to perform. The story is suitable for both student and adult audiences."

Raymond Ericson "Opera: Cinderella Spoof," *New York Times* (May 15, 1976), p. 15

> "*Back at Cinderella's* turns the fairy tale upside down. . . . the prince, a sad sack, and Cinderella are obviously made for each other. A narrator, a modern club-woman type, tries to tell the story straight, but without success and with many interruptions from the actors."

> "As much as one could get the text in the poor acoustics of the auditorium (a church), it sounded smoothly singable, and with Mr. Arlan's first-rate score it made a decidedly pleasant entertainment. The music, highly sophisticated in the scoring and some of the harmonies, still leaned toward Broadway in its breeziness and bright charm."

" . . . it has songs that can stand by themselves. The best one is 'Y' Know,' a duet for Cinderella and the prince, which is touching in its mixture of humor and pathos. This is a fine measure of Mr. Arlan's exceptional skill and taste."

Jan Bach (1937–)

THE STUDENT FROM SALAMANCA

Opera buffa. One act (50 minutes). Contrapuntal ensembles, rhythms of the cleverly rhymed text and musical repetition make this a conservative work in the seventeenth-century mold.

Libretto by the composer freely adapted from Cervantes' interludes: "La Cueva de Salamanca" and "El Viejo Celoso" as translated by S. Griswold Morley. Premiere: New York City Opera 10.9.80.

PLOT

Setting: Spain, early seventeenth century.

Cranky old Craccio prepares for a week-long journey, while his beautiful young wife, Marianna, and her maidservant, Cristina, secretly celebrate his leaving. No sooner has he gone, when Cristina reveals the fun-filled itinerary she has planned for the old man's absence. Marianna throws apprehension aside and agrees to the idea of entertaining a few younger gentlemen with a sumptuous feast, the likes of which the house has seldom seen. Their guests are none other than Craccio's chemist, Gonzalo (a pompous sort, always spewing meaningless Latin phrases) and the barber, Nicolas (a simpleminded thrill-seeker). Though they are hardly great "catches," Marianna agrees that they are safe choices, since the neighbors won't suspect these familiar visitors.

Gonzalo insists on performing a song for the occasion, with his terrible voice and badly tuned guitar. Fortunately for the women, a strapping, young passerby, Stephano, comes to call. The lost student from Salamanca is immediately invited to stay. Cristina quickly insists that he "help her" in the kitchen. The antics are interrupted by the return of the master, mud-caked and moaning that his carriage has had an accident. The guests quickly hide, but a noise arouses Craccio's suspicion. He demands to meet whomever the women are harboring in the kitchen.

Cristina introduces Stephano as a student who lived in the enchanted Cave of Salamanca, where he learned the secrets of black magic. Craccio plays along with the charade, demanding to see some magic. With Cristina's help, Stephano amazes Craccio by producing a sumptuous banquet served by two demons (in the guise of Craccio's own friends, Gonzalo and Nicolas). Awestruck, Craccio insists that Stephano remain in the household. All join in to celebrate this welcome turn of events.

PRODUCTION REQUIREMENTS

Major Roles. MARIANNA, a beautiful young wife (s): C♯3 to B4. CRISTINA, her buxom, middle-aged servant (m-s): A2 to A♭4.

Supporting Roles. CRACCIO, Marianna's aged husband (t): C2 to B3. GONZALO, Craccio's apothecary (t): B1 to B♭3. STEPHANO, a handsome young student (bar): G1 to F♯3. NICOLAS, Craccio's barber (bs-bar): F1 to G♭3 (with lower ossia).

Orchestra. fl, ob, cl, bsn, perc, harp, strings.

Material. FS–P and VS: contact composer through AMC. VS: American Music Center.

REVIEWS

Donal Henahan "Opera: 'An American Trilogy,' 3 One-Act Works," *New York Times* (October 10, 1980), p. 14

"The night's third and last gamble paid off. . . . Mr. Bach's aims were modest but he achieved them. The Illinois composer knows how to write a genuine allegro, a secret that seems to have been lost by contemporary composers. He sets words so that singers can enunciate them clearly, and his music's meaning generally runs parallel to his libretto."

Patrick J. Smith "New York City Opera: An American Trilogy," *Musical America* (February 1981), p. 21

"Bach is a thoroughly schooled academic composer who can set ensembles spinning and who can orchestrate for his chamber group. He has a tune for the opening, and a tune for the fugal finale, but, in between, his lack of melodic inspiration means that a lot must be spun out of very little."

THE SYSTEM

Black comedy. One act (50 minutes). Conventional modern idiom with some dissonant chromaticism, though mostly tonal. Generally lyrical, conjunct recitative style. Quasi ad-lib sections with each voice part singing its own tempo.

Libretto by the composer, freely adapted from a story by Edgar Allan Poe. Premiere: Mannes College, N.Y. 3.7.74.

PLOT

Setting: an asylum outside London, nineteenth century.

On a stormy night, Edgar Allen seeks refuge in a run-down mansion, whose inhabitants are having a banquet. Claiming to be a famous psychiatrist and his asylum staff, Warden McCoy describes his "system" for curing patients: letting them act out their fantasies. Each of the hosts steps forward to act out an example: Mrs. Henry clucks like a chicken; Dr. Green becomes a frog; Mr. Brayer, a donkey; the modest, mute Cordelia strips. As the muffled groaning from the dungeon grows louder, it gradually becomes evident that these hosts are actually the inmates, and that the revolution by the inmates has just taken place. The tarred and feathered wardens finally break out to restore things to their rightful order.

PRODUCTION REQUIREMENTS

Major Roles. HIRAM MCCOY, inventor of the system (bs): F1 to F♯3. EDGAR ALLEN, a young author (t): C2 to G3. MRS. HENRY, head nurse (s): D3 to D5 (F5 ossia). MADAME CHAUVENET, elderly dietician (m-s): G♯2 to A4. MR. BRAYER, hospital orderly (t): C2 to A3 (B♭3 falsetto). DR. GREEN (bs-bar): E1 to F♯3.

Mute Roles. CORDELIA, beautiful young girl.

Chorus. TB (minimum of 2).

Orchestra. 2 fls (picc), 2 obs, 3 cls (bs cl), 2 bsns, 3 hrns, 3 trps, 3 trbs, tuba, 2 perc, piano (cel), harp, strings. Onstage band: s sax, accord, bs trb.

Material. FS–P and VS: Galaxy Music.

REVIEWS

Jack Hiemenz "Mannes Opera: two premieres," *Musical America* (June 1974), pp. 29–30

> "a setup that allows for some amusingly grotesque characterizations, each individually and effectively colored by composer Bach's variable palette of musical styles. But, there's little chance under such circumstances for dramatic momentum to build; what began as an opera turns into something more like a vocal divertissement, a madman's vaudeville."

Leighton Kerner "New York," *Opera News* (May 1974), pp. 29–30

> "*The System* . . . is both jolly and ghoulish. . . . The score, also trimmed for this production, is full of music hall patterns, but some ensembles are a bit too thick to let the words always come through."

Seymour Judd "Mannes," *Music Journal* (May 1974), p. 54

> "The opera was a conglomerate of Mozart, ragtime, and modern musical. It had a bit of something for everyone and lacked continuity."

Seymour Barab (1921–)

FORTUNE'S FAVORITES

Comedy. One act (45 minutes). Conservative modern idiom, almost pop at times. Vocal lines easily delivered, mostly conjunct, with occasional chromatics supported by orchestra.

Libretto by the composer adapted from "Baker's Dozen," a short story by H. H. Munro (Saki). Premiere: After Dinner Opera, N.Y.C. 6.19.82.

PLOT

Setting: a restaurant, the present.

Richard and Emily, former sweethearts, meet in a crowded restaurant, when they are seated at the same table. Being superstitious people, they believe that fate has brought them together, especially when they learn that both have lost their spouses. Falling in love again, Richard proposes marriage and Emily immediately accepts. But a problem arises when they realize that, together, they would have *thirteen* children—Richard, five and Emily, eight. The topic becomes how to add or subtract a child so that the superstitious couple may wed. After many options are considered and the marriage nearly scrapped, Emily realizes that Richard has miscounted his children, that his sons "Junior" and "Richard" are one and the same. With twelve children, the wedding is on again, and the waitress can take their order!

PRODUCTION REQUIREMENTS

Major Roles. RICHARD (bar): B♭1 to F3. EMILY (m-s): B2 to A♭4.

Supporting Roles. WAITRESS (s): E♭3 to G4.

Orchestra. fl, ob, cl, bsn, 2 hrns, trp, trb, strings.

Material. FS–P and VS: Galaxy Music. VS: American Music Center.

REVIEWS

Edward Rothstein "Music: Four After-Dinner Operas," *New York Times* (June 25, 1982)

> "The most appealing, 'Fortune's Favorites' . . . deftly established its tone and farcical manners within minutes, as nearsighted, long-lost lovers find harmony in superstitious convictions and astrological signs. . . . Mr. Barab's musical and verbal wit at times overdid its somersaults, but his work always landed on its feet."

NOT A SPANISH KISS

Opera buffa. One act, one scene (30 minutes). Conservative tonal style with frequent allusions to Spanish dances and idiom. Simple diatonicism enriched by moments of impressionistic style as well as Broadway-style pop and jazz. Through-composed with recitative and arias, no orchestral overture or interludes. Lyrical vocal lines.

Libretto by the composer. Premiere: New York Singing Teachers Association 77. Performances: Golden Fleece Ltd, N.Y. 5.81; Association for Opera Awareness, N.Y. 11.82.

PLOT

Setting: a park or square in Spain on a sunny afternoon.

The young poet, Piero, strums his guitar and attempts to write a love song for Betta, the wife of the wealthy merchant, Crispin, whom he secretly admires. Crispin and his wife stroll by and Crispin is furious to learn that his wife is the subject of Piero's song. He threatens to kill the young man until Piero offers the businessman 1,000 pesetas for a kiss from his wife. When, after several tries, the kiss still does not meet Piero's expectations, Crispin threatens to kill him again, for impugning his wife's reputation. Piero confesses that he doesn't have 1,000 pesetas, but will come up with 750. Crispin agrees to lower the price and the couple strolls off, happily planning how to spend the money. Piero exposes his empty pockets, but smiles as he finally completes his love song, "how will I pay for the kiss . . . I don't know!"

PRODUCTION REQUIREMENTS

Major Roles. BETTA, the wife (s): B2 to A♭4. PIERO, the lover (t): C2 to A3. CRISPIN, the husband (bar): C2 to F♯3.

Orchestra. Orchestration to order; piano/vocal score available.

Material. VS: G. Schirmer and American Music Center.

REVIEWS

Bernard Holland "Chamber: Golden Fleece Ltd.," *New York Times* (May 7, 1981), section C, p. 15

> " 'Not a Spanish Kiss' by Seymour Barab was a pleasant, eclectic bit of operatic nonsense in the Spanish style—its love triangle spiced with narcissism, greed and a little sex, as well. It was never brilliantly funny; but at the same time it had the amiable good sense not to try too hard."

Tim Page "Opera: Awareness Unit with Donizetti's 'Rita'," *New York Times* (November 14, 1982)

> "This brief amusing tale . . . offered several real belly laughs, as well as subtler treats. Mr. Barab's score featured witty allusions to Spanish music, including a modern song of love, set to Bizet's famous habanera rhythm."

THE TOY SHOP

Children's opera. One act (45 minutes). Set pieces include dialogue, short arias, duets and an ensemble. Overture. Tonal, melodic vocal lines.

Libretto by the composer. Premiere: New York City Opera Theatre, N.Y. 6.3.78.

PLOT

Setting: a toy shop, the present.

The Toymaker speaks with Paul and Pauline, his life-size mannequins, as if they were his children. He promises that, for their birthday tomorrow, he will have a special present for them: a new doll named Paulette. When he leaves, Paul and Pauline come to life. Pauline expresses her jealousy about this beautiful new doll, Paulette, and her longing to leave the toy shop and see the world. Paul says he never wants to leave "Dad," the Toymaker, but wishes that "Dad" could hear him talk when he says, "I love you." Aaron Blunder, the classic villain, arrives to announce that he will be going on tour and would like to take one of the Toymaker's ingenious mechanical toys with him. Aaron tricks the Toymaker into showing him how Paul and Pauline can dance together. As the Toymaker winds them up he says, "I love you, my son . . . I love you, Pauline." Aaron Blunder is delighted by their dancing and decides that he must have Paul and Pauline in his show. The Toymaker angrily refuses. Aaron storms out, vowing that he will have the mannequins before the night is out. Aaron sneaks back in to grab Paul and Pauline, but when he finds the key, the screaming of the other toys alerts the Toymaker. When Aaron threatens to destroy the two mannequins, the Toymaker says he can have them, but he makes one last request: that he be able to show Paul and Pauline their birthday present before they go. Paulette enters. She is a beautiful gorilla who scares Aaron to death. Paulette gives Aaron a big hug and Aaron agrees to give back the key if Paulette will let him go. But when Aaron puts his hand in his pocket, he finds the key gone. The Toymaker, saddened that Paul and Pauline will never dance again, embraces Paul and Pauline, saying "I love you, my son . . . I love you, Pauline." Paul and Pauline step out of their boxes and begin to dance just as before. Paul realizes it was the Toymaker's "I love you" that wound them up. He responds with "Oh, I love you, Dad!" and the Toymaker hears him! Aaron concedes that anything is possible for love *is* magic.

PRODUCTION REQUIREMENTS

Major Roles. PAULINE (s): $E^{b}3$ to A4 [C5 opt]. PAUL (t): F2 to G3. TOYMAKER (bar): C2 to F3. AARON BLUNDER (bs): D2 to E3.

Minor Roles. PAULETTE (mime).

Orchestra. fl, ob, 2 cl in B^{b}, bsn, trp in B^{b}, 2 hrn in F, trb, timp, perc, strings.

Material. VS: American Music Center. FS–P and VS: G. Schirmer.

REVIEWS

Raymond Ericson " 'Toy Shop,' Opera for Children," *New York Times* (June 11, 1978), pp. 60–63

> "It is a simple, charming fable, adroitly written and composed by Mr. Barab, which rarely found the audience restless."

Samuel Barber (1910–1981)

ANTONY AND CLEOPATRA (REVISED EDITION)

Tragedy. Three acts, prologue and fourteen scenes (104 minutes). Modern conservative, tonal. Vocal rhythms patterned after speech. Vocal lines vary from wide leaps to melodic. Orchestral interludes introduce most scenes.

Text by William Shakespeare. Commissioned by The Metropolitan Opera Association. Premiere: Metropolitan Opera House, N.Y. 9.16.66. Revised: 75. Performances: Juilliard School, N.Y. 75; Spoletto 83. Recording: New World Records, 701 7th Ave. NY, NY 10036: NW 322/323/324.

PLOT

Act I, scene i: Cleopatra's palace, Alexandria; ii: The Senate, Rome; iii: Cleopatra's palace; iv: A Roman banquet hall. Act II, i: The Senate, Rome; ii: Cleopatra's garden; iii: Outside Antony's battlefield tent; iv: Inside

Antony's tent; v: The battlefield at Actium; vi: Cleopatra's palace; vii: A Battlefield; viii: Antony's ruined tent. Act III, i: Cleopatra's monument, ii: Inside the monument.

Bewitched by Cleopatra, Antony extends his stay in Egypt until he is urgently summoned back to Rome. To strengthen his tenuous position at home, Antony marries Octavia, the sister of Octavius Caesar. Cleopatra is angered by the news of Antony's marriage, but is reassured that her qualities are superior to those of Octavia. Strongly influenced by Egypt's attraction even after his marriage, Antony prepares to leave Rome, followed by Octavia. In Athens, he worries that Caesar is undermining his position and sends Octavia back to Rome as a safeguard. However, Caesar has already deposed the other Roman leader and plans to defeat Antony in Egypt. Despite his advisors' warnings, Antony is influenced by Cleopatra and decides to fight by sea, eventually losing the battle of Actium. Fearing Antony's anger, Cleopatra sends word that she has killed herself, driving Antony to suicide. Cleopatra soon follows him in death, unwilling to submit to Caesar's power.

PRODUCTION REQUIREMENTS

Major Roles. Cleopatra (s): B2 to B4. Antony (bar): G1 to G♭3 [A♭3 opt]. Caesar (t): D♯2 to B♭3 [C4 opt].

Supporting Roles. Charmian (m-s): C♭3 to G♯4. Iras (c): F2 to F4. Enobarbus (bs): G♭1 to F3.

Minor Roles. Agrippa (bs). Eros (a young man's voice, t or high bar). Dolabella (bar). Thidias (t or high bar). A Rustic (bar or bs). A Soothsayer (bs). Alexas (bs). Nine other small male roles: 2 t, 3 bar, 4 bs.

Chorus. Two full choruses, male chorus.

Ballet. Cleopatra's slaves' dance. Elaborate stick dance (cut when opera was revised).

Orchestra. 3 fls, 3 obs, 3 cls, 3 bsns, 4 hrns, 3 trps, 3 trbs, tuba, timp, 5 perc, piano, cel, harp, strings.

Material. FS–P and VS: G. Schirmer.

REVIEWS

John Ardoin "Charleston, S.C.," *Opera News* (October 1983), pp.94–96

"Musically, the revised *Antony* is a leaner, more swiftly moving piece. Though there are sections in which one feels Barber pruned too much, what was good—Antony's suicide, Cleopatra's farewell to life—stands out."

Peter G. Davis "Barber's Antony and Cleopatra Revised and Revived," *Ovation* (December 1984), p. 51

"[Cleopatra and Antony] now command the foreground more forcefully—a new love duet inserted into Act Two is the main addition, and a welcome one."

"Antony ['s] . . . most effective moment comes in the extended declamative arioso before he falls on his sword—an unusually striking scene accompanied by timpani and solo flute."

John W. Freeman "BARBER: Antony and Cleopatra," *Opera News* (November 1984), p. 64

"Barber's changes tend to make the work sound more romantic and old-fashioned, particularly in the love scenes, which . . . are now swollen with Puccinian orchestral perorations."

Irving Kolodin "Evenings With Carter, Rubinstein, and Barber," *Saturday Review* (March 22, 1975), pp. 33–34
Review of the Juilliard performance:

"Reduced in scale from a spectacular to a mini-music drama, it profited greatly from the participation of a mostly youthful cast."

"The revision. . . . does, appealingly and often compellingly, plead the case of love fettered by fate to an unhappy outcome. There is, however, much more to Shakespeare's *Antony and Cleopatra* than this. . . . The clash of arms is essentially tame; the sinew, the bite, the vigor in Shakespeare's text are insufficiently present in Barber's music to convey the place in literature occupied by these lovers."

Andrew Porter "Antony's Second Chance," *New Yorker* (February 24, 1975), pp. 123–124+

"I suspect that if the opera is revived a century or so hence, directors of the future will want to combine both scores in new arrangements . . . reinstating valued passages which the composer himself cut but retaining passages he strengthened by recomposition."

"[Antony] deserves a third chance: a large-scale production given preferably in France, Italy, or Germany, where the first hurdle—the dependence on Shakespeare's verbal poetry—could also be removed, and in a house . . . where the stage can hold big spectacle and the auditorium is small enough for the voices to tell strongly."

Dorle J. Soria "artist life," *Musical America* (September 1974), pp. 5–6

"If anyone doubts the moving beauty of the Barber score he has only to listen to the Price recordings of the soliloquoy . . . and the death scene."

Noah Andre Trudeau "An 'Antony and Cleopatra' from Spoleto," *Musical America* (February 1983), pp. 41–42

"It is the overall rightness of Barber's handling of [Act II] that convinces me of the greatness of this opera. Barber's revisions are all advantageous."

"Given stronger, more stage-wise singers, a freer approach to the letter of the score, and careful reconciliation of the various editions, a masterpiece will, I believe, emerge."

Edward Barnes (1957–)

FEATHERTOP

A fantasy parable. Two acts (100 minutes). Through-composed with traditional arias, duets and trios interspersed. Orchestral interludes between scenes and brief prelude to Act I. Contemporary idiom with melodious vocal lines.

Libretto by Maurice Valency from his play of the same name, based on short story by Nathaniel Hawthorne. Premiere: American Opera Center, Juilliard School N.Y. 2.7.80.

PLOT

Setting: New England, 1770.

Act I, scene i: Mother Rigby's kitchen; ii: The living room of Judge Bookin's house. Act II, i: A room in Judge Bookin's house adjoining the ballroom; ii: The ballroom and the adjoining room; iii: Mother Rigby's kitchen.

Mother Rigby completes her scarecrow by putting a pipe in its mouth, which it begins to puff: it has become human. She prepares Feathertop to go into the world, sending him to Judge Bookin's house. Upon his arrival, the Judge and two other foolish men confide their distrust of each other to Feathertop, believing that he has come to investigate them. Meanwhile, Feathertop has fallen in love with Polly, the Judge's daughter, and wants to marry her, despite her love for Bob. Although Feathertop's suit has the Judge's approval, Bob promises Polly that he will convince Feathertop of their love. However, Bob's courage fails when the scarecrow arrives to escort Polly to the ball. At the ball, Feathertop's awkward dancing is taken as the latest fashion. Alone with Polly, he declares his love for her, ignoring her protests that she loves another. However, when Feathertop's true image is revealed in a mirror, Polly's screams bring in the other guests. Feathertop presents Polly to Bob, overriding the Judge's protests by revealing his true image. As he prepares to leave, the three "straw men" ask him again about the investigation, not yet comprehending the situation. Returning to Mother Rigby, Feathertop destroys himself, not wishing to live as a mere scarecrow. Mother Rigby contemplates what the strawmen of the world might have learned from her creation.

PRODUCTION REQUIREMENTS

Major Roles. MOTHER RIGBY (m-s): B2 to A4. FEATHERTOP (bar): C2 to G♯3. POLLY BOOKIN (s): D3 to D5. Polly's father JUDGE BOOKIN (bs-bar): C2 to E♭3.

Supporting Roles. BOB ENDICOTT (t): D2 to B♭3. MAJOR WHITBY (bar): B♭1 to D3. MR. GRAHAM BELL (t): E♭2 to A3.

Minor Roles. SERVANT GIRL (col): E♭3 to D5.

Mute Roles. DICCON (dancer).

Orchestra. fl (picc), ob, cl in B♭, bsn, hrn in F, trp in C, women's voices (2 sop I, 2 sop II, 2 altos), 2 perc, piano, cel, strings.

Material. FS–P and VS: Belwin Mills. VS: American Music Center.

REVIEWS

Peter G. Davis "Opera: Juilliard Presents Premiere of 'Feathertop,' " *New York Times* (February 9, 1980), p. 14, column 3

"Mr. Valency and Mr. Barnes have not produced a startlingly original variation on this oft told operatic tale. . . . The action follows a predictable course . . . the characters lack personality, the satire is so gentle that . . . the piece as a whole is dramatically flat."

"Mr. Barnes' score shows that he has absorbed the manner of a great many twentieth-century composers . . . but the music has no style of its own and . . . ultimately seems little more than a talented student exercise."

Herbert Kupferberg "Juilliard: 'Feathertop' premiere," *Musical America* (May 1980), p. 35

" . . . a fresh and piquant work . . . although its stimulating qualities may have been due to the striking production."

Maurice Valency's libretto is "not only workable but elegant."

" . . .despite its percussiveness, the orchestration is both light-fingered and lighthearted, with lots of whimsical comments on the action."

Martin Mayer "America," *Opera* (May 1980), pp. 474–476

The first half hour of music was "an amalgam of skilled orchestral effects and imitatively chromatic vocal writing that typifies so much modern opera." But in the rest of the work, "Barnes began to give evidence of a considerable lyric gift. . . . all the duets and trios work . . . the orchestral writing is sharp."

Valency's libretto is "undistinguished and none of the characters develop."

Highlights: "a charming ball scene . . . a strophic folk-song . . . the duet between the girl and her human lover."

Andrew Porter "Musical Events," *New Yorker* (February 25, 1980), p. 124

"both the moral and the emotions are touched without emphasis. . . . It was hard to tell whether the composer's heart was engaged, whether he was drawn to the familiar material by more than its evident stage effectiveness."

" . . . his skill was not for a moment in doubt. The opera moves confidently, sings well and sounds good. . . . 'Feathertop' is a slight piece, but one of the most efficient first operas I ever heard."

Joyce Barthelson (1910–)

THE DEVIL'S DISCIPLE

Melodrama. Two acts, three scenes, three sets (135 minutes). Dissonant orchestral interludes, frequent key changes, mixed meters, and disjunct conversational passages contrast more conservative arias and ensembles that reflect music of American revolutionary war period.

Libretto adapted by the composer from the play by George Bernard Shaw. Premiere: Highlands School, White Plains, N.Y. 11.4.77.

PLOT

Setting: New England, the American Revolution.

As family members converge for the reading of Mr. Dudgeon's will, Tony tries to reassure his wife, Judith, about his involvement in revolutionary activities. Family members are shocked when the bulk of the will goes to the Dudgeon's oldest son, Richard, the black sheep of the family. British troops approach and Richard warns that someone will be hanged as an example to the rebels. Tony tries to caution Richard to leave town for safety, but is called away suddenly, leaving Richard and Judith alone. Their meal is interrupted by British soldiers who mistakenly arrest Richard in place of Tony. Richard willingly assumes his friend's identity, overwhelming Judith by his self-sacrifice. When Tony returns, Judith begs him to save his friend; however, the minister quickly leaves the village, leaving her to mourn Richard's certain death.

At the prison, Judith is permitted to visit her "husband." Although she expresses her grief that her real husband ran away, Richard is glad to hear that Tony is safe. Richard refuses her pleas that he identify himself, as well as her declaration of love. At the trial, Judith and another witness confirm that the prisoner is not Tony, but the British decide that Richard will be hanged as an example. Meanwhile, messages arrive from the rebels in Springtown demanding a safe conduct for their officer to arrange terms for the British evacuation of the town. Despite the rebel victory, the British general encourages his men to maintain their courage. At the gallows, Richard asks to be hanged immediately, but the general will not perform the act before the appointed hour. As the clock strikes noon, Tony rushes in and identifies himself. When the soldiers run to seize him, he waves the safe conduct papers and demands that Richard be released, defeating the British once again. The crowd joins the victory celebration.

PRODUCTION REQUIREMENTS

Major Roles. RICHARD DUDGEON, a village ne'er-do-well (bar): [A♭1 opt] C2 to G3. TONY ANDERSON, town minister and revolutionary leader, (bar): B1 to A♭3. JUDITH ANDERSON, Tony Anderson's wife (s): D3 to B♭4 [B4 opt]. ESSIE, Mrs. Dudgeon's niece (s): D3 to B♭4. GENERAL BURGOYNE (t): F2 to A3. SWINDON (bs-bar): A♭1 to E3. MRS. DUDGEON, Richard Dudgeon's mother (m-s): B♭2 to G4 [A♭4 opt].

Minor Roles. LAWYER HAWKINS (bar). CHRISTOPHER, Richard Dudgeon's brother (t). UNCLE WILLIAM (t). UNCLE TITUS (bar). MRS. WILLIAM (s). MRS. TITUS (a). SERGEANT (speaking). CHAPLAIN (bar).

Chorus. SATB (villagers) and Men's chorus with bar, bs, and t solos (soldiers).

Orchestra. 2 fls, ob, 2 cls, 2 bsns, 2 hrns, 2 trps, trb, timp, perc, piano or harp, strings. Stage band (may be students): 2 trps, trb, tuba, bs drum.

Material. FS–P and VS: Carl Fischer.

REVIEWS

Joseph Horowitz "A Shavian Play Becomes Opera that Succeeds," *New York Times* (November 7, 1977), p. 44, column 4

"Miss Barthelson's protagonists are softer, flashier, and less provocative than Shaw's rakish hero . . . and insipidly pure heroine. . . . Though much is lost, it is a tradeoff that caters to Miss Barthelson's considerable abilities as a composer."

"The duets for Dick and Judith are quite wonderful — melodious and warmly orchestrated in the modern-Romantic vein of, say,

Samuel Barber. There are also some well-turned diatonic hymn and march tunes.... Elsewhere the writing is more dissonant and abstract, but ... the fabric is virtually seamless."

Robert Sherman "Beguiling 'Devil's Disciple,' " *New York Times* (November 13, 1977), section 22, p. 16, column 1

"Among other pleasantries, there were some good tunes ... attractive singing and [a] kind of homespun patriotism."

"The connecting dramatic interludes are rather more in the operatic camp, but many solo and ensemble pieces are either influenced by, or taken directly from folklore sources, and are decidedly on the lyrical side. Technically they're arias ... but I would ... call them songs."

LYSISTRATA

Comic satire. One act, two scenes (60 minutes). Conservative, traditional tonality. Brief orchestral introduction and interlude between scenes. Through-composed, in a conversational style, with arias.

Libretto by the composer, based on the Aristophanes play. Premiere: New York University 3.27.81.

PLOT

Setting: Athens. Time: 411 B.C.

Gathered before the gates of the Acropolis, the young women of Athens bemoan the prolonged war with Sparta and their husbands' absence. Lysistrata announces that the men will be home that night, but must return to war the following morning. Lampito, the Spartan ambassador's wife, arrives to persuade the Athenian women to join the Spartan women in their search for peace. The women agree that peace can be achieved if they refuse to sleep with their husbands on their one night at home. They sequester themselves in the Acropolis.

Returning to find empty homes, Theodosius and the other leaders try to persuade their wives to come to them. But the wives refuse, teasing them about the joys of marriage and demanding an end to war. The Spartan ambassador arrives with his wife, Lampito, to sign a peace treaty: the women have won their war. The couples reunite, inviting the Spartans to join in the celebration.

PRODUCTION REQUIREMENTS

Major Roles. LYSISTRATA (s): C3 to B♭4. MAGISTRATE OF ATHENS (bs-bar): D2 to E♭3.

Supporting Roles. THEODOSIUS, Lysistrata's husband (t): D2 to B♭3. MYRRHINE (s): G3 to A4. KINESIUS, Myrrhine's husband (bar): C♭2 to E♭3. KALONIKE (m-s): C3 to G4. POLYDORUS, Kalonike's husband (bar): B♭1 to E3. ISMENE (s): D3 to G♯4. LAMPITO, the Spartan Ambassador's wife (m-s): C♯3 to F4.

Minor Roles. RAUCOUS ONE (m-s).

Speaking Roles. LITTLE THEO, Lysistrata's son.

Mute Roles. CHILDREN, six to ten years old. OLD CRONES, caring for children.

Chorus. SSA (Athenian women): 12 with principals. TBB (Athenian soldiers): 12 with principals.

Orchestra. 2 fls, 2 obs, 2 cls, 2 bsns, 2 hrns, 2 trps, 1 trb, harp, timp, perc, strings.

Material. FS–P: Carl Fischer. VS: American Music Center and Carl Fischer.

REVIEWS

Andrew Derhen "International Congress on Women in Music: Barthelson 'Lysistrata,' Rogers 'A Woman Alive' [premieres]," *Musical America* (August 1981), pp. 25–26

"The score, actually more a cantata than an opera, is in an agreeable conservative vein, and the vocal writing offers rewards to large and small roles alike."

Jack Beeson (1921–)

CAPTAIN JINKS OF THE HORSE MARINES

Romantic comedy. Three acts (120 minutes). Overture and set pieces. Contemporary light opera/musical theater idiom. Vocal and orchestral lines independent in ensembles. Strings orchestrated not to cover voices in arias. Juxtoposes contemporary original melodies with music from *La Traviata.*

Libretto by Sheldon Harnick, based on the play by Clyde Fitch. Premiere: Kansas City Lyric Theatre 9.26.75. Recordings: CMS Desto: DC7222/3L (2–record set with booklet) and DCX47222/3L (2–cassette set, no booklet).

PLOT

Setting: New York City, early 1870s.

The press meets Aurelia as she arrives in America for her operatic debut. Hearing her manager, Mapleson, boast of Aurelia's amorous exploits, Charlie bets that Jinks can seduce the opera star. When Jinks meets Aurelia, however, he realizes that she is not a socialite, but a dedicated artist and lonely woman. Recognizing the attraction between them, he tries to cancel the bet, but Charlie demands an IOU. Jinks tries to speed Aurelia's luggage through customs by tipping an official and is arrested for bribery.

Out on bail, the romance grows, and the lovers secretly become engaged. During a final rehearsal of *La Traviata,* Jinks' mother asks Aurelia not to marry her son. Aurelia agrees to consider this if Mrs. Jinks will attend that evening's performance. However, Belliarti arrives just then with the jealous Charlie, who produces the IOU. When Jinks admits that he signed it, Belliarti forbids him from seeing Aurelia again. In all the excitement, Jinks forgets to appear at his trial.

After the performance, Aurelia is too distressed to celebrate her triumphant debut. However, when Jinks explains what truly happened, she forgives him. A policeman arrives looking for the delinquent Jinks. Aurelia plays the dying Violetta, claiming that Jinks missed the trial because he was attending her illness. The celebratory party and the press soon arrive, looking for their heroine. Best of all, Mrs. Jinks, softened by the evening's performance, approves of Aurelia and Jinks' marriage.

PRODUCTION REQUIREMENTS

Major Roles. COLONEL MAPLESON, Aurelia Trentoni's manager (bass): F♯1 to E3 (B falsetto). JONATHAN JINKS, eligible bachelor and opera fan (t): D2 to A3. AURELIA TRENTONI, opera star (col s): C♯3 to D♭5 (F5 opt). "PAPA" BELLIARTI, Aurelia's uncle, guardian, and mentor (bar and violinist, if possible): C2 to F3.

Supporting Roles. Five reporters: THE TIMES (Irish t): D2 to C4. TRIBUNE (t): B1 to G3. SUN (bar): A1 to E3. HERALD (bar): A1 to E♭3. CLIPPER (bass): F1 to C3. MRS. GREENSBOROUGH [Mrs. Gee], Aurelia's chaperone (c and pianist, if possible): F♯2 to G♭4 (B♭4 opt). MRS. STONINGTON, of the "Anti-French Literature League" (dram s): C3 to A4. MRS. JINKS, Jonathan's mother: (m-s): B♭2 to G4.

Minor Roles. Jonathan's friends: WILLEM VAN BLEEKER (bs-bar) and CHARLES LAMARTINE (bar). MARY, "Annina" in *La Traviata* (s). CUSTOMS OFFICIAL (bs-buf).

Bit Roles. POLICEMAN (bs-buf). STAGE DOORMAN, STAGEHAND/SCENE PAINTER (doubled by Customs Official and Policeman).

Mute Roles. MISS MERRIAM, of the "Anti-French Literature League."

Ballet. Three or four couples.

Orchestra. 2 fls (picc, fl in G), 2 obs (Eng hrn), 2 B♭ cls (bs cl, cl in E♭), 2 bsns, 2 hrns in F, 2 hrns in B♭, euphonium, tuba, timp, perc, harp, piano (cel), strings.

Material. FS–P and VS: Boosey & Hawkes. VS: American Music Center.

REVIEWS

Alan Rich "Music," *New York* (November 15, 1976), p. 106

> "*Captain Jinks of the Horse Marines* (on the old Clyde Fitch melodrama), is a delightful piece, full of musical skill, especially in the handling of pastiche. (The heroine is a singer working on *Traviata,* whose music is woven into Beeson's own textures.)"

DR. HEIDEGGER'S FOUNTAIN OF YOUTH

Satirical tale. One act (40 minutes). Conservative music. Guests form a vocal quartet for ensemble singing, with narration by Dr. Heidegger.

Libretto by Sheldon Harnick, based on the story "Dr. Heidegger's Experiment" by Nathaniel Hawthorne. Commissioned by the National Arts Club. Premiere: National Arts Club, New York 11.19.78. Performances: Bel Canto Opera, New York 5.81. Recordings: Composers Recordings, CRI SD 406.

PLOT

Setting: Dr. Heidegger's study; mid-nineteenth century.

Dr. Heidegger entertains four elderly friends by pouring a youth potion on a dried flower, which immediately regains its bloom. He then gives the potion to his guests, who are soon restored to their youthful patterns and interests. The Colonel is drawn to Rachel, who can only admire her own beauty. Hannah condemns Rachel's self-absorbtion, resurrecting old jealousies. Reuben returns to his youthful shyness, loving Rachel from afar. As Rachel and the Colonel begin to dance, Hannah challenges Reuben to approach Rachel, but the Colonel refuses to relinquish his prize. The men break into a fight and cause the remaining youth potion to spill. Old once again, Dr. Heidegger's guests vow to seek the potion's source. As the Doctor toasts their search for the Fountain of Youth, he realizes that he has no wish to return to the pain of youth.

PRODUCTION REQUIREMENTS

Major Roles. RACHEL LOCKHART, a widow (lyr s): B♯3 to B4 (C5 opt). HANNAH MOODY, a spinster (m-s): G2 to A4. REUBEN WATERFORD (t): C♯2 to A3. COLONEL KILLIGREW (bar): A1 to F3. DR. HEIDEGGER (bs or bs-bar): G♯1 to E3 (F3 opt).

Minor Roles. A MAID (actress).

Orchestra. fl (picc and alto fl), cl in B♭ (bs cl), cl in B♭ and A (bs cl), perc, harp, piano (cel and harm), strings (1–1–1–1–1 [with C extension]).

Material. FS–P and VS: Boosey & Hawkes.

REVIEWS

Mark Blechner "N.Y. Arts Club: Beeson premiere," *Musical America* (March 1979), p. 22

"[The] plot could have been saved by irony, of which there was none, or by music that would paint vivid . . . portraits. . . . But Beeson paints with strokes too broad for his small canvas."

Orchestral music was "shapeless mood-setting, (although) writing for the voices is more assured."

Stephen Casale *Opera News* (January 29, 1979)

"Beeson's score, singable and well-constructed, shows a natural feeling for English speech rhythms."

"An offstage chamber orchestra . . . offers delicately scored, appropriately spooky music at the outset, grows in intensity and vivacity to the climactic fight . . ."

"The kernel of the piece is an extended waltz scene. . . . Unabashedly tonal and tuneful, it mirrors nicely the nineteenth-century setting."

Peter G. Davis "Opera: Bel Canto Troupe Offers Program of 3 One-Act Works," *New York Times* (May 7, 1981)

"The score is elegantly crafted in a conservative but attractively individual idiom and beautifully written to allow healthy voices an opportunity for some real singing."

John W. Freeman "Beeson: Dr. Heidgedgger's Fountain of Youth," *Opera News* (April 11, 1981). [Record review.]

"Beeson's piece, almost a madrigal opera, will prove a boon on the workshop circuit. . . . The libretto . . . is simplistic, less arresting than it would have to be to enliven Beeson's adroitly crafted but prosaic score."

Eric Salzman "Beeson: Dr. Heidegger's Fountain of Youth," *Stereo Review* (May 1980). [Record review.]

"Beeson's music is organized on a simple, effective premise: the music is twelve-tone until the elixir is quaffed, and then everything falls back into a youthful C Major."

Bill Zakariasen "English music a treat to ear," *Daily News* (November 1978)

"The evolution is predictable but fun all the same, and the music is delightful. None of Beeson's usual acidic social commentary ('Lizzie Borden' etc.) here—just a smoothly written piece of fluff that should prove very, very popular in small theatres."

Gimi Beni

FOREVER FIGARO

Biography of Rossini, with a pastiche of music from his operas with new lyrics. Premiere: Opera Theatre of St. Louis 78.

Thomas Benjamin (1940–   )

THE REHEARSAL

Romantic drama. One act (40 minutes). Chamber opera with traditional harmonies, mixed meters. Arias, ensembles, conversational in places.

Libretto by Cynthia MacDonald. Premiere: Lake George Opera, N.Y. 80.

PLOT

Setting: an opera rehearsal room.

Several young singers gossip as they gather for a rehearsal. Scott announces that Ottenberger, the director, has left his wife for Carlotta. Their gossiping ends abruptly with the entrance of the two lovers. The rehearsal of Mozart's *The Impressario* begins, but is disrupted by his wife's harsh criticism of Carlotta, as Madame struggles to control her emotions. During the break, Madame reminds her husband of their years together. But when Carlotta returns to rehearse an aria with Ottenberger, their deep relationship becomes evident. Tensions culminate when Madame openly reproaches Ottenberg in front of the cast. Ottenberg ends the rehearsal by suggesting that the cast contemplate death as found in *Suor Angelica* as their assignment. Alone, Madame concludes that death is an escape from pain, but that she is determined to learn to live with pain for her art.

PRODUCTION REQUIREMENTS

Major Roles. KURT OTTENBURGER (bar): A♭1 to F♯3. MADAME RENATA CANTRELLI (s): B♭2 to B♭4. CARLOTTA (s): C3 to A4.

Supporting Roles. MARIA (s): E♭3 to B♭4. HANK (t), C♯2 to F3. SCOTT (bar): B♭1 to D♭3. JENNIFER (m-s): D3 to F4.

Speaking Roles. REHEARSAL PIANIST.

Orchestra. fl, ob, cl, bsn, hrn, trp, trb, tuba, perc, piano, strings.

Material. FS–P and VS: the composer (address available through AMC). VS: American Music Center.

REVIEWS

Lisa R. Dominick "The Eighteenth Annual Festival/Conference of the American Society of University Composers: The Composer in the University Reexamined," *Perspectives in New Music* (Volume 21, Fall 1982–Summer 1983), p. 386

> "The pathos of unrequieted love was humorously relaxed by the incongruous bits of scenes culled from the opera under rehearsal, the Mozartean style of which contrasted effectively with the prevailing dramatic style of the work as a whole."

William Bergsma (1921–)

THE MURDER OF COMRADE SHARIK

Action packed comic satire. Prologue, two acts, six scenes, two sets (89 minutes). Dissonant, chromatic harmonic language, frequent meter changes. Conversational vocal style with frequent leaps. Orchestral interludes between scenes.

Libretto by the composer, based on the novel *Heart of Dog* by Mikhail Bulgakov, translated by Mirra Ginsburg. Premiere: Brooklyn, N.Y. 4.10.86.

PLOT

Setting: Moscow, 1925.

Dr. Danielov has perfected an operation that improves the sexual capabilities of his patients. When the Tenants Committee complains that the doctor occupies too much space, the doctor calls a devoted patient, Stalin, to straighten things out. The doctor decides to experiment by implanting human organs in the stray dog, Sharik. When Sharik recovers, he emerges as a human being, albeit a clumsy one. However, when he is registered as a state citizen and begins to espouse party propaganda, Sharik cannot understand why the doctor is no longer kind to him. In their mutual loneliness, Sharik and the doctor's cook, Darya, fall in love. When the doctor discovers them together, he orders Sharik out of the house. Exasperated, the doctor finally calls Stalin to report this evil creation. Unfortunately, the Soviet leader no longer needs the doctor's services and refuses to speak to him. Hearing this, Comrade Sharik begins to take over. But the doctor and his assistant, Blumenthal, sedate him and operate to reverse the initial procedure. The doctor is accused of murdering Comrade Sharik, but when the patient is produced as he turns back into a dog, the charges are dropped. The doctor and Blumenthal rejoice, Darya bemoans her loss, and Sharik howls.

PRODUCTION REQUIREMENTS

Major Roles. SHARIK sometimes a dog (t): D2 to A3 (with alternative F♯3, must bark, scream and make other dog noises). DR. DANIELOV, specialist in sex transplants (bar): A1 to F♯3. BLUMENTHAL, his assistant (bs): B1 to F3. DARYA PETROVNA, his cook (m-s): B♭2 to G4.

Supporting Roles. NURSE (s): D3 to F♯4. LUBINSKI (t): D♯2 to G3. NATASHA (s): C♯3 to A4. SHVONDER, chairman of tenants committee (bs): B♭1 to E3. WANDA/WOMAN'S VOICE (prologue) (s): C3 to F4. KLIM ("confused"): B♭1 to A2, C♯3 to C♯4 falsetto.

Orchestra. fl (picc), ob, cl (bs cl), bsn, hrn, piano, harm, perc, string quintet.

Material. FS–P and VS: Galaxy Music. VS: American Music Center.

Irving Berlin (1888–1989)

ANNIE GET YOUR GUN

Romantic comedy. Two acts, eight scenes (full evening). Musical theater with many dance numbers and a western flavor. Songs with talky verses and melodic refrains.

Lyrics by the composer. Book by Herbert and Dorothy Fields. Premiere: Imperial Theatre, N.Y. 5.16.46. Recording: MCA OC; RCA OC (1966).

PLOT

Setting: touring America in the 1880s.

Annie Oakley, a sharpshooting hillbilly, living outside of Cincinnati, is convinced to join Buffalo Bill's traveling Wild West Show. She falls in love at first sight with Frank Butler, the show's best shooter. But Frank doesn't return the affection when Annie becomes the better marksman. She finally decides that she must lose one in the name of love. She loses the match, but wins Frank's love.

PRODUCTION REQUIREMENTS

Major Roles. ANNIE OAKLEY (a): G♯2 to F4. FRANK BUTLER (bar): G1 to G♭3.

Supporting Roles.* COLONEL WM. F. CODY, "BUFFALO BILL" (bar). MAJOR GORDON LILLIE, "PAWNEE BILL" (bar). CHARLIE DAVENPORT (bar). DOLLY TATE (m-s).
*All supporting roles, more speaking than singing.

Minor Roles. Many other characters (including 7 children's roles) may be drawn from chorus.

Chorus. SATB with much unison or split between men and women.

Dance. Several Wild West Show numbers.

Orchestra. fls I–II (picc), ob (Eng hrn opt), cls I–II (bs cl), bsn, hrn, trps I–II, trp III, trb I, trb II, trb III, 2 perc, vlns A–B–C–D, vla, vcl, bs, harp, guitar.

Material. FS–P and VS: Rogers and Hammerstein.

Leonard Bernstein (1918–)

CANDIDE

Comedia dell'arte vignettes. One act (full evening). Musical theater. Various dance rhythms, folk, jazz, opera buffa influences. Choruses, ensembles of various sizes, unaccompanied vocal sections, much spoken dialogue, arias. Operatic overture and brief orchestral interludes.

Book by Hugh Wheeler, adapted from Voltaire's satire. Libretto by Richard Wilbur, John Latouche, Stephen Sondheim. Premiere: Martin Beck Theatre, N.Y. 12.1.56. Performances: Broadway Theatre, N.Y. 3.10.74 (revised); New York City Opera 82 (Opera House Version). Recordings: Columbia OC (1973), New World OC (1973), New World OC (1982), Random House (1957).

PLOT

Setting: a palace in Westphalia and around the world.

The palace tutor, Dr. Pangloss, teaches Candide, his beloved Cunegonde, her brother Maximillian and the maid Pacquette that everything is for the "best in this world." Their philosophy is tested when Candide is expelled from the palace, later learns that his beloved Cunegonde has died in a war, sets out on a journey, where he is nearly a victim of the Inquisition, is reunited with Cunegonde who, bedecked with jewels, has become the kept woman of a Jew and the Grand Inquisitor. Candide kills them both and he, Cunegonde and her Old Lady maid flee to the New World with a group of devout pilgrims. In Buenos Aires, the lovers are separated again, but Candide crosses paths again with the maid, Pacquette. He, Pacquette and the Old Lady acquire a wealth of gold in Eldorado. But, when they return for Cunegonde, she has set sail for Constantinople. The ship Candide purchases to pursue Cunegonde sinks off the coast. Candide, Pacquette and the Old Lady arrive in Constantinople at last, and are reunited with Cunegonde, Maximillian and Dr. Pangloss. Though Candide has squandered his fortune, the disillusioned young man finally realizes that the world is not perfect, and that one has to make the best of his own situation.

PRODUCTION REQUIREMENTS

Major Roles. DR. VOLTAIRE/DR. PANGLOSS/GOVERNOR/HOST/SAGE (bs-bar): G1 to B♭3. CANDIDE, a naive young man (bar): A1 to A3. PACQUETTE, the maid (m-s): A2 to G4. CUNEGONDE, Candide's beloved (col s): A2 to E5. MAXIMILLIAN, Cunegonde's brother (bs-bar): G1 to G3.

Supporting Roles. OLD LADY (a): D3 to A4. SAILOR/LION/GUEST (bs-bar): A1 to E3. HUNTSMAN/FIRST RECRUITING OFFICER/AGENT/SPANISH DON #1/CARTAGENIAN/PRIEST/SAILOR/EUNUCH (t): D2 to A3. SERVANT/ BULGARIAN SOLDIER/AGENT OF INQUISITION/SPANISH DON #2/ CARTAGENIAN/SAILOR (bar): C2 to F♯3.

Minor Roles. ARISTOCRAT/CARTAGENIAN/2ND SHEEP (male or female): A2 to B3. 2ND RECRUITING OFFICER/RICH JEW/JUDGE/MAN IN BLACK/ CARTAGENIAN/PIRATE/GERMAN BOTANIST/GUEST (bs-bar). LADY KNITTING/CARTAGENIAN/ FIRST SHEEP (a).

Chorus. Four men, five women playing various roles.

Orchestra. Reed I: picc, fl, B♭ cl, alt rec; Reed II: B♭ cl, B♭ bs cl, B♭ s sax; Reed III: fl, ob, bsn, B♭ cl; 2 B♭ trps (flugel hrn); trb; 2 pianos (cel); elec piano; perc; vln (vla); vcl; bs.

Material. FS–P and VS: Music Theatre International or Boosey & Hawkes (Opera House Version).

MASS

"Theater piece for singers, players and dancers." Seventeen divisions, thirty-two numbers (full evening). An amalgamation of compositional and musical styles: folk/guitar, rock and blues, live performance with prerecorded tape, full choral and orchestral writing, dissonance, and twelve-tone instrumental. Largely a choral work, with some solos, small ensembles, and instrumental movements.

Text from the liturgy of the Roman Mass, with additional texts by Stephen Schwartz and Leonard Bernstein. Commission: For the opening of the Kennedy Center of the Performing Arts, Washington, DC. Premiere: Kennedy Center 9.8.71. Recording: Columbia Records. Versions: Available for reduced orchestration and for chamber group.

PLOT

Setting: a surrealist altar setting, 1970s.

Voices heard on quadrophonic tape singing latin devotions before the Mass are interrupted by the strum of a young man's guitar. The Celebrant, in his mid-twenties, sings the famous "Simple Song." He dons a robe and the stage is suddenly flooded with a street chorus of people singing and dancing to the beat of a marching band. The Celebrant, then the church choir begin the formal confession, but members of the street chorus soon express their personal doubts about the church, their lives. The Epistle is read: individuals read letters about their own lonely experiences, and the Celebrant emphasizes that, no matter what, you cannot deny the word of the Lord. An old-fashioned Preacher gives the sermon about how it all began, gradually working the crowd into a frenzy. The Celebrant reappears, this time in more vestments, and the congregation becomes more pious. The Celebrant leads the Credo, only to be interrupted by the doubting Thomases. The Celebrant leads the Lord's Prayer, then attempts to regain his strength in the face of doubts. As always, the pure boy's choir is there to support and echo the word of the Sanctus. When the Celebrant leads the Agnus Dei, his strength is increasingly drained by the interruptions of the people. He finally breaks down and the people drop to the floor, leaving him alone. After the exhausted Celebrant leaves the stage, a small boy slowly rises to sing of peace. He is gradually joined by members of the chorus; even the Celebrant returns in plain clothes. The Boys' choir descends to spread the message to the audience, so that all may "go in Peace."

PRODUCTION REQUIREMENTS

Major Roles. CELEBRANT (bar): B♭1 to A3 (E1 sung sotto voce).

Supporting Roles. One solo each: PREACHER (t): F2 to B♭3; M-S: C3 to F4; BAR: C2 to F3; BOY S: C3 to A4. ROCK SINGER (t): F2 to C4; S: A3 to G4; M-S: C3 to G♭4.

Minor Roles. SOLOISTS WITH ROCK BAND (t, bar, high bar); SOLOISTS WITH BLUES COMBO (high bar, a, bar); Many soloists drawn from various ensembles, well-trained voices required.

Dance. Street chorus moves, separate dancers as well.

Chorus. Street Chorus: SATB (singers and dancers), divisi at times; Boys' Choir: SA, often divisi into choir I and choir II; Choir: SATB (60 members, robed), divisi up to 12 parts; countertenors (3–6)/ Descant Voices: 3 parts; pretaped choruses and soloists: SATB.

Orchestra. Stage musicians: 2 fls (picc), 2 obs (Eng hrn), 3 cls (3 sax (SAT), E♭ cl, bs cl), 2 bsns (cont bsn), 4 hrns, 4 trps, 3 trbs, tuba, 2 elec guitars, bs guitar, 2 elec keyboards, 2 perc. Pit: harp, 2 Allen org, timp, 3–4 perc, strings, prerecorded quadrophonic tape. Chamber version available.

Material. FS–P and VS: Boosey & Hawkes.

A QUIET PLACE

Domestic tragedy. Three acts, seven scenes (140 minutes). Through-composed with *Trouble in Tahiti* (in set numbers format) inserted as two flashback segments in Act II. Choral prologue, postlude: Act I; prelude: Act III. Vocal lines in larger work rhythmically difficult and disjunct.

Libretto by Stephen Wadsworth. Commissioned by Houston Grand Opera, Teatro Alla Scala, Milan, and John F. Kennedy for the Performing Arts. Premiere: Houston Grand Opera 6.17.83. Revised for performances: Milan: 6.84; Washington: 7.22.84. Recording: Deutsche Grammaphon, p. 1987, 419 762–2, CD.

PLOT

Setting: suburban America, early 1980s with flashbacks to early 1950s.

Dinah, Sam's wife, has been killed in an automobile accident. From the chatter of friends gathered at her funeral, we learn that Dinah had been drinking while driving. Dinah's brother Bill takes charge of the ceremony, as each of those close to Dinah reads or reminisces. Dinah and Sam's children arrive late. Dede and Junior now live in Canada with Francois, Junior's former lover, now Dede's husband. Junior, who has a history of mental illness, has not seen his father in twenty years. After the ceremony, with the family alone for the first time, Sam vents his thirty years of anger and grief at the young people. Rather than comfort him, the three reminisce about the time when they were close to their fathers. Junior interrupts by attacking his father, the two of them finally coming to blows. When the coffin lid is knocked shut, all exit, leaving Junior alone to tenderly touch his mother's coffin.

At home, later that evening, Sam sits alone in the master bedroom, reading Dinah's old diaries. Though they make him angry, he realizes that he still loves and misses her. The diary brings back memories of thirty years ago. In the first *Trouble in Tahiti* flashback, instead of seeing the ideal family of the 1950s the jazz trio describes, we see a marriage filled with bickering and lies. Sam's reverie is interrupted by Dede who comes to visit him. As they sort through the cartons and clothes, they start to reach out to each other and finally embrace. In the next room, Francois confronts Junior about his behavior at the funeral parlor. In another psychotic episode, Junior works through some painful associations, finally coming to the realization that he loves and needs his father. Dede and Francois meet in the hall, Dede comforting Francois who is overcome by the strain of the day. Sam goes into Junior's room. He tries to kiss his sleeping son but can't. A trophy on the shelf takes him back thirty years. Sam remembers the afternoon when, instead of going to Junior's school play, he competed for a handball trophy and won. But the feeling of victory lasted only until he approached his own front door, dreading the confrontation. But Dinah also avoided Junior's play. She went, instead, to a movie called *Trouble in Tahiti,* which she hated, but was able to describe frame-by-frame at the beauty shop. That night, rather than trying to communicate, the couple escaped again to the magic of the silver screen.

Early the next morning, Dede weeds Dinah's garden, remembering when she and her mother were close. Junior appears with breakfast. As brother and sister play games remembered from childhood, Francois (and eventually Sam) join in. Sam reads aloud from Dinah's diary, and all share a moment of laughter. The kids tell Sam they are thinking of staying a few days, but another argument ensues. Junior hurls Dinah's diary into the air. As they stop to pick up the pages, thinking of Dinah and her words, they realize that they must learn to communicate, to reach out for one another.

PRODUCTION REQUIREMENTS

Major Roles. SAM (bs): G1 to G3. DEDE (s): G2 to D5. FRANCOIS, Junior's former lover, now Dede's husband (t): B1 to B3. JUNIOR (bar): G1 to A♭3. DINAH (m-s): G2 to G4. YOUNG SAM (bs-bar): F♯1 to F♯3.

Minor Roles. FUNERAL DIRECTOR (t). BILL, Dinah's brother (bar). SUSIE, Dinah's best friend (m-s). DINAH'S ANALYST (t). DOC, the family doctor (bs). MRS. DOC, his wife (c). JAZZ TRIO (s/m-s, high t, high bar).

Chorus. In revised edition, SATB chorus positioned in orchestra pit, with supernumeraries playing guests in funeral scene.

Orchestra. 3 fls (2nd alt fl, 3rd picc), 2 obs, Eng hrn, cl in E♭ (cls in B♭ and A), 2 cls in B♭ (cl in A), bs cl, 2 bsns, cont bsn, 4 hrns in F, 3 trps in B♭, 2 t trbs, bs trb, tuba, timp, 3–4 perc, elec bs, piano (Yamaha DX-7 elec keyboard), harp, strings (6–4–3–3–3).

Material. FS–P and VS: Boosey & Hawkes.

REVIEWS

Philip Campbell "A New and Already Neglected American Opera," *Opera Monthly* (September 1988), pp. 50–53 (Record review.)

"the opera does steer a perilous course between brilliance and bathos. Wadsworth has built a shaky soap opera foundation that allows mawkish dialogue and murky motivation, but Bernstein delivers one of his best scores and, if that isn't cause enough for celebration, much of the drama works surprisingly well on its own terms. Many scenes resonate with deep emotional honesty. . . . *A Quiet Place* is a mightily effective work, warts and all."

Andrew Porter "Love in a Garden," *New Yorker* (August 27, 1984), pp. 60–62
A comparison of first and revised editions which cites several specific changes:

"It's a bold, ambitious, and very interesting opera, containing some of Berstein's most richly wrought music. . . . Bernstein and his librettist, Stephen Wadsworth, have worked with a candor that is almost shocking; they have 'bared their souls.' 'A Quiet place' is no opera for people who want art to keep its distance and behave with decorum."

" 'A Quiet place' is unlike any other opera I know . . . in its attempt to fashion a coherent work of art from the disorderly speech and disorderly thought of people who can't define their emotions clearly and don't even finish their sentences. The music makes clear what they are trying to say and gives form to their muddled lives."

Dorle J. Soria "Leonard Bernstein—His Opera 'A Quiet Place' opens, with glitter, in Washington," *Musical America* (December 1984), pp. 6–7+

"we found the score moving and impressive and the production and performances brilliant. Toward the end of the opera the characters engage in a wild game of symbolic 'stoop tag' in which, reverting to their childhood game, they tear about the stage, sing nostalgic words, try to find through the past some kind of contact or understanding. . . . It recalled the message of the Berstein *Mass.*"

WEST SIDE STORY

Tragedy. Prologue, two acts, fifteen scenes (full evening). Musical theatre. Set numbers, arias, duets, ensembles. Most roles require movement, many require dancers. Orchestra plays large role: mood setting, dance music, change of scenes, etc.

Libretto by Stephen Sondheim. Book by Arthur Laurents, based on a concept by Jerome Robbins. Premiere: Winter Garden Theatre, N.Y. 9.26.57. Performances: Music Theatre of Lincoln Center, N.Y. 68. Minskoff Theatre, N.Y. 80. Recordings: Columbia OC (1985); Random House (1958); Chilton (1973).

PLOT

Setting: New York City's West Side, the present.

A contemporized version of the Romeo and Juliet story—the native-born Polish gang feuds with the newly arrived Puerto Ricans. Tony, the former leader of the Jets, has outgrown the gang and is attempting to distance himself from it. When he meets and falls in love with Maria at the high school dance, he wants peace between the Jets and the Sharks more than ever. But Tony's old gang talks him into attending a rumble, where his efforts to break up the fight end in killing Maria's brother, Bernardo. Bernardo's grief-stricken girl friend, Anita, urges Maria to stay away from Tony. Finally, the Sharks kill Tony and the devastated Maria is left to cry out about the senselessness of hatred and violence.

PRODUCTION REQUIREMENTS

Major Roles. TONY, former leader of the Jets gang (t): $B^{b}1$ to $B^{b}3$. [C4 opt]. MARIA, sister of the Shark's leader, Bernardo (s): $B^{b}2$ to C5.

Supporting Roles. ANITA, Bernardo's girlfriend (ms): F2 to F4. RIFF, member of the Jets and Tony's best friend (bar): G1 to G3.

Minor Roles. ROSALIA (m-s). BERNARDO (bar). A GIRL (m-s). ACTION (bar).

Bit Roles. ACTION, BABY JOHN, A-RAB, SNOWBOY, BIG DEAL (small solos and dance).

Dance. All cast members must move; Shark women and Jet men must be dancers.

Chorus. Gang members and girlfriends, all chorus numbers involve movement or dance.

Orchestra. Reed I (picc, fl, alto sax, cl); Reed II (E^bcl, B^bcl); Reed III (bs cl, t sax, ob, B^bcl, Eng hrn); Reed IV (cl, fl, picc, bs sax); Reed V (bsn); trp I & II; trp III; trb I and II; vln I; vln II; vcl; bs; guitar; piano; perc; piano–conductor.

Material. FS–P and VS: Music Theatre International.

Chester Biscardi

TIGHT-ROPE

Drama. Nine scenes (89 minutes). Libretto by Henry Butler. Commission and premiere: University of Wisconsin, Madison 10.5.85.

Material. Theodore Presser Co. Audio and video tapes: Henry Butler. 56 Irving Place, New York, N.Y. 10003.

Marc Blitzstein (1905–1964) completed by Leonard Lehrman

IDIOTS FIRST

Fable. Thirteen scenes (60 minutes). Conversational vocal writing with mixed meters. Through-composed with brief orchestral interludes.

Libretto by Marc Blitzstein, based on a story by Bernard Malamud. Completed by Leonard Lehrman to be presented with Lehrman's own opera: *Karla*. Premiere: Marc Blitzstein Opera Co., Bloomington, Ind. 3.14.76. Performances: Cornell (concert preview) 8.74. Bel Canto Opera, N.Y.C. 1.22.78.

PLOT

Setting: New York.

Scene i: Mendel's room; ii: Pawnshop; iii: Fishbein's palace; iv: Park bench; v: Doorway; vi: Cafeteria; vii: Side Street; viii: Pawn Shop; ix: Synagogue; x: Pawnshop; xi: Train gate; xii: Coach seat; xiii: Train gate.

Mendel has been notified that he will die at midnight by Ginzberg, the messenger of death. Before he dies, Mendel wants to ensure that his son, Itzak, who is a simpleton, will be on a train to join a relative in California. Mendel unsuccessfully tries to raise the train fare by pawning his belongings and by begging from a wealthy man, though he is constantly stalked by Ginzberg. Finally, the poor Rabbi gives Mendel a new coat to pawn so that he can raise the needed amount. With ticket in hand, Mendel and Itzak are stopped at the train gate by Ginzberg. Mendel physically attacks his opponent and Ginzberg finally relents, allowing Itzak to board the train. When Mendel returns to the gate ready to meet death, he looks for Ginzberg, but dies alone.

PRODUCTION REQUIREMENTS

Major Roles. MENDEL (bar): A1 to A3. ITZAK (t): C♯2 to B♭3.

Supporting Roles. GINZBERG (bar): B1 to F♯3 (G3 opt). LEVINSON, Butler: (bs): G1 to D3. FISHBEIN (t): F2 to G♯3. PAWNBROKER (bar): A♭1 to D♭3. RABBI (t): F2 to A3. RUCHEL, Rabbi's wife (s): F♯3 to B♭4.

Non-singing Roles. WOMAN. POLICEMAN.

Mute Roles. PASSERSBY (5 people).

Orchestra. 2 fls (picc), 2 obs (Eng hrn), cl (E♭ cl opt), cl (bs cl), 2 bsns, 2 hrns, 2 trps, 2 trbs, tuba, 3 timp, chimes, perc, harp (opt), piano/celeste, vibraphone, strings (2–2–2–2–2 at least). May also be performed with 2 pianos plus chimes.

Material. FS–P and VS: Theodore Presser. VS: American Music Center.

REVIEWS

Stephen Casale "New York," *Opera News* (March 18, 1978), p. 49

> "The music for this powerful story does it full justice, and its unlikely mixture of Viennese Expressionism and American musical-theatre lyricism, particularly in the sensitive setting of the speech rhythms of Yiddish-American English, is expertly handled. To Lehrman's credit, one is unaware where Blitzstein ends and Lehrman begins."

Leighton Kerner " 'Idiots First' at Last," *Village Voice* (January 30, 1978), p. 55

> "It's a moving fablelike libretto, and the music makes it more moving. . . . Blitzstein's use of dodecaphony, as well as his drawing on ethnic characteristics in his score, are only starting points for an imaginative, healthily eclectic composer's transformation of the material into a musical language wholly natural and identifiable with this particular story."

Jerry Bock (1928–)

FIDDLER ON THE ROOF

Musical comedy. Two acts, two prologues, seventeen scenes, epilogue (full evening). Traditional with Jewish elements in music. Vocal style from lyrical to declamation.

Libretto by Sheldon Harnick, book by Joseph Stein based on stories by Sholem Aleichem. Premiere: Imperial Theatre, N.Y. 9.22.64. Recording: RCA (1964), Chilton (1973).

PLOT

Setting: Antevka, Russia, 1905.

Tevye, a common dairyman (would-be Rabbi or philanthropic rich man) is attempting to raise his five daughters, especially Tzeitel, Hodel, and Chava, with respect to the Jewish traditions. Golde, Tevye's wife, trusts the matches a local Yente has made for the girls, the first being Tzeitel to the butcher, Lazar Wolf. But Tzeitel and Hodel force Tevye to change with the times, as they choose their own husbands: Tzeitel, the tailor Motel, and Hodel, the student Perchik. A cloud hovers over the lives of these religious people, in the form of the anti-semitism that prevailed in revolutionary Russia. In the end, Tevye and Golde are forced to leave their beloved Antevka to find new lives in America.

PRODUCTION REQUIREMENTS

Major Roles. TEVYE, the dairyman (bar): $A^{\flat}1$ to $F^{\sharp}3$. GOLDE, Tevye's wife (m-s): A2 to E4.

Supporting Roles. TZEITEL, Tevye's oldest daughter (s/m-s): $B^{b}2$ to E4. HODEL, Tevye's second daughter (m-s): B2 to D4. MOTEL, the tailor (bar/t): E2 to $F^{\#}3$. PERCHIK, the student (bar): B1 to E3. LAZAR WOLF, the butcher (bar): C2 to $E^{b}3$. YENTE, the matchmaker (a): F2 to $E^{b}3$.

Minor Roles. CHAVA, Tevye's third daughter (m-s, dancer). GRANDMA TZEITEL (m-s). FRUMA-SARAH (m-s, character role). Several other small roles to be drawn from chorus.

Chorus. Pappas, mammas, sons, daughters: SATB, often split male/female.

Dance. Ensemble movement: tavern and wedding, dream/nightmare sequence.

Orchestra. Reed I: fl, picc; reed II: cl; reed III: cl, bs cl; *reed IV: bsn; *reed V: ob, Eng hrn; trps I & II; *trp III; trb; *hrn; accord; *guitar; perc; vlns A–B–C; *vla; *vcl; bs; piano-conductor.
*May be eliminated.

Material. FS–P and VS: Music Theatre International.

Heskel Brisman (1923–)

WHIRLIGIG

Satirical comedy. One act, two scenes, one set (35 minutes). Conservative modern, employing mixed meters, tonal harmonies. Conversational writing with duets, trios. No introduction, brief orchestral interludes.

Libretto by Jerome Greenfield, based on a story by O. Henry. Premiere: Ball State University, Muncie, Ind. 10.25.77.

PLOT

Setting: hillbilly country; anytime.

Justice of the Peace Widdup deplores his lack of cash as Ariela and Rance come to ask him for a divorce. Although Widdup cannot find guidance in the book of statutes, he agrees to unmarry them for a suitable fee. After Rance gives him five dollars, Widdup performs a divorce ceremony. As he finishes, Arelia demands alimony of five dollars. Since Rance has no more money, the court is adjourned until the next day. During the night, Rance returns to Widdup's place and steals back the five dollars he needs. When the unhappy couple returns the next morning, the divorce is completed. However, the finality of the divorce papers causes them to reconsider their action. They agree to compromise with each other and happily prepare to leave. Widdup reminds them that they are no longer entitled to the joys of matrimony. For a fee of five dollars, however, he happily remarries them.

PRODUCTION REQUIREMENTS

Major Roles. BENAJA WIDDUP, Justice of the Peace (bar): G1 to F#3. RANCE HILBO (t): B1 to B♭3 [falsetto]. ARIELA, Rance's wife (s): C#3 to A4.

Dance. RANCE has one dance.

Orchestra. fl, ob, 2 cls in B♭, bsn, 2 hrns in F, 2 trps, 2 trbs, perc (timp), piano, 2 vlns, vla, cello, cb.

Material. FS–P and VS: Theodore Presser. VS: American Music Center.

REVIEWS

Bernard Holland "Opera: From O. Henry," *New York Times* (June 14, 1982)

> "Heskel Brisman's 'Whirligig'—a treatment of divorce, country-style—was mercifully brief. Its characters went barefoot, drank out of jugs, brandished shotguns, spoke in double negatives, and, in general, ran the usual gamut of Dogpatch imitations."

Stephen Douglas Burton

THE DUCHESS OF MALFI

Three acts. Libretto by Christopher Keene adapted from John Webster's Jacobean tragedy. Commissioned by the National Opera Institute. Premiere: Wolf Trap, Vienna, Va. 9.18.78.

Robert Chauls (1942–)

ALICE IN WONDERLAND

Comic fantasy. Prologue and eight scenes. Shorter version (38 minutes) available for grade school audiences. Conservative twentieth-century idiom. Set numbers border on popular style. Spoken dialogue and sprechstimme. Orchestra provides musical interludes.

Libretto by the composer, based on "Alice's Adventures in Wonderland" by Lewis Carroll. Premiere: Valley Opera, Van Nuys, California 76. Performances: Valley Opera, Van Nuys, California 5.84.

PLOT

The libretto follows the well-known Lewis Carroll story, as Alice meets a host of comical characters on her bizarre adventure: the White Rabbit, the Cheshire Cat, the Queen of Hearts and her entourage, the Duchess, the Mad Hatter, the Gryphon, the Mock Turtle, the March Hare, etc. The Dormouse, the Mad Hatter, the Caterpillar and the March Hare are cut from the shorter version.

PRODUCTION REQUIREMENTS

Major Roles. ALICE (lyr s): B♭2 to B♭4.*

Supporting Roles. THE DUCHESS (bar): B♭1 to E3. QUEEN OF HEARTS (m-s or dram s): A2 to B4. CHESHIRE CAT (t or m-s): A1 to G♯3 or A2 to G♯4. GRYPHON (bs): F♯1 to D♯3. MOCK TURTLE (lyr t): E♭1 to F♯3.*

Minor Roles. THE DORMOUSE (s). THE COOK (m-s). THE WHITE RABBIT (t or s). THE MAD HATTER (bar). THE CATERPILLAR (bs), and THE MARCH HARE (bs) (can both be sung by the GRYPHON).*

Speaking Roles. THE KING OF HEARTS.*
*Role Doubling for Cast of Four in Shorter Version: ALICE (lyr s); WHITE RABBIT, CHESHIRE CAT, MOCK TURTLE (t or s); QUEEN OF HEARTS, COOK (m-s); DUCHESS, GRYPHON, KING OF HEARTS (bs-bar).

Chorus. Treble (unison and three part) (sops require B4).

Ballet. Cheshire cat dances a soft shoe, Gryphon and Mock Turtle dance.

Orchestra. 2 fls (picc), cl, bsn, 2 hrns, 2 trps, 2 trbs, perc, piano (harpsi), strings. Condensed orchestration available: fl, cl, bsn, hrn, trp, trb, piano, perc.

Material. FS–P and VS: Belwin Mills. VS: American Music Center.

REVIEWS

John Henken "Valley Opera Performs 'Alice'," *Los Angeles Times* (May 28, 1984), section 5, p. 2

"The truncated version of 'Alice' offered a series of broadly comic, weakly connected scenes, enlivened by Tara Sitser's slinky Cheshire Cat and David Darling's florid Duchess-in-drag. . . . Chauls and Sitser staged the piece with the jokes out front, credibility and coherence—of even the Wonderland sort—at best tertiary considerations. Children in the audience, though, seemed to like it."

Stewart Copeland

HOLY BLOOD AND CRESCENT MOON

Libretto by Susan Shirwen. Commission and premiere: Cleveland Opera 10.12.89.

Russell Currie (1954–)

THE CASK OF AMONTILLADO

Horror story. One act (30 minutes). Largely tonal with occasional chromatic sections. Through-composed except for a few conventional set numbers. Vocal demands range from lyrical to dramatic recitative to sprechstimme.

Libretto by Carl Laanes, based on a short story by Edgar Allan Poe.

Commission: Bronx Historical Society and Bronx Arts Ensemble. Premiere: Bronx Arts Ensemble, Bronx, N.Y. 4.3.82.

PLOT

Setting: Rome at Carnival time, the 1800s.

Montresor believes he has found the perfect opportunity to seek revenge upon Fortunato for an old insult. Montresor schemes about enticing Fortunato, a pompous, self-proclaimed wine expert, into his familial catacomb-turned wine cellar under the guise of sampling Montresor's newly acquired cask of Amontillado wine. The inebriated Fortunato agrees to leave the Carnival festivities and enter the catacomb. Though the nitre that clings to the walls proves hazardous to Fortunato's ill-health, the braggard follows Montresor deeper into the labyrinth, testing rare vintages along the way. Near exhaustion when he reaches the prized cask, Fortunato is surprised when Montresor quickly slaps him into chains. Fortunato takes this to be a joke, but Montresor reaches for mortar and bricks and slowly walls his "friend" into the crypt. As the last brick is set in place, Fortunato's cries are heard no more.

PRODUCTION REQUIREMENTS

Major Roles. MONTRESOR (bs): D$^{\flat}$1 to E3. FORTUNATO (t): B1 to A4.

Orchestra. fl, cl, bsn, hrn, vibes, timp, perc, strings.

Material. FS–P: contact composer through AMC. FS: American Music Center.

REVIEWS

Steven Phillips "New York," *Opera News* (June 1982), p. 38

> "The music conveyed an eerie, cavernous atmosphere that was appropriate and successful, but the goulash of tonal as well as atonal styles that followed defied explanation. . . . Passages evoked everything from Mozartean recitative to two- and three-part writing in the manner of Hindemith to nineteenth-century beer hall bantering."

Allan Davis (1922–)

THE DEPARTURE

Tragedy. Three acts, six scenes, two sets (180 minutes). Largely tonal with some dissonant, bitonal, modal passages and references to folk music. Vocal parts syllabic, limited in range. Orchestra provides atmosphere and dance music.

Libretto by the composer. Premiere: University of Montevallo, Alabama 4.24.75.

PLOT

Setting: New Orleans, post Civil War Mardi Gras season.

Therese Villiers grows more and more frustrated living with her aging husband, Henri. Having dealt with some hard times during the war, Henri has suffered a decline in status as well as the recent collapse of his bank. To make matters worse, Geraud, the opportunistic son of the Villier's gardener, turns his friendship with Henri to his own advantage and assumes control of the bank. In desperation, Therese sends Taffi, her maid, to hire the Voodooiene to cast a spell to bring about Henri's downfall, so that she can escape with Toni, a young gambler.

A week after the Voodoo ceremony is held, Mardi Gras arrives, and the Voodooiene returns for her pay. Since her spell has not worked, Therese refuses to pay. The angry Voodooiene places a curse on Therese. When Geraud arrives to demand that Henri sell his house in payment for his debts, the disillusioned Henri asks whether Geraud also covets his wife. Geraud responds that Therese is nothing more than a common whore. When Henri takes this accusation, seriously, Therese decides that she must leave Henri immediately. She discloses her plan to Toni: she will drug Henri, then Toni will lock Henri's body in the cellar, giving the two lovers time to escape in disguise into the Mardi Gras parade as it passes by. Taffy returns with Therese's disguise, the devil's mask worn by one of the Voodooiene's dancers the week before. Unfortunately, for the lovers, Henri overhears the plotting and confronts Therese. In his desperation to keep her, Henri asks how she can leave her home and the grave-site of their dead son. Therese is momentarily overcome, but in her hatred for her failed husband, she reveals that the boy was not Henri's child at all – he was Geraud's. Now truly a broken man, Henri leaps at Therese and strangles her. He covers her body with a shawl. Henri dons the mask Therese had planned to wear for her escape, when he hears a knock at the door. Toni enters assuming the masked figure is Therese, and proceeds to drag the body to the cellar. A shriek is heard when Toni learns the true identity of the corpse. Henri, still masked, slinks out of the door, to be lost in the Mardi Gras parade. The Voodooiene's price has been paid.

PRODUCTION REQUIREMENTS

Major Roles. HENRI VILLIERS, ex-confederate officer and one of New Orleans leading citizens before the Civil War (bar): A1 to G♯3. THERESE VILLIERS, Henri's wife, fifteen years his junior (s): B2 to B♭4 [ossia C5]. TONI, a young ne'er-do-well and gambler (t): C♯2 to C4. GERAUD, an opportunist who has bettered his civic status since the war (bs): F1 to F3.

Supporting Roles. TAFFY, Therese's teen-aged mulatto servant (m-s): B2 to G4 (ossia B♭4). THE VOODOOIENE, a Haitian priestess (c): G2 to G4.

Chorus. Followers of the Voodooiene, children of the neighborhood, Mardi Gras celebrants.

Ballet. Followers of the Voodooiene, children of the neighborhood.

Orchestra. fl (picc), ob, cl, bsn, hrn, trp, trb, timp, 3 perc, piano (cel), harp, strings. Stage band (tape recording may be used): 2 cls, 2 trps, 2 trbs, tuba, cymbals, sn drum, bs drum.

Material. FS–P and VS: E. C. Kerby, Ltd. VS: American Music Center.

REVIEWS

Robert Jones "THE UNIVERSITY OF MONTEVALLO STAGES A NEW OPERA: 'The Departure' highlights strengths, weakness of a small music department," *Musical America* (September 1975), pp. 34–35

> "no amount of expert playing could disguise the monotony of the vocal writing — entirely syllabic except for a few lines by the wife whose annoyance finally coaxed her into a welcome burst of melisma."

Oliver Roosevelt "Montevallo, Ala.," *Opera News* (June 1975), p.34

> "His book has promise, but the interminable setting of his libretto, arioso-style, was occasionally awkward."

Anthony Davis (1951–)

UNDER THE DOUBLE MOON

Science fiction. Two acts, ten scenes (full evening). Modern, dissonant idiom with jazz influences, mixed meters, rhythmic ostinatos. Overture, continuous texture with arias and ensembles. Vocal lines melodic in contour, rhythmically complex.

Story and libretto by Deborah Atherton. Commission and premiere: Opera Theatre of St. Louis 6.15.89.

PLOT

Setting: the planet of Undine, in the far future, the Year of the Empress 1332.

Krillig, the fisherman, complains that his wife, Kanaxa, the town fortune-teller has grown cold. Their twin children, Xola and Tarj, exhibit their mother's telepathic powers, but have been warned not to show them. A strange government inspector, sent by the Empress, searches for the twins, telling the villagers the young mind readers are dangerous. Actually, the Empress is dying and needs to be constantly revived by the powers of young people such as the twins. While sailing at sea, the twins are confronted by an amphibious creature, Gaxulta, who explains that he has transformed himself to live under the sea in a life of contemplation. He tells them that he is their real father, and that their mother will soon join him under the sea. Gaxulta confronts the Inspector on the beach, declaring that they will no longer tolerate children being taken and used by the Empress to feed her powers. Nevertheless, the Inspector tempts the twins with glowing "passports," crystal globes that enable them to travel to distant planets. Gaxulta meets his love, Kanaxa, on the beach, and she slowly transforms herself into a sea creature. Malek, a villager, sees the transformation, and summons Krillig, the twins and the Inspector to the beach. When Krillig attempts to stop Gaxulta and Kanaxa from disappearing into the sea, he is swallowed up by the waves. The Inspector uses his mental powers to take the twins by force, but he, too, is engulfed by the sea. The twins, left with the glowing passports, look ahead to the future.

PRODUCTION REQUIREMENTS

Major Roles. KANAXA, the village fortune-teller (m-s): C♯3 to B♭4. XOLA, Kanaxa's daughter (s): D3 to C5. TARJ, Xola's twin brother (bar): A1 to A♯3. INSPECTOR, the Empress' messenger (t): E2 to C♯4 (high tess).

GAXULTA, an amphibious creature, the twin's real father (bar): A1 to G♯3.

Supporting Roles. KRILLIG, a fisherman, Kanaxa's husband (t): E2 to B♭3. MELAK, a villager (bs): F♯1 to E3.

Mute Roles. THREE POLICEMEN (accompanied Inspector's entrance at premiere).

Dance. Six dancers represented undulating sea in premiere production.

Orchestra. 2 fls (picc, alt fl), ob, 2 cls (bs cl, bamboo fl opt), bsn, 2 hrns, trp, trb, timp (mallets), 3 perc (vibraphone, marimba, mallets, drum set, steel drums), harp, strings. Musician/Improvisors: reed, trb, bs, perc.

Material. FS–P and VS: G. Schirmer.

REVIEWS

James Wierzbicki " 'Double Moon' Uneven, Needs Polishing," *St. Louis Post Dispatch* (June 17, 1989), Section D, p. 4

> "Davis' music is repetitious, not just in its melodies but also in the jazzy rhythmic patterns that serve as foundations . . . for various sections. Repetitious music, of course, can be forceful; it can gain tremendous momentum when the material is not just repeated but somehow intensified and made to move relentlessly toward emotional peaks. And Davis knows how to do this."

> " 'Under the Double Moon' is an inconsistent opera, but its successful parts are worth hearing and seeing."

X (THE LIFE AND TIMES OF MALCOLM X)

Biography. Three acts, six to nine scenes (150 minutes). Varied musical styles from minimalism to jazz, blues, rap, African influence, some improvisation. Vocal lines have frequent meter changes, some chromaticism. Traditional set numbers, etc.

Story by Christopher Davis. Libretto by Thulani Davis. Premiere: New York City Opera, N.Y. 9.28.86 (revised edition). Performances: American Music Theatre Festival, Philadelphia 10.85. (workshop full performance).

PLOT

Setting: Harlem, Boston, 1950s, '60s.

As Malcolm Little, the child, participates in a church meeting, we learn of the early events that shaped his character: his preacher father's accidental death under questionable circumstances, his mother's breakdown, his sister Ella's view of life in Harlem, and Street, the hoodlum's influence on the young boy. The grown Malcolm moves to Boston and begins a life of petty crime, eventually spending an extended term in prison. While there, Malcolm is introduced to the Koran and his conversion to Islam brings him to drop his surname and adopt the letter X. Malcolm, the new man, emerges from prison, meets the head of the Muslim movement, Elijah Muhammed, and becomes an influential leader in his own right. Malcolm eventually becomes a threat to Elijah when he becomes more radical and independently outspoken. Malcolm visits Mecca, where he converts to orthodox Islam, taking a new name to signify his rebirth. Malcolm, now El-Shabazz, also travels through Africa and the Third World. He develops a broader view of the struggle not just for blacks in the U.S., but for human rights all over the world. His organizing of a religious/political group called the Organization of Afro-American Unity is simultaneous with the Harlem riot of 1964, depicted in the opera. Thus, his actions seem threatening to both the U.S. government's efforts to control black unrest and to Elijah. In 1965, Malcolm's radical efforts end in his assassination.

PRODUCTION REQUIRMENTS

Major Roles. MALCOLM X (bar): G1 to F♯3. ELIJAH, head of the Black Muslim movement (t): D2 to D4/STREET (t): E♭2 to B♭3 (these two roles played by same singer at premiere).

Supporting Roles. REGINALD (bar): A♭1 to E3. ELLA, Malcolm's sister (m-s): A♯2 to G4. LOUISE, Malcolm's mother/MUSLIM WOMAN/BETTY SHABAZZ, Malcolm's wife (s): C3 to C♯5.

Minor Roles. MALCOLM, as a child (boy s): G♯2 to B3. GARVEY PREACHER (bar). SOCIAL WORKER (m-s). QUEEN MOTHER (m-s). 3 POLICE OFFICERS (t,t,bar). REPORTER (spoken).

Chorus. SATB (3–4 part divisi). Large use of chorus, both black and white singers.

Orchestra. 2 fls, ob, 2 cls (2 sax), 2 bsns (cont bsn), 2 hrns, trp, 2 trbs, timp, 3 perc, celeste, piano, strings. Jazz band: fl, 2 cls, trp, perc, vcl, bs, piano, drums.

Material. FS–P and VS: G. Schirmer.

REVIEWS

Herbert Kupferberg "New York," *Musical America* (March 1987), pp. 22–23

"in addition to being sensitive to his people's history, the 35-year-old Davis is a musician of quality, susceptible to influences from Gershwin to minimalism, yet capable of molding his material into a stageworthy work with a profile of its own."

"Davis's music provides plenty of dramatic propulsion to go along with its distinctive ethnic flavor. No master of long lyric line, Davis gets his effects with pungent, short musical phrases set against a well-varied rhythmic background provided by the City Opera orchestra and his own instrumental group, Episteme."

Howard Mandel "X (The Life and Times of Malcolm X)," *Down Beat* (January 1987), p. 50

"Yes, opera can be a relevant musical theatre form of the late twentieth century, embracing (gasp!) jazz-like improvisation and idiomatic American English as well as serialism, contemporary social issues, and advanced stagecraft."

"A most gratifying aspect of Davis' music was his seamless inclusion in the orchestral score of jazz-related rhythms . . . and improvised passages."

Robert Massa "Philly Harmonics," *Village Voice* (July 17, 1984), pp. 83–84

"Davis' music is lush with atmosphere; the melodies are fragmented, the harmonies bend the ear a little, yet the score seems written through with one mad dash, melding the disparate rhythms of Malcolm's street life and religious conversion into a coherent whole."

Royce Dembo (1933–)

THE AUDIENCE

Comedy. One act (30 minutes). Contemporary idiom. Open harmonic structure with shifting tonal centers. Through-composed with mostly spoken dialogue, a duet, solo and trio. No overture or interludes. Vocal parts not overly difficult.

Libretto by Glen Miller. Commissioned by Meet the Composer Grant. Premiere: Soho Repertory N.Y. 5.82.

PLOT

Setting: Raymond and Martha's living room, c. 1900–1925.

As Martha practices her singing, Raymond taunts her for believing that she is singing to an audience "out there." Her new voice teacher, Arthur Romanoff, makes a grand entrance, bringing a full chamber orchestra to accompany Martha. Raymond is so disgusted by all this that he packs his bags and threatens to leave, unless Martha can return to her senses. Romanoff challenges Raymond to a test: if he is not a coward, he must look at the audience. Raymond complies and sees the audience for the first time. At Romanoff's urging, the reluctant Raymond finally joins his wife in song. The trio extols the power of song to open their souls and renew their love.

PRODUCTION REQUIREMENTS

Major Roles. MARTHA, a singer (m-s): D♭3 to G4. RAYMOND, her husband (bar): C♯2 to D♯3 [A♭3 falsetto]. MAESTRO ARTHUR ROMANOFF, the voice teacher (bar): C2 to F3.

Orchestra. ob, cl, vln, vla, vcl.

Material. FS–P and VS: Golden Fleece, Ltd., New York. VS: American Music Center.

REVIEWS

Edward Rothstein "Opera: Three One-Acters Get Premieres at SoHo," *New York Times* (May 11, 1982), section C, p. 16

"The slight plot had its minor modernist charms. Miss Dembo's skillful Menottian writing ... was suitably operatic and theatrical—though articulation difficulties prevented the message from being fully delivered."

Paul Dresher (1951–)

POWER FAILURE

Science fiction morality play. Two acts (90 minutes). Opera/theater piece mixing electronic, rock, jazz, minimalist styles. Vocal lines can be disjunct, chromatic, even improvised. Much spoken dialogue mostly with musical accompaniment.

Libretto by Rinde Eckert. Commissioned by the Walker Art Center, Musical Traditions, American Music Theatre Festival, the University of Iowa, and Robin Kirck. Premiere: American Music Theatre Festival 5.4.89. Performances: Paul Dresher Ensemble, Hancher Auditorium, Iowa City 10.27.89; Northrop Auditorium, Minneapolis 11.4.89.

PLOT

Setting: the present.

Merle Townsend, once a private detective, now a security guard at Delta Chemical, narrates the story. Charles Smithson built the mega-Delta Chemical from the ground up, never hesitating to cheat or lie to achieve wealth and power. Because he is dying of a rare blood disease, Charles uses his position to hire the bright young biochemist, Ruth Lehman, whose experiments with DNA and virus types eventually win her a Nobel Prize. Ruth develops a secret serum which can cure not only Charles' disease, but every affliction known to man. Smithson's personal secretary, Judith, reveals that Charles is already receiving treatments, and that he plans to keep the serum for his own personal use and financial gain—keeping it from the general public but selling it on the black market.

During one of Charles' treatments, held deep within the company's basements, Merle choreographs Smithson's demise. A power failure causes Ruth's apparatus to shut down, giving Merle his captive audience for the story of his daughter's painful death. On the verge of receiving a lifesaving liver transplant, the promised organ was rescinded. Merle's own investigation revealed that the organ was purchased by Charles for use in Ruth's experiments. When Ruth realizes that Charles has no intention of allowing her invention to help society, she leaves him helplessly attached to the machinery. Though Merle has the opportunity to finish him off in vengeance, he decides to let Charles die of the disease he tried so desperately to avoid.

PRODUCTION REQUIREMENTS

Major Roles. MERLE TOWNSEND, security guard at Delta Chemical (t): D2 to B♭3 [F♯3 to F♯4 fals]. RUTH LEHMAN, biochemist (m-s): G2 to A♭4. CHARLES SMITHSON, President of Delta Chemical (t): A1 to C4. JUDITH, Smithson's secretary (s): C♯3 to B♭4.

Orchestra. Four players: multi-woodwind performer (fl, bs cl, alt sax), electronic keyboard, synthesizer, perc.

Material. FS–P and VS: Paul Dresher Ensemble, 1937 Carleton Street, Berkeley, California 94103. (415) 843-4011

REVIEWS

Cary Mazer "Electricity and Red Socks," *Philadelphia City Paper* (May 12–May 19, 1989), p. 12

> "On the surface, *Power Failure* resembles a high-tech version of a 1920s German Expressionist play. Social forces are presented allegorically and satirically. . . . But Eckert holds all of this together with the same type of network of evocative images which made *Slow Fire* [premiered in 1986] so extraordinary."

> "At the center of the play is a remarkable musical solo, an imaginary dialogue about death between Merle and his daughter, with Merle singing alternately in each of their voices. . . . At such moments—indeed, whenever Eckert holds the stage—the play becomes . . . something beyond mere dystopian fantasy and satire: a haunting poetic fusion of acting, visual and verbal imagery and Dresher's music."

Miriam Seidel "Paul Dresher and Rinde Eckert," *High Performance* (Fall 1989), p. 72

> "It was in the staging, with its casually dreamlike accretion of elements, that the work found its signature. . . . Indeed the work is more about dreams, and how they underpin power and action, than about earthly power. All the characters revealed themselves

by describing their dreams. In these dream passages, Eckert and Dresher soared on long, sinuous melodic lines, the text filled with arresting images."

Howard Smith "Drug to make all world well is provocative tonic in opera 'Power Failure,' " *Minneapolis Star Tribune* (November 4, 1989)

"The action moves forward to the propulsive, rippling, multi-rhythmic chamber music of Dresher . . . its echoes range from Mike Oldfield to Indonesian gamelan effects."

"The music's lyrical moments, simple though they appear, are at least as impressive as the more general accompaniment. . . . the California composer shows elements in common with the lyric style of English composer Benjamin Britten."

"Dresher has sought to distance himself from standard opera, yet hardly anything here departs from opera technique and method. Projected images, open staging, acres of spoken dialogue, none of these is alien to operatic tradition."

Lesley Valdes "Contemporary opera by Eckert, Dresher," *Philadelphia Inquirer* (May 5, 1989)

"Eckert's articulately written libretto is one of the pluses; for its language is not only intelligently conceived, it is singable and witty. Dresher's music is another, a pulsing score that marries minimalist and rock idioms with some fairly traditional operatic writing that does not ignore the human voice."

"The second act Biblical allusions . . . notably weaken the structure although Dresher's four-man support system . . . keep[s] the momentum pulsing to a conclusion almost as highly charged as that which ends the vital first act."

SLOW FIRE

Developed by Paul Dresher in collaboration with librettist/performer Rinde Eckert. Owing to the unique nature of Eckert as a performer, the same ensemble would be required for future performances. Premiere: Theatre Artaud, San Francisco 2.88.

Material. Paul Dresher Ensemble (see address under *Power Failure*).

Paul Earls (1934–)

THE DEATH OF KING PHILLIP

Historical fiction. One act (70 minutes). Largely dissonant style with cluster chords, naturally and electronically generated "sound" pieces. Many notated "events" in which various combinations of instruments, voices or tape are played independently but simultaneously. Very disjunct, declamatory vocal lines often not aided by orchestral cues especially in "events" described above. Frequent meter changes, complex rhythms.

Libretto by Romulus Linney, based on the conflict between the Indian, King Phillip, and the Puritan settlers of New England. Premiere: New England Chamber Opera Group, Brookline, Mass. 3.26.76.

PLOT

Setting: New England, 1675–1676.

A psychological study which represents the varying points of view about the leader of the Wampanoag Indians of New England, who called himself King Phillip. Because he believed that the American Indian would be exterminated, he attempted to unite various Indian nations in war against the New England colonists. Reverend Joseph Rowlandson serves as spokesman for the Puritan view of King Phillip, as enemy to the cause of bringing God's Kingdom to America. The Reverend's wife is represented by two Marys: a sixty-year-old who reflects back on these events and as a thirty-year-old wife and mother. Held captive by King Phillip, Mary Rolandson grew to respect Phillip's bravery, convictions, his fears for his people, and his personal struggle with his own manhood.

In flashback, we see young Mary Rowlandson, an innocent captive who suffers many hardships: a wintry exile; the death of her baby; becoming the servant to Phillip. Finding strength in the purity of her faith, Mary's hatred for the enemy gradually turns to compassion for Phillip's own tragic life: the deaths of his friends and warriors; numerous defeats on the battlefield; the capture and selling into slavery of his own wife and child. After several battles, we finally witness Phillip's demise, not at the hands of an Englishman, but by one of his own people, a Christianized Indian.

PRODUCTION REQUIREMENTS

Major Roles. MARY ROWLANDSON, age 60 (dram s): G2 to B4. REVEREND JOSEPH ROWLANDSON, Mary's husband (t): C2 to D♭4. KING PHILLIP (bs): C1 to G♯3 (falsetto: E3 to D4.)

Supporting Roles. MARY ROWLANDSON, age 30 (1yr s): $B^{\flat}2$ to C5.

Speaking Roles. READER/VOICE (male) (supporting role).

Minor Roles. TWO WAMPANOAG WARRIORS I (t and bar).

Chorus. SATB (16 voices).

Ballet. WEETAMOO (female dancer).

Orchestra. fl (picc), cl (bs cl), hrn, trp, perc, accord, harp, portative organ, cello, tape, electronic processing.

Material. FS–P and libretto: American Music Center and the composer (contact through AMC).

REVIEWS

Ellen Pfeifer "BROOKLINE — New England Chamber Opera: 'The Death of King Phillip,' " *Musical America* (July 1976), pp. 24–25

"*King Phillip* is like a show-and-tell of visual technology with effects thrown in whether or not they enhance the dramatic moment."

"Musically, the opera also seems a catalogue of contemporary effects. The vocal line is jagged, featuring leaps and extremes of pitch at both the upper and lower ends of the singers' ranges. It failed to be interesting and often seemed painful for the singers to negotiate."

Andrew Porter "Musical Events," *New Yorker* (April 19, 1976), p. 120

"a more elaborate work, containing multiple scenes, multiple sound sources, and, in addition to 'regular' singing and playing, electronic effects both prerecorded and applied to the living performers."

"I found 'King Phillip' an adventurous, exciting, and very accomplished opera, enhanced by astonishing light effects devised by the M.I.T. Center for Advanced Visual Studies."

John Eaton (1935–)

THE CRY OF CLYTEMNESTRA

Tragedy. One act (75 minutes). Unusual requirements: two pianos, one tuned down a quarter-tone; quarter-tone accidentals in vocal parts indicating pitches which should be modified to match just intonation of live or taped electronic music. Recitative, some set numbers: arias, duets (singing as well as sprechstimme). No overture.

Libretto by Patrick Creagh, based on Greek tragedy by Aeschylus. Premiere: Indiana University Opera 3.1.80. Performances: Brooklyn Philharmonia 11.80.

PLOT

Setting: the bedroom of the palace of Argos and the garden beneath it, plus an area where Clytemnestra's dreams can be projected.

In a series of dream sequences, Clytemnestra recalls the sacrifice of her daughter, Iphegeneia, by her husband, Agamemnon. When the five Greek princes demand that Agamemnon sacrifice his daughter to ensure victory at Troy, he convinces Clytemnestra to send Iphegeneia to him, under the guise that she will be married to the great Achilles. Clytemnestra complies, separating Iphegeneia from her siblings, Orestes and Electra, and sending the unsuspecting girl to death at her father's hands. Clytemnestra wakes from her dream. She and her lover, Aegisthus, argue about her children, Electra and Orestes. In the heat of the argument, Aegisthus reveals that Agamemnon lies in Troy with Apollo's priestess, the Princess Cassandra. We see Agamemnon asking Cassandra to reveal what Apollo shows her. In a prophetic trance, Cassandra sees a woman weaving a robe, fit for a king. But the robe is a trap which brings him to a shameful death. This vision seems meaningless to Agamemnon. Electra and Orestes mourn their fate, and Electra vehemently rejects Aegisthus' advances. Aegisthus proclaims to Clytemnestra that they must be rid of Electra, because she refuses to be loyal to him. Electra's hatred finally drives Clytemnestra to ask her to leave their house, taking Orestes with her. Alone again, Clytemnestra falls unconscious, dreaming of Agamemnon's return. To welcome the King, Clytemnestra brings the prophesized robe, which strangles the King. Awaking from her dream, Clytemnestra hears the beacons, signaling Agamemnon's arrival. She goes to fulfill her destiny with robe in hand.

PRODUCTION REQUIREMENTS

Major Roles. CLYTEMNESTRA (m-s): F2 to C5. Clytemnestra's deceased daughter, IPHIGENEIA (col s): C3 to F5. Clytemnestra's husband, AGAMEMNON (bar): C2 to A3. Iphigeneia's younger sister, ELECTRA (s): F♯2 to C5 [D5 opt]. Clytemnestra's lover, AEGISTHUS (t): D♭2 [C2 opt] to C4.

Supporting Roles. Clytemnestra's son, ORESTES (t): D♭2 to B3 [C4 opt]. Agamemnon's lover, CASSANDRA (s): E2 to D5.

Minor Roles. FIVE GREEK PRINCES: ODYSSEUS, MENELAUS (tens); DIOMEDES, TEUCER (bars); AJAX (bs). CALCHAS (t). ACHILLES (t). ORESTES AS A CHILD (boy s).

Orchestra. Orchestra divided into groups a and b (b tuned down a quarter tone—half the distance between A and A♭): fl a and b (picc a and b), ob a and b, cl in B♭ a and b, cl in E♭b, bs cl in B♭ a and b (contbs cl in E♭), bsn a and b, hrn (B♭ and F), piano a and b, timp, perc, strings (2–2–2–2–1).

Material. FS–P, VS and Libretto: American Music Center and Shawnee Press.

REVIEWS

Harold Blumenfeld "Review: Two Opera Premieres," *Opera Journal* (1980), 13(2):13–14

> "The libretto's cimematic strategy comes across clearly enough. However . . . its prose is too often undermined by stylistic inconsistencies bordering on the soap opera."

> "The most remarkable feature of Eaton's score is the flexible, highly melismatic and often high-voltage vocal writing. The use of unusually high and taxing tessitura for all the leading roles helps maintain his angered characters at fever pitch . . . through much of the work . . . "

> "Electronic sound is marvelously panned throughout the hall as . . . action moves from one time frame to another."

Donal Henahan "Opera: Double Local Debut of One-Acters in Brooklyn," *New York Times* (November 15, 1980), p. 13, column 5

"[Mr. Eaton] employs all the cliches of Viennese Expressionism—the punishingly extreme vocal lines, the shapeless declamation, the instrumental roars and clatters, the rasping sonorities—and he has added to them his own generation's cliches."

"The opera was sung in English, but hardly one word in a hundred could be made out . . . "

Andrew Porter "Eleleleleu!" *New Yorker* (March 31, 1980), pp. 94–96

". . . hardly a 'chamber' opera. It makes a big sound. Its gestures are large. It has grandeur and force."

"His whole army of expressive devices. . . . includes different kinds of tuning, which can provide . . . telling inflections of melodic lines, curiously colored harmonies, and tonal oppositions between notes close yet different . . . his controlled enrichment of the traditional melodic and harmonic palettes sounds spontaneous and natural, not calculated."

"The vocal writing looks fiendishly difficult . . . One would have said that the composer had been recklessly extravagant in his demands had not those demands been so ably met."

Charles Staff "Indiana University: Eaton's 'Cry of Clytemnestra,' " *Musical America* (June 1980), p. 29

"Eaton rises above the inept libretto with a seething, volcanic score which erupts with superbly calculated electronic effects and then subsides into artfully written lyric moments. . . . The results are often so thrilling that the words seemed even sillier by comparison with the originality and strength of the music."

DANTON AND ROBESPIERRE

Historical fiction. Three acts, thirteen scenes (120 minutes). Eclectic, mostly atonal; extreme chromaticism. Solo roles demand quarter tones mixed with normal intonation; frequent wide, dissonant leaps; intricate rhythms; and quick succession of meters. Chorus parts also very difficult—quarter-tones with little or no support from orchestra. Structure more traditional. Non-traditional notation used frequently throughout.

Libretto by Patrick Creagh. Premiere: Indiana University, Bloomington, Ind. 4.21.78.

PLOT

Setting: Paris, 1792, beginning of the Reign of Terror.

In the tumultuous years just after the storming of the Bastille, two of the revolution's heroes have now parted company, subscribing to different ideologies. Robespierre's Reign of Terror contrasts with Danton's heroic life, idealism and patriotism. Together with his compatriot Camille Desmoulins, Danton, as friend of the People, is cast against the evil power Robespierre has gained through the guillotine. The promise of happiness and brotherhood for which the revolution was fought has now left little in France but hunger and blood-stained streets. Gabrielle, Danton's wife, holds her husband somewhat responsible when he appears unwilling to challenge Robespierre. But, finding strength in his new love, the young Louise, Danton returns to Paris in all its chaos to confront Robespierre. Welcomed by the populace as a saviour figure, Danton quickly earns Robespierre's hatred and distrust. Robespierre's henchmen, St. Just and Couthon, spread rumors of treason, and Danton and Camille are brought to trial. The two heroes bravely go to the guillotine, but not without formally denouncing Robespierre, and blaming him for the terror that holds Paris captive. After their deaths, all Paris cries for revenge and it is Robespierre who is finally brought to trial. Seeing his hopes and plans crumble before him, Robespierre meets with the same end to which he had sentenced the innocent Danton: death by the guillotine.

PRODUCTION REQUIREMENTS

Major Roles. Note: † = ½ sharp, 𝄳 = ½ flat. DANTON, leader in Legislative Assembly (t): C𝄳2 to B3 [C♯4 opt]. ROBESPIERRE, leader in L.A. (bs-bar): F𝄳1 to A3 [falsetto: E3 to A♯3 and higher if possible]. CAMILLE DESMOULINS, leader in L.A. (t): D2 to B3 [D♭4 opt]. LOUISE, Danton's mistress (s): C3 to C5 [E♭2 opt parlando, D♯5 opt]. LUCILLE (col s): C♭3 to D♭5 [D♯5 opt].

Supporting Roles. GABRIELLE, Danton's wife (m-s): G♭2 to G4 [D2 opt]. ST. JUST (bs): E𝄳1 to F♯3. COUTHON (t): D2 to C4 [C2 opt]. DRUNK (bar): G1 to F♯3 [G3 opt].

Minor Roles. MARAT (t): to B3 [E5 opt]. A FISHWIFE (s). BAKER'S WIFE (s). PROSTITUTE (m-s). TALLIEN (t). MADAME TALLIEN (m-s).

Bit Roles. Small solo roles drawn from chorus: ROLAND (bar), A SOLDIER (bar), 3 MEN, 2 SPEAKERS, 2 WOMEN, 3 THUGS; MESSENGER.

Chorus. Full Chorus: SATB [divisi up to 10 on each part], Mixed Ensemble: SSATB [4–3–3–4–4 at least], Male Chorus, Female Chorus.

Orchestra. 4 fls (picc, a^{b}fl), 4 obs (Eng hrn), E^b cl, 4 cls, bs cl, 4 bsns, 2 cont basns, 4 hns, 4 trps, 4 trbs, 2 tubas, timp, perc, 2 pianos, 3 harps, strings, elect music. Stage band: 4 trps, 4 trbs, perc.

Material. FS–P and VS: G. Schirmer.

REVIEWS

Andrew Porter "Enflam'd with Hope," *New Yorker* (May 22, 1978), pp. 118–121

" 'Danton and Robespierre' . . . is a large, exciting, adventurous, and vividly theatrical piece. . . . The composer's and librettist's visions . . . were carried out to thrilling effect."

"Except in steady and exposed solo lines, it was hard to take conscious cognizances of the quarter-tones. One tended to 'read' them as the nearest regular note, slightly 'bent' for the purpose of expression."

"For all the intricacies of Eaton's score, it is direct and readily comprehensible. . . . His writing for the chorus is adventurous and exciting. His writing for the orchestra is varied and very colorful. Moreover, and perhaps most important of all, 'Danton' is a mellifluous opera, composed of lyrical vocal gestures that reveal character and are also good to sing. Without that quality, an opera does not live."

John Rockwell "Opera: 'Danton' by John Eaton," *New York Times* (April 24, 1978), section 3, p. 20

"(The opera) had a genuine epic sweep last night. Particularly in the final act, when the stirring passions of the time, Mr. Eaton's music and the mass tableaus . . . really came to life."

"The larger problems lay in the libretto and the music. Danton and Robespierre emerge in Mr. Creagh's vision too stereotypical. . . . In Mr. Eaton's case, 'Danton and Robespierre' is yet another new opera with undistinguished, recitativelike vocal lines. Mr. Eaton's ear for imaginative instrumental effects is so considerable that one fervently hopes he tries opera again."

THE TEMPEST

Fantasy. Three acts, twelve scenes (full evening). Contemporary idiom includes electronics and electronic manipulation of live singers, quarter-tone sonority, elements of aleatoric writing in the orchestra, jazz band within orchestral fabric. Continuous texture with arias and ensembles. Vocal writing difficult melodically and rhythmically, often at registral extremes.

Libretto by Andrew Porter after Shakespeare. Premiere: Santa Fe Opera 7.27.85.

PLOT

Setting: at sea, on a deserted island, during the Italian Renaissance.

Following Shakespeare's story, briefly: Prospero, the former Duke of Milan, was deposed by his brother, Antonio, and Alonso, the King of Naples, and cast out to sea. Prospero, with his books of magic and his daughter, Miranda, has inhabited this deserted island ever since. With the aid of Ariel, the chief island spirit, Antonio, Alonso and their royal party are shipwrecked near the island. Miranda meets Prince Ferdinand, Alonso's son, who believes he is the only survivor of the shipwreck, and it is love at first sight. But Prospero intervenes, forcing Ferdinand into menial labor. Meanwhile, the other courtiers attempt to cheer Alonso, who believes his son has perished. While Alonso sleeps, Antonio and Sebastian plot to kill him for his crown. But Ariel works her magic once again, to wake Alonso in time. Caliban, the man-monster of the island, and slave of Prospero, hides from his master's torments. Trinculo, a jester from the shipwrecked party, followed by Stephano, the ship's butler, who floated ashore on a keg of wine, proceed to share their drink with Caliban. Drunk for the first time, Caliban swears he will serve these new masters anywhere.

Prospero works his magic and presides over each party. Miranda and Ferdinand profess their love, Caliban enlists Stephano and Trinculo in a plot against Prospero's life, and Ariel appears to frighten and accuse Alonso, Antonio and Sebastian of their plot against Prospero. The drunken trio interrupt the trembling courtiers. But Prospero, pleased with the proceedings, promises that Ariel will soon have her freedom. Prospero gives his daughter's hand to Ferdinand, forgives those who plotted against him, and all look forward to returning to their rightful positions in Milan.

PRODUCTION REQUIREMENTS

Major Roles. PROSPERO, former Duke of Milan (bar): F1 to B3 (opt C♯4 fals). MIRANDA, Prospero's daughter (lyr s): B2 to E5. ARIEL, chief spirit of the island (col m-s): F2 to E5 [must sing with live electronic manipulation of voice: echo, reverb, harmonize]. FERDINAND, Alonso's son (spin t): B1 to D4 (F♯4 fals).

Supporting Roles. CALIBAN, man-monster of the island ("jazz singer," male or female): F2 to E5 in score (writing is skeletal, part may be adapted for singer). TRINCULO, the ship jester (ct or t): E♭2 to D4 (opt G♯4). STEPHANO, the ship's butler (buf bar): A♭1 to A♭3 (opt G4 fals). SEBASTIAN, Alonso's brother (high t): C2 to B3. ANTONIO, Prospero's brother (t): D♭2 to B3. ALONZO, King of Naples (bs): F1 to G3. GONZOLO, faithful court councillor (bs): D1 to F3. IRIS, Juno's messenger (col s): D♭3 to E5.

Minor Roles. CERES (m-s): F2 to A4. JUNO (c): F2 to D4.

Bit Roles. MASTER OF THE SHIP (bs): BOATSWAIN (bar). Roles to be drawn from chorus: t, t, 2 bar, 2 bs).

Chorus. Mixed. Includes: Chorus of Spirits (SI and II, M-S, A), Chorus of Seamen (2 T, BAR, BS) (2 persons per part max); 4 Courtiers (listed above).

Orchestra. 2 fls, 2 obs, 2 Eng horns, 2 bs cls. cont bsn, 4 hrns, 3 trps, 2 trbs, bs trb, tuba, timp, perc, 2 harps (opt), 2 pianos, strings (9 vlns–6–6–4), Renaissance ens (shawm, lute), jazz trio, electronic music.

Material. FS–P and VS: G. Schirmer.

REVIEWS

Joan La Barbara "At Santa Fe," *Musical America* (January 1986), p. 25

> "Each of the characters has special music associated with an aspect Eaton wished to portray: Miranda and Ferdinand, the young lovers, sing in different tempos and have solo strings playing *cantabile;* Caliban, the island's resident monster, scat sings with jazz band accompaniment; Ariel and the spirits are accompanied by a Renaissance ensemble playing a quarter-tone above the orchestra . . . Alonzo, Gonazalo, and the courtiers are accompanied by brass players who have been instructed to slide around pitch fields searching for notes."

John Rockwell "Opera: World Premiere of Eaton's 'Tempest,' " *New York Times* (July 30, 1985), p. 14

> "it is worth cataloguing the various ways in which 'The Tempest' is an interesting, even admirable work. Mr. Porter's libretto is a truly ingenious, sensitive condensation of Shakespeare. . . . Mr. Eaton's music, too, has much to commend, at least in its isolated components. He writes often in microtones, which can lend a rare color and even untempered consonance to music. His use of electronics, both for coloration and to disperse voices, especially Ariel's, around the stage is promising. . . . But for all the occasionally piquant detail—especially some of the atmospheric orchestral effects coupled with electronics—the pervasive impression is of dissonant sludge."

Michael Walsh "When the Style is No Style," *Time* (August 19, 1985), p. 61

> "*The Tempest* is a rich blend of Renaissance music, jazz and electronics that is surrounded by an uncompromisingly modernist microtonal framework."

> "What Eaton has done is not merely to set Porter's concise, three-act libretto, but to retell it in musical terms, creating a cognate of Shakespeare's play. It is a formidable intellectual as well as musical accomplishment."

Duke Ellington

QUEENIE PIE

"Street opera or opera buffa." Unfinished at the time of Duke Ellington's death in 1974—completed by George C. Wolfe (libretto), George David Weiss (lyrics), Maurice Peress and Barrie Lee Hall (adaptation and development of music for the Duke Ellington Orchestra), Mercer Ellington (orchestra leader and production coordinator). Premiere: American Music Theatre Festival, Philadelphia 86.

Harold Farberman (1929–)

THE LOSERS

Contemporary drama. Two acts, four or five scenes, three sets (120 minutes). An avant-garde work employing organized sound, frequent meter changes, cluster chords, simultaneous use of live and taped music. Very chromatic, disjunct vocal lines often not aided by orchestral cues. Video tape of motorcycle riders opens Act II.

Libretto by Barbara Fried. Commissioned by Juilliard American Opera Theatre. Premiere: Juilliard American Opera Theatre, N.Y. 3.26.71.

PLOT

Setting: a small town in California, 1970s.

Focusing on the violent, decadent lives of a motorcycle gang called the "Losers," the audience witnesses the beating of a gas station owner; the subsequent meeting of the gang at Gino's Bar, the gang's hangout; a violent initiation of a new member; the arrest of Buzz, the gang leader; and finally, in Buzz's absence, the gang-rape of Donna, the naive girl who loves him. Gino, the bar owner, and Marie, the waitress, stand idly by, afraid to get involved. Meanwhile, Ken, a pacifist hippy, tries to defend Donna, and is beaten by the gang. When Buzz arrives, Ken revives to tell him that Donna is being raped in the back room by his own companions. Buzz, who cannot believe his gang would betray him, starts a fight with Ken. Ken accidently kills Buzz in the struggle. But when the Losers see their dead leader, they all descend on Ken and beat him to death. Finally, all run from the scene and Donna is left alone. She stumbles over to Buzz's lifeless body and collapses in tears.

PRODUCTION REQUIREMENTS

Major Roles. BUZZ, leader of the Losers (bar): F$^{\#}$1 to G3. DONNA, Buzz's girl (s): A2 to D5. JOKER, a Loser (bs): E^{b}1 to F3 (D^{b}1 ossia).

Supporting Roles. KEN, not a gang member, a pacifist (t): A^{b}1 to B^{b}3. MARIE, a waitress (m-s): G^{b}2 to B4. GINO, owner and bartender of Gino's/JUNKIE, a Loser (t): B1 to B^{b}3. THE DUO, performers with on-stage jazz combo who comment on action (s): C3 to A4 and (m-s): G2 to A^{b}4.

Minor Roles. Gas Station Owner (t). Tiny Alex, a Loser (bar). Bo, new Loser initiate (bs-bar). Losers' gang members: Chinkie, Angel, Stretch, Axer, Wino (comfortable bari-tenor range).

Chorus. TTBB (sung by minor roles to which additional chorus may be added).

Ballet. Initiation ballet: soloist and ballet corp, drug "trip" ballet: soloist only.

Orchestra. 2 fls (picc), 2 obs, 2 cls (bs cl), alt sax, t sax, 4 fr hrns, 3 trps in B^{b} (3 E^{b} trps), 3 trbs, 2 tubas, 6 perc, elec guitar, piano, string trio. Jazz quartet: trp, alt sax, bs, dance drums; vocal duo.

Material. FS–P: Belwin-Mills Pub.

REVIEWS

Irving Kolodin "In Vespa Veritas, or Verismo on Wheels," *Saturday Review* (April 10, 1971), p. 16+

> "As for lyric theatre in the Farberman phase, it is a theatre in which Varese has supplanted Verdi, the drum has taken the place of the violin as melodic instrument, and *vocalise* is based upon Schoenberg rather than Sacchini. When coloratura is called for . . . it is derived not from *Lakme* but from *Lulu.*"

> "*The Losers* operates best, functions finest, and penetrates most profoundly in those episodes when verbal communication is suspended, when attitudes, emotions, and involvements are conveyed by sound and movement. . . . In these situations, Farberman's basic training as a percussion player . . . equipped him richly with the means to evoke momentum."

Frank Merkling "New York," *Opera News* (May 15, 1971), p. 22

> "Two other groupies . . . puncture the action like a deadpan Greek chorus and in Sprechstimme murmur the Losers' central philosophy. . . . They are endearing, since everybody else is given to expressing himself in snarls or that jagged vocal idiom beloved by composers from Schoenberg to Gunther Schuller."

> "one expected and got a percussive, wind-oriented orchestra that made Pendereckian noises."

William Ferris (1937–   )

THE DIVA

Drama. One act, two scenes, two sets. Neo-romantic twentieth-century idiom. Through-composed with dramatic ariosos and set pieces in "concert" within the drama. Much transpires in recitative-like vocal style with some rapid meter changes, complex rhythms, and chromatic vocal lines, though lyricism is the norm. Orchestra has brief introduction and interlude.

Libretto by John Vorrasi, based on an original scenario by the composer. Premiere: New Works Showcase, Chicago Opera Theatre (workshop production with two pianos) 6.13.87.

PLOT

Setting: Island Bay, the present.

The Diva, retiring after an unimpressive farewell concert tour, returns to her home town, Island Bay. Nearly everyone gathers at the depot to greet her: the band and the chorale from the Conservatory; its President, Dr. Williams; its musical director, Foster Dowd; the Mayor, Mr. Crane; the local critic, Oliver Stark (with harsh appraisal of the Diva's career); and David Brown, the Diva's first manager and ardent admirer. David has, in fact, coaxed the Diva into giving one last performance in Island Bay. But the town, persuaded by Stark's biased opinions, is convinced that the Diva is long past her prime. Stark convinces all that the star of the evening will be Miss Agnes Whitmar's young student, Loretta Norris, an untalented beauty who has caught the eye of Stark's dandy friend, Duane Jordan.

The concert opens with a madrigal by the Conservatory Chorale, followed by Loretta's debut. No amount of coaching by Miss Whitmar can keep Loretta on pitch as she wails through a melange of classic Italian art songs. Despite these musical assassinations, Stark and Jordan lead audience applause. David introduces the Diva as the highlight of the evening, but she chokes with emotion after the first line of her aria. Stark quickly denounces her cheap theatrics, but the Diva begins again. This time, all are transfixed by her crystalline tones, surely her best performance in years. In a trance, David moves to her with a single rose, exclaiming, "Diva!"

PRODUCTION REQUIREMENTS

Major Roles. DAVID BYRON, the Diva's first manager and admirer (t): D2 to B3. THE DIVA, a famous singer (s): D3 to C♯5.

Supporting Roles. DR. ARTHUR WILLIAMS, President, Island Bay Conservatory (t): D2 to G♯3. MAYOR PETER WINSLOW CRANE (bar): A1 to F3. OLIVER STARK, music critic (bar): A1 to D3. LORETTA NORRIS, young singer (col s): D3 to C♯5.

Minor Roles. MISS AGNES WHITMAR, Loretta's coach (m-s) (should accompany Loretta at piano). FOSTER DOWD, director of the Conservatory band and chorale (bs). DUANE JORDAN, a young dilatente (bar).

Chorus. SATB with divisi at times.

Orchestra. 2 fls (picc), 2 obs (Eng hrn), 2 B♭ cls (bs cl in B♭), 2 bsns, 4 hrns in F, 2 trps in C, 2 t trbs, bs trb, tuba, 2 perc, harp, strings. On-stage band: 2 cors in B♭, t trb, tuba, field dr, piano.

Material. FS–P: contact composer through AMC. FS: American Music Center.

REVIEWS

Howard Reich " 'Diva' gets a polished first performance," *Chicago Tribune* (June 16, 1987), section 5, p. 5

> "it even has a climatic duet . . . redolent of late nineteenth-century opera in general and Puccini in particular. . . . Yet the pulse of the work is utterly twentieth-century American. . . . the blue-note thirds and sevenths of Gershwin's music, the soaring vocal phrases of Samuel Barber's, the dissonances and shifting meters of Marc Blitzstein's."

> "the pacing is a shade breathless in the first scene: too much unfolds a bit too quickly. Nevertheless, 'The Diva' . . . stands as a compelling opera worthy of a fully staged production."

Vivian Fine

WOMEN IN THE GARDEN

One act (60 minutes). Libretto by the composer based on writings by women writers. Premiere: Port Costa Players, San Francisco 78. Performances: San Francisco Opera Center: 4.82.

Material. Catamount Facsimile (obtain address from AMC); American Music Center.

Myron Fink (1932–)

CHINCHILLA

Light operetta. Three acts (140 minutes). Conservative modern idiom with period jazz/blues influences in rhythms and harmonies. Includes songs, conversational vocal lines, as well as spoken dialogue. Overture and closing music sung by the M.C. Brief orchestral interludes.

Libretto by Donald Moreland. Premiere: Tri-Cities Opera, Binghamton, New York 1.18.86.

PLOT

Setting: New York City, 1920s.

Nick and Delia Ashton are planning a farewell party for their best friends, Ramon and Chi-chi Castillian, who are leaving New York, where Ramon has served as a Latin American diplomat. Each man sends a chincilla coat to his wife, and one to his secret lover—his best friend's wife. The furrier mixes up the orders and the accompanying cards. Although the wives do not recognize their husbands' pet names for their lovers, they vow to find out who the lovers are. Many antics, having to do with the mistaken identities, ensue.

At the farewell party, Mrs. Betterbotham is recognized by the Consul General as a lover from long ago. Meanwhile, Chi-chi and Delia discover the identity of their husbands' lovers. Fyodor, the furrier arrives, demanding his money, and each wife persuades her husband to pay for the coat he gave her, but refuses to keep her lover's gift. The Consul General purchases the third coat for Mrs. Betterbotham. When Delia's maid reveals that she and Fyodor are going to be married, the husbands buy the fourth coat as a wedding present. The couples eventually toast friendship and acknowledge their love for their own spouses.

PRODUCTION REQUIREMENTS

Major Roles. DELIA ASHTON (s): B♭2 to B♭4. RAMON CASTILLIAN (t): C♯2 to B♭3. NICK ASHTON (bar): B♭1 to A♭3. CHI-CHI CASTILLIAN (m-s): G♯2 to G♯4.

Supporting Roles. MASTER OF CEREMONIES (t): C2 to G3. SOLANGE, Delia's maid (s): B♭2 to A4. FYODOR, the furrier (bs): F1 to E3. MRS. BETTERBOTHAM, the Ashton's neighbor (m-s): A♭2 to E4. SENOR VARGAS, the Consul General (bs-bar): B♭1 to E3.

Minor Roles. JACK, the window washer (bs). MRS. VANDERWYCK (s). Chi-chi's hairdressers, FREDDY (t) AND BOBBY (t). TWO MANICURISTS, (s, m-s). Many other small roles such as Furriers' Assistants, Delivery Men, Party Guests, Servants, may be cast from chorus.

Chorus. SATB.

Ballet. Much period choreography: modern, jazz, ballet and tap dance. Several orchestral dance sequences at party scene.

Orchestra. 2 fls, 2 obs, cl, 2 bsns, hrn, trp, perc, harp, strings (5–4–3–2–1). Jazz ensemble: cl, sax, trp, trb, piano, banjo (guitar), tuba, double bs, perc.

Material. FS–P: Composer (contact AMC for address). VS and libretto: American Music Center.

REVIEWS

Leighton Kerner "Tri-Cities Opera: Fink 'Chinchilla,' " *Musical America* (June 1986), pp. 41–42

"The stuff is fluff, but it works more often than not, thanks less to Moreland's efficient but uninspired words than to Fink's sometimes catchy and often interestingly off-center music."

"Almost the entire second act and a big slice of the third could disappear immediately, and *Chinchilla* could then be adopted comfortably and maybe profitably by any good regional company."

William West "Binghamton," *Opera News* (April 12, 1986), pp. 43–44

> "Fink's music has fascinating moments, especially in its feel for the period's jazz idiom. Too often, however, it provides a mildly dissonant accompaniment to vocal lines that rarely captivate the ear."

JoElyn Wakefield-Wright "*Chinchilla* by Myron Fink," *Opera Journal* (1986), 19(1):31–33

> "There are some truly lovely moments, especially in his ensemble writing. The breezy, sophisticated rhythms are reminiscent of Bernstein's *Trouble in Tahiti,* but without his musical inventiveness and brevity."

> "This could be a fine one-act opera, entertaining and interesting, but there is not enough first-rate material to sustain three acts."

Thomas J. Flanagan

STATUES ON A LAWN

Libretto by Matthew Calhoun based on his own short story. Premiere: Golden Fleece, Ltd., New York 3.24.83.

Carlisle Floyd (1926–   )

BILBY'S DOLL

Romantic tragedy. Three acts, eight scenes (210 minutes with 2 intermissions). No overture. Through-composed with arias, duets, trios, choruses. Conservative modern idiom, atonal in parts.

Libretto by the composer, based on the novel, *A Mirror for Witches,* by Esther Forbes. Commissioned by Houston Grand Opera. Premiere: Houston Grand Opera 2.27.76.

PLOT

Setting: Cowan Corners, Massachusetts, 1671–1673.

Act I, scene i: The Black Moon Tavern interior and exterior, surrounded by other shops, a harbor in the background; ii: Bilby's house, interior and exterior. Act II, i: Cowan Corners Cemetery; ii and iii: Bilby's house; iv: the Thumb's house. Act III, i: Meeting house in Salem; ii: Salem jail.

Deacon Thumb proposes that his son, Titus, marry Bilby's adopted daughter, Doll. Bilby rejects the idea at first, but accepts it after witnessing a woman's arrest for witchcraft. Meanwhile, Bilby's wife, Hannah, denounces Doll's pagan ideas and maliciously claims that, when Bilby brought the girl home to live with them, Doll cursed Hannah's unborn child. Bilby comes home with new dresses for Doll, ignoring Hannah's jealousy. Hannah threatens that she will take all when Bilby dies, including Doll's half. Doll is shocked and frightened when Titus arrives with a marriage proposal, but Doll assures Titus that if she marries a mortal, it will be he. She also describes how Bilby had adopted her just after her parents were burned as witches.

Months later, all except Doll gather for Bilby's funeral. Hannah claims that Bilby died from Doll's curse, but Mister Zelley, a clergyman, confirms a natural death. Doll later visits the grave, begging the Kings of Heaven or Hell to send her a sign about her future. She is later entranced by a striking young man and joyfully accepts that he was sent by the King of Hell. They secretly marry in a pagan ceremony and Doll receives his medallion as a wedding gift.

Some time later, Titus' twin sisters fall into convulsive fits, and Hannah accuses Doll of cursing them. When Doll is arrested, Hannah claims Bilby's possessions for her own. While Doll awaits trial, Titus and Zelley both offer to save her through marriage. She informs them that she is married and pregnant, showing them her medallion. Zelley recognizes it and realizes that Doll has been misused by his wayward son, Shad. Disillusioned and abandoned, Doll refuses to renounce her past life, condemning herself to die as a witch. When she goes into labor, Titus begs Zelley to give Doll a reason for living. As labor progresses, Zelley and Doll remember Shad together. Zelley intentionally describes him incorrectly, convincing Doll that her husband was, indeed, the demon lover she had imagined. Thus, the misguided girl is allowed to die in peace.

PRODUCTION REQUIREMENTS

Major Roles. TITUS THUMB (bar): D2 to G3 ($G^{\#}$ opt). DEACON THUMB, Titus' father (t): E2 to A3. MISTER ZELLEY, a clergyman (bs-bar): $A^{\#}1$ to F3. DOLL BILBY, Jared Bilby's adopted daughter (s): B2 to $C^{b}5$ (C5 opt). HANNAH BILBY, Jared Bilby's wife (m-s): G2 to $B^{b}4$.

Supporting Roles. JARED BILBY (bs): $B^{b}1$ to $F^{\#}3$. SHAD, Mister Zelley's son (t): E2 to $B^{b}3$.

Minor Roles. SILAS, the tavern owner (bar). TOWN CRIER (t). SORROW and LABOUR, Deacon Thumb's twin daughters (girl s). MISTER KLEAVER (bar). GOODY GOOCHY (c). INCREASE MATHER (bs). CAPTAIN BUZZEY (t).

Non-singing Roles. JUDGE BRIDE, JUDGE LOLLIMOUR, NURSE, GOODY GREEN.

Chorus. SATB.

Orchestra. 2 fls, 2 obs, 2 cls, 2 bsns, 4 hrns, 2 trps, 2 trbs, tuba, timp, perc, harp, piano, strings.

Material. FS–P and VS: Belwin-Mills. VS and libretto: American Music Center.

REVIEWS

William Bender "Houston's *Doll*," *Time* (March 8, 1976), pp. 59–60

"Floyd is ambivalent about his uses of music. He gives Doll a sweet ditty to sing as she makes dolls for two neighbors' children, but in a mad scene she is totally silent. . . . Floyd relies on his orchestration—expert in its post-romantic, pre-*Elektra* style—for most of his emotional impact. Yet that emotion is expended on shallow comments on the action, rather than on getting inside the characters."

Carol Cunningham "Houston Opera: *Bilby's Doll*," *Musical America* (February 1976), pp. 25–26

"*Bilby's Doll* premiered as an extremely long stage work, cluttered with subsidiary cardboard characters, and far more remote emotionally than Floyd's masterful *Of Mice and Men* or his passionate *Susannah*."

"Floyd has largely forsaken his formerly direct tonal musical language for an atonalism that has a certain self-conscious sterility and occasionally conflicts with baldly diatonic means, especially in a maudlin Broadway love song . . . sung by . . . [Titus]."

"But Floyd's skill as a composer and musical dramatist is still stamped in scene after scene of the score. His vocal lines are masterfully and lyrically shaped and he has drawn powerful, deeply faceted portraits of the opera's two main characters: vulnerable, deranged Doll Bilby, . . . and the humane preacher, Mr. Zelley."

Allen Hughes "Opera: *Bilby's Doll* Opens in Houston," *New York Times* (February 29, 1976), p. 45, column 3

" . . . the libretto, devised by the composer himself, reads well, and if it had been matched with music of equal strength, the opera might have been quite successful."

"only towards the end of the opera are there moments that really seize the listener's attention."

Andrew Porter "Going to the Devil," *New Yorker* (March 22, 1976), pp. 120–123

"The word setting is flexible, not tied to the bar lines, natural in its response to what would be the spoken inflections of the text but unnatural, much of the time, in its slowness."

"in two scenes he has most delicately mirrored, and with his music enhanced, the irony of the original novel. . . . the young pirate, Shad, appears to her lit by the glare of a blazing barn. During the second act, in Doll's bedroom, the two enact a childish demonic marriage rite, which Doll recalls from the nonsense with which her head has been stuffed. The action is realistic—nothing supernatural is happening—but the music can suggest to us, as it were, Doll's view of the events and portray her mystic rapture as she surrenders to her demon lover."

WILLIE STARK

Historical fiction. Three acts, nine scenes. (Full evening). Chromatic tonalities and mixed meters with vocal lines not doubled in accompaniment. Highly conversational, including unmeasured recitative, though arias, ensembles, and choruses exist.

Libretto by the composer, based on Robert Penn Warren's *All the Kings Men*. Commissioned by the Kennedy Center, Washington, D.C. 1976. Premiere: Houston Grand Opera 4.24.81.

PLOT

Setting: a Southern state, the depression thirties.

The state legislature is preparing to take an impeachment vote against Willie, who is accused of corruption. Hearing that the respected Judge Burton endorses the impeachment, Willie attempts to gain his support. Jack idealistically tries to convince his father that his boss stretches the law to help the poor, but the Judge will not sanction Willie's methods. When the Judge denies Willie's request for support, the Governor orders Duffy to search for dirt from the Judge's past. Meanwhile, Jack's dedication to his work for Willie leaves him no time to spend with Anne. Questioning whether Jack really wants to marry her, Anne decides to see Willie again, in secret meetings.

Duffy finds proof that the Judge once accepted a bribe. Jack confronts his father and is shocked when the Judge admits to accepting the bribe. Jack warns him that the evidence will be published, but the Judge refuses to change his stand on the impeachment. After his disillusioned son leaves, the Judge shoots himself. Meanwhile, Willie's right-hand woman, Sadie, jealously quits when Willie announces that he and Anne will marry. She tells Jack of the engagement, and he becomes even more dazed by Willie's deceit and corruption.

At the capitol, crowds cheer when they hear that Willie has won the impeachment vote. As he gives a triumphant speech, Jack emerges from the crowd and shoots him. Willie's bodyguard, Sugar Boy, immediately kills Jack. Anne fights through the crowd to get to Willie, who dies in her arms.

PRODUCTION REQUIREMENTS

Major Roles. Willie Stark, Governor (bar): A1 to G3 [A3 opt]. Sadie, Willie's assistant and advisor (s): C3 to B4. Anne (s): C3 to C5. Jack, Judge Burton's son (t): C♯3 to A4. Judge Burton (bs): G1 to G3.

Supporting Roles. Duffy, the Lieutenant-Governor (t): D2 to B3. Sugar Boy, Willie's bodyguard (t): F2 to B3.

Minor Roles. Jeff (t). Hugh (bar). Mrs. Stark (m-s or c). Lucy (treble, child). Radio Announcer (actor). Jarvis (actor). George William (actor). Mayor (actor). Little Boy (mute).

Chorus. SATB.

Orchestra. fl, picc, ob, Eng hrn, cl, bs cl, bsn, cont bsn, 2 hrns, 2 trps, trb, tuba, harp, celeste, timp, perc, strings.

Material. FS–P and VS: Belwin-Mills.

REVIEWS

Leland Fox "Carlisle Floyd's 'Willie Stark,' " *Opera Journal* (November 3, 1981), 14(3):39–44

> Through the novel "we know the outcome, the event, but the drama resides in the struggle. . . . Stark struggles with his conscience to determine what is right . . . we are reminded of the nobility of the man. The ultimate scene of the opera depicts the shooting of Willie Stark on the courthouse steps. . . . the event is central, not the people caught up in its wake."
>
> " 'The law is like a single-bed blanket,' is an excerptable 'hit' and beautifully expressive of the poet's (Warren's) original text."
>
> "Space must be reserved for Timothy Nolen in the title role. Without an actor of consummate skill, whose movements were fluid yet energized, a singer of range, volume, subtlety, and presence, and a musician who made each of these attributes servants to a complex score, the opera would not have been attempted."

Donal Henahan "Opera: Floyd's 'Willie,' " *New York Times* (Monday, April 27, 1981), p. 21

> "The overall effect of both decor and direction is Brechtian, but that leaves one sorely wishing for music of at least Weillian distinction to give the evening operatic point."

Scott F. Heumann "Houston," *Opera News* (August 1981), p. 30

> "[This] is a subject calling for musical treatment of a distinctly American sort. This challenge was brilliantly met. . . . Not that the piece lacks musical high points, but for long stretches music takes a back seat to the drama."

Annalyn Swan "Grand Opera, Texas Style," *Newsweek* (May 11, 1981), pp. 96, 99

> "There are a few tuneful numbers, as in the 'Come back, Willie, come back home' refrain, and there are pleasing references to jazz and American hymnody. But mostly the music simply patters along . . . never getting inside the characters or breaking away in lyrical abandon."

"Except for a top-heavy first act, it moves along briskly and there are deft comic touches . . . And Floyd's libretto does well by the novel. The plot is condensed and changed, but its moral complexity remains."

Margaret Garwood (1927–)

THE NIGHTINGALE AND THE ROSE

Fairytale. One act (60 minutes). Conservative modern idiom. Chromatic vocal lines range from speech inflection to soaring melodies.

Libretto by the composer, based on a story by Oscar Wilde. Commissioned by Franklin Concerts, Inc. Premiere: Pennsylvania Opera Company 73. Performances: National Federation of Music Clubs 12.2.78.

PLOT

Setting: abandoned garden at the edge of a forest, fourteenth century.

Rossignol is crushed when she overhears her love, Stefan, telling his friend, Mark, of his love for Narcissa. The fickle Narcissa agrees to attend the grand ball with Stefan only if he can present her with a perfect red rose the next day. Stefan is left to bemoan this challenge, since no rose has bloomed in the garden for fifteen years. Moved by Stefan's love, Rossignol emerges from her hiding place and promises to consult her Grandmother, a witch, to learn how to find a rose. Her "Grandmother" reluctantly reveals that she found Rossignol under the rose tree fifteen years ago and that another rose will bloom only when its thorn pierces Rossignol's heart. Rossignol sacrifices her life for the happiness of Stefan and a rose miraculously appears the following day. Stefan picks it, but when he offers it to Narcissa, she spurns his love. Stefan realizes that he was destined to love Rossignol and runs off to find her. But Mark remains to lament, "Poets are truly fools. Beauty once denied is beauty lost forever." The barren tree grows bright with new roses.

PRODUCTION REQUIREMENTS

Major Roles. ROSSIGNOL, a young girl (col s): C♯3 to E♭5. STEFAN, a poet (t): D2 to B3 (C3 opt).

Supporting Roles. MARK, a playboy (bar): B1 to F3 [A♭3 falsetto].

NARCISSA, a beautiful flirt (s): D3 to B^{b}4. GRANDMOTHER, Rossignol's guardian (m-s): A^{b}2 to A4.

Orchestra. 2 fls (picc), 2 obs, 2 cls, 2 bsns, 2 hrns, 2 trps, 2 trbs, timp, perc, harp, strings.

Material. FS–P and VS: Carl Fischer, Inc. VS: American Music Center.

REVIEWS

Joseph Horowitz *New York Times* (December 4, 1978), p. 18

> "a miniature 'Frau ohne Schatten.' Her mastery of Strauss's idiom — the sultry chromaticism, the sinuous lines, the alert marriage of text and music — is really quite startling. Though it is a dated idiom, and one that works better on a more pretentious scale, the opulence of *The Nightingale and the Rose* is thoroughly absorbing."

RAPPACCINI'S DAUGHTER

Tragedy. Two acts, six scenes, one set with scrims (120 minutes). Conversational style with frequent large skips. Orchestral sections more dissonant, chromatic, with frequent meter changes.

Libretto by the composer, based on the story by Nathaniel Hawthorne. Premiere: Pennsylvania Opera Theatre, Philadelphia 11.23.81 (with piano); 5.6.83 (with orchestra).

PLOT

Setting: Padua, turn of the nineteenth century.

New to Padua, Giovanni takes rooms at Lizabetta's house, entranced by the garden next door. He is even more entranced by Beata as she helps her father, Rappaccini, tend to the garden plants. Baglione warns that Rappaccini is a dangerous scientist and Giovanni should beware of Beata and the garden. Nevertheless, when Giovanni next sees Beata, he gives her flowers. He remembers the warning when he sees the flowers wilt and a butterfly falls dead after touching her, but he is too smitten to renounce his love. Baglione warns that Rappaccini is using Giovanni experimentally, but the young man refuses to listen. In fact, when Lizabetta tells him a way into the garden, Giovanni hastens there to meet his love. They pledge themselves to each other, but when Giovanni tries to touch Beata, she runs away. Baglione finds that his friend is ill and tells Giovanni an old story about a young maiden who had been nurtured on poisons since birth and would kill anyone who touched her. Giovanni refuses to acknowledge the importance of the story until Baglione reveals that flowers from Beata's garden caused Giovanni's illness. Baglione gives his friend an antidote which he hopes will cure Beata. When Giovanni angrily confronts Beata with the truth, she convinces him that she was unaware of her father's plan to include him in the experiment. Out of love for him, she takes the antidote, knowing that it will kill her. When Rappaccini joins them to declare his experiment a success, his daughter dies.

PRODUCTION REQUIREMENTS

Major Roles. Beata, Rappaccini's beautiful daughter (s): C3 to C5. Giovanni, a student (t): D2 to C4. Baglione, a professor and friend of Giovanni's parents (bar): B1 to A♭3. Rappaccini, a scientist (bs-bar): B♭1 to F♯3.

Supporting Roles. Lizabetta (m-s): B2 to G4. Sister Plant (offstage m-s or s): F3 to G4.

Orchestra. 2 fls (picc), 2 obs (Eng hrn), 2 cls (bs cl), 2 bsns (cont bsn), 2 hrns, 2 trps, 2 trbs, timp, perc, harp, strings.

Material. FS–P and VS: American Music Center and composer (contact AMC for address).

REVIEWS

William Ashbrook "Philadelphia," *Opera* (October 1983), 34(10):1122–1123

"More problematic was the work's derivation from Hawthorne's tangled allegory with its cumbersome symbolism and ornate nineteenth-century diction. . . . A more neutral verbal style would have added a welcome sense of understatement to the potentially provocative plot. . . . But to say all that is not to deny to *Rappacini's Daughter* some moments where action, music and atmosphere fused to produce powerful impressions."

Edward Rothstein "Opera: 'Rappaccini' Opens," *New York Times* (May 14, 1983), section 1, p. 17

"The success of Margaret Garwood's opera . . . is partly due to the impact of the story itself. Hawthorne's tale is so well-suited to an operatic treatment."

> "The conservative, lyrical score approached its themes in the style of both Debussy and Berg. . . . her composition did not display a strikingly original musical conception, but gave the entire opera a passionate integrity."

Gary Schmidgall "Philadelphia," *Opera News* (August 1983), p. 38

> "[notable for] the richly evocative, Delius-like descriptions of the Doctor's exotic flora and the surreal choreography . . . for the loving, balletic 'plants' it contains. Miss Garwood's ingratiating score shows care in pacing and variation, eschewing memorable gestures in favor of shimmering, oblique understatement."

George Gershwin

STRIKE UP THE BAND

Premiere: American Music Theatre Festival 84. From the original 1927 version which requires legit singing, in an edition prepared by Eric Salzman (the published version is the 1930 revision).

Material. Eric Salzman, 29 Middagh St., Brooklyn, N.Y. 11201.

Philip Glass (1937–)

AKHNATEN

Historical pageant. Three acts with prelude and epilogue, ten scenes, seven sets (150 minutes). In the language of the audience, the narrator describes what is being sung. Minimalist with repetitions of phrases, harmonies, text, and small- and large-scale sections. Tonal harmonies sounded through broken chords in accompaniment. Entire work has orchestral emphasis — several scenes contain orchestra and narration only.

Book by Philip Glass in association with Shalom Goldman, Robert Israel, and Richard Riddel. Libretto drawn from original documents of the Armarna period in their original languages: ancient Egyptian, Akkadian, and Biblical Hebrew by Shalom Goldman. Premiere: Stuttgart State Opera 3.24.84. Performances: Houston Grand Opera 10.12.84, and New York City Opera 11.4.84 (joint American premiere production). English National Opera 85. Recordings: Recording by Stuttgart State Opera Orchestra and Chorus, Dennis Russell Davies, director. CBS Masterworks, M2K 42458.

PLOT

Setting: Egypt, the Amarna period, 1375–1358 B.C. (the reign of Akhnaten).

Act I, Prelude; scene i: Funeral of Amenhotep III; ii: The Coronation of Akhnaten; iii: The Window of Appearances. Act II, i: The Temple; ii: Akhnaten and Nefertiti; iii: The City/Dance; iv: Hymn. Act III, i: The Family; ii: Attack and Fall; iii: The Ruins; Epilogue.

With the death of Amenhotep III in 1875 B.C., Akhnaten succeeds to the Egyptian throne. The funeral procession of Akhnaten's father, depicting the traditions of Amon ritual, reappears throughout the opera as a contrast to the ideas of the new regime. The new king is crowned by the Amon High Priest and ascends to the throne as Amenhotep IV. As king, he abolishes the pantheistic traditions of the past and asks all to join him in worshipping the monotheistic God, Aten. Thus, Akhnaten revolutionizes history by introducing the first abstract concept of God. In further reforming acts, Akhnaten deposes the priests of Amon, refuses to practice polygomy for the love of his wife, Nefertiti, and builds Akhetaten, a temple of art and beauty, in honor of Aten. However, Akhnaten's obsessions isolate him from the suffering of the Egyptian people. Unrest builds until the priests of Amon urge the overthrow of the king. After the crowd carries off the royal family and destroys Akhetaten, the priests restore the traditions of Akhnaten's forefathers. (The ruins of Akhetaten, uncovered in this century, provide few clues to Akhnaten's achievements and far-reaching ideas.) Akhnaten and his family wander among the ruins until they join the funeral procession, accepting that their epoch has passed.

PRODUCTION REQUIREMENTS

Major Roles. AKHNATEN (ct): E3 to E4. NEFERTITI, wife of Akhnaten (c): A2 to F4. QUEEN TYE, mother of Akhnaten (s): A3 to B4. HOREMHAB, General and future Pharoah (bar): E2 to D3. AMON, High Priest (t): $A^{b}2$ to $A^{b}3$. AYE, father of Nefertiti and advisor to the Pharoah (bs): A1 to E3. AMENHOTEP, son of Hapu, the scribe (male speaker).

Chorus. SIX DAUGHTERS (women's voices). FUNERAL PARTY (8 men's voices). LARGE CHORUS (mixed voices).

Orchestra. 2 fls (picc), 2 obs (2 ob d'Amour), 2 cls in B^{b}, bs cl in B^{b}, 2 bsns, 2 fr hrns, 2 trps in B^{b}, 2 trbs (bs trb), tuba, 3 perc (4 tuned tom toms, sn drum, bs drum, etc.), synth (cel), strings (vla, vcl, bs only).

Material. FS–P and VS: Dunvagen, c/o Theodore Presser (rental).

REVIEWS

Edward Greenfield "Glass's 'Akhnaten' at ENO wows the British," *Musical America* (October 1985), p. 38

"the production itself, directed by David Freeman . . . and the performance conducted by Paul Daniel exerted a magnetism which made Glass' minimalist repetitions into something more than trance-like and mindblowing. . . . In absolute terms, the music may be a mere adjunct in this style of music theatre, but that seems to be exactly what Glass was aiming at."

Highlights "the ravishing duet for Akhnaten and Nefertiti in Act II."

K. Robert Schwarz "GLASS: Akhnaten," *Musical America* (July 1988), pp. 65+ (Record review)

"With genuinely Wagnerian scope, it reworks unified musical material: the 'Knee Plays' of *Einstein,* for instance, return in *Akhnaten*'s epilogue. And *Akhnaten* shares with *Satyagraha* a mythic, ritualistic aura, as the vast, granitic tableaux build up slowly, inscrutably."

"Yet *Akhnaten* relates to Western conventions more closely than does *Satyagraha*. . . . The vocal and orchestral complements are larger, and . . . of an increasingly emotional rhetoric. . . . Akhnaten's narrative structure is also far more traditional . . . We have a conventional chronological presentation, albeit one fragmented into static, isolated vignettes."

Patrick Smith "New York City Opera: Glass 'Akhnaten,' " *Musical America* (February 1985)

"The opera is largely static — a series of tableaux come to life. The only character protrait is that of Akhnaten. . . . The vocal roles of the others . . . are restricted, and they seem more like statues than people."

"Glass' score continues to impress one with . . . the growing mastery of . . . coloristic handling of instruments, and the control of the ethos of the piece. His writing for the voice is more assured than in either of his two earlier stage works."

"The highlight of the score, [Akhnaten's] 'Hymn to the Sun' . . . was especially beautiful."

The CIVIL WarS, Act V

Abstract, symbolic pageant with Latin, Italian, and English text. One act, four scenes, four sets (110 minutes). Minimalist: rhythmic motion in orchestra contrasts with longer, sustained tones in vocal parts. Instrumental use of voices: repeated rhythms on one syllable.

Book by Robert Wilson. Act V, the Rome section, is final act of a 12-hour multimedia project conceived by Robert Wilson to be performed at the Los Angeles Olympics in 1984 (complete performance never came to pass). Premiere of Act V: Teatro Dell'Opera, Rome 3.25.84. Performances: New York Opera Repertory Theatre 5.20.84; Los Angeles Philharmonic and Master Chorale 11.24.84.

PLOT

Setting: not specified.

The Rome act of this large-scale work focuses on leaders of the American and Italian civil wars, including Garibaldi, Lincoln, Mrs. Lincoln, and Robert E. Lee, as well as Hercules, the founder of the Olympics. Each scene, independently representing a view of war, features anachronistic and fantastical settings, impossible encounters between ethnic groups, and the convergence of real and mythical characters, in order to heighten the symbolism of the act as a whole. Thus, Garibaldi looks on as Lincoln, a Snow Owl and the Earth Mother join together to express their hope for peace (Prologue); Hopi Indians dance with Garibaldi's men while Garabaldi sings of his past (Scene A); Robert E. Lee floats in a spaceship as Mrs. Lincoln describes him after his defeat (Scene B); and Hercules comes to earth to help mankind as Mrs. Lincoln, as a girl, recites a speech announcing the end of the war, and Lincoln reiterates his earlier speech. Finally, Hercules, having defeated destruction, raises the Olympic torch as he ascends back to heaven (Scene C).

PRODUCTION REQUIREMENTS

Major Roles. ABE LINCOLN (bar): C2 to F3. EARTH MOTHER/MRS. LINCOLN (a): B2 to A^{b}4. SNOW OWL/ALEMENA (s): A3 to C5 (many, repeated C5s, but offers A4 ossia). GARIBALDI (t): A2 to B3 (many repeated high notes). HERCULES (bs): G1 to B2.*
*Please note that roles are designated only by voice type in the score, rather than by names of characters.

Chorus. SATB (large), vocal octet.

Orchestra. 2 fls (picc), 2 obs, 2 cls in B^{b}, bs cl, 2 bsns, 4 hrns, 3 trps, 3 trbs, tuba, 3 perc, harp, strings.

Material. FS–P and VS: Dunvagen, c/o G. Schirmer.

REVIEWS

Luigi Bellingardi "*ITALY* American Saga," *Opera* (June 1984), pp. 664–665

Contains mainly a detailed synopsis of work. "The CIVIL WarS was a great success . . . "

Richard S. Ginell "American Music Weekend," *Musical America* (April 1985), p. 19

"a performance of considerable power and drive."

"What the text was supposed to represent was unclear without the stage action or a coherent synopsis. But there was little doubt that, in particular, Section A could stand on its own as a concert work."

Robert T. Jones "New York Opera Repertory Theatre: Wilson/Glass 'The CIVIL WarS,' " *Musical America* (September 1984), pp. 19–20

"The vocal parts, especially the soprano and tenor ones, . . . take the singers into cruel and uncomfortable tessituras. . . . Perhaps Glass himself might be coaxed into a rewrite, or at least some transpositions, to bring . . . an imposing and beautiful work into more musical and vocal focus."

Deborah Jowitt "Dance: To End All Wars," *Village Voice* (December 30, 1986), p. 92

"the city where each section was created influenced subject and style—Rome in this case. . . . The elaborate panorama of trees, the arias, the librettos that must be consulted, the opulent ballet with bows afterward, refer to the Italian opera tradition. Glass' score is often suffused with the grandiose or florid emotionality of opera. Fragments of beautiful melody rise through the turbulent pulsing."

Gregory Sandow "An Echo, Not a Choice," *Village Voice* (June 12, 1984), pp. 76–77

"Glass . . . is a consummate theatre composer. There are striking and, for him at least, strikingly new things in the score for *CIVIL WarS:* sharp contrasts between sections of a single scene for example . . . and forceful, even Italianate vocal declamation."

"The Hopi scene reminded me of movie Indians, the kind who dance to simpleminded rhythms and hackneyed open fifths, though I have to admit that even if Glass did hint at the old cliche, he also refreshed it with his own irresistible brand of cosmopolitan verve."

EINSTEIN ON THE BEACH

Abstract, symbolic pageant. Four acts, nine scenes, and five connecting "knee plays" (4 hours, 45 minutes). No traditional operatic vocal display. Sung text utilizes solfege syllables and counting of rhythmic patterns. Spoken texts are repeated paragraph stories used alone or in canon with two voices.

Conceived and designed by Robert Wilson. No traditional "libretto," per se. American premiere: Metropolitan Opera House, N.Y. 11.21.76. European premiere: Avignon Festival, France 7.76. Recording: CBS M4 38875.

PLOT

Scenery, images, and repeated gestures relating to Einstein's biography form substance of work. Various Einstein figures appear: a violinist made up to look like an old man plays a brilliant solo in the orchestra pit, another writes mathematical formulae on a blackboard. Other images and themes are: a train (in various tranformations), first as a locomotive, then disappearing in the distance, finally transforming into a building, where a character inside does calculations; a trial scene with a huge bed that slowly rises out of sight; a field with floating dancers and a spaceship.

PRODUCTION REQUIREMENTS

Roles. Four principal actors, twelve singers who dance and act, a solo violinist dressed as a grey-haired Einstein. The above includes two speaking female dancers, a small boy, and an old man.

Dance. See above.

Orchestra. 2 s sax (2 fls), t sax, 3 elec organs, vln, s soloist.

Material. FS–P and Choral score: G. Schirmer.

REVIEWS

Mary Effie Burnham "Opera Scientifique," *National Review* (January 21, 1977), pp. 99–100

"THE OPERA has a meditative quality, which, paradoxically, is achieved by ceaselessly flowing activity. . . . But all the while the faces of the performers are calm: they are on a carefully structured frenetic path, like particles surrounding a nucleus. This impassivity, plus the colors Wilson has used — tan, grey, black, white — gives Einstein a certain asceticism. But the fabric is shot through with levity at the same time — a sort of stately zaniness."

Patricia Ensworth "New York," *Music Journal* (February 1977), 25(2):34

"The three main tableax . . . presented a dream landscape rich enough in symbolic detail that one enjoyed making an intuitive personal sense out of them even if their logical meaning remained veiled in Wilson's imagination. Glass' music, like medieval chanting, often succeeded in evoking the inward state of mind suitable for the contemplation of such subjects."

"There were moments when this lack of narrative progression sent the audience out to the lobby for drinks and sandwiches, but there were also moments when it worked. . . . simple actions had a mythic resonance that was quite powerful."

Dale Harris "Einstein on the Beach," *Musical America* (December 1976), pp. 36–37

"By 'opera' I suspect that Wilson simply means a piece for the stage released from the confines of a single genre — neither play nor ballet, spectacle nor happening, but a mixture of diverse theatrical forms."

"Wilson, it must be emphasized, has not let his unconscious run wild. . . . *Einstein* is a very carefully structured piece of work."

John Rockwell "Robert Wilson's Five-Hour Operatic Dream," *New York Times* (August 1, 1976), p. 15+

"The overall theme of the play might be said to be a consideration of the same moral and cosmic issues that concerned Einstein himself in his later years, principally the role of science in the modern world and the relation of science to religion."

David Stevens "Paris," *Opera News* (December 11, 1976), pp. 46–47

"The work moves in an inexorable lentissimo, animated by a proliferation of mini-events, a huge theatrical machine propelled by feverishly spinning inner parts."

THE FALL OF THE HOUSE OF USHER

Horror story. Prologue, two acts, ten scenes (110 minutes). Minimalist idiom throughout with simple syllabic, but melodic vocal lines. Clearly separated scenes with continuous texture within each. Orchestral preludes and interludes. No recitative.

Libretto by Arthur Yorinks, based on a story by Edgar Allan Poe. Commission and premiere: American Repertory Theatre, Cambridge, Mass. 5.18.88; and Kentucky Opera, Louisville 5.88.

PLOT

Setting: a decaying stone mansion, mid- to late-nineteenth century.

William comes to the house of Usher at the request of his boyhood friend, Roderick, who is suffering from an unnamed affliction. Roderick reveals that his sister, Madeline, whom William has never seen, is near death. During his stay, William begins to hear a mysterious voice and has several nightmares. Roderick, however, seems to be in better spirits. When William suggests that the three of them get out of the house for some fresh air, Roderick casually remarks that his sister has just died.

Roderick and William carry Madeline's coffin to the family vault in the dungeon. A few evenings later, in Roderick's studio, William hears the strange voice and clanking of chains again. Roderick finally confesses that he, too, has heard the sounds and that he has buried Madeline alive in the tomb. Madeline returns from the grave, and falls from the balcony, crushing her brother to death. The house of Usher crumbles, as William flees.

PRODUCTION REQUIREMENTS

Major Roles. WILLIAM, childhood friend of Roderick's (bar): B1 to F3. RODERICK USHER (t): C2 to B^{b}3. MADELINE USHER, Roderick's twin sister (s): C3 to C5 (largely off stage vocalises).

Minor Roles. PHYSICIAN (t). SERVANT (bs).

Orchestra. fl (picc), cl in B^{b}, bsn, hrn in F, guitar, perc, strings (2–1–1–1), synthesizer.

Material. FS–P and VS: G. Schirmer.

REVIEWS

Andrew Adler "Louisville," *Musical America* (November 1988), pp. 40–41

"So what hath Glass wrought? Essentially, a piece that is conventional in structure, lyrically scored, and possessed of surprising restraint, considering the lurid subject matter. Music and theatre are admirably balanced, and if the early performances were dramatically tepid, this seems more the fault of the director, Richard Foreman, than of Glass."

"Glass has composed evocative, nuanced music that belies the simplistic description of 'minimalism.' He shows a keen sense of instrumental timbre, and his melodic development is unusually expressive, given his past tendencies. Glass seems to have benefited from the discipline imposed by a chamber ensemble."

Richard Dyer "America Audible wallpaper," *Opera* (August 1988), pp. 934–6

"The music . . . is sophisticated in some respects, primitive in others. The rhythmic developments are characteristically kinetic; the instrumental colors compelling. . . . The way the themes interlock reflects the web of relationships among the three characters. On the other hand, the vocal lines reveal what Glass' famous operas in ancient and oriental languages conceal — his prosody is unskilled. The notes 'read' Yorink's lines in false rhythms no singing-actor could animate. Glass's style can suggest extremes of activity and stasis and their union in ecstasy, but it is less apt to other operatic purposes."

William Mootz "Louisville," *Opera News* (October 1988), p. 46

"The libretto, by Arthur Yorinks, is based on Edgar Allan Poe's famous tale ... though Yorinks fleshes out the original with Freudian flourishes.... Such embellishments underpin Poe's prevailing mood of nameless horror without betraying it."

"The vocal writing for the three main characters ... is grateful, the orchestration ... deft. But Glass supports the narrative thrust of the libretto with music that is repetitious and bland.... Foreman's staging attempted to create the drama missing in Glass' music; ... the director invented intriguing visual effects."

THE JUNIPER TREE (*GLASS/MORAN*)

Morality drama. Prologue, two acts, five scenes and epilogue, 1 set (90 minutes). Minimalist: repetitive patterns in rhythms, melodies, and text with frequent metric shifts; tonal harmonies. Vocal lines syncopated against accompaniment. Spoken and sung dialogue; one extended ensemble, several duets. Orchestral intro and long interludes, no intermission. Instrumental use of chorus (i.e., repeated rhythms on one syllable).

Libretto by Arthur Yorinks, based on a Brothers Grimm fairy tale. Premiere: American Repertory Theater, Cambridge, Mass. 12.17.85. Performances: American Music Theatre Festival, Philadelphia, Pa. 86.

PLOT

Setting: landowner's house and yard.

The landowner's wife feeds baby birds to alleviate her frustration at having no child of her own. When she finally bears a son, she dies and is buried under the juniper tree. The landowner's second wife obsessively dotes on her daughter, whom she intends to inherit her husband's wealth. Because she jealously fears that the boy reminds her husband of her predecessor, the stepmother slams the top of a chest shut on him, cutting off his head. When the daughter asks why the boy sits so strangely, the stepmother tells her to box his ears. The daughter is horrified by the result and blames herself, but her mother assures her that she will hide everything, and proceeds to cook the boy for dinner. The father is confused when told that his son has gone to visit relatives, but he voraciously eats his dinner. The daughter lays the boy's bones at the base of the juniper tree.

The boy returns as a bird, singing of his tragedy. His beautiful song attracts several townspeople, who bring a gold chain, some shoes and a millstone to make him sing more. The bird delights his father with the gold chain and his sister with the shoes. However, when the stepmother goes outside, the millstone drops and kills her. The son is joyfully reunited with his father and sister, watched over by the juniper tree.

PRODUCTION REQUIREMENTS

Major Roles. THE HUSBAND, a wealthy landowner (lyr bar): B1 to E3. THE STEPMOTHER, landowner's second wife (m-s, high tessitura): (B2 opt) C3 to A4 (B4 opt). THE SON/THE JUNIPER BIRD (boy s:) D3 to G4. THE DAUGHTER (girl s): D3 to G4.

Supporting Roles. THE WIFE, landowner's first wife (lyr s): F♯3 to A♭4. THE MILLER (bs): G1 to B2. THE COBBLER (bar): G2 to E3.

Minor Roles. MAMA BIRD (s). THE GOLDSMITH (t).

Chorus. Offstage SATB and children's choruses.

Orchestra. fl, cl in B♭, bsn, hrn, trp, trb, 3 perc, harp, 2 synth, celeste, strings (1–1–1–1–0).

Material. FS–P and VS: G. Schirmer.

REVIEWS

Debra Cash "Boston," *Opera News* (March 29, 1986), p. 42

> "*The Juniper Tree* is tailor-made for those who protest they enjoy Philip Glass' music—but only in small doses."

> "its paradigmatic events transpire as 'faits accomplis,' outside musical comment. The 'good' First Wife's dying words are no different from her previous pronouncements. . . . The composers keep to conventional dynamics and dampen the musical potential of human speech."

Andrew L. Pincus "American Repertory Theatre: Glass/Moran 'The Juniper Tree' [premiere]," *Musical America* (April 1986), pp. 18–19

"Glass's instrumental writing, of course, enthrones the arpeggio, while Moran goes in for ominous syncopation. But the two styles mesh and fit the syncopation and the scenes they set. Glass' vocal parts achieve some tender moments in kind of wan, Menotti-like lyricism. But, overall, the music is relentlessly repetitive, diatonic, and even saccharine . . ."

Michael Walsh "The Maturing of Minimalism," *Time* (December 23, 1985), p. 73

"Today, Glass' relentless, repetitious music has become gentler, smoother, subtler and more flexible."

"Based on an especially grisly Brothers Grimm fairy tale. . . . Glass and Moran have chosen to emphasize the tale's elements of love and redemption, instead of its gruesome aspects."

"In dividing the opera's six scenes roughly equally between them, the composers have maintained stylistic integrity even while sharing melodic motifs and a unified dramatic plan. The interplay between them is slickly accomplished, especially in the final scene. . . . Glass' hypnotic arpeggios and Moran's dry Stravinskian syncopations are harmoniously soldered in a chamber opera that should prove practical and durable."

THE MAKING OF THE REPRESENTATIVE FOR PLANET 8

Science fiction. Three acts, seventeen scenes (180 minutes). Repetition of short motivic cells with small rhythmic variations, but melodic themes emerge from orchestra. Simple repetitive vocal melodies contrast with use of much spoken dialogue, long monologues.

Libretto by Doris Lessing, based on her novel of the same title, book four of her 5-part series, *Canopus in Argos: Archives.* Co-commissioned by Houston Grand Opera and English National Opera. Premiere: Houston, Texas 7.8.88. Performances: UK 11.9.88.

PLOT

Setting: Planet 8, a once Eden-like paradise, now caught in a second Ice Age.

Allegory and symbolism run high in this story, reflecting the perils faced by our own civilization and its environment. Planet 8, once inhabited by a tranquil, civilized race of agrarian peoples, is caught in a cosmic occurrence which alters its natural orbit, casting it into a second Ice Age. Helpless in their attempts at survival, and knowing only the simple life of constant springtime, the natives are offered aid and direction from their protectors, the Canopean representatives. Johor, the chief cosmic agent, arrives on Planet 8 to announce the certainty of doom if the populace does not immediately move to build a wall around their troubled planet. Though building begins, all gradually realize that the end is near. The hardships, tragedies and disillusionments of Planet 8 are seen in microcosm through the characters of Alsi and Nooni. Doeg, the leader of the ill-fated race, can offer little solace to his people. Dragging and beaten, they trek from one end of the globe to the other in search of whatever might be harvested, always aware of the encroaching ice. They die in hordes, hoping against hope that a Canopean spacecraft will come to their rescue. Finally, the souls and knowledge of the remaining representatives unite in the being of a single "representative for Planet 8."

PRODUCTION REQUIREMENTS

Major Roles. JOHOR, the Canopean agent (bs): G1 to E3. DOEG, memory-maker and keeper of records (bar): C2 to F3 (long spoken monologue). ALSI, a young woman (s): E3 to B♯4.

Supporting Roles. NOONI, a young man (t): G♯2 to F♯3.

Minor Roles. The following roles may be drawn from chorus: RIVALIN, custodian of the lake (s); KLIN, Fruit-maker (m-s); BRATCH, Representative for health (a/m-s); MASSON, The Builder (t); PEDUG, Representative for education (bar); MARL, Keeper of the herds (bs).

Chorus. SATB (some divisi S) plays large role. Minor roles above drawn from chorus.

Orchestra. 2 fl (picc), 2 cl in B♭, bs cl in B♭ (E♭ cl), 2 obs, 2 bsns, 3 trps in B♭, 4 hrns in F, 2 trbs, bs trb, tuba, 3 perc, harp, vln I and II, vla, vcl, bs.

Material. FS–P and VS: G. Schirmer.

REVIEWS

William Albright "Houston," *Opera News* (December 24, 1988), p. 36

> "Philip Glass's theatre piece is ... enriched by fragrant flowerings of melody, subtle yet vivid orchestral colors and tex-

tures . . . and a fluent setting of Lessing's prose that alternates and combines speech and song."

"HGO's production was visually compelling and musically superb. John DeMain's crisp conducting mined the color and mesmeric magnetism of Glass' writing, though Domberger's staging failed to inject life into the often static opera. But the projections—boiling snow clouds, galloping rhino-like cattle, drifting asteroids . . . were striking."

Manuela Hoelterhoff "Opera: Glass's 'Planet 8,' " *Wall Street Journal* (July 15, 1988), p. 9

"Ms. Lessing wrote six versions of the libretto and a seventh may be needed. . . . Ms. Lessing seems to like her words a bit too much to cut very many of them."

"Whenever characters are asked to deliver a Significant Thought . . . the singing stops and the declamation starts."

"Such shortcomings are . . . puzzling, given the generally inspired level of so much of 'Planet 8's' music. . . . The arpeggio exercises Mr. Glass used to turn out by the mile are trimmed back and subdued to give the opera a melancholy undercurrent. . . . In an affecting scene showing shivering folks hauling boats filled with life-giving magic flowers . . . muted trumpets and drums send up their emanations from the pit."

SATYAGRAHA

Abstract, symbolic pageant. Three acts, seven scenes (120 minutes). Many minimalist characteristics similar to Glass's *AKHNATEN.* Vocal lines generally simple musical phrases of limited range. Homophonic ensembles. Each scene based on a basic musical cell or structural device such as ostinato, theme and variations, modal scale patterns, or rondo-like structure.

Book by Philip Glass and Constance de Jong. Lyrics adapted from the Bhagavad-Gita by Constance de Jong. Commissioned by the City of Rotterdam for De Nederlandse Operastichting. Premiere: Netherlands Opera 9.5.80. Performances: Artpark, N.Y. 81; Brooklyn Academy of Music 11.6.81; New York City Opera; Lyric Opera of Chicago 9.28.87. Recordings: Recording by New York City Opera, Christopher Keene, director, copyright 1985. CBS Masterworks, M3K 39672.

PLOT

Setting: South Africa, 1896–1910.

Act I, scene i: The Kuru Field of Justice; ii: Tolstoy Farm (1904); iii: The Vow (1906). Act II, i: Rescue (1896); ii: Indian Opinion (1906); iii: Protest (1908). Act III, i: Newcastle March (1910).

As Tolstoy watches from above, a mythological battle is depicted between two royal families at the Kuru Field of Justice. The duty and honor of fighting are emphasized, despite what the outcome may bring. The scenes that follow depict the way Gandhi led the Indian people of South Africa to secure their civil and human rights through establishing the self-sufficient, collective called Tolstoy farm in 1904, as well as gathering to protest and resist the severe restriction of civil rights imposed by the British in 1906.

As the Indian poet, Tagore, looks on, European prejudice against Gandhi, as well as the bravery of those who helped him, is depicted. The movement strengthened and educated its followers by publishing the weekly newspaper, the *Indian Opinion,* beginning in 1906. In 1908, the Indian population burned their registration cards as a unified gesture of resistance to offensive British laws.

Watched by Martin Luther King, in 1910, the Satyagraha women assisted the Newcastle miners in a strike. Finally, the entire group of workers marches back to Tolstoy farm led by Gandhi, who instructed them in non-violent resistance. During the march, Gandhi and his helpers settle down to sleep as the Satyagraha army appears in the night sky.

PRODUCTION REQUIREMENTS

Major Roles. GANDHI (t): C2 to A3. MISS SCHLESEN, Gandhi's secretary (s): G♯3 to C♯5 (sustained high tessitura). MRS. NAIDOO, Indian co-worker (s): G♯3 to A4. KASTURBAI, Gandhi's wife (m-s): D♯3 to E4. MR. KALLENBACH, European co-worker (bar): C2 to F3. PARSI RUSTOMJI, Indian co-worker (bs): C1 to E3.

Supporting Roles. MRS. ALEXANDER, European friend (c): F3 to D♭4. ARJUNA, mythical figure (t): D2 to E♭3. KRISHNA, mythical figure (bs): B♭1 to B♭2.

Mute Roles. LEO TOLSTOY, RABINDRANATH TABORE, MARTIN LUTHER KING, JR.

Chorus. SATB (40 voices).

Orchestra. 3 fls, 3 obs, 3 cls in B♭, bs cl, 2 bsns, electronic organ, strings.

Material. FS–P and VS: Dunvagen, c/o G. Schirmer.

REVIEWS

Menno Feenstra "The Netherlands," *Opera News* (January 17, 1981), pp. 38–39

"Sanskrit verses from Gandhi's bible and ideological starting point, the *Bagavid Gita,* having nothing to do with the African locale, but which inspired that specific scene's action, were sung. . . . The words had no direct relation to the story, but [David Pountney's] direction was so imaginative that he created an extra sense of understanding by doing so."

"Glass' hallucinatory music reduces time speed to nearly zero, intensifying the audience's sensitivity to the tiniest change in harmony, rhythm, melody or color and to the drama's undercurrents."

Robert Jacobson "New York," *Opera News* (February 27, 1982), pp. 30–32

"The orchestral colors, the timbres Glass creates, are often arresting, as are his basic musical germs in terms of capturing a particular situation . . . but his resistance to taking them further, as opposed to merely restating them, is a serious detriment."

Robert T. Jones " 'Satyagraha' — A New 'Parsifal'?" *Musical America* (December 1980), pp. 32–33

"Glass' new opera, though, lies within operatic tradition. It has a plot, trained voices, and an orchestra that is only mildly unconventional. . . . Glass's music here is as propulsive as it was in *Einstein,* but minus the aggression, the about-to-blow-up quality. *Satyagraha* is a beautiful, radiant work, filled with ecstacy."

Leslie Lassetter "The Position of *Satyagraha* in the Operatic Trilogy of Philip Glass," *Opera Journal* (1987), 20(1):3–13

"composer and librettist were careful to avoid the sort of threefold repetition that occurs when the sung text explains the action while the music enhances the word-painted action and the text. Their intent was rather to let the 'elemental power' of words, plot, and music function contiguously without overlapping."

"Time is treated from the point of view of eternity, a realm in which past, present, and future are not binding forces. As if to reinforce this, the three historical figures . . . form a trinity of time and passively observe the action on stage: Tolstoy represents Gandhi's past, Tagore his present, and King the future beyond him."

1000 AIRPLANES ON THE ROOF

Performance art. Libretto by David Henry Hwang. Premiere: American Music Theatre Festival, Philadelphia 9.21.88.

Lee Goldstein (1952–1990)

THE FAN

Comedy in buffa tradition. Two acts (130 minutes). Contemporary tonal idiom with some dissonant neo-classicism, even jazz influences. Sung introduction, frequent intricate, rhythmically complex ensembles. Care taken for clever libretto to be understood.

Libretto by Charles Kondek, based on *Il Ventaglio* by Carlo Goldoni. Commissioned by Lyric Opera of Chicago. Premiere: Lyric Opera Center for American Artists 6.17.89.

PLOT

Setting: the square of a small town in Italy on a summer day, mid-1700s.

A buffo plot filled with love triangles, and one complication after another, cleverly narrated by the ensemble itself. Candida's fan fell and broke, so Evarist (her true love) takes the fan to Susanna (because she is a milliner) to get a new one. Candida sees Evarist with Susanna and suspects the worst. Evarist then gives the new fan to Nina to return to Candida. Of course, Coronado and Crispino (who both love Nina) observe this act by spying. Hence, they are both sure that Nina loves Evarist. The distraught Candida, bent on revenge, agrees to marry the Baron (who loves her, even though she loves Evarist). Geltrude, Candida's stern and protective aunt, fancies Timoteo and he feels the same, but neither knows the other's feelings. Poor Susanna is desperate for romance and the Count loves himself! But, lo and behold, the fan crosses everyone's hands, it seems, and all resolves itself happily in the end!

PRODUCTION REQUIREMENTS

Major Roles. CANDIDA, ward of Geltrude (s): C3 to E♭5. NINA, a peasant girl (m-s): A2 to B♭4. COUNT ROCCA MARINA (t): C2 to C4. SIGNOR EVARIST, a gentleman (t): C2 to B3. CRISPINO, a shoemaker (bar): A♭1 to G3.

Supporting Roles. SUSANNA, a milliner (s): C3 to C5. GELTRUDE, a woman of means (m-s): G2 to A♭4. TIMOTEO, an apothecary (t): C2 to A3. CORONATO, an innkeeper (bar): B♭1 to F♯3. BARON DEL CEDRO (bs): G1 to G3. MORRACCHIO, Nina's brother (bs): G1 to F♯3.

Orchestra. fl (picc, alt fl), ob (Eng hrn), cl (bs cl), bsn, hrn, trp (flugelhrn), timp (perc), piano, strings (1–1–1–1–1).

Material. FS–P and VS: Lyric Opera Center for American Artists, 20 N. Wacker, Chicago, IL 60606

REVIEWS

Wynne Delacoma "Lyric's breezy 'Fan' stirs fresh air," *Chicago Sun-Times* (June 19, 1989), p.32

> "the stuff of comic-opera cliche. But 'The Fan' came to life with its richly detailed score and witty dialogue."

> "the opera sparkled with speedy pacing and inventive staging that required its 11 singers to pop in and out of character as they chatted directly with the audience."

Dorothy Samachson "Chicago," *Opera Magazine* (October, 1989)

> "Whether *The Fan* can fit on to a major stage, I'm not sure. But I am sure that it will find a welcome place on many regional stages, here and abroad."

John von Rhein "Chicago," *Opera News* (October 1989)

> "The comedy faithfully evoked the buffa conventions of Rossini and Donizetti while remaining a product of our time in its slick theatricality and eclectic musical blend."

"Goldstein took pains in his transparent scoring to make sure the words came through clearly."

"The music acknowledges neoclassic Stravinsky, as well as today's musical comedy. . . . it is brilliantly scored, grateful to sing, rewarding to hear, tonal in its harmonies though not beholden to predictable formulas. Energy never flags."

Robert Gross (1914–   )

PROJECT 1521

Science fiction satire. Three acts, two scenes (130 minutes). Mostly conservative modern writing, contrasts with pointilistic, electronic Act III. Recitative-like vocal style with chamber orchestra in Acts I and II. Act III: spoken and half-sung dialogue with prerecorded tapes and percussion only.

Libretto by the composer. Premiere: Occidental College, Los Angeles, California 11.74.

PLOT

Setting: "not quite mythical Ur University."

Recent scientific advancements, producing (through regimented dieting) a strain of intellectually superior earthworms, lead the Dean and President Cumak to begin an experiment of their own. Having just lost one of the most brilliant minds on their faculty (Dr. Verano), who left everything (including his body) to the University, the administrative duo decide to liquify Dr. Verano's brain to a vitamin formula, to be administered secretly to the football team. The experiment is later titled "Project 1521," the date of the historically convenient "Diet of Worms."

Within a semester's time, three of the students have improved so much that their teachers suspect cheating. But the Verano-elixir begins to run out. In order to replenish the supply, Cumak arranges an honorary banquet for the university's most respected retired faculty members, to be held in the dilapidated science building. Conveniently, an explosion in one of the labs brings down the roof, convincing the Board of Trustees of the need for more modern facilities as well as replenishing raw materials for the secret vitamin.

Ten years pass, and the Dean is now President of the University (Cumak perished in the explosion and is now merely "food for thought"). As the new President escorts Mrs. Kindern, his Chief Dietician, through the new science building, they meet several students, who only converse through a gibberish of vowel sounds and are taught wholly by computers. The elderly Dr. Artesia, who began the experiments with earthworms years earlier, feels alien from the Project 1521 and stops by to request a tour. The new President is happy to oblige. As Artesia enters the secret vault, the door slams behind him and the sound of mechanical grinding begins.

PRODUCTION REQUIREMENTS

Major Roles. THE DEAN (later the NEW PRESIDENT) (t): B♯1 to G♯3. PRESIDENT CUMAK (bar): B1 to G3.

Supporting Roles. STUDENT ALFER (t): D2 to A3. STUDENT BAITER (s): G3 to F♯4. STUDENT GYMEL (bs): D2 to E3. MS. KINDERN, the dietician (m-s): A3 to F♯4. DR. ARTESIA (bar): E2 to F♯3.

Speaking Roles. STUDENT HOLLYMAN. STUDENT EARLYMAN. STUDENT MITCHMAN. INSTRUCTOR NICKSMAN.

Chorus. Speaking student chorus (Act III only).

Orchestra. fl (picc), ob, cl in B♭, bsn, hrn in F, perc, strings (1–1–1–1–1), tape.

Material. FS–P: contact composer through AMC. FS: American Music Center.

REVIEWS

Lewis Segal "Gross' 'Project 1521' at Occidental College," *Los Angeles Times* (November 5, 1974), section 4, p. 13

> "except for a lively student ensemble in the last act, Gross' current text is wholly, relentlessly expositional."

> "his 15-piece chamber ensemble maintains a lively dialogue of its own, often commenting on themes initiated by the singers."

> "Like his dramatic premise, Gross' musical ideas display wit and talent—but not much focus or sense of theatrical proportion."

Philip Hagemann

THE ASPERN PAPERS

Drama. Two acts, eight scenes (90 minutes). Chromatic vocal lines in speech-like rhythms often supported by accompaniment. An ongoing dialogue structure with ensembles appearing as set numbers. Recurring motives in arias, duets, ensembles.

Libretto by the composer, based on the novella by Henry James. Premiere: Northwestern University, Evanston, Illinois 11.19.88.

PLOT

Setting: Venice, 1888.

Two literary critics, John Cumnor and Henry Jonson, arrive at the dilapidated palazzo of Juliana Bordereau in Venice. Miss Bordereau, once the beauty who inspired the American poet, Jeffrey Aspern, to write great love poems, is now a wheelchair bound, shrewish woman of some ninety years. The two men believe that Juliana still holds unpublished works by Aspern, and momentos that might shed light upon his otherwise obscure life. The old woman has denied this outrightly and has refused all visitors. Henry, however, has conceived a plan to gain entrance: he is willing to pay handsomely for a few rooms off the garden courtyard of the palazzo, knowing that Miss Bordereau needs the income. Once a tenant, he shall seduce Miss Bordereau's spinster niece, Tina, who cares for the old woman, in the hope that he might gain information about the Aspern papers.

One month later, after having hired a gardener and cultivated flowers to send daily to the ladies, Henry is still no closer to his objective. Finally, Juliana admits him to her company, wishing to sell a valuable miniature painting: a portrait of Aspern himself. Juliana even reads Henry one of Aspern's love poems, hitherto unknown to the public. Henry quickly offers to purchase the portrait of Aspern, and when Juliana retires, he absconds with the poem. However, Juliana suffers a mild stroke, believing that the poem has been misplaced. Nevertheless, Henry has his proof that she might be concealing other papers, and entreats Tina to help him remove them from the house before Juliana might eventually destroy them. He wins Tina's affection, providing the lonely woman with friendship she has not known for years.

When the opportunity arises, Henry steals into the parlor and locates the remainder of Aspern's papers. Juliana discovers him, and is stricken again, this time fatally. Henry flees, though he does attend the old woman's funeral. Miss Tina, now sole owner of the Aspern papers, proposes that Henry may see the papers if he will become part of the family. Marrying Miss Tina, of course, is a price too high for Henry to pay. She is left to spend the remainder of her years in isolation. As the curtain falls, a half-crazed Tina burns Aspern's papers, realizing that she had been used by Henry in the same way Juliana was used by Aspern.

PRODUCTION REQUIREMENTS

Major Roles. Henry Jonson, an American literary critic (bar): G1 to G3. Miss Tina, Juliana's niece (s): C3 to C5.

Supporting Roles. Juliana Bordereau, the beauty that inspired the poetry of Jeffrey Aspern, now a bitter old woman (m-s): A♭2 to A4. John Comnor, a British literary critic (t): E2 to B♭3.

Minor Roles. Gondolier (t). Gardener (bar). Giovanna, the maid (s).

Orchestra. 2 fls, 2 obs, 2 cls, 2 bsns, 2 trps, 2 hrns, 2 trbs, tuba, piano (cel), perc, timp, strings.

Material. FS–P and VS: Philip Hagemann, 35 Riverside Dr., Apt. #3, New York, NY 10023

REVIEWS

Andrew Porter "From Page to Stage," *New Yorker* (December 26, 1988), pp. 69–71

> "It's a 'well-made opera,' with both the good and bad points implicit in that phrase. Hagemann is a proficient composer, and a well-made opera is preferable to a badly made one. There is intelligent use of motifs. . . . But the music does not take command. . . . The opera seemed to be not much more than James's 'Aspern Papers' ably dramatized and set to music."

John Harbison (1938–)

A FULL MOON IN MARCH

Tragedy. One act (45 minutes). Set numbers: duets and arias. Opens with orchestral fanfare. Atonal with changing meters.

Libretto adapted by John Harbison from W. B. Yeats' play. Based on an age-old tale, originally written as a dance play by Yeats. Premiere: Boston Musica Viva, Cambridge, Mass. 4.30.79. Recordings: Boston Musica Viva, Richard Pittman, cond. Composers Recordings Inc. SD 454.

PLOT

Setting: defined setting not required.

The opera is based on an old tale of a Queen who will marry the man whose song she likes best. Should she not like the song, the suitor will lose his life.

The opera begins with a commentary by two attendants on the foolishness of men in love. The Queen enters to meet a Swineherd who has come to offer his song. The Swineherd tells of his tribulations to reach her; the Queen warns of her cruelty. The Queen softens and agrees to hear his song, but is shocked by his confidence. She orders his severed head brought to her.

For the remainder of the opera, the attendants describe the action, a dancer replaces the Queen in a ritualistic dance around the head.

PRODUCTION REQUIREMENTS

Major Roles. First Attendant (s): B2 to D5. Second Attendant (t): D2 to D4. The Queen (m-s): A2 to A4. The Swineherd (bar): B♭1 to A3.

Ballet. Dancer replaces the Queen toward the end of the opera.

Orchestra. fl, ob, bs cl, perc, vln, vla, vcl, piano (with preparations).

Material. FS–P and VS: Associated Music Publishers.

REVIEWS

John Freeman "Records," *Opera News* (March 16, 1985), p. 44

> "The Turandot-Salome subject matter tends to stretch the chamber-opera format, but Harbison's old-fashioned vocal lines, with fashionably contemporary-sounding orchestral fabric and patterns, are not out to shock anyone."

Ellen Pfeiffer "Boston Musica Viva: Harbison 'Full Moon in March' premiere," *Musical America* (September 1979), pp. 23–24

> "*Full Moon* is based on a late verse play by W. B. Yeats, . . . (not exactly a) compelling operatic libretto."

"Harbison's music, on the other hand, is extraordinarily attractive . . . it is sensual, almost exotic, what with . . . the Eastern quality of its prepared piano sonorities."

Andrew Porter "Words for Music Perhaps," *New Yorker* (May 28, 1979), pp. 111–117

[Gives background of Yeats' play of the same name (1935). Its origin as a dance play discussed at length.]

"(Harbison's) excellent score asserts and justifies the musician's prerogative to rape a poem or play, to invest 'the plain fable' with his own kind of 'secret.' . . . *Full Moon in March* is an opera that holds the ear and stirs the mind. It moves surely and it sounds beautiful. It should have a future."

Barbara Kinsey Sable "Harbison, John, *Full Moon in March*," *The NATS Bulletin* (November/December 1984), p. 57

"Here is a work that might be attractive to opera workshops . . . The instrumental requirements are demanding in quality but not in quantity. The music provides more promise than the tale, for it is difficult to empathize with the characters . . . In spite of the difficulties, the work is a good one."

"The writing for the Queen incorporates a number of low notes that are difficult to be heard over the orchestral sounds."

Robert Schwarz "Dodge: Cascando. Harbison: Full Moon in March," *Musical America* (December 1984), p. 44

"Harbison has an innate dramatic gift that enables him to portray this action in deeply moving musical terms, while employing only limited resources. The vocal lines are highly expressive . . . they are grateful, singable, memorable."

"*Full Moon in March* is tonal in an attenuated sort of way, utilizing expressionistic atonality, Eastern sonorities . . . , and a propulsive Stravinskian rhythmic component, all mingled with operatic conventions such as aria, recitative, and strophic song."

WINTER'S TALE

Tragedy. Two acts (75 minutes). Atonal writing through-composed in dialogue form with arias, duets, trios, and choruses. No overture. Wide skips as well as lyrical vocal lines. Much action takes place in dumb shows, with ritualized, symbolic movement accompanied by prerecorded tape of a small chamber ensemble.

Libretto by the composer, based on the play by William Shakespeare. Premiere: San Francisco Opera 8.20.79. Recording: Tape available through American Opera Project, San Francisco Opera.

PLOT

Setting: Italy and Bohemia, Elizabethan times.

Act I, scene i: Sicily, before Leontes' palace; ii: A room in Leontes' palace; iii: Courtroom in Leontes' palace. Act II, i: Bohemia, sixteen years later, a meadow with farmhouse; ii: Sicily, a room in Leontes' palace; iii: Sicily, a chapel.

When Polixenes, the King of Bohemia, ignores Leontes' pleas to stay, Leontes directs his wife, Hermione, to change his departing guest's mind. But when Hermione is successful, King Leontes is convinced of his wife's infidelity. He condemns Hermione to prison, accusing her of being pregnant with Polixenes' child, and sends to Delphi for confirmation of his actions. Hermione gives birth to a daughter and the enraged King orders that the child be left in the desert. The child is carried away, protected by Hermione's mantle and necklace. At Hermoine's trial, the Queen defers to the oracle, which upholds her innocence. Furthermore, Leontes is warned that he shall live without an heir if the lost child is not found. The King denies the oracle until the news arrives that his son has died. Finally acknowledging his injustice, Leontes begs Apollo's forgiveness, but the Queen also dies.

Sixteen years later, Florizel, Polixenes' son, wants to marry Perdita, the Queen's daughter, who was taken in by a shepherd after being abandoned. The shepherd agrees that they should marry, but Polixenes, who is visiting the island, forbids the wedding on pain of death. The couple is advised to seek Leontes' help. King Leontes, still mourning the loss of his wife, is introduced to Perdita. He is transfixed by her beauty and her resemblance to Hermione. Polixenes is announced, and Florizel quickly beseeches Leontes to be his advocate against his father. When Polixenes enters, he threatens his son, but is interrupted when the shepherd places Hermione's necklace around Perdita's neck. Leontes kneels joyously before his daughter, and both fathers give their blessings to the children's union. All gather to see the previously unrevealed statue of Hermione. After Perdita kisses the statue's hand, the Queen is miraculously brought back to life to embrace Leontes and bless her daughter's marriage.

PRODUCTION REQUIREMENTS

Major Roles. LEONTES, King of Sicily (bar): G1 to G3 (much falsetto A3 to C♯4). HERMIONE, Queen to Leontes (s): B2 to A4. FLORIZEL, Son of Polixenes (t): E2 to A♭3. PERDITA, Daughter of Leontes (s): C♯3 to C5.

Supporting Roles. TIME (bs): B1 to C♯3. POLIXENES, King of Bohemia (bar): B1 to A♭3. PAULINA, Wife of Antigonus and servant to King Leontes (m-s): E3 to A♭4.

Minor Roles. Lords of Sicily: CAMILLO (bs), ANTIGONUS (t). SHPHERD (bs).

Mute Roles. MAMILLIUS, Young Prince of Sicily (mute).

Orchestra. 2 fls (picc or alt fl), 2 obs (Eng hrn), 2 cls, 2 bsns, 2 hrns, 2 trps, perc, strings (6–6–4–4–3).

Chorus. SATB

Dance. Small group.

Material. FS–P, VS, and tape: Associated Music Publishers and American Music Center.

REVIEWS

Marilyn Tucker "San Francisco. American Opera Project: Harbison's 'A Winter's Tale,' " *Musical America* (December 1979), pp. 20–21

> "He cunningly telescoped the more-than-sixteen-year time element in the play by the use of dumb show for several key scenes. . . . This worked very well theatrically."

> "Musically, the opera, with Harbison's vivid score, is very substantial."

> "Harbison created a fully dimensioned group of characters to play out the action."

Stephanie Von Buchau "San Francisco," *Opera* (December 1979), p. 1185

"Harbison writes in a conservative idiom, with most of the musical substance and interest reserved for the orchestra. His woodwind and brass writing, with piquant coloration from the percussion, is varied and inventive. But the vocal lines, though lyrical and not too difficult, fail to ignite the imagination."

William Harper

SNOW LEOPARD

Libretto by Roger Nieboer and the composer inspired by Peter Matthiesen's written account of his trek through the Himalayas. Premiere: Minnesota Opera New Music-Theatre Ensemble 11.9.89.

Derek Healey (1936–   )

SEABIRD ISLAND

Mythical drama. Two acts, six scenes, four sets (100 minutes). Unique, twentieth-century style with chromatic melodic lines. Frequent grace notes, glissandi, jagged angular vocal lines creates primitive effect. Colorful orchestration with many timbral effects. Scored for instrumental ensemble and tape. Some unconventional notation.

Libretto by Norman Newton, based on a Tsimshian story. Commissioned by the Edward Johnson Music Foundation. Premiere: Guelph Spring Festival, Ontario 77.

PLOT

Setting: country of Tsimshian, on the northern coast of British Columbia near the mouth of the Skeena, mythical times.

Though several young maidens have disappeared into the sea at night, the princess remains outside to buy arrows from an old shaman. A charming prince declares his love for the princess, but the willful girl falls in love with the shaman, who has disguised himself as a magnificent youth. She soon falls under his spell and leaves with him, becoming his servant and lover in a nighttime world. The prince and the maid travel to find her, but they are led astray by the sorceror's obstacles. The princess finally uncovers her lover's masked face and realizes that he is really the old shaman. Repulsed, she begs him to take her home. On their journey, the shaman leaves the princess on an island, to be eaten by the birds. The princess hides from the birds and, when the shaman returns, she takes off in his canoe, leaving him to the same fate. Because of her murderous act, the princess must don the mask of an old woman and assume the shaman's role: she is doomed to live off the bodies of young men to sustain her life.

PRODUCTION REQUIREMENTS

Major Roles. PRINCESS (s): C3 to C5. SHAMAN (t): $B^{b}1$ to $B^{b}3$. MAID (s): B2 to A4. PRINCE (bs-bar): G1 to F3 [G3 falsetto].

Supporting Roles. KING (bs): G1 to F3. QUEEN (m-s): C3 to G4.

Mute Roles. WARRIORS. VILLAGERS.

Orchestra. 2 fls (picc), cl (bs cl), bsn (cont bsn), 2 hrns, 3 perc, harp, piano (cel), piano accordian, string quintet, tape.

Material. FS–P and VS: the composer (address available through AMC). VS: American Music Center.

REVIEWS

Ruby Mercer "Guelph: Guelph Spring Festival," *Opera Canada* (September 1977), 18(3):31–32

"The score, kind to the singers, presented authentic-sounding music that was, nevertheless, original. Basically tonal, the music was varied by the use of percussion, rattles and electronic distortions, all woven together with sound technique and creative mastery."

"It is a work that bears hearing again, for its first impressions linger on."

F. B. St. Clair "Canada: An Indian Legend," *Opera* (October 1978), 29(10):1008

"The concise and unaffected language of the libretto is supported, if not exactly illuminated, by Derek Healey's score. . . . The music was more successful in creating mood than specific dramatic comment, but the combination of a taut and gripping drama given adequate musical support made for an evening of real excitement."

Alva Henderson (1940–   )

THE LAST OF THE MOHICANS

Tragedy. Three acts, ten scenes, one set (180 minutes). Use of chromaticism and dissonance, though neo-Romantic feeling prevails. Several dramatic choral and ensemble sections, including Act I and Act III finales.

Libretto by Janet Lewis, dramatic concept by Robert Darling, based on the novel by James Fennimore Cooper. Commission: Wilmington Opera Society for American Bicentennial. Premiere: Wilmington Opera Society, Delaware 6.12.76. Performances: Lake George Opera Festival, N.Y. 77.

PLOT

Setting: Pioneer America during the French and Indian War, 1757.

A crowd mourns the double murder of Cora (a beautiful, young Scottish girl) and Uncas (the Mohican who secretly loved her), as the events which lead to this scene follow in flashback.

Cora and her younger sister, Alice, are en route to join their father, Munro, who is commander of Fort William Henry. Their guardian, Heyward, who has fallen in love with Alice, enlists the aid of the Indian, Magua, to conduct the party on the dangerous journey. Once a mighty chieftain himself, Magua now seeks vengeance on Munro, swearing to break his heart, just as Munro had broken Magua's spirit and reputation. Magua leads the party into the dark woods, where he abandons them at dusk. Heyward, Cora and Alice take refuge in a cavern, where they meet some friendlier natives who agree to help them complete their journey: Chingatchgook (chief of the Mohican tribe), his son Uncas (the last of the Mohican leaders), and Hawkeye (the last of another race).

The party arrives just as Munro surrenders his besieged fort to the Frenchman, Montcalm. But the surrendered party is ambushed in a bloody surprise attack led by Magua, who mercilessly slaughters nearly all but Cora and her sister, with the intent of taking Cora for his wife and slave.

Back at the smoldering ruins of the fort, Heyward again enlists the aid of Chingatchgook, Uncas, and Hawkeye to rescue the women. They find them at the camp of the wise and feared Lenape tribe, where Magua has left Cora, to learn the ways of being a proper squaw. The aged and omniscient Tamenund is called in to make a just decision about their fates. Tamenund decrees that Heyward, Alice, and the other Indians may leave in peace, but that Cora must remain as Magua's prisoner-bride. All are horrified by the judgment. When Uncas, Chingatchgook, and Tamenund realize that they are all members of the nearly extinct Mohican tribe, fervent belief in the "law" forces even Uncas to relinquish his feelings for Cora. But when Magua finally drags Cora off, Uncas swears revenge. He and the others follow Magua's trail.

Alone with Magua, Cora chooses death rather than to serve Magua. She cries out for Uncas, who lunges out of hiding to her defense. Cora is stabbed by the warriors who held her; Uncas is slain by Magua's dagger. Magua's victory is short lived—Hawkeye levels his musket and kills Magua with a single shot. The scene dissolves back to that of the opening of the opera. Hawkeye pledges his devotion to the grief-stricken Chingatchgook and the weary Tamenund goes off to die. The age of the Red Man has come and gone.

PRODUCTION REQUIREMENTS

Major Roles. CORA, a beautiful young Scottish girl (s): A♯2 to C5. UNCAS, the last of the Mohicans (t): Al to B♭3. HAWKEYE, the last of another race (bar): Al to G3 [A♭3 ossia]. MAGUA, once a mighty chieftain, now Munro's bitter servant (bar): B♭1 to G3 [A♭3 ossia]. HEYWARD, military aide to Munro (t): Al to B♭3.

Supporting Roles. ALICE, Cora's younger sister (s): A♯2 to C5 (D5 ossia, much ensemble singing). CHINGATCHGOOK, Unca's father and former Mohican chief (bs-bar): F1 to F3 (F♯3 ossia). TAMENUND, wise sage and lost brother of Chingatchgook (bs-bar): B1 to B♭3.

Minor Roles. MUNRO, English general, Alice and Cora's father (bar). MONTCALM, French military leader (bar). Two SAGES OF THE LENAPE TRIBE (bars).

Chorus. SSAATTBB.

Orchestra. 2 fls, ob (Eng hrn), 2 cls (bs c1), 2 bsns (cont bsn), 2 hrns, 2 trps, 2 tubas, timp, 2 perc, cel, harp, strings.

Material. FS–P and VS: contact Wilmington Opera Society through AMC. VS: American Music Center.

REVIEWS

Robert Baxter "Philadelphia and Wilmington," *Opera* (October 1976), 27(10):914–916

"[Henderson] has written a lush, densely orchestrated music, laced with dissonance. For all his inventive skill . . . his jagged, wide-ranging vocal lines tend to obscure the words."

Robert Jacobson "Wilmington," *Opera News* (September 1976), p. 66

"[Henderson] and particularly his librettist, Janet Lewis, needed editorial blue-penciling to bring this lengthy opus into more concise, workable shape."

"the expertly handled mood painting and static exchanges tended to dominate in a Wagnerian, almost hectoring way. But the composer's ability to make time stand still worked to splendid effect in the sextet near the end of Act I and the Act II male quartet."

"with a pulsing sense of melody and stirring emotional commitment. . . . His careful building of ensembles . . . aspires to greatness—particularly in the final act, where Cora's dramatic farewell forms the basis of a richly layered, thrilling outburst with principals and chorus."

Andrew Porter "Music at the Falls," *New Yorker* (July 5, 1976), pp. 69–71

"it is a work on a different level . . . more imaginative, more romantic, nobler in intention."

"The effect is almost as of a choral drama with solos, kin to those music-dramas of Handel that he called oratorios. . . . Offstage choruses echo, amplify, provide a background to thoughts that are voiced and moods that are felt onstage. Henderson's aim seems to have been to find and sustain those 'musics' that are never long absent from Cooper's pages."

"[Henderson's music] has many virtues: lyricism, vocal lines that are flexible and good to sing, liveliness and color in orchestral writing. But many of the tunes are just not quite good enough."

MEDEA

Greek tragedy. Two acts, one scene, one set (95 minutes). Neo-Romantic with chromaticism and dissonance. Vocal lines chromatic with some wide and dissonant leaps. Largely an extended, through-composed soliloquoy for Medea. Choral sections simpler, more chordally conceived. Orchestra and Greek chorus important in projecting drama.

Libretto by the composer, based on an adaptation of Euripides' *Medea* by Robinson Jeffers. Premiere: San Diego Opera 11.29.72.

PLOT

Setting: Corinth, ancient Greece.

When Jason returns to Corinth with the Golden Fleece he is declared a hero and is betrothed to Creon's daughter. But Medea, who helped him capture the Golden Fleece, and bore Jason two sons, is now cast aside. Creon, who hates her solely by virtue of her presence, banishes her from his kingdom. Jason gives Medea no consolation, but grants her one evening more to say farewell to the children. Dejected and alone, Medea swears her vengeance. Only the Nurse, knowing how deeply Medea has been wounded, perceives the hideous plot Medea plans as retribution.

Medea sends the Nurse and her two sons off to their new mistress and mother, bearing a golden wreath and veil she offers as gifts from her own treasures. When Jason's new bride dons the gifts, the gold turns to fire, and the blaze spreads throughout Creon's palace. Jason rushes to Medea's door, determined to kill her and retrieve his sons who had escaped the fire. Medea presents the children to Jason—two bloodied corpses she murdered with her own hands. Mad with grief, Jason lunges at her, but Medea walks safely across the blood-stained threshold of her darkened house, cursing Jason, and sending him to his once enchanted ship that has now begun to rot. Jason's fickle love has caused his downfall.

PRODUCTION REQUIREMENTS

Major Roles. MEDEA (m-s): F$^{\#}$2 to B^{b}4. (Demands flexible voice with wide dramatic capabilities.)

Supporting Roles. JASON (t): C2 to B^{b}3 (ossia B3). CREON (bs): A1 to E$^{\#}$3. THE NURSE (m-s): A2 to A^{b}4.

Minor Roles. THE TUTOR (bar).

Mute Roles. MEDEA'S CHILDREN (2 boys). TWO SERVING WOMEN.

Chorus. Greek Chorus: SSAA (16 total): Jason's men: TTBB (16); Citizens of Corinth: SATB (28).

Orchestra. 2 fls, ob, 2 cls (bs cl), 3 bsns, 2 hrns, 2 trps, 3 trbs, tuba, timp, 2 perc, harp, strings.

Material. FS–P and VS: San Diego Opera, P.O. Box 988, San Diego, CA 92112-0988. VS: American Music Center.

REVIEWS

S. A. Desick "San Diego," *Opera News* (January 20, 1973), p. 27

> "Except for a few dissonances, *Medea* is quite traditional. . . . there are strong traces of Britten, Strauss, Barber. The orchestral writing, at times busily self-indulgent, tends to distract the ear from the singing or to engulf the solo parts in ensemble just as you expect them to ascend dramatically. Yet I liked the opera. Henderson's mixture has bite — effective syncopation in vocal entrances, especially good choral writing. . . , theatrical tension."

Karen Monson "A new 'Medea' by Alva Henderson, with Irene Dalis," *Musical America* (March 1973), p. 22

> "Considered as a first effort, *Medea* is no minor accomplishment. It is sufficiently well-crafted, the work of a young eclectic obviously under the influence of the more conservative moderns. Henderson may take credit for moments of significant melodic effect. But *Medea* does not sustain."

WEST OF WASHINGTON SQUARE

Two acts (120 minutes). Libretto by the composer and Janet Lewis based on two short stories by O. Henry, *The Last Leaf* and *Room Across the Hall*. Commission and premiere: Opera San Jose 11.26.88.

Jerry Herman (1933–   )

HELLO, DOLLY!

Romantic comedy. Two acts, fifteen scenes (full evening). Musical theater with grand ensembles, many dance segments and orchestral interludes. Vocal writing ranges from lyrical to patter style.

Lyrics by the composer. Book by Michael Stewart, based on Thornton Wilder's "The Matchmaker." Premiere: St. James Theatre, N.Y. 1.16.64. Recording: RCA OC (Various cast recordings include Channing, Bailey and Martin as "Dolly.")

PLOT

Setting: New York City, 1898.

The recently widowed Dolly Levi has turned to a new career: matchmaking. She is hired to find a suitable wife for the wealthy merchant, Horace Vandergelder. Dolly (who is interested in Horace herself) does make an effort to arrrange a meeting in New York between Horace and Mrs. Molloy, owner of a fashionable shop. Unbeknownst to him, Vandergelder's two company clerks, Cornelius and Barnaby, also steal away to New York. When his clerks are discovered in Mrs. Molloy's store, Dolly turns Horace's chagrin to her own advantage. She fixes Cornelius up with Mrs. Molloy, and Barnaby with Minnie Fay, for an evening at Harmonia Gardens restaurant. Dolly, absent from the social scene for too long, makes a gracious entrance and all the waiters join in the welcome. As the evening progresses Dolly wins Horace's affection. Thus, the match Dolly really had in mind—Horace and herself—is made.

PRODUCTION REQUIREMENTS

Major Roles. Dolly Levi (m-s): G2 to G$^\sharp$4.

Supporting Roles. Horace Vandergelder (bar): B$^\flat$1 to D3. Irene Molloy (m-s): G2 to F4. Cornelius Hackl (bar-t): B$^\flat$1 to G$^\sharp$3.

Minor Roles. Minnie Fay (s). Barnaby Tucker (high bar). Ambrose Kemper (bar, mostly speaking).

Bit Roles. Several from chorus.

Chorus. SATB separates into men's and women's choruses.

Ballet. Many dance numbers.

Orchestra. Reed I: fl, picc, cl, alt sax; Reed II: cl, alt sax; Reed III: cl, t sax; Reed IV: cl, bs cl, bar sax; trp I and II; trp III; trb I; trb II; optional tuba; perc I and II; guitar and banjo; piano-conductor; 2 vln I; vln II; vla; vcl; bs. (Orch. parts cued also for min. no. of parts: 3 reeds, 2 trps, trb, perc, bs, piano.)

Material. FS–P and VS: Tams-Witmark Music Library.

Bernard Herrmann

WUTHERING HEIGHTS

Lyric drama. Four acts and prologue. Libretto by Lucille Fletscher. Premiere: Portland Opera, Oregon 11.6.82. Recording: Unicorn/Kanchana records: UNB-400 (1971).

Material. Libretto: Novello & Co.

Lee Hoiby (1926–   )

THE ITALIAN LESSON

Satire. One act (50 minutes). Through-composed with vocal lines and accompaniment that support and highlight comic text. Declamatory throughout with occasional lyricism.

Libretto from a monologue by Ruth Draper. Premiere: Baltimore Opera 1.85.

PLOT

Place: New York penthouse apartment unspecified time.

A wealthy New York society woman is delighted that she has progressed in her Italian lessons to reading Dante's *Divine Comedy*. Enthusiastically translating the opening lines, she is enthralled by the simple way in which Dante expressed how easily one becomes lost amidst life's complexities. However, although her enthusiasm continues, the lesson disintegrates into a series of interruptions which represent the normal course of her day. During her "lesson," she handles gossipy telephone calls, gives orders to the cook, arranges for the delivery of her husband's golf clubs, greets a new puppy, talks to her son's teacher, and discusses a portrait with an artist, while she intermittently deals with her children and has a manicure. All of a sudden, she realizes she is late for a funeral and dismisses her Italian teacher, manicurist and children in order to get ready. However, the whirlwind continues as she gives orders to her secretary, makes luncheon plans, and discretely arranges to meet her lover. In fact, at the same time that Dante's profundity is forgotten, it is depicted by her uncountable interests, commitments and activities: as the complexities of her life tangle about her, she is unaware that she is in any way lost amongst them.

PRODUCTION REQUIREMENTS

Major Roles. Woman (m-s): A2 to G4 (A4 high version).

Orchestra. fl, ob, cl in B^b, bsn, hrn, harp, piano, strings (1–1–1–1–0).

Material. FS–P and VS: Aquarius Music Co., RD 1, 71 Rock Valley Rd., Long Eddy, NY 12760. VS: American Music Center.

REVIEWS

Charles Jahant "Baltimore," *Opera* (May 1985), 36(5):502–503

> "Hoiby [is] a careful craftsman who composes operas only when there is a strong book or play to fuel his imagination. Ruth Draper, now called a diseuse, was in her own way a genius at creating a character with scant help from anything save her own penetrating observation. Setting her words to music was an ungrateful job. Hoiby solved part of the problem by scoring lightly over the punch lines."

> "As a sketch this was hilarious, but the material is so frail as to be not easily transferred from the originator's persona. . . . Wretchedly staged, the whole affair seemed bogus, even though the Hoiby score was genteel enough."

Karen Monson "Baltimore Opera: Pasatieri/Weisgall/Hoiby triple bill," *Musical America* (May 1985), p. 20

"Hoiby's music, which leaves plenty of room for approximate pitches, is beige, unprepossessing, eminently forgettable."

David Patrick Stearns "Baltimore," *Opera News* (April 13, 1985), 49:43

"Hoiby's musical language skillfully supports the stage action, tellingly inflecting the vocal lines but never fading into innocuousness. Though the composer has fun at his heroine's expense . . . he is mostly warm and affectionate. Especially memorable was the lady's telephone conversation with her extramarital lover, in which the music soars with Straussian lushness, lifting this daffy caricature to a Central Park West Marschallin."

THE TEMPEST

Fantasy. Three acts (150 minutes). Conservative contemporary idiom with many chromatic passages. Through-composed with set arias, ensembles, choruses. Vocal lines chromatically and rhythmically complex. Orchestra plays large role in providing atmosphere.

Libretto by Mark Shulgasser after Shakespeare. Premiere: Des Moines Metro Opera 6.21.86. Performances: Lyric Opera of Kansas City 4.13.88 (revised).

PLOT

Setting: at sea, on a deserted island, during the Italian Renaissance.

Following Shakespeare's story, briefly: Prospero, the former Duke of Milan, was deposed by his brother, Antonio and Alonso, the King of Naples, and cast out to sea. Prospero, with his books of magic and his daughter Miranda, has inhabited a deserted island ever since. With the aid of Ariel, the chief island spirit, Antonio, Alonso and their royal party are shipwrecked near the island. Miranda meets Prince Ferdinand, Alonso's son, who believes he is the only survivor of the shipwreck, and it is love at first sight. Bur Prospero invervenes, forcing Ferdinand into menial labor. Caliban, the man-monster of the island, and slave of Prospero, hides from his master's torments. Trinculo, a jester from the shipwrecked party, followed by Stephano, the ship's butler, who floated ashore on a keg of wine, proceed to share their drink with Caliban. Drunk for the first time, Caliban swears he will serve these new masters forever.

The courtiers attempt to cheer Alonso, who believes his son has perished. While Alonso sleeps, Antonio and Sebastian plot to kill him for his crown. But Ariel works her magic once again, to wake Alonso in time.

Prospero works his magic and presides over each party. Miranda and Ferdinand profess their love, Caliban enlists Stephano and Trinculo in a plot against Prospero's life, and Ariel appears to frighten and accuse Alonso, Antonio and Sebastian of their plot against Prospero. The drunken trio interrupt the trembling courtiers. But Prospero, pleased with the proceedings, promises that Ariel will soon have her freedom. Prospero gives his daughter's hand to Ferdinand, forgives those who plotted against him, and all look forward to returning to their rightful positions in Milan.

PRODUCTION REQUIREMENTS

Major Roles. PROSPERO, the rightful Duke of Milan (bs-bar): $F^{\#}1$ to $G^{\flat}3$. MIRANDA, his daughter (s): $C^{\#}3$ to B4. ARIEL, an airy spirit (col s): C3 to F5. CALIBAN, a savage and deformed slave (dram t): $D^{\flat}2$ to $B^{\flat}3$.

Supporting Roles. FERDINAND, son of the King of Naples (lyr bar): $C^{\flat}2$ to $G^{\#}3$. ALONSO, King of Naples (bs-bar): $A^{\#}1$ to $E^{\flat}3$. GONZALO, an honest old councillor (t): D2 to B3. TRINCULO, a jester (bar): $A^{\flat}1$ to G3 [F3 to D4 fals]. STEPHANO, a drunken butler (buf bs): F1 to G3.

Minor Roles. SEBASTIAN, Alonso's brother (bar). ANTONIO, the usurping Duke of Milan, Prospero's brother (bar). Goddesses: IRIS (s), CERES (m-s), JUNO (c).

Chorus. SATB off-stage chorus of spirits and courtiers (small men's chorus) appear on-stage.

Ballet. Small corps required.

Orchestra. 2 fls, 2 obs, 2 cls, 2 bsns, 4 hrns, 2 trps, 2 trbs, tuba, timp, perc, harp, piano, strings; reduction in preparation.

Material. FS–P and VS: G. Schirmer.

M. A. Feldman "Indianola, Iowa," *Opera News* (November 1986), pp. 56–57

> "rarely did the evocative orchestration compete for supremacy with the voices."

> "Hoiby's unabashedly extravagant spectacle attests to the composer's passion for the genre and courage to preserve its cherished traditions. . . . Hoiby's score is crammed with musical events: Ariel's swift, airy coloratura displays . . . a vengeance

aria for Caliban . . . an affecting Verdian duet with Miranda . . . a *Der Rosenkavalier* offshoot as three goddesses entertain the bridal pair."

Kenneth LaFave " 'The Tempest' a pleasing and worth effort," *The Kansas City Star*

"There is much to credit the three-hour score . . . most of all the deeply moving chorus that ends the piece."

"Mark Shulgasser's libretto is a canny job that leaves a lot of the original intact. . . . He and Hoiby know how to frame the most familiar lines in touching fashion. The setting of Prospero's 'We are such stuff as dreams are made on' . . . gave away the sage magician's whole character and illuminated the entire evening."

Stanley Hollingsworth (1924–   )

HARRISON LOVED HIS UMBRELLA

Fantasy. One act (25 minutes). Loosely tonal with some chromaticism and non-functional harmony. A jazzy feeling lends to "tongue in cheek" quality. Through-composed in a natural recitative style. Chromatic and disjunct vocal lines often supported by accompaniment. Choral sections less demanding. The opera was "conceived for students at the high school and college levels, but would work very well with a cast of pre-adolescent children and adults."

Libretto by Rhoda Levine based on her book of the same title. Premiere: Students from Oakland University, Rochester, Minn., Spoleto Festival, Charleston, SC 5.24.81. Premiered as Trilogy with Hollingsworth's "The Mother" (premiere: 1954) and "The Selfish Giant" (also a premiere).

PLOT

Harrison's love for his umbrella (he carries it rain or shine, bragging of its beauty) causes a craze that has the town's parents in a quandry. Now all the children, envious of Harrison's prize, want to carry umbrellas everywhere. No amount of coaxing, bribing, scolding, and scheming can alter the children's fixation. Nothing, that is, until Harrison marches in sporting his new prize—a bright red yo-yo.

PRODUCTION REQUIREMENTS

Major Roles. HARRISON (boy s or t): C3 to G4 or C2 to G3.

Minor Roles. HARRISON'S MOTHER (s). HARRISON'S FATHER (t).

Bit Roles. MOTHERS, FATHERS AND CHILDREN (played by members of the chorus, many could play multiple roles).

Chorus. SATB chorus plays major role (premiere production employed 12 MOTHERS and FATHERS and 6 CHILDREN).

Orchestra. fl, ob, 2 cls, bsn, 2 hrns, trp, solo string quintet (may be augmented), piano, harp (opt), 2 perc.

Material. FS–P and VS: Belwin Mills, VS: American Music Center.

REVIEWS

Robert Jacobson "Charleston," *Opera News* (October 1981), pp. 34, 36

> "The world premiere of *Harrison Loved His Umbrella,* 'a musical cartoon for children,' impressed one more with Miss Levine's adroit concept than with anything musical, since Hollingsworth's minimal use of winds and percussion lent no sense of structure."

Kegi "Hollingsworth Trilogy," *Variety* (June 10, 1981), p. 80

> "Another world premiere, 'Harrison Loved His Umbrella' . . . was much more successful. Dealing with teenage fads and parents' efforts to cope, a remarkable cast . . . delighted the audience."

THE SELFISH GIANT

Fairy tale. One act. Conservative contemporary style with recitative-like dialogue. Through-composed with arias, duets, short orchestral prelude and interludes between scenes. Many spoken lines for children.

Libretto by Herbert Moulton and the composer, based on the fairy tale by Oscar Wilde. Premiere: Spoleto Festival, Charleston, S.C. 5.24.81. Premiered as Trilogy with Hollingsworth's "The Mother" (premiere: 1954) and "Harrison Loved His Umbrella" (also a premiere).

PLOT

Setting: the Giant's garden.

A group of children, welcomed by a linnet bird in a tree, begin to play in the Giant's garden, despite the "no trespassing" sign. When he returns home, he chases them away, warning them never to return. Once the garden is empty, the flowers and birds vanish and everything is covered with a blanket of snow. A little boy dressed in white enters the garden and tries unsuccessfully to climb one of the trees to look for his star. The lonely Giant is strangely moved, and asks if he can help. The boy describes his own garden where there are no walls, and everyone who comes in peace is welcome. The Giant lifts the boy into the tree. Miraculously, the tree blossoms into full flower. The next day, the little boy is gone, but the other children return. This time, the Giant steps out to greet them and, for a time, his garden becomes one of the children's favorite play spots. Finally, the little boy in white returns, wounded. The child reassures him that the wounds are wounds of love, not hate. The Giant asks the boy to take him to his garden far away. When the other children return to the garden, they find the Giant lying peacefully under a tree. Thinking that he is asleep, they leave the gifts they had brought him and quietly slip away.

PRODUCTION REQUIREMENTS

Major Roles. GIANT (bs-bar): A1 to F3. LITTLE BOY (boy s): C3 to F♯4.

Supporting Roles. CHILD 1, the leader; CHILD 2; CHILD 3, the youngest; CHILD 4 (child s): E♭3 to G4. (Additional children can divide child 2 and 4's parts.)

Minor Roles. LINNET (s).

Mute Roles. FROST, a mime (optional).

Orchestral. fl, ob, cl, bsn, hn, trp, 2 perc, harp, piano, celeste, strings (1–1–1–1–1).

Material. FS–P and VS: Belwin Mills. VS: American Music Center.

REVIEWS

Robert Jacobson "Charleston," *Opera News* (October 1981), pp. 34, 36

> "The libretto, based on Oscar Wilde, is a saccharine one about love, generosity and tearing down barriers, going on far too long to sustain real interest."

Kegi "Hollingsworth Trilogy," *Variety* (June 10, 1981), p. 80

> " 'The Selfish Giant' . . . failed to make much sense to either children or adults, although the five children were charming."

Mark Houston

HAZEL KIRKE

Two acts. Libretto by the composer based on a 19th-century melodrama by the American playwright Steele MacKaye. Premiere: Lake George Opera Festival 7.31.87.

Andrew Imbrie (1921–)

ANGLE OF REPOSE

Historical fiction. Three acts, seven scenes, four sets (180 minutes). Atonal without strict serial procedures. Western song styles incorporated to represent earlier period. Vocal writing arioso-style of dramatic recitation, motivic and rhythmic densities in accompaniment require independent soloists. Orchestra plays prominent role.

Libretto by Oakley Hall, based on the novel by Wallace Stegner. Commission and premiere: San Francisco Opera 11.6.76.

PLOT

Setting: California, Colorado, and Idaho, 1976, 1876–1890.

Lyman Ward, an historian and cripple convalescing on the California estate of his grandparents, finds some solace from his troubled life and recently dissolved marriage by charting the story of his grandparent's lives. With the aid of his daughter, Shelly, who is rebounding from her own relationship, we learn of the parallel hardships faced by Lyman's Victorian-turned-pioneering grandparents, Oliver and Susan. Susan Ward, a refined woman, a writer, brought up in the East, faithfully follows her enterprising husband to the savage American West. Oliver Ward, an honest engineer, knows little of his wife's needs, which are described through Susan's heartfelt letters home to a trusted friend. Through the letters we learn how Susan, ignored by Oliver, falls in love with Frank Sargeant, an old admirer. Tragically, she becomes so caught up on her own feelings that she fails to watch her young child, who drowns in a canal. This catastrophe causes the couple to spend the next fifty years in grim silence. With the help of his daughter, Shelly, Lyman realizes that he must not duplicate the mistakes of the past, and finally reconciles his own relationship with his wife.

PRODUCTION REQUIREMENTS

Major Roles. LYMAN WARD (bar): G1 to F♯3. SUSAN WARD, Lyman's grandmother (s): C3 to B4. SHELLY WARD, Lyman's daughter (m-s): A2 to A4. OLIVER WARD, Lyman's grandfather (bar): G♯1 to F♯3.

Supporting Roles. FRANK SARGEANT, Susan Ward's admirer (t): D2 to B♭3. BILLY DALY, Oliver's business partner (bar): C2 to F♯3.

Minor Roles. ADA, Lyman's nurse (m-s). ANTONIO (bar). DAHL (bs-bar). JOACHIM MILLER (bar). HELEN HUNT JACKSON (m-s). ELLEN, Lyman's wife (m-s).

Speaking Roles. AGNES (child).

Bit Roles. KING (bar). CHINESE FISH PEDDLER (buf t). 3 GUESTS (bars).

Chorus. SATB plus offstage men's and women's choruses.

Dance. Nob Hill ballroom scene w/chorus, soloists.

Orchestra. 3 fls, 3 obs, 3 cls, 3 bsns, 4 hrns, 3 trps, 3 trbs, tuba, timp, perc, harp, strings.

Material. FS–P and VS: Shawnee Press.

REVIEWS

Arthur Bloomfield "San Francisco," *Opera* (March 1977), pp. 271–274

"While a sensitive linear contrapuntalist, a composer of 'class,' Berkeley professor Imbrie does not have a strong feeling for theatre. His score falls back much too often on busywork musical gestures."

Robert Commanday "A Glowing World Premiere," *San Francisco Chronicle* (November 8, 1976), p.37

"The eloquence of Hall's words is heightened in Imbrie's melodious music, perfectly capturing their rhythm and feeling. Lyman's opening aria . . . returns in the final scene . . . a grand cello-like theme framing the opera."

"Within the opera, an episodic panorama of the west unfolds, authentic yet personalized and different from any other. We see Oliver and his bride greeted by an earthy shivaree. There is an awesome trip into the mine's depths with stirring incidents and music, a Nob Hill salon with guests dancing . . . a giant Joaquin Miller singer, a paean to the Bay and Gate."

Alfred Frankenstein "Andrew Imbrie's 'Angle of Repose'," *Musical America* (March 1977), pp. 30–31

"There were, to be sure, some effective moments, especially some long-spun aria-like passages wherein there really was a vocal line. But most of it was atonal declamation."

"There was one really magnificent moment in this opera. When Oliver brought his dead child across the stage, the action was accompanied entirely by percussion instruments, and for the duration of that moment we were in the world of modern music."

Martin Kalmanoff (1920–)

THE HARMFULNESS OF TOBACCO

Satirical comedy. One act (30 minutes). Through-composed in a harmonically tonal style which grows more dissonant as the lecture becomes more emotional. Recitative-style with short arias.

Libretto by Eric Bentley, based on the novel by Anton Chekhov. Premiere: Manhattan Opera Singers, Tully Hall, NY 3.22.79.

PLOT

Setting: Russia, turn of the century.

A lecture that is ostensibly about the dangers of tobacco becomes a forum through which the speaker vents his frustrations with his life. As he randomly discusses one thought after another, a complete picture of his unhappy existence unfolds. The main difficulty for this henpecked man is his domineering wife. As he describes his duties, which include running their household and teaching all the classes in her school, his confidence builds, and he fantasizes about running away. But, when his wife enters the wings, his moment of independence is over. He lamely finishes the lecture, trying to pretend that he has merely informed his audience of the harmfulness of tobacco.

PRODUCTION REQUIREMENTS

Major Roles. LECTURER (bar, bs, or t "any male voice with the indicated range. . . . alternate notes . . . and adjustments can be arranged"): F♯1 to G3.

Orchestra. fl, ob, cl, bsn, hrn, trp, trb, timp, perc, strings.

Material. FS–P and VS: Martin Kalmanoff, 392 Central Park West, New York, NY 10025. VS: American Music Center.

REVIEWS

Jack Heimenz "Manhattan Opera Singers: Kalmanoff premiere," *Musical America* (August 1979), p. 27

"The music is a well-knit and amusing pastiche of styles and quotes of composers from Rossini to Rachmaninoff."

"Because of its economy of means this opera could find its way onto many a concert program. It could become . . . a sort of comic equivalent for basses and baritones of *La Voix Humaine.* My only reservation is that it goes on a mite long."

Ulysses Kay (1917–)

JUBILEE

Historical fiction. Three acts, five scenes (180 minutes). Conservative contemporary idiom. Mildly dissonant, employing folk, spiritual and hymn tunes. Continuous texture with some spoken parts. Vocal lines patterned after speech. Extensive choral sections.

Libretto by Donald Dorr, based on the novel *Jubilee* by Margaret Walker. Commissioned by Opera/South for the American Bicentennial. Premiere: Opera/South, Jackson, Miss. 11.20.76. Performances: Opera/South, Jackson 11.19.77. A Tribute to Ulysses Kay, Lehman College, The City University of New York, Bronx N.Y. 6.10.89. (piano only).

PLOT

Setting: American South; before, during and after the Civil War.

Act I, scene 1: Dutton plantation, Christmas eve, 1859; ii: Swampland near Dutton plantation, July 1860, iii: Dawson, Georgia, July 4, 1860. Act II: Dutton plantation, Spring 1865. Act III: Brown homestead, Alabama, Summer 1870.

On Christmas eve, 1859, guests gather at John Dutton's Georgia plantation to celebrate the engagement of his daughter, Lillian, to the young school teacher, Kevin MacDougall. However, John Dutton has prohibited the marriage of his daughter by his slave mistress, Vyry Dutton, to Randall Ware, a free black man to whom she has borne a son. Vyry rejects Randall's pleas to escape north and leave her son, Jim, behind. In July 1860, Vyry agrees to escape with Randall, but she is captured on her way to a clandestine church meeting. The meeting is discovered and bloodily put to a stop, but Randall escapes, thinking that Vyry has not kept her promise to meet him. In a Fourth of July tableau, Mandy is publicly hanged for poisoning her master and Vyry is flogged as a runaway. By the spring of 1865, war has swept across the south. Lillian's suitor, Kevin, is killed in battle, and Lillian and Vyry are the only remaining Duttons. Federal troops overrun the plantation, freeing the slaves in the year of the Jubilee. But one of the slaves, Innis Brown, offers to stay to protect Vyry. Lillian, destitute after being savagely attacked by a looter, grows mentally unstable. Because of her dependent son, and no trace of Randall, Vyry agrees to marry Innis. In the summer of 1870, at their Alabama homestead, the struggle for independence after the war has left hostility between Jim and Innis. A gathering of neighbors celebrating Vyry as their midwife and nurse is interrupted by Randall Ware, demanding his son. In her pleas for understanding, Vyry reveals the scars from her flogging. When Randall realizes her suffering, they are reconciled. Vyry sends her son, Jim, away with his father with the promise of schooling and a better life. Vyry and Innis, now mature in their love, face the future together.

PRODUCTION REQUIREMENTS

Major Roles. LILLIAN DUTTON, John Dutton's daughter and Vyry's half-sister (s): D3 to B♭4. VYRY, John Dutton's daughter by his slave mistress (m-s): A2 to A4. INNIS BROWN, freed slave who marries Vyry (t): E2 to A3. RANDALL WARE, father of Vyry's son, Jim (bar): C2 to F♯3.

Supporting Roles. MANDY, cook on the Dutton plantation (s): C3 to B♭4. JOEY, servant on the Dutton plantation (t): E2 to B♭3. BROTHER ZEKE/UNION OFFICER/BLACK FIDDLER (bs): C2 to E3. KEVIN MACDOUGAL, Lillian's suitor (t): F2 to A♭3. JOHN DUTTON, Lillian and Vyry's father (bs): B♭1 to D3.

Minor Roles. FIRST PLANTER/WHITE PREACHER (bar). JIM, Vyry and Randall's son (boy s): F♯3 to F4.

Bit Roles. LIZA (s), SECOND PLANTER (bs) (drawn from chorus).

Chorus. SATB [divisi SSS, AAA, etc.] Extensive choral parts for slaves, planters, buckra, soldiers, townspeople.

Orchestra. 2 fls, 2 obs, 2 cls, 2 bsns, 4 hrns, 2 trps, 3 trbs, timp, perc, strings.

Material. FS–P and VS: Carl Fischer, Inc.

REVIEWS

Richard Freis "World Premiere A Triumph For Opera," *The Clarion-Ledger* (December 22, 1976)

"The work emphasizes lyric and meditative rather than epic dimensions. . . . This is especially noticeable in Kay's orchestration, which eschews lushness in favor of spareness and precision. The orchestral restraint throws strong emphasis on the vocal line."

"Kay's most notable triumphs are perhaps the choral and ensemble passages. . . . Some of the individual roles and passages are handled in a strikingly successful manner."

Michael Redmond "A stirring concert honors U.S. composer," *The Newark Star-Ledger* (June 12, 1989), p. 32

"the composer's style is conservative in the best sense of the word. The music, while quite challenging, is written for, not against, the voice. One has a sense of natural declamation and of honest emotion. The music rises to clear climaxes, many of them stirring. Dorr's libretto is eloquent."

Nancy Tipton " 'Jubilee' Marks Cultural Union," *Jackson Daily News* (November 22, 1976), p. 5

"And we saw in the world premiere of Ulysses Kay's 'Jubilee,' an inspiring story of a life, indeed the collective lives of a race, rising up Phoenix-like from the ashes of slavery. . . . And, if not great, it is at times exceedingly good."

"Of particular merit are Vyry's 'Golden Door' aria of the gallows scene, Innis Brown's touching 'I Can Make a Bare Field Grow' proposal to Vyry, Lillian's militaristic-flavored 'mad' scene and Vyry's climactic revelation of 'I Reckon I Knows a Thing 'Bout Hell.' "

Jerome Kern (1885–1945)

SHOW BOAT

Drama. Two acts, fifteen scenes (full evening). Musical theater which captures various Southern styles: spiritual, blues, rag. Several variety show song and dance numbers for solos and chorus. Large role for orchestra: overture, dances, interludes, etc.

Libretto and book by Oscar Hammerstein II. Premiere: Ziegfield Theatre, N.Y. 12.27.27. Performances: Music Theatre of Lincoln Center, N.Y. 1.5.46. Houston Grand Opera 83. Recordings: Columbia OL (OC), many others.

PLOT

Setting: Levee at Natchez on the Mississippi river aboard the steamboat, "Cotton Blossom;" Chicago; mid-1880s through 1927.

Magnolia Hawks, daughter of Captain Andy Hawks, who runs the showboat, "Cotton Blossom," is attracted to Gaylord Ravenal, a good-for-nothing riverboat gambler. Fate brings them together when the sheriff reports that the showboat's star, Julie, is a mulatto involved in a forbidden mixed marriage. When Julie and Steve are forced to leave, Magnolia and Ravenal are recruited to take their places. They fall in love on the showboat, marry and move to Chicago. Years later, Captain Andy and Parthy visit Magnolia and Ravenal, who now have a daughter of their own, Kim. But Ravenal reveals their marital problems, due to his gambling debts. Finally deserted, Magnolia's friend, Julie, helps her once again by leaving her job at the Trocadero nightclub so that Magnolia can have the job to support her child. On New Year's Eve, Magnolia has a humbling reunion there with her father, who convinces her to return to the showboat. Ravenal is waiting for her there, and the couple reunite at last. Their daughter, Kim, becomes the new star of the showboat.

PRODUCTION REQUIREMENTS

Major Roles. Magnolia Hawkes, Captain Andy's daughter (s): C♭3 to G4. Gaylord Ravenal, riverboat gambler (t): B1 to B♭3. Julie, mulatto showboat performer (s/m-s): B♭ to F4. Joe, a black stevadore (bs): G1 to F♯3.

Supporting Roles. Queenie, black showboat performer (m-s): G2 to E♭4. Ellie, showboat singer/dancer (s/m-s): B♭2 to F4.

Speaking Roles. Captain Andy Hawkes, runs the showboat, "Cotton Blossom." Parthy Ann Hawkes, Andy's wife.

Minor Roles. Steve Baker, Julie's husband. Frank (dancer). Jake. Pete.

Chorus. Large role: SATB (unison and 2-part).

Dance. Several solo and chorus dance numbers.

Orchestra. fl (picc), ob (Eng hrn opt), 2 cls, bsn, 2 hrns, 2 trps, trb, perc, strings (4–1–1–1), banjo-guitar.

Material. FS–P and VS: Rodgers & Hammerstein.

Leon Kirchner

LILY

Three acts (90 minutes). Libretto by the composer based on Saul Bellow's "Henderson the Rain King." Premiere: New York City Opera 4.10.77.

Material. Associated Music Publishers.

Frederick Koch (1928–)

THE SHEPHERDS

Religious drama. Prologue and one act (60 minutes). A modal effect created through use of fourths and fifths in harmonies and vocal lines. Homophonic ensembles (duets and trios). Sudden half-step shifts of tonal center. Conversational, syllabic setting. Orchestra accompanies and doubles vocal line.

Libretto by Seymour Reiter, based on the fifteenth-century *Second Shepherd's Play* by the anonymous Wakefield Master. Premiere: Koch School of Music, an affiliate of Cleveland Music School Settlement 12.1.85.

PLOT

Setting: on the moors, the first Christmas.

In the prologue, Truth, Mercy, and Justice debate whether mankind should survive, but learn from Peace that God intends to redeem man. Overwhelmed by hunger, poverty, and the oppression of their masters, Coll and Gib protest their difficult lives. They are joined by the youngest shepherd, Daw, who reports that a lamb has been stolen, an offense punishable by death. Believing that Mak is the offender, the three set off to claim their property. In fact, Mak stole the lamb in order to feed his hungry children. He and his wife, Gill, dress the lamb to look like a newborn child and pretend that Gill has just given birth. The shepherds are nearly fooled. However, when Daw returns with a gift for the baby and tries to kiss it, he discovers the trick. The shepherds forgive Mak, understanding that he stole to help his family survive. Out on the moors, the three shepherds stop to rest. An angel comes to tell them that Jesus has been born. They go to the stable bringing gifts, as Mary sings that the Lord lent his son to the world to restore love and peace.

PRODUCTION REQUIREMENTS

Major Roles. COLL, the oldest shepherd (bar): A1 to G3. GIB, the second shepherd (high bar): B1 to E3. DAW, the youngest shepherd (t): B1 to F3. MAK, the sheep stealer (bar): B1 to D3. GILL, his wife (m-s): C3 to E4. ANGEL (s): E3 to G4.

Supporting Roles. MARY (s): $E^{\flat}3$ to G4.

Chorus. SA division (s, s, m-s, a sing roles of TRUTH, MERCY, JUSTICE and PEACE in Prologue and comprise chorus).

Orchestra. fl, perc, harp, string quartet.

Material. FS–P and VS: Carl Fischer.

REVIEWS

Phillipa Kiraly "Miracle plays are similar though 8 centuries apart," *Parma Sun Post* (December 19, 1985), p. C4

> "Koch wrote for the same types of instruments as would have been played — a few strings to accompany the angel, and in other melodic sections; tambourine and drum, harp, flute and bells (or xylophone). . . . He used the same simple, sturdy rhythms and long phrases, and his music fits the words easily and idiomatically. While it was basically modal, using open harmonies, some of the latter were emphatically twentieth century, which gave the work freshness and individuality."

> "It worked. This is a charming mild little mystery play, with attractive music and simple, effective line. The audience loved it."

John La Montaine (1920–)

BE GLAD THEN AMERICA

Choral opera/oratorio. Two acts (80 minutes). Largely tonal, conservative modern writing centering around two hymn tunes by William Billings. Narrative joins independent vignettes. Vocal lines mostly conjunct, easily executed. Hymn-like choral writing with chorus playing largest role.

Libretto by the composer, drawn from documents and historical sources concerning the American Revolution. Premiere: The Institute for the Arts and Humanistic Studies/Pennsylvania State University 2.6.76.

PLOT

Setting: colonial America, 1776.

Written from the colonist's viewpoint, the Town Crier sets the stage for each event representing the birth of the nation: the Stamp Act, the Boston Tea Party, the Battle of Lexington, the signing of the Constitution, etc. We also meet prominent figures of the time: King George III, Patrick Henry, Sam Adams, Thomas Paine, and a host of minor characters. The Muse for America (Freedom) is represented by a folk singer. Yet the chorus takes the largest role, representing "We the People:" providing commentary on the patriotic events (in Greek chorus fashion) or splitting into double choirs to represent the opposing views of the Rebels and Loyalists.

PRODUCTION REQUIREMENTS

Major Roles. Town Crier (t): D2 to B♭3 (much recitative-like declamation).

Supporting Roles. King George III (t): D2 to B♭3. Muse for America (m-s): D3 to A4 (folk singer). Patrick Henry (and other minor roles) (bar): C♭2 to F3.

Minor Roles. Several; can be drawn from chorus.

Chorus. SATB (divisi at times, double chorus at others).

Orchestra. 3 fls, 2 cls, 2 obs, 3 bsns, 6 trps, 3 trbs, tuba, timp, 2 perc, strings.

Material. FS–P and VS: P. J. Sifler, 3947 Fredonia Drive, Hollywood, CA 90028. VS: American Music Center.

REVIEWS

Allen Hughes "Penn State Celebrates Bicentennial in Opera," *New York Times* (Sunday, February 8, 1976), p.45

> " 'Be Glad Then, America' is definitely not an opera in the conventional sense, but it is filled with drama, both implied and overt, and it would be a hardhearted American indeed who did not feel a lump in his throat as the singing of the Declaration of Independence began the climactic conclusion of the work."

> "Mr. La Montaine is a master of choral writing, and the 200-voice Penn State Chorus was the star of the production."

Daniel Webster "Penn State: La Montaine premiere," *Musical America* (June 1976), p. 30

> "Using the massive resources of the University and director Sarah Caldwell's theatrical wizardry, the piece became a grand, grand pageant of the Revolution and an interesting try at becoming an opera without the usual operatic means."

> "The composer developed a work of high literary quality. . . . the music, by comparison, was of less importance and tended to magnify William Billings. . . . In a sense, it was a baroque opera, with historical sweep and the appearance of mythic figures—in this case Sam Adams (etc.)."

Ezra Laderman (1924–   )

AND DAVID WEPT

Biblical drama. Eleven sections (50 minutes). Conservative modern style with orchestration closely related to vocal lines. Eleven closed sections with spoken narration, arias, duets, trios.

Libretto by Joe Darion. Commissioned by CBS News. Premiere: CBS-TV 4.8.71 (unstaged). Jewish Opera at the Y, 92d Street YMHA, N.Y. 5.31.80 (staged).

PLOT

Setting: biblical story of King David.

Through a series of flashbacks mimed by dancers, the tormented David and distanced Bathsheba relate their tragic love story, with Uriah adding his perspective from the grave. Bathsheba describes how she had bathed on the palace roof in order to seduce the King. Although she experienced love with him as she never had with her husband, she feared the death penalty when she became pregnant with his child. David tried to entice Uriah to sleep with his wife to cover the adulterous affair. However, despite Uriah's former love for his King and the favor he would gain by abetting David's plot, he could not force himself to sleep with his wife. In a fit of madness, David ordered that Uriah be killed to save Bathsheba. In retribution, the Prophet Nathan cursed David with numerous punishments that occurred throughout his life, including the death of his favorite son, Absolom. Now in old age, all three believe that David has been punished enough and pray that he may finally find peace.

PRODUCTION REQUIREMENTS

Major Roles. DAVID (t or bar): A1 to G3. BATHSHEBA (m-s): A2 to A4. URIAH (bs-bar): G1 to F3 [D1 opt].

Orchestra. fl, ob, 2 cls in B♭, bsn, 2 hrns in F, trp in C, harp, piano (harpsichord), 2 perc, strings.

Material. FS–P and VS: Oxford University Press.

REVIEWS

Peter Davis "Opera: And David Wept," *New York Times* (June 2, 1980), section 3, p. 13, column 5

> "By distancing the principals from the action in this fashion—the technique strongly recalls the studied ritualism of Stravinsky's 'Oedipus Rex'—Mr. Darion is able to give the tale a timeless quality."

> "If Mr. Darion has not exactly offered any novel insights, he at least presents the inevitable conflicts of passion, outrage and guilt succinctly, theatrically and with a minimum of cliche."

> "The score is tonal, melodic and clearly the work of a craftsman who never makes a false step. While the style is quite eclectic—

Bloch and Vaughan Williams frequently come to mind with more than a hint of the popular side of Kurt Weill."

Herbert Kupferberg "Jewish Opera at the Y: Laderman stage premiere: 'And David Wept'," *Musical America,* 30 (September 1980), pp. 23–24

"Laderman's music . . . follows a smooth and lyrically attractive course without any great feeling of depth or originality. Most of the impact seemed to come from the expert orchestration, with strong but not obtrusive percussion passages that provide a certain rugged quality and kept two young players busy."

Bert Wechsler "New York," *Music Journal* (August 1980), 37:56

"Ezra Laderman has provided music full of instrumental color: harp, harpsichord and two busy percussionists who had traffic problems of their own as they raced to their various noisemakers without colliding. It was also deeply unmemorable. A very short romantic section did work."

GALILEO GALILEI

Historical drama. Three acts and an epilogue (120 minutes). Dialogue between the main characters and chorus tells the story. Through-composed. No overture. Atonal, mostly declamatory, with a few melodic passages.

Libretto by Joseph Darion, based o the life of Galileo Galilei. Commissioned and premiered as the opera-oratorio, *The Trials of Galileo,* CBS Television Network 5.14.67. Stage Premiere as *Galileo Galilei:* Tri-Cities Opera and the State University of New York, Binghamton, NY 2.2.79.

PLOT

Setting: Rome, seventeenth century.

In his old age, Galileo curses his blindness as he remembers events in his life. He tried to share his telescope with other professors at the University, but was accused of trying to show the unshowable. He remembers being mocked in Rome and accused of heresy. When tried, Cardinals Bellarmine and Barberini defended Galileo as a brilliant scientist and follower of the church. The church decreed that he could speculate, but he could not prove. But Bellarmine begged Galileo to be discreet about his discoveries and to better treat his women, whom he used and abandoned. These women appear to him: Marina, his mistress; his two daughters; and even his friend, the Roman noblewoman, to recount their stories.

When Barberini became Pope Urban VIII, he no longer wanted to be bothered about Galileo. New interrogation led to new accusations against the scientist. Because Bellarmine was now dead and the earlier document proclaiming Galileo's innocence ignored, the interrogator and torturers finally convinced Galileo to confess his heresy. He was sentenced to prison, although several of the Cardinals refused to sign the condemnation. Released now, as a blind old man, Galileo convinces his friend that before he dies, she must take his book to Holland to be published so that the world may know the truth.

PRODUCTION REQUIREMENTS

Major Roles. GALILEO (bs-bar): F♯1 to E♭3. THE FRIEND (m-s): B♭2 to A4. CARDINAL BELLARMINE (bar): C2 to G♯3. CARDINAL BARBERINI (t): C2 to G3. THE INTERROGATOR (high t): E♭2 to A♯3.

Supporting Roles. THREE PROFESSORS (t): singing in unison or choral trio. POPE PAUL (t). TWO JESUITS (t, bar). TWO DOMINICANS (t, bar). TORTURERS (b). MARINA (m-s). Galileo's daughters: LIVIA (lyr s) and VIRGINIA (m-s). FIRST AND FOURTH CARDINALS (t).

Chorus. SATB

Orchestra. 2 fl, 2 ob, 2 cl in B♭, 2 bsn, 2 hrn in F, 2 trp in B♭, 2 trb, tuba, harp, organ, 3 perc, timp, strings.

Material. FS–P and VS: Oxford University Press. VS: American Music Center.

REVIEWS

Leighton Kerner "Tri-Cities Op: 'Galileo Galilei'," *Musical America* (June 1979), p. 24

> "Theatrically apt, lyrically expansive music." Laderman "uses his relatively unambitious musical language to tighten the not very distinguished rhetoric of his librettist, to give it sinew and accent, and to propel the action as it takes place in Galileo's mind."

> "In a scene where the women in Galileo's life . . . variously accuse him of heartlessness and forgive him, (he) achieves the re-

vised opera's most sustained flights of melodic and harmonic beauty."

Andrew Porter "Tableaux," *New Yorker* (March 19, 1979), pp. 132–133

"There is no theatrical action. There is little conflict except in dialogues between Galileo and his Friend, a mezzo-soprano role and less a character than a sharer of what would otherwise be soliloquies. Nevertheless, *Galileo Galilei* worked well in the theatre and held the attention securely. The score is arresting and the staging was brilliant."

"Laderman's forte is writing catchy jingles . . . jingles apart, the music is hard to describe. It is decent, satisfying, intelligently and strongly made . . . But I hear no note of passion in it. . . . At the last, in Galileo's final solo, some emotion does shine out."

Harold Schonberg " 'Galileo Galilei' has Upstate Premiere," *New York Times* (February 5, 1979), section 3, p.13, column 5

"Most of the tension, drama, and emotion in *Galileo Galilei* came from the libretto instead of the music, much of which ended up almost as a background function. Yet Mr. Laderman's secure technique cannot be easily dismissed, and his score will occupy an honorable place in the annals of American opera."

Burton Lane (1912–)

FINIAN'S RAINBOW

Musical. Two acts, ten scenes. Musical numbers inserted into straight play with three main characters and chorus carrying nearly all of the singing. Highlights are: "How are things in Glocca Morra," "Look to the Rainbow," and "Old Devil Moon."

Libretto by E. Y. Harburg, based on a book by Harburg and Fred Saidy. Premiere: New York 1.10.47.

PLOT

Setting: Rainbow Valley, Missitucky—an imaginary rural setting near Fort Knox, 1940s.

Finian McLonergan has just arrived in America from Ireland, bringing his lovely daughter, Sharon, and a pot of gold that he stole from the leprechauns. He chooses to settle near Fort Knox, believing that the soil near there is suitable for "growing" gold. In reality, Rainbow Valley is somewhat impoverished. Woody Mahoney and the local sharecroppers are banking on the Negro inventor, Howard's experiments with tobacco crops to save their lands. But their plans are thwarted by the bigoted Senator Billboard Rawkins, who wants to usurp their lands, especially now that he has learned that the soil contains gold (just the pot of gold "planted" by Finian himself).

Og, a leprechaun, has followd Finian to Rainbow Valley to retrieve the stolen gold. He reveals that, with the pot, come three wishes. The first wish transforms the bigot Senator into a black evangelist; for the second, Og wishes that his love, Woody's deaf-mute sister, Susan, regain her speech and hearing. The third wish is for Sharon and Woody's happiness.

In the end, Howard's experiments succeed, enabling the sharecroppers to keep their lands. With the gold's magical powers exhausted, Finian decides to leave the valley. But the lovers are united: Sharon stays with Woody; and Og, whose taste for love transforms him into a human being, finds happiness with Susan.

PRODUCTION REQUIREMENTS

Major Roles. Sharon McLonergan (m-s): $A^{b}2$ to D4 [in solos], to A4 (ensembles only). Woody Mahoney (bar): $B^{b}1$ to F3. Og, a leprechaun (bar/t): $B^{b}1$ to $F^{\#}3$.

Minor Roles. A Preacher (t). Senator Billboard Rawkins (t).

Speaking Roles. Finian McLonergan (bar). Howard, a Negro inventor. Many other minor speaking roles.

Mute Roles. Susan Mahoney (dancer).

Chorus. Simple unison, 2- and 3-part singing; occasional SATB.

Ballet. 16 dancers in original cast.

Orchestra. fl (picc, cl), ob (Eng hrn), cl, cl (fl, picc), bs cl (cl, bsn), 2 hrns, 2 trps, 2 trbs, harp, perc, piano, guitar, strings.

Material. FS–P and VS: Frank Music Corp.

Libby Larsen

CLAIR DE LUNE

Two Acts. Libretto by Patricia Hampl. Premiere: Arkansas Opera Theatre, Little Rock 2.22.85.

Material. Contact composer through American Music Center.

Leonard Lehrman (1949–)

IDIOTS FIRST
[See BLITZSTEIN]

KARLA

Light drama. One act, three scenes (45 minutes). Conversational style in ensembles, chromatic vocal lines. Brief orchestral intros: scenes 1 and 2.

Libretto by Leonard Lehrman, based on "Notes from a Lady at a Dinner Party" by Bernard Malamud. Intended to be presented with Lehrman's completion of Blitzstein's opera: *Idiots First.* Premiere: Marc Blitzstein Opera Co., Bloomington, Indiana 3.14.76. Performances: Cornell Univ. (concert preview) 8.74; Bel Canto Opera, N.Y.C. 1.22.78.

PLOT

Setting: Hempstead, "recently."

Clem and Karla Harris have invited several guests to dinner: Ralph and Ada Lewin; Clem's former student, Max, and Clem's secretary, Shirley. When Max meets Karla, he expresses surprise that Clem married such a young woman. Karla immediately begins to flirt with him, secretly placing a note in his pocket at dinner. As the evening progresses, Shirley observes the continuing flirtation, growing more and more jealous of Karla. Karla and Max eventually meet and embrace in the nursery, agreeing to meet later that night. Before the dinner party ends, Karla gives Max another note, which falls to the floor. Shirley dramatically hands it to Karla's husband, Clem, who returns it to Max, unopened. The awkward moment breaks up the evening. Afterward, Max reads the note: Karla has broken off their meeting.

PRODUCTION REQUIREMENTS

Major Roles. CLEM HARRIS (bs-bar): E♯1 to F♯3. RALPH LEWIN (t): D♯2 to B3. ADA LEWIN (m-s): B2 to G4. KARLA HARRIS (lyr s): B2 to D5. SHIRLEY FISHER (high c/ "gutsy" m-s): G2 to F♯4. MAX ADLER (lyr bar): F♯1 to A♭3.

Non-singing Roles. STEPHANIE.

Orchestra. 2 fls (picc), 2 obs (Eng hrn), 2 cls (bs cl), 2 bsns, 2 hrns, 2 trps, 2 trbs, tuba, 3 timp, chimes, perc, harp (opt), piano/celeste, vibraphone, strings (2–2–2–2–2 at least). May also be performed with 2 pianos plus chimes and castanets.

Material. FS–P and VS: Theodore Presser. VS: American Music Center.

REVIEWS

Stephen Casale "New York," *Opera News* (March 18, 1978), p. 49

> "Musically the idiom is close to that of Blitzstein, with perhaps less of Middle European 'Angst' and more American-style forthrightness. The role of Karla, with its high tessitura in crucial moments, carries echoes of Berg's *Lulu.*"

Leighton Kerner " 'Idiots First' at Last," *Village Voice* (January 30, 1978), p. 55

> "The banter and double entendres that carry its story . . . needs a lighter, more graceful touch and less 'operatic' phrases. But there are moments when it seems that such a touch is not beyond the composer's means and that some careful rewriting might be useful."

Willian Allin Storrer "Bloomington," *Opera News* (June 1976), pp. 43–44

> "Lehrman's own musical proclivities were evident — angular vocal lines and an excellent grasp of rhythm suitable to setting spoken language."

Willian Allin Storrer "Bloomington," *Opera* (July 1976) 27(7):650–651

"The evening was, ultimately, Lehrman's, first for having successfully followed Blitzstein's lead, then for having written a highly entertaining opera of his own."

Mitch Leigh (1928–)

MAN OF LA MANCHA

Musical. Two acts and epilogue. Emotional, lyrical music with a Spanish flavor. Many set numbers connected by spoken drama. Orchestra plays important role, not only in intros, etc., but also programmatically describes Quixote's adventures.

Lyrics by Joe Darion. Musical play by Dale Wasserman, based on the life and works of Miguel de Cervantes (Don Quixote). Premiere: New York 11.22.65.

PLOT

Setting: A prison in Seville and other places imagined by Cervantes, sixteenth-century Spain.

Miguel de Cervantes entertains other prisoners with tales of his imaginary hero, Don Quixote (the "Man of La Mancha"), while he awaits execution at the hands of the Spanish Inquisition. Quixote, the aging idealist and romantic, fancies himself to be a glorious knight, setting out with his trusty squire, Sancho (a neighborhood friend) to right the troubled world. He fearlessly combats windmill giants; finds his beloved "Dulcinea" in the common whore, Aldonza, and takes on countless magical evildoers.

Cervante's story gradually moves beyond simple entertainment to arouse deep feelings of hope for justice in the other condemned prisoners. As Cervantes himself is called to his death, the jail resounds with the message of Don Quixote — to fearlessly pursue the "impossible dream."

PRODUCTION REQUIREMENTS

Major Roles. Don Quixote/Cervantes (bar): B1 to E3. Aldonza/Dulcinea (m-s): A♭2 to A♭4 (A4 in final chorus). Sancho (high bar/t): C2 to A3 [B3 opt].

Supporting Roles. The Padre (bar): C2 to G3. Antonia (s): C3 to F4.

HOUSEKEEPER (m-s): F2 to F4. INNKEEPER (bs): G1 to C3 [E3 in chorus]. BARBER (t): D2 to G3. PEDRO (bar): D2 to D3. ANSELMO (bar): F♯2 to F♯3.

Minor Roles. DR. CARRASCO (bar).

Non-singing Roles. MARIA, Innkeeper's wife; FERMINA, a slavey and Moorish dancer; CAPTAIN of the INQUISITION; GUITARIST.

Chorus. Guards and Men of the Inquisition. Women's choral parts sung by cast members.

Ballet. Moorish dance.

Orchestra. fls (picc), ob, cl, bsn (cl), 2 hrns, 2 B♭ trps, 2 trbs (t and bs), 3 perc, 2 spanish guitars, cb.

Material. FS–P and VS: Cherry Lane Music Co., Inc.

Dan Locklair (1947–)

GOOD TIDINGS FROM THE HOLY BEAST

Mystery play. One act (50 minutes). Open harmonies, dance sections, and rhythmic patterns reflect medieval models; while modern chromatic harmonies mark climaxes. Vocal lines range from chant to angularly chromatic. Choral portions less demanding. Set pieces include arias, duets, ensembles, interludes. Composer states that a church is preferable for the performance, though not necessary.

Libretto by the composer, based on the "Wrightes Play" from the Chester Miracle Cycle, as edited and translated by Suzanne Locklair. Premiere: First Plymouth Congregational, Lincoln, Nebraska 12.21.78. Performances: First Presbyterian Church, Binghamton, N.Y. 81.

PLOT

Setting: Bethlehem, the first Christmas.

The events leading to the birth of Jesus Christ are told in the style of a medieval liturgical drama or an English mystery play—replete with choral interjections, liturgical dancing, and a concluding carol in which the congregation/audience is called upon to participate.

PRODUCTION REQUIREMENTS

Major Roles. MARIA (s): C3 to C♯5 (high tessitura with D5 in descant of final carol). JOSEPH (bar): A♭1 to F3 (role requires wide leaps and sprechstimme).

Supporting Roles. GABRYELL (t): B1 to A3. ELIZABETH (a): F♯2 to E4 (low tessitura).

Minor Roles. Two midwives: TEBELL (a), SALOME (s).

Chorus. SATB.

Ballet. Liturgical dancers (8 in premiere production).

Orchestra. s rec (t rec), fl, cl, bsn, hrn, trp in C, 2 perc, piano, organ (opt), strings.

Material. FS–P and VS: Seesaw Music Corporation. VS: American Music Center.

REVIEWS

Delores V. Koch "Binghamton: First Presbyterian Church: Locklair 'Good Tidings from the Holy Beast,' " *Muscial America* (April 1982), p. 20

"Dan Locklair's 'Good Tidings from the Holy Beast,' a one-act opera on the Nativity story, is fresh and new, medieval and stylistic, colorful and gracious."

"Orchestral support was effective and meticulous in an imaginative score molding several harmonic idioms into an impressive cohesion."

Larry Lusk Church Opera Review," *Diapason* (April 1979), 70(s):5

"Locklair's new work would certainly fit comfortably under the oratorio label."

"What makes this work so appealing is the effective blending of musical and dramatic styles from the medieval and contemporary idioms. . . . The opera opens, for example, with a delightful *Estampie* for orchestra and dancers. The orchestral writing employs the lyric simplicity and open sonorities associated with the form. . . . By the end of the dance, however, the music becomes extremely chromatic and utilizes the free dissonance in a decidedly contemporary way."

Frank Loesser (1910–1969)

GUYS AND DOLLS

Romantic comedy. Two acts, seventeen scenes (full evening). Musical theater with many dance numbers and orchestral interludes. Vocal writing ranges from lyrical to nightclub-comic presentation.

Lyrics by the composer. Book by Jo Swerling and Abe Burrows, based on the characters in Damon Runyon's short story "The Idyll of Miss Sarah Brown." Premiere: 46th Street Theatre, N.Y. 11.24.50. Recording: Decca 9023; 79023.

PLOT

Setting: New York City and Havana, Cuba, 1950.

Nathan Detroit, in charge of the infamous floating crap game, has been engaged to Adelaide, a nightclub singer, for fourteen years. Sky Masterson, a gambler and womanizer, bets his cronies that he can coax the pure Sarah Brown, a mission worker for the Salvation Army, into taking a trip with him to Havana. Sarah agrees to go when Sky promises to help her raise money for the floundering mission her father runs. In Cuba, Sky gets Sarah drunk, but he can't take advantage of her, as he intended; instead, the two fall in love. Back in New York Sarah discovers that she was a victim of Sky's bet. But Sky redeems himself by calling all his friends to the mission just as the authorities appear for inspection. Finding the mission filled to the brim, the Salvation Army allows it to remain open. Sarah and Sky are reunited, and even Nathan and Adelaide finally decide to get married.

PRODUCTION REQUIREMENTS

Major Roles. SARAH BROWN (s): $B^{\flat}2$ to $G^{\#}4$. SKY MASTERSON (bar): $B^{\flat}1$ to $E^{\flat}3$. MISS ADELAIDE (a): $A^{\flat}2$ to $E^{\flat}4$.

Supporting Roles. NATHAN DETROIT (bar): D2 to F3. NICELY-NICELY JOHNSON (t): $D^{b}2$ to $B^{b}3$. ARVIDE ABERNATHY (bar): D2 to F3. BENNY SOUTHSTREET (high bar): D2 to G3.

Minor Roles. RUSTY CHARLEY (bar).

Bit Roles. Several gamblers, the Salvation Army band, nightclub girls, drunk and waiter.

Chorus. SATB with divisi especially for male voices.

Ballet. Many dance numbers, Adelaide and chorus girls, melodrama scene in Havana.

Orchestra. Reed I: fl, alt sax, cl; II: alt sax, cl; III: t sax, cl, ob, Eng hrn; IV: bar sax, bs cl; trp I & II; tr III; trb; fr hrn; vln A–C; vln B–D; vcl; bs; perc.

Material. FS–P and VS: Music Theatre International.

THE MOST HAPPY FELLA

Musical with operatic characteristics. Three acts, eleven scenes. Set numbers: arias, duets, ensembles. Popular and jazz oriented harmonies. Many international interludes.

Lyrics and libretto by the composer, based on Sidney Howard's "They Knew What They Wanted." Premiere: New York 5.3.56. Performances: New York 79.

PLOT

Setting: a vineyard in Napa Valley and a restaurant in San Francisco, 1950s.

Tony, an aging Italian vintner, becomes infatuated with a young waitress who waited on him during a visit to San Francisco. Tony decides to propose to Rosabella in a letter. Insecure about his age, Tony encloses a photo of Joe, the handsome foreman of his ranch. Rosabella immediately agrees to leave her waitressing job at a San Francisco restaurant in order to marry the man she believes is Tony. Upon her arrival, she runs into the arms of Joe, who explains that he is not Tony. When Tony is brought in on a stretcher, after a car accident on the way to meet Rosabella at the station, Tony wins her sympathy. Even though she feels she has been deceived, Rosabella agrees to marry Tony.

In her confusion, Rosabella turns to Joe's younger arms for one night. But, as she nurses Tony back to health, Rosabella grows to love him. Tony even imports her waitress friend, Cleo, to keep her happy. Just as Tony fully recuperates, Rosabella discovers that she is pregnant with Joe's child. She immediately tells Tony, assuring him of her love. But, Tony's old-maid sister, Marie, has already made him paranoid about his being too old for Rosabella. Rosabella boards the bus for San Francisco, but Tony finds her in time for a reconciliation. Even Cleo's romance with Herman, the ranch hand, reaches a happy conclusion.

PRODUCTION REQUIREMENTS

Major Roles. TONY, aging Italian vintner (bar): B1 to G3. ROSABELLA (s): C3 to G4. JOE, foreman of Tony's vineyard (bar): B♭1 to F3.

Supporting Roles. CLEO, Rosabella's waitress friend (m-s): G♭2 to A4. MARIE, Tony's old-maid sister (s): C3 to F♯4. HERMAN, a ranch band (t): E2 to A3.

Minor Roles. POSTMAN (bar). DOCTOR (t). Ranch hands (ensemble singing): JAKE (high bar). CLEM (bar). AL (bs-bar). Joe's Italian servants: PASQUALE (bar). GIUSEPPE (t). CICCIO (bar). Other small roles sung by chorus members.

Chorus. Townspeople and vineyard workers: SATB, unison or 2 parts.

Ballet. Tarantella, 1920s dances, hoedown.

Orchestra. Reeds: #1: fl, picc, alto fl; #2: ob, Eng hrn; #3: cl, s sax, fl; #4 cl, bs cl; #5 bsn; 2 B♭ trps, t trb, bs trb, 3 hrns, accord, harp, strings (2–2–1–2–2).

Material. FS–P: Music Theatre International. VS: Hal Leonard or widely available.

Frederick Loewe (1901–   )

BRIGADOON

Romantic fantasy. Two acts, two scenes (full evening). Musical theater with Scottish/folk music atmosphere. Extensive use of four-part chorus.

Libretto by Alan Jay Lerner. Premiere: New York 3.13.47. Performances: New York City Opera 86. Recording: RCA OC (1947); Chilton (1973).

PLOT

Setting: May of this year.

Two American tourists, Tommy Albright and Jeff Douglas, happen upon a misty Scottish town. When Tommy falls in love with a local girl. Fiona MacLaren, he and Jeff learn that the unusual town only awakens one day every hundred years. Though they stay to enjoy the day, witness a wedding and a funeral, Tommy decides he must return home to New York. But his love for Fiona makes him return to find Brigadoon. Miraculously, he does just that.

PRODUCTION REQUIREMENTS

Major Roles. TOMMY ALBRIGHT (legit bar): B♭1 to F♯3. FIONA MACLAREN (legit s): B2 to A4. JEFF DOUGLAS (actor, chorus). MEG BROCKIE (a): G2 to F4 (patter songs). JEAN MACLAREN (dancer, actress). CHARLIE DALRYMPLE (legit t): D2 to G3.

Supporting Roles. MACGREGOR (bar-t): E♭2 to G3. STUART DALRYMPLE (t): D2 to G3. SANDY DEAN (bs-bar): C2 to D3 [C1 opt].

Minor Roles. Townsfolk of Brigadoon: many minor solo roles.

Chorus. SATB chorus plays large role.

Ballet. Dance sections include bagpipers, sword dancers, folk and country dances.

Orchestra. fl (picc), ob, 2 cls, bsn, hrn, 3 trps, trb, perc, piano (cel), strings (2–1–1–1–1). (Available in Bandstration as well.)

Material. FS–P and VS: Tams-Witmark Music Library, Inc.

CAMELOT

Legend. Two acts, twenty scenes (full evening). Orchestra plays important role: musical interludes, programmatic music with mimed or danced action. Singing ranges from parlando, recitative-like, to lyrical.

Book and lyrics by Alan Jay Lerner, based on T. H. White's *The Once and Future King.* Premiere: Majestic Theatre, N.Y. 12.3.60. Performances: N.Y. 80; N.Y. 81. Recordings: RCA OC, Random House (1961). Film: 1967.

PLOT

Setting: Arthurian times, England.

Soon after King Arthur marries the beautiful Guenevere, he creates his immortal Round Table in the hope of keeping peace throughout his realm and happiness in his court at Camelot. Lancelot, a young French knight, jousts for a position at the Round Table, and in emerging victorious, he gains the love of the King's bride. The ensuing affair is no secret, and Arthur's illegitimate son, Mordred, uses the embarrassing situation in his scheme to usurp the throne of England. Lancelot is cast into a dungeon, while Guenevere is sentenced to burn at the stake. Arthur is not able to intercede on his wife's behalf for fear of breaking his own laws, but Lancelot escapes and rescues Guenevere, though his men kill many knights and the dream of the Round Table in the process. At war with France, Arthur meets Lancelot and Guenevere on the battlefield, and can only forgive them. Wary of the battle's outcome, Arthur be-knights a young stowaway, sending him back to England to keep the dream of the Round Table alive.

PRODUCTION REQUIREMENTS

Major Roles. King Arthur (bar): A1 to E♭3. Guenevere, Arthur's queen (s): B♭2 to G4. Sir Lancelot, Knight of the Round Table (bar): A1 to D3.

Supporting Roles. Mordred, King Arthur's illegitimate son (bar) (speaks rhythmically to music).

Speaking Roles. Merlyn, magician and soothsayer, councillor to the King. Morgan Le Fey, Guinevere's sister (speaks rhythmically to music).

Minor Roles. Nimue (s) (offstage voice). Several minor speaking roles involve no musical solos.

Chorus. SATB (20 in original production).

Dance. 21 in original production.

Orchestra. fl (picc), ob (Eng hrn), B♭ cl (bs cl), B♭ cl (E♭ cl, bs cl, fl), bsn,

3 hrns, 3 trps, 2 trbs, 2 perc, guitar (lute, mand), harp, strings (10–2–2–2).

Material. FS–P and VS: Chappell Music Co.

MY FAIR LADY

Musical theater. Two acts, eighteen scenes (full evening). Vocal styles from lyrical to vaudeville to recitative presentation for Higgins. Overture, entr'acte, several dance numbers.

Libretto and book by Alan Jan Lerner, based on George Bernard Shaw's play "Pygmalion." Premiere: Mark Hellinger Theatre, N.Y. 3.15.56. Performances: Broadway revivals 76 and 81. Recordings: Columbia OC (1976); London SC (1987).

PLOT

Setting: London, 1912.

Linguistics professor, Henry Higgins, makes a bet with his friend, Colonel Pickering, that he can pass a scruffy cockney flower seller off as a sales girl in a high-class florist shop merely by teaching her how to speak the English language properly. After much suffering on Eliza's part, Higgins' experiment proves to be a success — Eliza passes as nobility at a royal ball. She even captures the heart of a young dandy, Freddy Eynsford-Hill, but Eliza falls in love with her teacher. The stubborn bachelor attempts to end the relationship in the businesslike fashion it began, but he finally admits that he has grown "accustomed to her face." Eliza's scraggly father, and his own approaching wedding day, provide comic relief and lots of dancing crowds.

PRODUCTION REQUIREMENTS

Major Roles. Eliza Doolittle (s): A2 to G4. Henry Higgins (bar): A1 to F3.

Supporting Roles. Colonel Pickering, Higgins' friend (bar): C2 to F3. Freddy Eynsford-Hill, a young dandy (bar-t): C2 to F3. Alfred P. Doolittle, Eliza's father (bs-bar): G1 to E3.

Speaking Roles. Several speaking roles such as Mrs. Higgins, Henry's mother and Mrs. Pearce, Henry's maid.

Minor Roles. Two cockneys: HARRY (bs), JAMIE (t). Other small solos can be drawn from chorus.

Chorus. SSAATTBB: street people, cockneys, servants, society guests.

Dance. Street dancing for cockneys, ballroom dancing for society guests.

Orchestra. fl (picc), ob (Eng hrn), 2 B^b cls, bsn, 2 hrns, 3 trps, 2 trbs, tuba, perc, harp, vlns A & B, vlas, vcls, bs.

Material. FS–P and VS: Chappell & Co., Inc.

David Huston Macbride

POND IN A BOWL

One act (40 minutes). Libretto based on Chinese poems by various authors. Premiere: New York 3.24.83.

Material. American Composer's Alliance; American Music Center.

Tod Machover (1953–   )

VALIS

Modernist psychological drama. Two parts, twenty-two sections (77 minutes). Broad stylistic palette: 'New Age' open harmonies; intense lyricism and chromaticism founded on late Romanticism; computer-generated and transformed sounds, both live and prerecorded; popular style drawn from hard and soft rock; minimalist elements. Varied vocal styles: freely or rhythmically spoken, smoothly melodious, chant, angular and chromatically complex.

Libretto by the composer, Catherine Ikam, and Bill Raymond, based on the novel by Philip K. Dick. Commissioned for the tenth anniversary of the Pompidou Center in Paris by IRCAM, Pierre Boulez's Center for Experimental Music. Premiere: Pompidou Center, Paris 12.1.88 (French language version). Premiere: MIT Experimental Media Facility, Boston,

Mass. 2.88 (concert performance of revised English language version). Recording: Bridge Records: BCD 9007 (DDD) 1988 (88) (revised version).

PLOT

Setting: the present.

The opening explosion of sound and light is explained by the Narrator, Philip K. Dick, to be a mystical vision or a nervous breakdown experienced by the protagonist, Horselover Fat. The narrative focuses on the mental wanderings of Fat, as he attempts to reconcile his friend, Gloria's suicide. (Fat is actually the split side of Phil's personality, as is learned later in the opera). Horselover Fat is haunted by mystical visions, something neither he nor his analyst, Dr. Stone, can explain, but which Fat believes are encounters with the divinely supernatural. Fat keeps a journal called his "Exegesis," in which he tries to explain the mysteries of the universe. In his search for the eternal truths, Fat fancies himself a modern-day Parsifal. Dr. Stone's advice is hardly helpful, but Fat finds some answers when he chances to see a rock video of a song called "VALIS" (an acronym meaning "Vast Active Living Intelligent System") sung by the Lamptons. Linda and Eric Lampton are joined by the song's crippled computer-music composer (Mini), as they quiz Fat about the film's secret message, finally assuring him that his pain will soon be over. Mini weaves magic with his sounds, until they form a pure female voice. Thus, the otherworldly Sophia is created. She alone can see that Phil/Fat's own multiple personalities have finally come together. Tension rebuilds as the Lamptons, Mini, Sophia and the united Phil/Fat debate the existence of VALIS. Just as Phil/Fat triumphs in his acceptance of VALIS as real, Sophia vanishes in an explosion of light, as in the beginning of the opera. Phil and Fat are once again torn asunder — Fat goes back to his dazed wandering, and Phil sits down to his TV set. Yet, Phil now has a peaceful feeling inside. In a dream, he hears a beautiful song (Gloria's music from Part I); perhaps it is Sophia saying goodbye. Phil is rejuvenated by his belief in the "goodness of men," and is willing to wait.

PRODUCTION REQUIREMENTS

Major Roles. HORSELOVER FAT/PHILIP K. DICK, Narrator (Narrator's part largely spoken, prerecorded) (bar): A1 to F3 (B^{b}3 falsetto).

Supporting Roles. GLORIA (m-s): C3 to B^{b}4. DR. STONE (bs): D^{b}1 to E^{b}3 (low tessitura). LINDA LAMPTON (s): $G^{\#}$2 to C5. ERIC LAMPTON (bar): B^{b}1 to B^{b}3. SOPHIA (s): C3 to B4.

Minor Roles. VOICE OF "GESEGNET SONG" (t): D2 to A3.

Speaking Roles. READER OF THE "EXEGESIS."

Mute Roles. MINI (conductor of the opera).

Orchestra. piano, perc, prerecorded tape, and live computer manipulation.

Material. FS–P: Ricordi, c/o Boosey and Hawkes.

REVIEWS

Charles Pitt "France Technological truth?" *Opera* (February 1988), pp. 212–213

"For this listener . . . the story was pungently nauseating and naive, the images little more than strip-cartoons, and all the music created by so much technology pretentious and shallow."

Andrew Porter "Magic Mirrors," *The New Yorker* (July 31, 1989), pp. 67–69 (Record review)

" 'Valis' is one of the brightest and most intelligent of new American operas. There is no monotony or meagreness of sound. The score is cast in numbers that build into two well-shaped, carefully paced acts. There are cross-references; there is variety of tempo, texture, tone, and intensity."

Jonathan Richmond "*Valis* points to exciting possibilities for growth of opera," *The Tech* (June 27, 1989), p. 9 (Record review)

"new ways are used to cast fresh light on ancient human themes, and a deliciously black humor adds substance and entertainment to what might otherwise be statements of the obvious."

"The closing passages of Part II contain some of the opera's strongest music (there's a passacaglia of monumental proportions), and also some of the most psychologically revealing moments."

Patrick J. Smith "Inner Landscape," *Opera News* (July 1989), pp. 20–22 (Record review)

"if the subject matter (on whatever level) seems to come directly from a California sensibility (and that's where Dick lived) under the influence of drugs, the opera does transcend the immediate and achieve a kind of universality—even if Sophia's message is a banal 'Love one another.' "

Andrew Stiller " 'VALIS' UNVEILED,' " *Musical America* (March 1989), pp. 75–76 (Record review)

"Machover amputated nearly a third of *VALIS* . . . following the opera's December 1987 Paris premiere, and he reworked both the score and libretto. . . . whatever the initial travails, *VALIS* in its final form has become a work of bold imagination, individual personality, and undeniable emotional impact."

"Sophia's dream-farewell to Phil/Fat packs a considerable wallop in its very simplicity and unexpectedness. It is the strongest possible testimony to Machover's musico-dramatic abilities that he is able to bring this sequence off, tiptoeing as he does right to the edge of treacly sentimentality."

"Machover, an IRCAM veteran, has a well-earned reputation as the wunderkind of the computer-music world, and his extraordinarily sophisticated software is capable of true ensemble performance, turning individual singers into choruses and single instruments into multitimbred ensembles."

William Mayer (1925–)

A DEATH IN THE FAMILY

Dramatic tragedy. Three acts, thirteen scenes, three sets (150 minutes). Conservative, contemporary style with references to folk/spiritual melodies. No overture, conversational with arias, ensembles.

Libretto by the composer, based on the novel by James Agee. Premiere: Minnesota Opera 3.11.83. Performances: Opera Theatre of St. Louis 6.4.86 (revised).

PLOT

Setting: Knoxville, Tennessee; 1915.

Frequent flashbacks depict contrasts between the reality of the present and dreams of the future, through scenes of simple American life. Mary and Jay's marriage is troubled by problems stemming from their differing backgrounds and religious beliefs, and Jay's drinking problem. Mary's pregnancy adds to the tension, since she and Jay disagree on how to share news of the baby with their son, Rufas. However, the coming baby soon strengthens their relationship. By the time that Jay is summoned to his father's sickbed, they have reconciled some of their differences, and Mary agrees to tell Rufas about the baby. However, Jay never returns after visiting his father. After Mary hears about the fatal accident, she alternately prays and lashes out at God, but is comforted when Jay's ghost appears for a final farewell. Jay's death forces Mary to finish reconciling the problems of their marriage on her own: initially, rumors that Jay was drunk when he died send her into hysterics, but she soon hopes he had, at least, enjoyed his last moments. Mary finally tells Rufas about the baby, rather than heeding Father Andrew's advice to call it a surprise from heaven. When she decides to show Rufas where the baby is within her, she acknowledges Jay's final wish and her love for him. Jay's sudden death also forces Rufas to mature. No longer able to depend on his father to calm him from nightmares or to share his excitement over treasured belongings, Rufas looks ahead to his adulthood.

PRODUCTION REQUIREMENTS

Major Roles. JAY (bar): F♯1 to G3 (A3 falsetto). MARY (s or m-s [ossias]): (A♯2 to B2 opt.) C3 to B♭4 (C5 opt.). RUFAS, as a boy (boy s): B2 to F4.

Supporting Roles. SALLY, Ralph's wife (high m-s): B♭2 to F♯4, RALPH, Jay's brother (bar): A1 to F♯3, RUFAS, as a man (t): B1 (opt) D2 to A♭3. FATHER JACKSON (bar): A♭1 to G♭3 (falsetto). AUNT HANNAH (m-s): F♯2 to A♭3. ANDREW, Mary's brother (t): C♯2 to A3.

Important Smaller Roles. CATHERINE, Mary's mother (s). JESSE, Jay's mother (m-s). VICTORIA, Rufas' black nanny (low m-s). JOHN HENRY, Jay's father (low bar). JOEL, Mary's father (bs).

Minor Roles. Main cast can double many of these roles: GREAT GRAMMAW (actress). AUNT SADIE (c). BARTENDER (bar). SENTIMENTAL DRUNK (t). TEMPERANCE LADIES (s, a). VOICE OF DARKNESS (t or m-s). WCTU LEADER (m-s). TEENAGERS (3 boys, 2 girls). BANJO PLAYER (t). STRANGER (bs). COUNTRY GIRL (m-s).

Chorus. SATB, may be comprised of cast.

Orchestra. 2 fls (picc), 1 ob (Eng hrn), 2 cls (bs cl), 1 bsn, 2 hrns, 1 trp, 2 trbs, harp, piano, 2 perc (timp), strings.

Material. FS–P and VS: Music Associates of America. VS: American Music Center.

REVIEWS

Harold Blumenfeld "Opera Theatre of St. Louis Starts its Second Decade," *The Opera Journal* (1986), 19(3):27–29

> "elegant, eloquent language is made to leap off the peopled stage as it leaps off Agee's printed page. But much of the opera is laced with words and tunes of the hill country, lending the work its pervasively homespun and sometimes earthy quality."

> "Mr. Mayer has shaped his material into a virtual dream-opera realized by cinematic ebb and flow of flashbacks, fades, split-screen images, and freeze-frame ensembles, making possible a fluid movement from place to place and from reality to illusion and back."

Robert Jacobson "Minneapolis," *Opera News* (April 9, 1983), p. 38

> "it held hypnotic sway . . . because within its emotional-psychological fabric are people and situations with which an American public can identify."

> "Mayer's tonal, melodic style, in the Barber-Copland mold, brings together gentle expression with power and angularity for a full palette of expression . . . "

Gilbert Johns "St. Louis," *Opera News* (October 1986)

> "The music, conservatively tonal and indebted to the American folk idiom, is in itself unmemorable, yet it serves the action and is strikingly apt for the projection — in a blessedly non-maudlin way — of both public and private emotions shared by all who have experienced the sudden loss of a loved one."

Kirke Mechem (1925–)

TARTUFFE

Comedy. Three acts, four scenes, (140 minutes). Conservative, contemporary with traditional harmonies and tonalities, modeled on classical Rossini/Mozart operas. Clear-cut tempo and key changes designate sections. Many ensembles: S,S duet; S,S,T trio; Bs,BAR,T,M-S fugue especially memorable. No overture, short orchestral intros.

Libretto by the composer, based on the comedy by Moliere in contemporary language. Premiere: San Francisco Opera 5.27.80. Performances: Arizona State University Lyric Opera Theatre 11.14.86; Lyric Opera Theatre of Baton Rouge 1.9.87; Northwestern University Opera 11.13.87.

PLOT

Setting: Orgon's house in Paris, seventeenth century.

Orgon orders his daughter, Mariane, to marry his guest and mentor, Tartuffe, despite the fact that she has already received permission to marry Valere. The decree horrifies Orgon's family, who consider Tartuffe to be a hypocrite and a cheat. When Tartuffe later meets with Orgon's wife, Elmire, his show of piety soon gives way to amorous pursuit. Damis reveals this disloyalty to his father, but Tartuffe's penitence moves Orgon to denounce his son, decreeing that the wedding will take place that day. Moreover, Damis is disinherited when he refuses to apologize to the hypocrite, and Tartuffe is named the legal heir. In an attempt to reveal Tartuffe's true character, Elmire tempts Tartuffe with Orgon as a hidden witness. In the course of his pursuit, Tartuffe disclaims his piety and his friend. Enraged, Orgon orders his guest to leave. However, Tartuffe claims his right to Orgon's property through a deed that had been signed over to him. He brings officers of the law, who are really Damis, Valere and Mariane in disguise, to evict the family. However, once Tartuffe unknowingly puts the deed in their hands, the trio quickly calls for his arrest. All is forgiven within the family, and they celebrate success.

PRODUCTION REQUIREMENTS

Major Roles. TARTUFFE, a hypocrite (bar): G♯1 to G3. ORGON (bs): F♯1 to F3. ELMIRE, Orgon's wife (m-s): B♭2 to A4. DAMIS, Orgon's son, Elmire's stepson (high bar): B♭1 to F♯3 (G3 falsetto). MARIANE, Orgon's daughter, Elmire's stepdaughter (s): C3 to C5. VALERE, in love with Marianne (t): D2 to B3. DORINE, Mariane's maid (s): C3 to C♯5. MADAME PERNELLE, Orgon's mother (m-s): B♭2 to F♯4.

Minor Roles. FLIPOTE, Mme. Pernelle's maid (mute).

Orchestra. 2 fls (picc or alt fl), 2 obs, 2 cls (bs cl), 2 bsns (cont bsn), 2 hrns, 1 trp, 1 trb, tuba, perc, harp, strings.

Material. FS–P: G. Schirmer. VS: American Music Center and G. Schirmer.

REVIEWS

Stephanie Von Buchau "San Francisco," *Opera News* (September 1980), p. 56

> "*Tartuffe* may find an audience, for it is conservative and attractively orchestrated, with a slick, glossy surface, and has many clever touches.
>
> "There are charming moments, such as Orgon's duet with Dorine and Mariane's Act II aria, but for a comic opera the score moves slowly."

Gian Carlo Menotti (1911–   )

THE EGG

Light children's opera in the form of a parable. One act (60 minutes). Through-composed conversational writing, only one aria. Chorus used as Greek chorus to set the stage and comment on the action. No overture.

Libretto by the composer. Premiere: Washington Cathedral, Wash., D.C. 6.17.76. Performances: Brooklyn Academy of Music, N.Y. 11.13.80.

PLOT

Setting: Byzantine Empire; fifth century.

Manuel asks his uncle, who meditates atop a pillar, about the meaning of life. St. Simeon explains that when he asked God that question, he had been given an egg and told that upon opening it, he would learn the meaning of life. After many years of trying to open the egg, he had thrown it away. St. Simeon agrees to help Manuel find the egg so that Manuel can try his luck at opening it. When Manuel tells the story to Areobindus, the Empress Basilissa's lover, he is arrested for blasphemy and brought before Basilissa. Before Manuel is hanged, the Empress challenges her cook, her treasurer and her lover to try to open the egg. When all three fail, she banishes Manuel and the egg. Meeting a beggar-woman, Manuel offers her the egg, which immediately opens to save her starving child. Realizing that the egg would only open when given away, Manuel returns to tell Basilissa. Nevertheless, he is sentenced to death. St. Simeon leaves his pillar to save Manuel, since he now understands the meaning of life: to share with one's fellowman. St. Simeon and Manuel go together to share their blessings with others.

PRODUCTION REQUIREMENTS

Major Roles. St. Simeon (t): E2 to A3. Manuel, St. Simeon's nephew (bar): C2 to G3. Basilissa, the Empress of Byzantium (s): D3 to B♭4.

Supporting Roles. Areobindus, Basilissa's lover (bass): B1 to F3. Gourmantus, Basilissa's cook (bs-buf): C2 to E♭3. Chief Eunuch (t): D2 to F♯3. Panchomus, the treasurer (t): E♭2 to F3.

Minor Roles. Basilissa's Sister (s). Beggarwoman (m-s).

Orchestra. fl, ob, cl, bsn, hrn, trp, trb, perc, harp, organ, vln, vla, vcl, cb.

Material. FS–P and VS: G. Schirmer.

REVIEWS

Donal Henahan "Opera: Double Local Debut of One-Acters in Brooklyn," *New York Times* November 15, 1980), p. 3

> "After [Eaton's] *Clytaemnestra,* Mr. Menotti's slight little opera seemed almost masterly. This is another of the composer's parables about Christian love, in the philosophical vein of *Amahl and the Night Visitors,* but breezier and less offensively sanctimonious. Aiming at childlike innocence, it frequently falls over the side into childish joking. . . . This is simple stuff, but at least Mr. Menotti knows the potential of human voices and how to score for them."

Robert Parris "Washington Cath: Menotti prems," *Musical America* (November 1976), p. 21

"*The Egg* lends itself so obviously to the misplaced giggle that, to his credit, Menotti himself, to some extent disarming his critics, lets us know that he is not unaware of the slapsticky possibilities in this otherwise unbearably sanctimonious morality play."

"Menotti prefers a continuous recitative, and a kind of continuous unschoenbergian Sprechstimme."

Lawrence Sears "Debut and Premieres at Washington Cathedral," *Music* [American Guild of Organists] (October 1976), pp. 48–49

"Both of Menotti's operas turned out to be deeply religious, dealing with the world as we find it rather than with some picture book representation of never–never land. Each has a sense of immediacy about the melodic lines which characterizes this composer, much to the constant despair of his critics, and to the delight of his worldwide audiences."

"The two processions of the Basilissa — the entry of her court, and her progress to the cathedral — are given over to an unseen chorus and organ. Here Menotti has created forceful scores of rugged strength which do not rely on complexity for effectiveness.

"A hilarious comedy role for the cook Gourmantus, sung by bass-buffo Gimi Beni, calls for him to cut off a finger (actually an uncooked hotdog) and throw it away. This touch was added just before the first performance and caused an instant audience reaction."

Charles Timbrell "Philadelphia/Washington," *Opera News* (October 1976), p. 64

" . . . the music is scrappy, especially in the second scene, which consists of a tedious succession of unaccompanied recitatives, interrupted only occasionally by innocuous punctuating ideas in the orchestra."

GOYA

Historical fiction. Three acts (full evening). Tonal, colored by chromaticism, Neo-Romantic arias, duets, ensembles. Rhythms follow speech accents, requiring frequent meter changes. Orchestra important as accompaniment, dance music and programmatic backdrop.

Libretto by the composer, freely based on the life and paintings of Francisco Goya (1746–1828). Commission and premiere: Washington Opera/Kennedy Center, Wash., D.C. 11.15.86. Performances: PBS "Great Performances" series 86.

PLOT

Setting: Spain, late eighteenth, early nineteenth century.

Goya, a young thrill-seeker and womanizer, and his friend, Martin, frequent the local taverns seeking adventure. In a tavern near Madrid, Goya meets a maiden who agrees to pose for him in the nude. This maid turns out to be the Duchess of Alba herself—hated by the Queen of Spain for her beauty, wealth, and free will. Goya falls in love with his new patroness, though she continues her carefree ways. The Queen, jealous that the duchess should have such a famous talent in her employ, summons Goya to a royal ball, where he is to be appointed court painter. When the Duchess appears at the ball with her ladies-in-waiting intentionally wearing the same gown as the Queen, the Queen faints. Just before the Duchess is evicted, Goya is devastated by a confrontation with the callous woman, over his unrequited love for her. When the King approaches Goya with his new appointment, Goya is overcome by a fit which renders him deaf.

Years later, Goya's fame has grown immensely. The Duchess (presumably poisoned) is visited on her deathbed by the Queen and Prime Minister Godoy. When she dies, they abscond with some of her treasures just before Goya and Martin arrive. Though his love is lost, Goya continues to paint scenes of the painful times he has seen throughout Spain. On his own deathbed, Goya is tormented by his inadequacies, as a host of images from his life and his paintings are to haunt him. The spirit of his beloved Duchess appears to absolve him of his self-inflicted guilt. Redeemed by the knowledge that he has brought truth to the canvas, if not always through his own life, Goya dies in peace.

PRODUCTION REQUIREMENTS

Major Roles. DON FRANCISCO GOYA Y LUCIENTES, the painter (t): D♭2 to B♭3. DONA CAYETANA, Duchess of Alba (m-s): A2 to A4.

Supporting Roles. MARTIN ZAPATER, Goya's friend (bar): C2 to F3. CHARLES IV, King of Spain (t): D♯2 to A3. MARIA LUISA, Queen of Spain (s): C♯3 to D♭5. DON MANUEL GODOY, Prime Minister of Spain (bs): A1 to E3.

Minor Roles. A Tavern Singer (m-s). The Duchess of Alba's Maid (m-s). Innkeeper (bar). Major Domo (t). Leocadia (m-s).

Chorus. SATB.

Orchestra. picc, 2 fls, 2 obs, Eng hrn, 2 cls, bs cl, 2 bsns, 4 hrns, 3 trps, 3 trbs, tuba, timp, perc, piano, harp, strings.

Material. FS–P: G. Schirmer.

REVIEWS

Manuela Hoelterhoff " 'Goya': A Portrait in Monotony," *The Wall Street Journal* (November 20, 1986) p. 24

"('Goya') is airplane music, written between engagements and tethered to a silly libretto. Mr. Menotti stretched his gifts still further by doing triple duty, as composer, librettist and director. Even so, his theatrical flair flashes inventively here and there."

Charles Jahant "Washington," *Opera* (March 1987), 38:276–277

"There is nothing new here, but Menotti has concluded it with a superbly theatrical idea: the dying Goya is visited by visions drawn from some of his more memorable works, The 5th of May, Witches' Sabbath, Burial of the Sardine and various and sundry monsters."

David Patrick Stearns "Washington, D.C.," *Opera News* (March 14, 1987), p. 38

"much of *Goya* seemed the work of last-minute inspiration or no inspiration at all."

"Essentially, Goya is a generic nineteenth-century opera hero. Accepting that, there were some genuinely engaging moments in the second act, where Menotti explored the bitchery between Queen and Duchess, the obsessiveness of Goya's love and the onset of his deafness, portrayed by all sound stopping except for a searing high-pitched violin tone. In these moments, drama and music melded in the best Menotti tradition and made for riveting theatre."

THE HERO

Satire. Three acts (full evening). Through-composed in a conservative modern idiom. No overture. Conversational writing with a variety of textures: substantial arias, duets, choruses, and orchestral bridges. Orchestra often doubles vocal parts.

Libretto by Gian Carlo Menotti. Commissioned by the Opera company of Philadelphia. Premiere: Opera Company of Philadelphia, 6.76.

PLOT

Setting: David Murphy's bedroom, 1976.

For most of the ten years David has been asleep, his wife, Mildred, and their neighbors have promoted his illness as a tourist attraction. His cousin, Barbara, who loves him, decides to leave the day before he will become the world champion of uninterrupted sleep, since his recovery seems remote and the exploitation of his illness disgusts her. Barbara gives David a good-bye kiss which awakens him. Concerned about the financial implications of his recovery, Mildred calls the doctor and the Mayor. David rejects their suggestions that he go back to sleep, refusing to take a sleeping pill the doctor leaves for him. He pretends to sleep when Mildred and the doctor return to erase the evidence of his recovery, discovering that they are in love and plan to leave the country with their profits. When they leave, David and Barbara are free to express their love for each other.

At a ceremony the next day, David greets the crowd just as a monument honoring the local hero is to be unveiled. He asks them to respect his honesty and the American spirit that it reflects, but the people accuse him of fraud. The crowd stampedes the ceremony, but David is at peace with himself because of his honesty. Mildred and the doctor accuse David of ruining their reputations and wonder how to resolve the mess. But after David and Barbara openly admit their love for each other, Mildred and the doctor are able to acknowledge their love and all is well.

PRODUCTION REQUIREMENTS

Major Roles. BARBARA (s): D♭3 to B4. MILDRED MURPHY (m-s): A♭2 to A♭4. DAVID MURPHY (bs-bar): F♯1 to G3.

Supporting Roles. DR. BRAINKOFF (t): D♭2 to B♭3. THE MAYOR (bar): G1 to F3.

Minor Roles. WHITE WOMAN TOURIST (m-s). WHITE MAN TOURIST (bs).

Black Woman Tourist (s). Black Man Tourist (t). The Jeweler (t). A Shopkeeper (bs-bar).

Chorus. SATB.

Orchestra. 3 fls, 2 obs, 2 cls, 2 bsns, 4 hrns, 3 trps, 3 trbs, tuba, perc, harp, strings.

Material. FS–P: G. Schirmer. V-S: American Music Center and G. Schirmer.

REVIEWS

Robert Baxter "Philadelphia and Wilmington," *Opera* (October 1976), pp. 914–916

"*The Hero,* like all of Menotti's stage works, is a clever fusion of word, music and action. Taken separately, the music and the text of *The Hero* are not very memorable. . . .

"*The Hero* is very much a singer's opera with lyrical arias and duets."

Daniel Webster "PHILADELPHIA: Opera Co.: Menotti premiere," *Musical America* (September 1976), pp. 21–22

"The text is clever to the exreme of overeshadowing the music. Despite the presence of showy duets and ensembles, the score's chief distinction seems to be the deftness with which it provides musical speech."

LA LOCA

Historical drama. Three acts, eight scenes (full evening). Through-composed, conversational writing, with several monologues for soprano. No overture.

Libretto by the composer about the daughter of Spain's Ferdinand and Isabella. Premiere: San Diego Opera 6.3.79. Performance: New York City Opera 9.16.79.

PLOT

Setting: sixteenth century.

Juana, future Queen of Castile, and Filipe, her betrothed, fall in love at first sight and are married immediately. When Juana inherits the crown, she remains in her husband's land. Her father sends Ximenes to complain that Filipe has been intercepting his communications to her and to request that she sign a letter that would allow him to govern until she returns to Castile. Juana's loyal servant, Miguel, begs her not to sign the letter. He also warns that Filipe covets her throne and has been unfaithful to her. When Filipe enters, he sees the letter and accuses her of plotting to hand Castile to her father. She assures Filipe of her love, but refuses to sign a similar letter that would give her power to him. Filipe declares that she will be locked up until she makes him the same offer she made to her father. On his deathbed, Filipe asks to see Juana. When Juana enters, she finds Manuela, her servant, fondly caressing Filipe and realizes that this is her husband's lover. She hysterically cuts Manuela's hair and strikes at her with the scissors. Her despair stuns Filipe, who asks for her forgiveness before he dies.

In Castile, Juana's father realizes that his dream to unite Spain is thwarted by Juana's hold on her crown. Ximenes suggests that he declare his daughter mad and lock her up. Juana's eldest child, Carlos, is taken from her, and she and her daughter are locked away. When Carlos has been king for many years, he visits Juana's cell to request that she sign away her power in exchange for her freedom. Again she refuses. Miguel, who has become a priest, visits the mad queen and offers her the solace of God's love. Juana prays to God to take the cursed crown which has kept her prisoner for so long and to grant her freedom at last.

PRODUCTION REQUIREMENTS

Major Roles. JUANA, daughter of Castile's Ferdinand and Isabella, heir to the throne (s): D3 to D5. FILIPE, Juana's husband; FERNANDO, Juana's father; and CARLOS, Juana's son (played by the same bar): $A^{b}1$ to G3.

Supporting Roles. Juana's servants: MIGUEL (t): D2 to $B^{b}3$ and MANUELA (m-s): C2 to $F^{\#}4$. XIMENES, Bishop of Toledo and counsel to Fernando (bs): A1 to E3.

Minor Roles. LADY I (s). LADY II (m-s). NURSE (m-s). CATALINA, Juana's grown daughter (m-s). MARQUIS OF DEMIE, jailkeeper during Juana's imprisonment (bs or bar).

Non-singing Roles. CARLOS, Juana's son as a child.

Chorus. SATB (backstage).

Orchestra. 2 fls (pic), 2 obs, Eng hrn, 2 cls, bs cl, 2 bsns, 4 hrns, 3 trps, 2 trps (offstage), 3 trbs, tuba, timp, 2 perc, harp, piano, strings.

Materials. FS–P and VS: G. Schirmer.

REVIEWS

Martin Bernheimer "San Diego," *Opera* (August 1979), pp. 787–789

"[Menotti] writes modern music for people who hate modern music. It is lush and sweet; it never unsettles the listener with pesky surprises; it steadfastly refuses to stretch the ears or challenge the cerebellum. . . . he peppers the musical broth with pinches of dissonance. He is, without question, a master craftsman, and he commands a telling theatrical gift. In the final analysis, however, he seems merely to have stitched together a network of easy devices."

"Menotti still may want to reconsider some details: the fitful addition of a piano to the pit band sounds more like desperation than intention; the dramatic gaps between some scenes jolt credibility; the libretto could use the helping colloquial hand of a good editor."

"Obviously, this is the role of any prima donna's lifetime. The heroine, essentially, must be a virtuoso actress, a resourceful technician, and an artist with sufficient stamina and intelligence to pace the cumulative vocal hurdles."

Manuela Hoelterhoff "Beverly Sills Retires From a Lustrous Career," *Wall Street Journal* (September 28, 1979), p. 23

"It's obviously a tale of some dramatic potential, but Mr. Menotti unfortunately didn't have the good sense to let a poet write the libretto, and his own concoction turns Juana's interesting conflict into libidinous mush and melodrama. . . . The libretto's failing is doubly unfortunate since the opera contains some pretty music."

"The issue by now really isn't whether Mr. Menotti has anything new to say musically, but whether he can repeat himself and late nineteenth-century composers effectively, and often he can. . . . listen well, for instance, to Juana's beseeching of her husband, or her poignant lament at his casket, beautifully rendered by Ms. Sills."

Leighton Kerner "Walk out like a Queen," *Village Voice* (September 24, 1979), p. 78

"As with all his better stage pieces, the composer has built his libretto with an unerring sense of how fast to feed information to the audience, how tight to pull tension toward a climax, and just where to end a scene. But as with even his best operas, he has saddled the drama with sentences not quite English but made of his own special Librettoese, whose metaphors constantly lock bumpers in traffic jams."

"And as with all but his most inspired operas, *The Medium* and possibly *The Old Maid and the Thief*, the music is not so much invented as manufactured. . . . In *La Loca* the manufacture is smooth and expert . . . Everything works and not a note is wasted."

TAMU TAMU

Bilingual drama in Indonesian and English. Two acts (70 minutes). Overture. Through-composed, conversational writing with one set piece.

Libretto by composer. Commission and premiere: International Congress of anthropological and Ethnological Sciences, Chicago, Ill. 9.5.73.

PLOT

Setting: the apartment of a contemporary American couple.

Mr. Hudson and his wife coldly greet each other over breakfast, apologizing for the angry words of the previous night. In order to coax his wife out of her depression, Mr. Hudson shows her a picture of an Indonesian family fleeing from armed soldiers, pointing out the contrast to her own relatively fulfilled life. Although the wife is shocked by the sight, the husband questions whether her feelings can truly reach out to embrace such distant people and problems.

After her husband leaves for work, Mrs. Hudson answers the doorbell and is confronted by the family from the picture. Initial shock gives way to compassion as Mrs. Hudson helps the strangers inside and calls for her doctor to tend to their wounds. When her husband calls, she tells him of the strange happening and requests that he bring food. He arrives with rice, confused about the appearance of their guests. The doctor arrives, but refuses to treat the family, quickly withdrawing from the mysterious situation. The Indonesian grandfather dies and is tended by an Indonesian priest. The family's life entwines with the Hudson's. Ananto describes the family's flight, convincing his host that he is equally confused about their strange arrival at the Hudson's. Mrs. Hudson and Indra surprise and anger their husbands by exchanging clothes, but the confrontation is interrupted by Ratna's initial labor cries. Mrs. Hudson's frenzy is calmed by Nenek's experienced control of the situation. As all celebrate the birth of a son, armed soldiers enter. They push the Indonesian family outside and shoot them.

The Hudsons are again at breakfast. Mrs. Hudson asks whether anything interesting is in the paper. Mr. Hudson replies negatively and leaves for work as she begins to clean.

PRODUCTION REQUIREMENTS

Major Roles. MR. HUDSON (bar): C1 to G♯3. MRS. HUDSON (s): B2 to B♭4.

Supporting Roles. ANANTO (bar): C2 to G♭3. Ananto's wives: INDRA (s): D♭3 to B♭4; RATNA (s): B2 to C5. NENEK (m-s or c): A♭2 to E♭4, the grandmother.

Minor Roles. DOCTOR (t).

Non-singing Roles. Ratna's children: DJOKO (boy); SOLIMA (girl). KAKEK, the grandfather.

Orchestra. fl, cl, hrn, trp, perc, piano, harp, 3 vlns, 3 vcl, cb.

Material. FS–P and VS: G. Schirmer.

REVIEWS

Peter Davis "Menotti's Hard Blow to the Gut," *New York Times* (September 16, 1973), p. 17

"*Tamu-Tamu* tells us little that we haven't already learned about Menotti's art. Like all of his operas, it is a vulnerable piece, easily dismissed by those who dislike having their emotions manipulated so flagrantly. Still, it does 'work,' one is engaged after a fashion, and audiences are going to love it. . . . it is a crafty, neatly made piece that aims at the gut and rarely misses."

" . . . the outward events are fashioned into a tightly ordered, swiftly paced unit. . . . But isn't it all a bit artificial and contrived? Perhaps it's a mistake to look too hard at works of this sort that do indeed offer an evening of well-made diversion, but Menotti always invites such scrutiny simply because he invariably strikes such moralizing attitudes."

"In Menotti's 'Gesamtkunst' populist opera world, his easy-to-grasp music has always been of secondary importance, underlining rather than illuminating. . . . very little time is wasted on arias, duets and the like. There is only one real set number, a rather pretty lullaby for the wife . . . "

"For the Indonesians, Menotti uses an exotic gamelan-flavored idiom to contrast the 'western' song-speech arioso. . . . it does the job economically and effectively, no more, no less."

Jack Kroll "Anthroperalogy," *Newsweek* (September 17, 1973), p. 90

"The Asians . . . take refuge right there in the apartment. And the tragic tone quickly turns into comedy, a kind of Oriental 'Beverly Hillbillies.' . . . . It's not all comic. The Eastern family cannot escape the fate foreshadowed by the newspaper picture . . . "

"Musically Menotti utilizes song-speech, liberally laced with recitative. Arias are rare, melody suggested rather than developed."

Karen Monson "Chicago's Menotti premiere," *Musical America* (December 1973), p. 16

"The score holds a few attractive melodies, but the strength of *Tamu-Tamu* rests in the shock value of a series of ultra-theatrical tableaux. Between these moments of effect, Menotti has allowed mundane silliness to undermine his essential seriousness and he has missed his chance to make the music work on behalf of the drama."

Henry Mollicone (1946–)

THE FACE ON THE BARROOM FLOOR

Melodrama. Three scenes (25 minutes). Through-composed with references to saloon music, barroom jazz. Conversational, recitative-like vocal style with lyrical arias, duets, and trios. Orchestral overture underscores dialogue and provides background for scene changes. Three orchestral players can be part of saloon environment.

Libretto by John S. Bowman. Commissioned by the Central City Opera

House Association. Premiere: Central City Opera, Colo. 7.22.78. Performances: Houston Opera Studio 4.81; Chamber Opera Theatre of New York 12.17.82; San Diego State Univ. Opera Theatre 4.24.86.

PLOT

Setting: the Teller House Bar, Central City, Colorado; the present and 100 years ago.

Larry and Isabelle enter a bar, entranced by its western charm. Larry notices a woman's portrait on the floor and demands that Tom, the barman, relate its history. As Tom begins, the three of them become the characters in the tale. John and Madeline enjoy their successful business as Matt, a traveling artist, enters their bar. After ordering drinks for the house, Matt demands a song, not recognizing Madeline until she begins to sing. Sensing tension between them, John demands that the artist pay and leave. Matt has no money, but offers to paint a portrait of his love on the floor. When John sees Madeline's face there, he jealously realizes that she and the artist had been lovers. Matt tries to convince Madeline to come with him, and a fight breaks out. As the three struggle, a shot is fired and Madeline slumps dead across the portrait. The scene reverts to the present, displaying Larry, drunk and entranced with Madeline's portrait, refusing to leave despite Isabelle's pleas. Tom tries to avoid a scene, but he inevitably discloses that he and Isabelle had been lovers. As in the story, a fight begins, a shot is fired, and Isabelle falls dead over the portrait on the floor.

PRODUCTION REQUIREMENTS

Major Roles. ISABELLE/MADELINE (lyr s): D3 to C5. TOM/JOHN (bar): B♭1 to F3. LARRY/MATT (t): D2 to A3 (opt B3, C3.)

Orchestra. fl (picc), cello, piano.

Material. FS–P and VS: Belwin-Mills. VS: American Music Center.

Recordings. Composer's Recordings Inc. CRI SD-442, 170 W. 74th St. New York, NY 10023.

REVIEWS

John W. Freeman "RECORDS," *Opera News* (April 11, 1981), p. 52 (Record review).

"The music, unpretentious and apt, bites off less than it can chew, and one is left willing to hear more, which is always a good sign."

"Like the cast, the instrumental accompaniment forms a lively, tension-poised threesome . . . "

Ken "The Face on the Barroom Floor (Mollicone) and The Old Maid and the Thief (Menotti)," *Variety* (January 6, 1982), p. 76

"Mollicone's music, with an equally individual profile, proves that the interaction between Broadway and 'serious' music is still alive and well."

Leighton Kerner "Tex-Op," *Village Voice* (May 13, 1981), pp. 92+

"Both Mollicone pieces have lots of easy, lyrical charm and sometimes avoid identification with music you've heard before. . . . But the Western ballad-style tunes and rhythms pour out like watered whiskey, without much kick."

Bill Zakariasen "Central City," *Musical America* (December 1979), pp. 18–19

"The libretto . . . is clever indeed. Mollicone's music, despite the modest forces . . . exudes the sort of passion one might find in the last act of Barber's *Vanessa,* building to a truly knockout final ensemble."

THE STARBIRD

Fantasy. One act (50 minutes). Mostly conservative modern, conversational writing; some aria-like passages; ensembles. Uses mixed meters, long "blues" section. A brief orchestral introduction with optional cut of the only orchestral interlude. Requires taped sound effects: sirens, spaceship "blast-offs," etc.; visual effects: explosion/flash.

Libretto by Kate Pogue. Commissioned by the Houston Grand Opera. Premiere: Houston Grand Opera Studio 5.17.79.

PLOT

Setting: New York and outer space, present day.

Three animals dejectedly meet after they are displaced from their jobs by mechanical devices. They bicker amongst themselves, each finding fault with the others. After nightfall, they are awakened by the starbird, who comes from the planet Arcturus. When the animals ask to go there, the bird warns that she had been an earth bird before spacemen took her to Arcturus and changed her into a metal being. The robots return and take off for home. When they realize that the animals are on board, they try to seize them for use in their experiments. But the bird saves the frightened animals by telling them how to deactivate their captors. After their escape, the animals continue to argue — the cat wants to go to Arcturus, while the others want to go home. The spaceship lands, and the three animals finally agree to face the unknown together as friends. As they look around, they realize that they are back on earth. The starbird explains that she guided the ship back to earth when she realized that the animals had learned to value their faults, their friends, and their home. As the starbird returns to the stars, the animal friends rejoice at being back on earth.

PRODUCTION REQUIREMENTS

Major Roles. BIRD (s): C3 to D5. CAT (m-s): G2 to G4. DOG (t): C2 to C4 [falsetto]. MULE (bs-bar): G1 to F♯3.

Supporting Roles. ROBOT I (t): F2 to G♯3 and ROBOT II (bs): F1 to E3 (sing together).

Minor Roles. ACTURION (amplified offstage speaking voice).

Orchestra. fl (picc), cl in B♭, fr hrn, violin, cello, cb (5 string), perc (large role), piano.

Material. FS–P and VS: Belwin Mills.

REVIEWS

Leland Fox "Carlisle Floyd's 'Willie Stark,' " *Opera Journal* (November 3, 1981), 14(3):39–44

> "To a skintight libretto by Houston's Kate Pogue, a script that could stand alone as poetry, Henry Mollicone has grafted a score that realizes its full potential and, despite a small cast and orchestra, provides a wealth of sound in which to revel."

> "Although in no way avant-garde, Henry Mollicone has given us a score that suspends our awareness of opera and heightens our perception of drama."

Scott F. Heumann "America: Birthday Premieres," *Opera* (September 1981), 32(9):939–942

"(Mollicone's) style manages to be both ingratiating and sophisticated, a la Leonard Bernstein. *Starbird* . . . proved to be a science-fiction variation on 'The Bremen Town Musicians' with a delightful, pop-flavored score that appealed to children without condescending to them."

Annalyn Swan "Grand Opera, Texas Style," *Newsweek* (May 11, 1981), pp. 96, 99

"The children in the audience loved 'Starbird,' and so did the adults. Mollicone should go far; he can't seem to write a note that doesn't sing."

Robert Moran

THE JUNIPER TREE
[See GLASS]

Thea Musgrave (1928–)

A CHRISTMAS CAROL

Two acts, thirteen scenes, unit set (105 minutes). Through-composed, conservative modern style. Mainly conversational writing, although arias and choruses exist. Short orchestral introduction, brief dance sequences, orchestra rarely doubles voices. Minimum cast needed: twelve (with many roles doubled).

Libretto by the composer, based on the Dickens' tale. Commissioned by The Virginia Opera Association. Premiere: Virginia Opera Association 12.7.79.

PLOT

Setting: London, nineteenth century.

The classic Dickens' *A Christmas Carol* with a few adaptations. The Ghosts of Christmas Past, Present and Future are played by a dancer. The last scene of Act I, Belle's farewell, is expanded.

PRODUCTION REQUIREMENTS

Major Roles. SCROOGE (bar): A1 to F♯3 (G3, G♯3 opt).

Supporting Roles. Each of these roles can double those in brackets plus other small roles listed in score. SPIRIT OF CHRISTMAS (dancer). FAN, young Scrooge's sister (LIZA FEZZIWIG, BELINDA CRATCHIT, LUCY) (s): F3 to C♯5 (D♯5, E5 opt). BELLA FIZZIWIG, young Ben's fiancee (MARTHA CRATCHIT, ROSIE) (s): D2 TO B♭4 (C5 OPT). MRS. CRATCHIT (MRS. FEZZIWIG, AUNT LOUISE) (m-s): B♭2 to A4. BOB CRATCHIT (MR. DORIT) (t): E2 to A3 (A♯3, B3 opt). BEN, Scrooge as a young man (FRED, Scrooge's nephew) (bar): C2 to F♯3.

Minor Roles. These double other small roles as well. MR. FEZZIWIG (TOPPER) (bs-bar or bar). MARLEY'S GHOST (actor). PAPER BOY (boy, 12 or 13). MOLLIE FEZZIWIG (girl, 11 or 12). TINY TIM (Scrooge as a boy) (boy, 9 or 10).

Chorus. Made up of cast members. Children's offstage chorus in finale is optional.

Orchestra. fl (picc), ob (Eng hrn), 2 cls in B♭ (bs cl), hrn in F, 2 perc, harp, piano, strings (played by solo string quintet or small string orchestra).

Material. FS–P and VS: Novello. VS: American Music Center.

REVIEWS

Harold Blumenfeld "Christmas Carol," *Opera Journal* (1980), 13(2):15–18

> "In her incarnation of the Dickens' tale, Musgrave has succeeded in avoiding . . . dual pitfalls: . . . an all-too-hastily defrosting of Scrooge's character, and a general goody-goody sentimentalization of all concerned . . ."

> "(Musgrave's) vocal writing is splendid, allowing the text audibility and comprehensibility along with its wide range of expression. The acid recitative of old Ebenezer is counterbalanced by the lyric outpourings of the young Belle-enamoured Ben."

"Musgrave has touched down on two mutually reinforcing familiarities — the tale itself and two well-known tunes . . . "

Andrew Porter "Carol," *The New Yorker* (December 24, 1979), pp. 84–87

" 'A Christmas Carol' is, on all counts, a well-made opera. There is variety and contrast of pace, mood, and texture. Lyricism and declamation, closed forms and straight-line dialogue are deftly balanced. The instrumentation is masterly. The word setting is sensitive, the lines are singable, the roles rewarding."

"Nothing in the music replaces the important scenes a chamber opera could not compass. . . . The focus is held close on Scrooge and those immediately around him, and the range and scope of the 'Carol' are diminished."

Annalyn Swan "Christmas Cheer," *Newsweek* (December 17, 1979), pp. 88–90

"Musgrave's characteristic dissonance, with its echoes here and there of Benjamin Britten, underscores Scrooge's misanthropy. But, as befits the sentimental theme, Musgrave has created the most melodic of her five operas."

"Dickens' story is as full of sounds as it is sights, and Musgrave gives them their full measure."

HARRIET, THE WOMAN CALLED MOSES

Historical drama. Two acts (full evening). Modern musical style utilizing several spirituals. Through-composed with arias and duets surfacing throughout. Rapid scene changes can be acted out to depict Harriet's journeys.

Libretto by the composer, freely based on the life of Harriet Tubman, with quotations from two books by Sarah Bradford: "Harriet, the Moses of her People" and "Scenes in the life of Harriet Tubman." Commission: The Royal Opera House, London and The Virginia Opera Association. Premiere: Virginia Opera, Norfolk 3.1.85. Revised: Summer of 1985.

PLOT

Setting: Civil War years.

Harriet Tubman was an escaped slave who helped over 300 slaves to freedom as a "conductor" on the Underground Railroad. The hardships of Harriet's family life on the plantation are revealed through a series of flashbacks. The Master's concern for his slaves is not shared by his son Preston — a drunkard, gambler, and womanizer. Preston beats Harriet for not responding to his sexual advances; beats Harriet's father, Ben; decides to sell the slaves to the ruthless Mr. Covey in order to pay his gambling debts; and attacks Harriet for protecting her lover, Josiah, when he escapes. When the Master seems near death, Harriet's brother, Benji, convinces her to escape. She finds her way to the home of Thomas Garrett, a Quaker. Safe at last, she dreams of being reunited with Josiah. But Harriet decides to follow her heart and return South to help other slaves escape. She rescues her father from prison and helps to free Josiah again after he is recaptured. Finally, Harriet attempts to rescue her entire family, though her mother, Rit, sees little hope in the escape. When the entourage reaches the bridge to Canada, Harriet is recognized to be the renegade "Moses." The patrols fire at Harriet, but it is Josiah who is fatally wounded. Harriet is devastated, crying that she cannot continue alone. But Harriet is consoled when Rit vows to join the fight for freedom.

PRODUCTION REQUIREMENTS

Major Roles. HARRIET (s): C3 to C♯5. JOSIAH, a friend (bar): C2 to G3. RIT, Harriet's mother (m-s): G2 to A4.

Supporting Roles. THE MASTER (bar): B1 to F♯3. PRESTON, the Master's son (t): D2 to B♭3. BENJIE, Harriet's brother (t): E2 to A3. BEN, Harriet's father (bs): G1 to D♯3.

Minor Roles. THOMAS GARRETT, a Quaker (bar). EDWARD COVEY, leader of the patrol (bs). MR. MCLEOD, THE OVERSEER (t).

Minor Speaking Roles. CATO, a young black man; JAILKEEPER; TWO BOUNTY HUNTERS; SUELLEN, Preston's wife; POLICE SERGEANT.

Chorus. SATB chorus participates on stage throughout.

Orchestra. 2 fls (picc), 2 obs (Eng hrn), 2 B♭ cls, 2 bsns (cont bsn), 3 hrns in F, 3 trps, 3 trbs, harp, piano, timp, 2 perc, strings.

Material. FS–P and VS: Theodore Presser.

REVIEWS

Peter G. Davis "Prime Time," *New York* (April 1, 1985), pp. 79–80

"Musgrave has responded instinctively and honestly to the interior spirit of the drama without neglecting its theatrical potential."

"Like previous Musgrave operas seen, heard, and admired hereabouts . . . the composer's latest effort is more notable for its solid professional craft, good intentions, agreeable music, and firm grasp of operatic convention than for any inspired flights of lyricism or scenes of dramatic originality."

Shirley Fleming "Harriet, The Woman Called Moses," *Musical America* (August 1985), pp. 21–22

"Musically, 'Harriet' is easy on the ear, in Musgrave's proven fashion. Like *Mary, Queen of Scotts* — only tighter. . . . there are warm episodes that come into sharp focus — a love duet between Harriet and Josiah, Harriet's lullaby . . . and a despairing outpouring from Rit."

"The orchestration is alive and full of bite. . . . But Musgrave still betrays an inordinate fondness for the cliches of 'dramatic' writing."

Robert Jacobson "Norfolk," *Opera News* (June 1985), pp. 35–36

"(Musgrave) writes more mellifluous vocal lines than many other contemporary composers, but one waits in vain for that lyric release, that burst of truly inspired melody. . . . What lends the score its happiest episodes are the traditional American tunes that Musgrave weaves into her tapestry . . . Like Sir Michael Tippet, Musgrave shares a fascination with spirituals as set into a modern idiom, and often these timbres fall gratefully on the ear."

Allen Shaffer "Harriet, The Woman Called Moses by Thea Musgrave," *The Opera Journal* (1985), 18(1):31–37

"The story line is clear and easy to follow, and the flashback technique . . . is largely successful. However, the libretto's actual literary quality is variable at best."

"Musically, the score is generally more successful, and in many places is genuinely powerful."

"The choral writing throughout the opera is thrilling and dramatically effective. The well-trained chorus of twenty-two local black singers was a nearly constant presence on stage."

MARY, QUEEN OF SCOTS

Historical fiction. Three acts (129 minutes). Chromatic patterns, tone clusters and free improvised orchestral passages. Vocal writing generally linear with many tritone intervals, unmeasured recitative, and counterpoint in ensembles.

Libretto by the composer based on *Moray,* a play by Amalia Elguera. Commissioned by the Scottish Opera. Premiere: Edinburgh Festival 9.77. Performances: Virginia Opera 3.29.78; San Francisco Spring Opera 79; Hinsdale Opera Theatre, Ill. 6.20.80.

PLOT

Setting: Edinburgh, 1561–1668.

When Mary returns to Scotland to assume her crown, she is welcomed by her people, but must contend with her half brother, James, and the Earl of Bothwell, who both vie for her favor. A year later, Mary dances with Lord Darnley to the consternation of Bothwell and James, who feel that Darnley is unsuitable for her. Mary spurns James' pleas to send Darnley away, and when Bothwell draws his sword against Darnley, she banishes him. After the royal wedding, it becomes clear that the drunken Darnley can never be named King, even though Mary carries his child. Mary summons James, but when he demands her power, she knows that she must rely on her own strength. Meanwhile, two of James' men convince Darnley that Mary's secretary, Riccio, has fathered the child Mary carries. Drunk and jealous, Darnley bursts into Mary's chambers and stabs Riccio. Some feel that James should take power, and he begins to do so when it appears that Mary has fled. However, she reemerges, accusing James of usurping her position and of inciting Darnley to commit murder. The people, led by Lord Gordon, turn against James, and Mary banishes him.

After Mary's son is born, James enters Scotland with an army. Gordon unsuccessfully urges the Queen to flee, begging her not to trust Bothwell whom she has summoned. Gordon's worst fears prove true when Bothwell seduces Mary as the price she must pay for his protection. When James discovers his sister with her seducer, he overpowers and wounds Bothwell, but convinces the Scots that Mary encouraged his advances. The people demand her abdication. After hiding the baby, Lord Gordon finally convinces Mary to flee to England. As James takes power,

Gordon stabs him. James's friend, Morton, takes the child, assuming power as Regent of Scotland.

PRODUCTION REQUIREMENTS

Major Roles. MARY, QUEEN OF SCOTS (s): B2 to C5 [C♯5 opt]. JAMES STUART, Mary's half brother (bar): C2 to G3. EARL OF BOTHWELL (t): C2 to B♭3. LORD DARNLEY (t): D2 to A3.

Supporting Roles. DAVID RICCIO (bs-bar): G1 to E♭3, CARDINAL BEATON (bs-bar): C♯2 to E♭3 (these two roles may be doubled by one singer). LORD GORDON (bs): C♯2 to E3. EARL OF MORTON (bar): A1 to F3. EARL OF RUTHVEN (t): D2 to A3. MARY SETON (m-s): D3 to F4 [C3 opt].

Minor Roles. The other three Marys (s,s,c).

Chorus. Minimum 32. Monks, soldiers, courtiers, Lords of the Congregation, and the people of Edinburgh.

Ballet. Courtiers and leading roles participate in court dancing.

Orchestra. 2 fls (2 piccs), 3 obs (2 Eng hrns), 2 cls in B♭ (bs cl), 2 bsns (cont bsn), 3 hrns in F, 2 trps in C, tenor trb, 4 timp, 2 perc, chamber org, harp, strings (8–6–5–4–2). Stage band: fl (picc), ob, Eng hrn, bsn, trp in C, perc (can be drawn from pit orchestra).

Material. FS–P and VS: Novello.

Recordings. Moss Music Group, MMG 301. Live recording of Virginia Opera performance.

REVIEWS

Shirley Fleming "Virginia, 'Mary Queen of Scots,' " *Musical America* (September 1978), p. 19

> "Miss Musgrave isn't afraid of some cliches: the smash of timpani, the punctuation of brass. . . . These broad brush strokes are balanced by some very particular writing for individual instruments, especially woodwinds, for which the composer has a keen ear."

David Hamilton "Music," *Nation* (July 22–29, 1978), pp. 92–93

"(Musgrave) really knows how to write operatic continuity, and that's rare these days. Here and there the writing will turn briefly inert and dutiful . . . but the sureness with which the big ballroom scene in the first act is built . . . bespeaks genuine command of the stage as well as of the musical materials."

"Musgrave makes strong vocal lines for dramatic situations, supporting them rather than smothering them with the orchestra as the climaxes arrive."

K. M. "Musgrave, Mary, Queen of Scots," *High Fidelity* (January 1980), pp. 83–83

"The grace with which the text and the music dance together demonstrates that the composer made the final decisions about the two simultaneously."

"The fact that the three acts revolve around scenes in the ballroom, at court, and at table, might suggest that *Mary, Queen of Scots* is grandiose, not just grand. In fact, the work is easily managed, both by companies of modest size and by first-time listeners."

Andrew Porter "Mary in Virginia," *New Yorker* (May 1, 1978), pp. 136–138+

"a suite of sixteenth-century court dances counterpointed by keen, personal commentary that cuts through the antique harmonies—at once an attractive period spectacle and a potent dramatic device."

"Musgrave gives her heroine many chances to be commanding, yielding, merry, melancholy, tender, severe, brave, broken."

Alan Rich "Even in California, Small Can Triumph," *New York* (April 30, 1979), pp. 103–104

"Musgrave's script is a magnificent framework for stage effects of the most endearing, if old-fashioned, sort: confrontations, sudden revelations, stages divided as sinister undercurrents flow through the gaiety."

THE VOICE OF ARIADNE

Supernatural tale. Three acts, five scenes, three to four sets (132 minutes). Complex, layered rhythms. Chromatic vocal lines with wide leaps contrast with more conjunct, lyric ones. Near aleatoric, unmetered "ad lib" solos and ensembles, some coordinating with prerecorded tape.

Libretto by Amalia Elguera, based on "The Last of the Valerii" by Henry James. Commissioned by Royal Opera House, London. Premiere: English Opera Group, Aldeburgh, England 6.15.74.

PLOT

Setting: Rome, 1870s.

The Count and Countess Valerios host a celebration to commemorate the unearthing of an ancient statue the Valerio family has, for generations, been searching for on their land. Mrs. Tracy, the Countess' American friend, wanders through the grounds exclaiming about each lavish detail, hounded by her Italian admirer, Baldovino. The old gardener, Gualtiero, tells the guests of the superstition that whoever uncovers the lost relic will reap the happiness that the statue might bring. However, only a pedestal is found, bearing the inscription "Ariadne," not the name of one of the goddesses the guests had speculated about, but rather a simple woman. The Count ruminates over the find on his own. He is startled by a distant voice that only he can hear, the voice of the missing statue, Ariadne, who claims to be lost on a faraway island, calling to her lover, Theseus, for rescue. The Count becomes obsessed with Ariadne, vowing to find her, even if it means spilling his own blood. Marchesa Bianca Bianchi, learning of this new obsession from Gualtiero, decides to use the information to fuel the Countess' jealousy, so that the Count might turn away from his wife, and turn to her instead. Depressed and alone, the Countess still has faith that the Count will return to his senses. Gualtiero convinces the Count to make a sacrifice to the Gods in his effort to find the statue. The encouraging words of Mr. Lamb, her elderly admirer, convince the Countess to take on the guise of Ariadne so that when the Count makes his sacrificial offering, he might be united with his own wife, rather than the lost statue. The voice of the statue fades, the noble couple is reunited, as the unrequieted lovers, Mr. Lamb and the Marchesa, look on.

PRODUCTION REQUIREMENTS

Major Roles. COUNT MARCO VALERIO (bar): B♭1 to F♯3. (D4 falsetto lx). THE COUNTESS, his American wife (s): A2 to B♭4 (many notes in low end of range). GUALTIERO, the old gardener (bs): E1 to E♭3.

Supporting Roles. MR. LAMB, an elderly American gentleman (bar): C2 to F3. MARCHESA BIANCA BIANCHI (m-s): G2 to F♯4.

Minor Roles. MRS. TRACY, the Countess' American friend (c). BALDOVINO, Mrs. Tracy's blundering admirer (t). GIOVANNI (t). THE STATUE, The voice of Ariadne (m-s) (prerecorded tape).

Orchestra. fl (picc), ob (Eng hrn), cl (bs cl), bsn (cont bsn), hrn, perc, harp, piano (Hammond chamber org), strings (1–1–1–1–1 or 7–5–4–3–2), elec tape.

Material. FS–P and VS: Theodore Presser. VS: American Music Center.

REVIEWS

Winton Dean "Festivals: ALDEBURGH — The Voice of Ariadne," *Musical Times* (August 1974), 115:678–679

"the merging of natural and supernatural offers excellent operatic material."

"The librettist has added a subplot, to provide a Roman background, comic relief and an opportunity for ensembles. . . . The aim is understandable, but it is not well worked out, especially as regards the caricatured figures of Mrs. Tracy and Baldovino. . . . nevertheless, this is in many ways a viable text, and Miss Musgrave has made a great deal of it."

"The last act is full of powerful music, and the whole score, while continuously intersting to the ear, sustains a theatrical grip."

George McElroy/Jane Stedman "Aldeburgh," *Opera News* (October 1974), pp. 56–57

"The dialogue, in free verse and rhymed stanzas, gives Miss Musgrave's inventiveness full scope. The melodic line is firmly wedded to text."

"As (the Countess') voice first blended with, then replaced that of the fading Ariadne, shivers went through the house."

Harold Rosenthal "The Voice of Ariadne," *Opera* (December 1974), 25:1106–1107

> "There is much in it musically which gives great pleasure, not least of all the atmospheric and other-worldly sounds . . . especially effective was the use of electronic tape. . . . Miss Musgrave is a contemporary composer who knows how to write for the human voice without asking her singers to do the impossible."
>
> "Yet like many composers, Miss Musgrave is handicapped by libretto that does not hold up dramatically for three acts. . . . A two-act setting would surely have made the climax to the piece more effective dramatically."

Nicolas Nabokov (1903–1978)

LOVE'S LABOUR'S LOST (VERLOR'NE LIEBESMUH)

Comedy. Three acts, six scenes (120 minutes). Vocal lines disjunct, chromatically complex with frequent meter changes. Many ensembles modeled on the English madrigal.

Libretto by W. H. Auden and Chester Kallman (German by Claus H. Henneberg) from the Shakespeare play. Premiere: Deutsche Oper, Theatre de la Monnaie, Brussels 2.7.73. Performances: Deutsche Oper, West Berlin 9.17.73.

PLOT

Setting: park, palace and grounds in Navarre, sixteenth century.

The King decrees that love shall be against the law, so that his subjects might contemplate higher things. His reluctant Lords finally sign the pact just as the Princess of France arrives with her beauteous entourage to discuss matters of state. The noblemen try to disguise the fact that they have fallen hopelessly in love: the King with the Princess, Berowne with Rosaline, Dumaine with Katherine, and the Spanish guest-at-court, Don Armando, with the maid Jaquenetta. The ladies are not impressed with the near silent welcome nor the poor poetry they receive in secretly delivered letters. Moth, acting as Cupid, the messenger, confounds things by getting the letters mixed up. Now bound together by their illegal quest for love, the men disguise themselves as foreigners in order to pursue their lovers. The women, forewarned by Boyet, really confuse their suitors by adopting their own disguises. The double charade ends when Boyet solemnly announces the death of the Princess' father. With this turn of events, the fact that the women must depart immediately now seems devastating. All is resolved when the women invite the men to woo them again, this time in earnest.

PRODUCTION REQUIREMENTS

Major Roles. PRINCESS OF FRANCE (m-s): A♯2 to A♭4. Ladies attending the Princess: ROSALINE (dram s): B♯2 to C5 and KATHERINE (lyr s): C♯3 to C♯5. KING OF NAVARRE (dram bar): G♯1 to G♭3. Lords attending the King: BEROWNE (high bar): B1 to G♯3 (A3 falsetto) and DUMAINE (t): D2 to C♯4.

Supporting Roles. DON ARMANDO, a Spanish guest (lt bar): A♯1 to G3. JAQUENETTA, a maid (lt s): B♯2 to C5. BOYET, advisor to the Princess (bs): F1 to F♯3. MOTH, Armando's page who symbolizes Cupid (lyr s/a): C3 to A♭4.

Orchestra. 3 fls (3 piccs), 3 obs (Eng hrn), 3 cls (bs cl), 2 bsns (cont bsn), 4 hrns, 3 trps, 3 trbs, tuba, timp, perc (3–10 players), piano, cel, mand, guitar, harp, strings, prerecorded music on tape.

Material. FS–P and VS: Bote & Bock. VS: American Music Center.

REVIEWS

Kenneth Loveland "Brussels," *Musical Times* (April, 1973), 114:411

> "the real mastery of *Love's Labour Lost* is the libretto, on which it is not too much to say that Auden and Kallman have done a Boito job.... what remained was a concise distillation of the play's finest elements—the lyricism, romance and humanity."

John McCann "Belgium: Climax of the Season," *Opera* (April 1973), pp. 24:317–320

> "I suspect that ... Auden and Kallman became overexcited by the musical possibilities of the famous change of mood when the King of France's death is announced.... This opportunity was certainly seized by Nabokov and the last fifteen minutes of the work was undeniably successful as music."

"Nabokov also writes gratefully for the voice and a number of intriguing sounds brighten up the orchestral testure."

James Helme Sutcliffe "West Berlin," *Opera News* (December 8, 1973), pp. 57–58

"(the music) sets off at a jog-trot and never lets up, rhythmically or harmonically, until the solemn finale, sounding like everyone along the way. The librettists have done a fine job of reducing eighteen characters to ten and five acts to six shortish scenes that cry out for more substantial musical treatment."

William Neil (1954–   )

THE GUILT OF LILLIAN SLOAN

Tragic courtroom drama. Two acts, nine scenes (90 minutes). Conservative twentieth-century idiom. Tonal yet chromatic, rhythmically complex, frequent tempo and meter changes. Vocal styles range from declamatory to lyric arioso. Effective ensembles with principals over chorus. No overture, orchestra generally serving as backdrop.

Libretto by Frank Galati. Commissioned by Lyric Opera of Chicago. Premiere: Lyric Opera Center for American Artists 6.6.86.

PLOT

Setting: a London courthouse, prison, etc., 1922.

Owen Evans and Lillian Sloan are found guilty of the murder of her husband, Howard Sloan. The details leading up to this event are told in flashback as Lillian dreams in her prison cell, or takes part in the trial. Lillian remembers her first encounter with the young sailor, Evans; the Solicitor General and the Defense Attorneys each describe the murder; Howard forces himself upon his desolate and unhappy wife; a letter from Lillian to Evans reveals their passionate love affair and their desire to free Lillian from her unhappy marriage. Lillian's mother visits her in prison, where Lillian becomes hysterical and must be sedated. As her mother sings her a lullaby, the trial continues. Lillian is questioned by the Solicitor General and reveals her desire to kill her husband, as well as the commitment from Evans to help her. The Solicitor then relives the night of the murder with Lillian and Evans. The scene comes to a dramatic conclusion when Lillian reveals that it was she, and not Evans, who picked up the knife and murdered her husband. Lillian mourns her failed would-be hero, while Evans expresses shame and guilt over his attempt to make the court believe that he was the murderer. The death sentence turns into a dramatic ritual as the ropes are placed around the lovers' necks, hoods over their heads, and finally, the lights and their lives extinguished.

PRODUCTION REQUIREMENTS

Major Roles. LILLIAN SLOAN (s): B2 to E♭5. OWEN EVANS, Lillian's lover, a young sailor (t): D♭2 to D4. THE SOLICITOR GENERAL (bar): A1 to G♯3.

Supporting Roles. HOWARD SLOAN, Lillian's husband (bs): F1 to D♭3. DEFENSE ATTORNEY SITWELL (t): E♭2 to B3. JUDGE CASSEL (bar): A♭1 to G♭3. LILLIAN'S MOTHER (m-s): B2 to F♯4.

Minor Roles. COURT CLERK (t). THE MATRON (m-s). A NURSE (s).

Chorus. SATB, sometimes separate men's and women's.

Orchestra. fl, cl, ob (Eng hrn), bsn (cont bsn), 2 hrns, trp in C, trb (T/B), celeste, harp, timp, 2 perc, strings.

Material. FS–P and VS: William Neil, 1415 Balmoral Street, Chicago, IL 60640.

REVIEWS

Nancy, Malitz "New Opera sparks new hope," *Detroit News* (June 9, 1986), section B, pp. 1–2

> "The opera begins with the jury delivering its verdict of guilty to some of the most rhythmically aggressive and generally exciting music in the entire show."

> "Whether consciously or unconsciously, Neil's and Galati's debt to Benjamin Britten and Alban Berg was forcefully acknowledged."

> "The texture of Neil's own music during these Act I scenes is also quite thick and homogenous. One would appreciate a few moments of simple lyric abandon like those he so readily provides

in Act 2. . . . Yet it is impossible to deny the essentially attractive musical personality of Neil and the sharp theatrical instincts and poetic ear of Galati."

John von Rhein "Lyric's 'Lillian Sloan' needs more work," *Chicago Tribune* (June 9, 1986), p. 8

"An effective opera certainly could be distilled from such lurid, melodramatic ingredients. But the Galati-Neil narrative, in its present, severely condensed form, leaves the opera almost no room in which to develop."

"The composer writes in a tonal, conservative, mildly dissonant style that does not always exploit the most effective part of the singers' ranges nor guarantee that the vocal lines project intelligibly through the chamber orchestration. There are moments, notably Owen's ballad and the lullaby that Lillian's mother sings to her in prison, when the music almost breaks into real song."

Hall Overton

HUCKLEBERRY FINN

Two acts. Premiere: Juilliard American Opera Center, New York 71.

Material. American Music Center (full score only).

Richard Owen (1922–)

ABIGAIL ADAMS

Historical drama. Two acts and epilogue (75 minutes). Through-composed. Tonal yet chromatic with dissonant harmonies, frequent metric shifts. Recitative-like vocal style throughout with occasional disjunct lines and dissonant skips.

Libretto by the composer from letters of Abigail, John and John Quincy

Adams. Premiere: New York Lyric Opera 3.18.87 (in honor of the Bicentennial of the Constitution of the U.S.A.).

PLOT

Setting: New England and Paris (1762 to 1845).

Through the eloquent and insightful letters of Abigail, John and John Quincy Adams, the personalities, influences and interrelationships between members of this important family in early American history are portrayed. The central figure is Abigail, John's beloved wife and John Quincy's mother. The collage of letters, dating from 1762, when Abigail and John are courting, to 1845, when John Quincy is an old man remembering his past, depicts important events in the protagonists' lives, presented so that they overlap, complement, and explain one another: (1) Abigail and John teach John Quincy to have leadership qualities; (2) John mourns Abigail's mortal illness; (3) Abigail and John decide to marry; (4) John defends the British captain in the Boston massacre trial; (5) Abigail urges John to support women's rights and the independency of the colonies at the Continental Congress; (6) John is appointed Commissioner to France and is accompanied there by John Quincy; and (7) John Quincy's brother, Charlie, dies from excessive drinking. Strong love and honest values support the family members through the difficulties they encounter and the separations they endure while helping to mold the United States.

PRODUCTION REQUIREMENTS

Major Roles. ABIGAIL (s): B2 to C♭5. JOHN ADAMS (t): C2 to B♭3. JOHN QUINCY ADAMS (also REVEREND SMITH, CAPTAIN PRESTON, NATHAN and LOVELL) (bar): G1 to F♯3. JOHNNY (boy s): C3 to G4.

Orchestra. fl, hrn, trp, vln, vcl, timp, piano.

Material. FS–P and VS: Music Associates of America.

REVIEWS

Will Crutchfield "Opera: 'Abigail Adams,' " *New York Times* (March 25, 1987), section 3, p. 18, column 5

> "The opera, which deals mostly with the experiences of our second President and his wife . . . has the great advantage of a good text, the words being mostly drawn from Abigail's own letters."

"The score is firmly rooted in the arioso-parlando idiom that typifies American opera . . . wanting in variety of texture and subtlety of instrumental writing, satisfyingly laid out for the voices. There are several effective touches."

THE DEATH OF THE VIRGIN

Drama with tragic tone. One act, five scenes (50 minutes). Through-composed, in a conservative modern style, with many meter changes. Short orchestral introduction and interludes before each scene. Conversational linear vocal writing with one aria-like section.

Libretto by Michael Straight, based on the Caravaggio painting. Premiere: New York City Lyric Opera Company 3.31.83.

PLOT

Setting: Rome, 1600.

Scene i: Dining room of Cardinal Del Monte; ii: Caravaggio's studio; iii: A Courtroom; iv: A beach on the river Tiber; v: A side Chapel of the Santa Maria della Scala.

The Cardinal boasts about his servant, Caravaggio, the painter, proudly displaying a prestigious commission for an altar painting. However, the artist, involved with his work, refuses his master's summons. Caravaggio is attempting to paint the Cardinal's vision of the Virgin Mary, represented by the barmaid Lena, dressed in velvet and satin, rather than his own, simpler view. The Cardinal confronts Caravaggio for disobeying him, but forgives the artist when he sees the new work. However, when he demands that the Virgin be given a halo, the frustrated painter slashes the canvas. The Cardinal orders Caravaggio to leave, claiming the paintings as his property. Nevertheless, the artist takes one painting with him. When tried for stealing it, Caravaggio denies taking property that is not his. However, Lena returns the work in order to gain the release of the man she loves. Caravaggio accuses her of stealing for the Cardinal and vows never to see her again as he is led away to prison.

Lena's drowned body is brought to the hut of a fisherman. Caravaggio comes to see the body, but denies that her death was his fault. Although disabled by prison, he vows to paint the Virgin from this tired, bloated model. When the finished work, The Death of the Virgin, is presented to Father Pietro and the Brothers as their altarpiece, they cannot comprehend Caravaggio's choice of model, denouncing the decomposed body of the whore who killed herself. After the picture is removed,

Caravaggio turns to thoughts of Lena, remembering her love which inspired him, even in death, to artistic freedom.

PRODUCTION REQUIREMENTS

Major Roles. THE CARDINAL (t): B1 to A3. CARAVAGGIO (bar): B♭1 to G3. LENA (s): C2 to B♭4.

Supporting Roles. THE PRINCE (bar): C2 to E♭3. FIRST FISHERMAN (bar): C2 to E3.

Minor Roles. ANDREA (t or boy s). FATHER PIETRO (t). THE MAGISTRATE (t). BROTHER DOMINIC (bs-bar). BROTHER SEBASTIAN (t). BROTHER FERDINAND (bs-bar). FOUR FISHERMEN (t, t, bar, bar).

Orchestra. 3 fls (picc), 2 obs, 2 cls, 2 bsns, 3 hrns, 2 trps, 3 trbs, harp, timp, perc, cathedral chimes, strings.

Material. FS–P: The Composer (contact AMC for address) VS: American Music Center.

REVIEWS

Robert Jacobson "New York," *Opera News* (June 1983), p. 48

> "Owen's music offers a bevy of cliches and empty string writing, the whole lacking profile or even dramatic tension."

Kurt Saffir "New Argento and Owen Operas Premiered in New York," *The Opera Journal* (1983), 16(2):25–27

> "Mr. Straight's libretto is highly dramatic, consisting of six short scenes full of confrontations, accusations, and denunciations. John Haber's staging and Mr. Harrison's ingenious use of a laterally split stage worked beautifully in combination with realistic acting by all concerned."

> "(Owen's) musical style is a kind of neo-verismo, with restlessy shifting meters and tonalities, frequently dissonant . . . but often marked by long, beautifully arching vocal lines and expressive string writing. . . . Mr. Owen continues an unbroken Italianate chain."

Gregory Sandow "The Unreality Principle," *Village Voice* (April 26, 1983), p. 68

"(Caravaggio) throws fits, slashes paintings, and slaps Lena around only because he's an artist . . . because that's how artists are supposed to act. Baloney—and precisely because the music was an honest and well-crafted response to such a preposterous tale it was baloney, too, full of climatic outbursts too stagey and too much alike."

MARY DYER

Historical fiction. Three acts, nine scenes (full evening). Many orchestral interludes, chromatic vocal lines often doubled by orchestra, frequent meter changes. Vocal writing mostly in recitative style with occasional arias, effective duets, dramatic ensembles.

Libretto by the composer from actual trial manuscripts, diaries and letters. Premiere: Eastern Opera Company and Hudson Valley Philharmonic, Suffern, NY 6.12.76.

PLOT

Setting: New England, 1650s.

Act I, scene i: A square in Boston, June 1654; ii: A Quaker meeting in Rhode Island; iii: In front of the Boston prison; iv: An assembly of the Massachusetts Bay Council. Act II, i: Mary's home in Rhode Island; ii: The governor's chambers; iii: In front of the Boston prison. Act III, i: Boston Common; ii: Mary's cell.

When Anne reports to her Quaker friends in Rhode Island that she has been publicly whipped in Boston for her Quaker beliefs, they resolve to change the laws that endorse such persecution. Christopher goes to speak to the governor, but his words cause him to receive fifty lashes and lose his ear. When Mary addresses the governor, her strong argument is viewed as insolence, and she, too, is imprisoned. Anxious about the increasing opposition to their laws, the governor and council pass a motion which banishes the Quakers from the Commonwealth, on pain of death if they return. Although Mary returns to her home with the understanding that she may not return to Boston, she hears that a Quaker, Robinson, who has refused to leave Boston, is to be hanged. Even her great love for her husband and her home cannot dissuade her from trying to save the man. She returns to Boston to speak in his defense, but is immediately imprisoned. The governor is horrified that she must die. Several women are also outraged that Mary will die and openly protest the shameful decision. Such persecution was the reason that they were forced to come to the colonies; they fear that word of similar persecution will discourage others from coming. The next morning, three women petition the governor to pardon Mary. He is troubled by the open resistance and stops the proceedings until he speaks to her. However, when the governor offers Mary her freedom, she refuses it since he will not repeal the law. When he offers to spare Robinson's life as well, she is torn. However, Robinson has already been led to the gallows and his death strengthens Mary's resolve. Mary is led to the gallows where she is hanged.

PRODUCTION REQUIREMENTS

Major Roles. MARY DYER (s): G♯2 to B4. GOVERNOR JOHN ENDICOTT (bar): A1 to G♭3. MAGISTRATE NORTON (t): C2 to A♭3 [B♭3 opt].

Supporting Roles. ANNE COLEMAN/ABAGAIL CLARK (m-s): B♭2 to A4 (low tess). WILL DYER/SERGEANT (bar): C2 to G3. CAPTAIN WALKER (bar): C2 to F♯3.

Minor Roles. CHRISTOPHER HOLDER/THE CORPORAL (t). Remaining solo roles played by chorus members: 5b, 2t, 2s, 2m-s.

Chorus. SATB

Orchestra. 2 fls (picc), 2 obs, 2 cls, 2 bsns, 2 hrns, 2 trps, 2 trbs, perc, harp, strings.

Material. FS–P and VS: Music Associates of America. VS: American Music Center.

REVIEWS

J. H. "Eastern Opera Co.: 'Mary Dyer,' " *Musical America* (October 1976), 26:23

> "Owen's libretto treats the subject with integrity—it is economical, direct, and devoid of extraneous 'love interest.' The result, however, is a certain glumness and leadenness in the proceedings."

> "Owen's music is also a serious, well-integrated affair, written in a pre-serial, post-Hindemithian vein; but its lack of memorable melodic profile likewise militates against operatic effectiveness."

Delores Koch "Suffern, N.Y.," *Opera News* (September 1976), 41:67–68

> "(Mary Dyer's) Act II solo scene in her cell gave Mr. Owen his most lyrical pages, a soliloquy and prayer for courage. Another

fine passage was the duet between Mary and her husband, Will. . . . Otherwise, there was more action than lyricism in this performance."

Mark "New York," *Music Journal* (September 1976), 34:41

"To get right to the point, Richard Owen's *Mary Dyer* . . . is one of the most noteworthy American operas of recent years."

"Mary Dyer and Governor Endicott . . . are given three-dimensionality, largely because the sophisticated libretto avoids painting anyone in either all black or all white. The scenes . . . are tersely constructed and move forward swiftly, with strong climaxes for each of the three brief acts."

"here is a composer who knows how to flatter the voice—and this is the opera's real strength."

Thomas Pasatieri (1945–)

BEFORE BREAKFAST

Dramatic monologue. One act (40 minutes). Recitative and aria-like passages with overture and orchestral interludes (both prerecorded and live). Prerecorded music represents Victrola playing. Tonally conservative.

Libretto by Frank Corsaro based on the play by Eugene O'Neill. Premiere: New York City Opera 10.9.80.

PLOT

Setting: an apartment, mid-twentieth century.

Failing to wake Alfred, Charlotte nags him for being such an inadequate husband. She puts dancing music on the Victrola and continues to describe her marriage to her poet-husband. They met at a dance marathon and married when she became pregnant. After the wedding, Alfred stayed away for weeks at a time. When the baby was stillborn, he returned, but soon became interested in another woman, Helen. Helen has become pregnant, but Charlotte refuses to get a divorce. She grows hysterical, demanding that Alfred answer her. As she screams into the bedroom, a policeman enters the apartment. Checking the bedroom, he confirms that no one is there. The landlady sadly attributes Charlotte's condition to loneliness.

PRODUCTION REQUIREMENTS

Major Roles. CHARLOTTE (s): C3 to $B^{b}4$.

Minor Roles. POLICEMAN (actor). LANDLADY (actress).

Orchestra. 2 fls, 2 obs, 2 cls, 2 bsns, 2 hrns, 2 trps, 2 trbs, perc (timp), harp, piano, strings.

Material. FS–P and VS: Belwin-Mills. VS: American Music Center.

REVIEWS

Gerald Clarke "Opera is Still Alive in New York," *Time* (October 20, 1980), pp. 86–87

Describes a plot adaptation made at this performance. Charlotte actually runs into the bedroom at the end, to discover that Alfred has cut his throat. She returns with "his blood on her hands."

"It is an intense work, musically and dramatically, and both the composer and the singer make the most of it. Pasatieri's music is pleasing rather than profound, but his lyrical gift is real. . . . The influence of Gian Carlo Menotti is obvious, but in this, his fourteenth opera, Pasatieri speaks nonetheless in a voice all his own."

"There are beautiful swelling orchestral lines in *Before Breakfast,* and a touching, plangent piano solo."

"(Marilyn) Zschau is a fine actress, as well as singer, and her only fault, a major one, alas, is her inability to enunciate clearly all of Corsaro's words."

Alan Rich "Three operas in search of a trash bin," *New York* (November 3, 1980), pp. 90–91

" . . . this deformed off-spring of the over-the-hill Italian *verismo* in which even the requisite minimum of creative technique—how to end a phrase, say, or how to set a line of declamation to a line of melody—cannot be heard."

"... (the) words couldn't be heard because you cannot sing English—and certainly not the logy English of Eugene O'Neill even as smoothed out as in the Frank Corsaro libretto—to the strains of second-hand Mascagni."

MARIA ELENA

One act (70 minutes). Libretto by the composer. Commission and premiere: University of Arizona Opera Theatre, Tucson 4.6.83.

THE SEAGULL

Serious drama. Three acts, four scenes (full evening). Conservative contemporary idiom with lush harmonies. Through-composed with some spoken dialogue as well as set pieces: arias, duets, ensembles. Melodious writing for the voice with the orchestra often doubling the vocal line. Contains overture and orchestral interludes.

Libretto by Kenward Elmslie, based on the play by Anton Chekhov. Commission and premiere: Houston Grand Opera 3.5.74.

PLOT

Setting: the garden of Sorin's estate, 1890s.

Medvedenko, the boring school teacher, begs Masha to marry him, but she does not love him and rejects his offer. Constantine is nervous about his mother, Arkadina's reaction to the premiere of his play, which is to take place that evening. Nina, the girl he loves, is nervous about having to perform before the famous writer, Trigorin. That evening, Arkadina interrupts the performance with remarks and jokes until her humiliated son leaves. When Nina is introduced to Trigorin, they are mutually attracted to each other. As the audience leaves, Masha confesses her love for Constantine to Dr. Dorn. At a picnic, an argument erupts between members of the party. Jealous of Nina's attention to Trigorin, Constantine lays a dead seagull at her feet, threatening to shoot himself. When Trigorin arrives, the dead seagull inspires him to tell Nina a story about a man who destroys a young girl for the hell of it. Several days later, Masha decides to marry Medvedenko, although she is shaken by Constantine's recent suicide attempt. Constantine and Arkadina argue about her lover, Trigorin, whom she defends despite his infatuation with Nina. However, when Trigorin asks to remain longer, Arkadina angrily reveals her jealousy and they agree to leave together. When saying farewell to Nina, Trigorin learns that she will also be leaving for Moscow.

Two years later, Medvedenko and Masha argue about caring for their baby. Constantine and Sorin discuss Nina, who has written desperate letters signed "The Seagull" to Constantine since Trigorin ended their affair. Nina secretly arrives to see Constantine. Both confess that they are still in love: Constantine with Nina, Nina with Trigorin. After she leaves, Constantine burns his manuscripts. While the rest of the party listens to Arkadina describe old acting triumphs, a shot is heard. Dr. Dorn discovers that Constantine has killed himself.

PRODUCTION REQUIREMENTS

Major Roles. IRINA ARKADINA, a famous actress (s): B2 to C5. CONSTANTINE, Arkadina's son (bar): A1 to G3. NINA, a would-be actress (m-s): G♯2 to C5. MASHA, Shamrayeff's daughter (s): B2 to C5. TRIGORIN, Arkadina's lover, a writer (bar): B1 to F♯3 (G3 opt.).

Supporting Roles. SORIN, Arkadina's brother, a semi-invalid bachelor (bs): A1 to E3. MEDVEDENKO, a school teacher (t): E2 to F3.

Minor Roles. SHAMRAYEFF, Sorin's estate manager (bar). PAULINE, Shamrayeff's wife (m-s). DR. DORN, Sorin's Doctor (t).

Mute Roles. YAKOV, a servant; A MAID; OTHER SERVANTS.

Chorus. SATB (offstage).

Orchestra. 2 fls, 2 obs, 2 cls, 2 bsns, 4 hrns, 2 trps, 2 trbs, tuba, timp, perc, harp, strings.

Material. FS–P and VS: Belwin-Mills.

REVIEWS

Peter G. Davis "They love him in Seattle," *New York Times Magazine* (March 21, 1976), pp. 42–42

"*The Seagull,* Pasatieri's most acclaimed score to date, is a comparatively subdued opera. . . . The opera's lyrical, conversational style is a good demonstration of Pasatieri's two strongest suits, his fluent prosody and theatrical cunning."

"Highlights Masha's lyrical outburst at the end of Act I. 'He loves the voice. He never uses it in an instrumental manner,' says Evelyn Mandac, who will sing the title role in *Ines de Castro.*"

Shirley Fleming "Chekhov is set with intensity and the old-fashioned virtues," *Musical America* (June 1974), pp. 32–33

"There are, to be sure, some small, bothersome things in *The Seagull* . . . but the opera as a whole is a warm and communicative work, and the music carried the emotional burden of the play successfully."

Pasatieri uses "obvious devices to make dramatic points . . . luscious harmonies, orchestrations contrived . . . never to interfere with singers . . . and set pieces which provide fine bravura moments for his cast."

"Act I got off to a slow and rather confusing start . . . when nine or ten individuals come onstage and only three of them have a chance to define themselves. [Act I showed] Pasatieri's way of setting cosy little nuggets of familiar sounding music amidst the kind of ongoing Everyman's melody line which keeps the action moving. . . . Act II moved more fluidly. . . . The biggest emotional crescendo of all was reserved for the last act, when Nina and Constantine . . . are reunited briefly for the last time. Their love duet is tender, passionate and searing."

Hubert Saal "Chekhov From the Heart," *Newsweek* (March 18, 1974), p. 75

"In Chekhov's quiet, but tense world, melodramatics take place offstage. . . . what Pasatieri and his librettist . . . have done is to try to bring the subterranean Chekhov to the surface. But Chekhov is made of sturdy stuff and it is Pasatieri's reliance on that, along with his well-placed faith that musical values will pinch-hit for necessary abbreviations, that turns the opera into a splendid success."

"Because he's young, Pasatieri's music often resounds with echoes of Puccini . . . , Strauss . . . , Tchaikowsky, and a disconcerting Hollywood-Broadway penchant for the superficial. . . . Things come too easily for him and Chekhov is sometimes . . . tenderized, melodramatized."

SIGNOR DELUSO

Opera buffa. One act (30 minutes). Tonal, conservative musical style. Set numbers (arias, duets, ensembles), although orchestral texture appears to be continuous. No overture.

Libretto by the composer, based on Moliere's *Sganarelle.* Premiere: Wolf Trap Company, Greenway, Virginia 7.27.74.

PLOT

Setting: a public place in a small town outside of Paris.

A comic mix-up, where each character accuses his love of being unfaithful with someone else. Celie leaves Gorgibus' house crying that she will never marry Valere, because she loves Leon, whose picture she carries in her locket. When she faints, dropping the locket, Rosine, the maid, enlists Deluso to watch Celie as she rushes off to get help. When Deluso's wife, Clara, peers out of the window, just in time to see Deluso holding Celie in his arms, she instantly suspects her husband of being unfaithful. Clara runs outside to catch Deluso in the act. In the meantime, Deluso carries Celie into her own house. While Clara bemoans the faithlessness of husbands, she finds the locket Celie had dropped. Just then, Deluso enters and sees his wife gazing at the handsome young man's picture in the locket. He quickly decides that she must be unfaithful and runs after her. Leon enters, still hopeful about winning Celie's hand. But his hopes are dashed when Deluso enters carrying the locket, claiming that he got Leon's portrait from his wife. Leon assumes that he is indeed too late, that Celie has married Deluso. Meanwhile, Deluso accuses Leon of amorous intrigues. To complete the circle, Celie asks Deluso if he knows that young man, and Deluso answers that he is in love with his wife. Thinking she has been rejected, Celie agrees to marry Valere. The ensemble gathers with accusation from all sides. Rosine brings the nonsense to a halt, clearing up the mess for a happy conclusion.

PRODUCTION REQUIREMENTS

Major Roles. CELIE (s): D♯3 to B4. SIGNOR DELUSO (bar): B♭1 to F3 (F♯ opt). CLARA (s): B2 to G♯4. LEON (t): E♭2 to A♭3.

Supporting Roles. GORGIBUS (bs-bar), TOWN MAGISTRATE (bs-bar): both of these roles may be performed by the same singer. ROSINE (m-s).

Orchestra. fl (picc). ob (Eng hrn), cl in B♭, hrn in F, vln, vla, vcl, piano.

Material. FS–P and VS: Belwin-Mills.

REVIEWS

Donal Henahan "Pasatieri's 'Signor Deluso' Shares Bill With Holst Work at Theatre Club," *New York Times* (December 11, 1974), p. 57, column 1

> "*Signor Deluso* . . . is a good example of Mr. Pasatieri's facility and professionalism. Unfortunately, it is also a good example of a composer who has decided to aim at commercially safe targets. The musical style might be characterized as simplified Puccini, and the approach to comedy—the fatigued opera buffa tradition."

Robert Jacobson "Vienna, Va.," *Opera News* (October 1974), p. 50

> "A delightful contemporary comic opera entered the ranks with the world premiere of . . . *Signor Deluso* . . . thirty minutes of comic concision and captivating music."

THREE SISTERS

Tragicomedy. One act, two scenes, one set (105 minutes). Through-composed syllabic, conversational style links lyrical arias, duets, ensembles. Vocal lines are tonal, yet chromatic with disjunct leaps. Orchestra often doubles the vocal line. Folk-like themes unify the work.

Libretto by Kenward Elmslie, based on the play by Anton Chekhov. Premiere: Opera/Columbus, Ohio 3.13.86. Recordings: Battery Records, PS1333 (2), 74-09 37th Ave. Jackson Heights, N.Y. 11372.

PLOT

Setting: small town in Russia, around 1900.

Three intelligent, cultured sisters stagnate in a small town far from their native Moscow. Since the death of their parents, dreams of the life they had hoped for color all their decisions and activities. When their brother, Andrei, marries the shrewd, uneducated Natasha, the sisters condescendingly ridicule her. In their daily lives, the sisters are frustrated by loneliness and worthlessness: Olga as a teacher, Irina as a worker, and Masha as a wife. Olga plans a move back to Moscow, Masha has an affair with Vershinin, and Irina agrees to marry the Baron. But, as their apathy increases, their control over their lives decreases: Natasha takes over their home; Olga is tied down as headmistress of her school; Vershinin must leave the town and Masha; and Irina's fiance is killed in a duel. Overwhelmed by failure, they cling to one another for support, mourning their wasted, lonely lives.

PRODUCTION REQUIREMENTS

Major Roles. MASHA (s): A2 to C5. IRINA (s): B♭2 to C5. OLGA (m-s): A♭2 to A4. ANDREI, brother to the three sisters (bar): A1 to A3. NATASHA, Andrei's wife (s): B♭2 to C5. THE BARON, Irina's fiance (t): D2 to B♭3. VERSHININ, Masha's lover (bar): A1 to G3 [A♭3 opt]. NANNA (m-s): G2 to F4.

Supporting Roles. FYODOR, Masha's husband (t): E♭2 to G3. CHEBUTKIN, doctor friend of the sisters (bs): G1 to D♯3. SOLYONY, admirer of Irina (bs): F1 to D♯3.

Minor Roles. YAKOV (t) and VLADIMIR (t), friends of the sisters.

Mute Roles. SELMA, the maid.

Chorus. Small SATB.

Orchestra. 2 fls (picc), 2 obs (Eng hrn), 2 cls (bs cl), 2 bsns (cont bsn), 4 hrns, 2 trps, 2 trbs, tuba, perc, timp, harp, strings.

Material. FS–P and VS: Belwin-Mills.

REVIEWS

Marajean Marvin "Pasatieri Premiere in Columbus," *Opera Journal* (1986), 19(2):23–27

> "There was no lack of lyrical moments of expansion for the arias, yet these did not sacrifice the dramatic motion, except in the last scene. Here the action moved from one introspective aria to another, giving one the feeling of having suddenly wandered into the world of *opera seria.*"
>
> "Pasatieri's music. . . . is at its best in the arias, particularly that of Olga which opens the last scene, and in the trios of the sisters."
>
> "The fire described by Nana . . . and the duel which takes place offstage in the final scene are so much a part of the general texture that one is not aware of these as important events. . . . The most exciting music was the property of the sister-in-law, Natascha."

Barbara Zuck "Columbus," *Opera News* (June 1986), p. 34

"Elmslie's libretto soars poetically through Chekhov's bleak domestic drama, preserving its ensemble character, maintaining the essence of its fatalistic plot. . . . Chekhov, however, lacks theatrical grandeur and denies the audience any catharsis at the close."

"Pasatieri's emotional style brims with lyricism and lush orchestration, complete with Pucciniesque doublings of the vocal line. Even with its updated dissonances and chromaticism, devotees of nineteenth-century opera should find the score palatable."

"One of Pasatieri's talents is character portrayal, so it is especially disappointing that he failed to allow the individual self-expression of the major characters to be developed in more memorable arias and ensembles."

WASHINGTON SQUARE

Tragedy. Three acts and epilogue (110 minutes). Music is tonal at times and atonal at others. Each scene through-composed. Contains dialogue, arias, trios, and duets. Brief prelude to Act I. Melodious vocal lines with orchestra frequently doubling the voice. Traditional recitative sections patterned after speech.

Libretto by Kenward Elmslie, based on the novel by Henry James. Commissioned by the Michigan Opera Theatre. Premiere: Michigan Opera Theatre 10.1.76. Performances: New York Lyric Opera Company 10.13.77 (revised); Augusta Opera Company 3.79.

PLOT

Setting: nineteenth century.

Act I, scene i: Garden of the Harrington House; ii: A carriage; iii: Parlor of the Sloper House; iv: The front hall; v: Parlor; vi: Front hall, then Parlor. Act II, i and ii: Parlor; iii: Front hall, then Parlor; iv: Parlor. Act III, i: Balcony in Venice and Dr. Sloper's study; ii: Catherine's bedroom and Front hall; iii and Epilogue: Parlor.

Morris attracts Dr. Sloper's attention by his interest in the doctor's shy daughter, Catherine. The doctor invites the young suitor to dinner, but his brusque rebuff causes Morris to leave angrily. When Catherine and Morris tell her father about their decision to marry, the men argue and the doctor refuses to give his approval. The doctor harangues Morris' sister until she admits that her brother is shallow and selfish, warning the doctor to prevent the marriage. Catherine agrees to delay the wedding until she and her father return from a European tour. Morris urges Catherine to win her father's approval during the trip.

In Venice, Dr. Sloper angrily turns on Catherine after reading a letter she has received from Morris, causing her to realize that her father never loved her. When they return home, Morris learns that the doctor is still against the marriage and abruptly leaves. When Catherine finally understands that she has been jilted, she resolves to be free of manipulative men and to rely solely on herself. Twenty years later Morris returns, fat and balding, to ask her to forget the past. Catherine serenely spurns his advances.

PRODUCTION REQUIREMENTS

Major Roles. CATHERINE SLOPER (s): $B^{b}2$ to C4. Catherine's father, DR. AUSTIN SLOPER (bs-bar): A1 to F3. The Sloper's housekeeper, LAVINIA DAVENPORT (m-s): $G^{b}2$ to $F^{\#}4$. MORRIS TOWNSEND (bar): C2 to $A^{b}3$.

Supporting Roles. ELIZABETH HARRINGTON (m-s). MARIAN HARRINGTON (s): A2 to C4. ARTHUR TOWNSEND (t or bar), Morris' sister, MRS. MONTGOMERY (s).

Orchestra. fl (picc), ob (Eng hrn), cl in B^{b} (bs cl), bsn (cont bsn), hrn in F, trp in B^{b}, trb, piano (cel), harp, strings, perc.

Material. FS–P and VS: Belwin Mills.

REVIEWS

John Harvey "Michigan Opera Theatre: Pasatieri's Washington Square," *Musical America* (January 1977), pp. 21–22

" . . . details such as these [phrasing, orchestration, etc.] attest to Pasatieri's skill in musico-dramatic construction, and his ability to reveal the essential attributes of his characters. Considered by itself, however, his music impressed more with its facility than its depth."

Robert Jacobson "Detroit," *Opera News* (December 4, 1976), pp. 57–58

" . . . the public, not exactly weaned on contemporary opera, reacted with rapt attention and ovations, and it was obvious the new piece exercised great appeal . . . In the scoring for fifteen players, textures are kept lucid and generally delicate even in big climaxes, but often there is not enough instrumental weight to achieve what the composer was after."

Alan Rich "Music and Dance," *New York* (November 7, 1977), pp. 82–84

" . . . his mucilaginous music ozzes through and around the text, defining no characters, lending no outline to any possible dramatic situation. Of musical shaping there is none; pieces and whole scenes do not end, they merely stop."

Oliver W. Roosevelt "Augusta Op.: Washington Square," *Musical America* (May 1979), p. 23

In the orchestration, "built-in problems of voices versus brass sometimes created problems. If Pasatieri is weak in this regard, he is masterful in shaping his music to word rhythms; the vocal lines are not always easy, but they always have a natural quality."

" . . . the Catherine Sloper role is inhibited through most of the opera. It all comes together, though, in that remarkable singing *tour de force* at the end of Act III, when Catherine finds freedom from mens' dominion."

Stephen Paulus (1949–)

THE POSTMAN ALWAYS RINGS TWICE

Classic tragedy in a contemporary setting. Two acts (130 minutes). Set pieces linked by conversational vocal writing. Vocal style varies from "parlando" to chromatic and disjunct to melodic. Several orchestral interludes.

Libretto by Colin Graham, based on novel by James M. Cain. Commissioned by Opera Theatre of St. Louis. Premiere: Opera Theatre of St. Louis 6.17.82. Performances: Fort Worth Opera 3.1.85; Minnesota Opera 10.31.87; Greater Miami Opera 3.14.88.

PLOT

Setting: California, 1934.

A series of flashbacks tell the story of the ill-fated lovers as Frank awaits execution for killing Cora. The young hobo, Frank, comes to work for Nick Papadakis, owner of a gas station-diner. The attraction between Frank and Cora, Nick's discontented wife, is apparent immediately. As in a Greek tragedy, the two obsessed lovers are destined to doom. Cora convinces Frank that getting rid of her unsuspecting husband, Nick, will solve their problems. They clumsily stage a car crash in which Nick appears to have been killed. The murder charges are dropped, because the corrupt lawyers and police see an opportunity to cash in on the settlement of Nick's life insurance policy. But the lovers are not really free. Their life together is filled with distrust and haunted by Nick's ghostly voice. When Cora reveals that she is pregnant, the lovers attempt to regain the love they had once had. Ironically, Frank takes her for a drive, and Cora is killed. Although this crash may, indeed, have been an accident, Frank is sentenced to death for Cora's murder.

PRODUCTION REQUIREMENTS

Major Roles. Frank Chambers (bar): A1 to G3. Cora Papadakis (sop): A♭2 to A4 (B4 opt).

Supporting Roles. Nick Papadakis (t): C♯2 to C4. Sackett (bs): F♯1 to D3. Katz (t): C♯2 to B4.

Minor Roles. Cop (bar). Kennedy (actor).

Orchestra. 2 fls (picc), ob, cl in B♭, alto sax in E♭, bsn, hrn in F, 2 trps in B♭, trb, t/bs trb, timp (perc), perc, guitar, harp, piano, strings (8–6–4–4–2).

Material. FS–P and VS: European American Music Corp. VS: American Music Center.

REVIEWS

Michael Anthony "St. Paul," *Opera News* (March 28, 1987), pp. 38–39

> "Tasteless but apt—Cain's novel is more about lust than love. Still, the production . . . failed to have the impact it might have had. There are terror and violence in this story, too."

"What finally emerged was the strength of the work itself. Perhaps because Graham is a seasoned stage director, his libretto is a demonstration of what works, while Paulus' canny score never wastes a note."

Harold Blumenfeld "THE ST. LOUIS SEASON," *The Opera Journal* (1982), 15(4):19–22

"Graham's extraordinary 'Postman' libretto conveys its tawdry tale of amoral lovers with brilliant structure and relentless cinematic flow."

"the libretto masters the tricky matter of taking down-in-the-mouth, naked Depression vernacular and shaping it . . . into language the lyricism of which exceeds the sum of its words."

Michael Fleming "Fort Worth," *Opera News* (June 1985), pp. 36–37

"For this run, the composer trimmed the score, resulting in a tauter work than was heard at the 1982 premiere. . . . The genre scenes had the greatest impact: the wailing saxophone solo . . . the fragments of the rinky-tink piano."

Donal Henahan "Opera: 'Postman Always Rings Twice' in St. Louis," *New York Times* (June 20, 1982), p. 50

"most of the musically interesting ideas come from the pit, where the scoring is invariably expert and sometimes exceptionally imaginative."

"Dramatically, if not musically, the most gripping moments come in confrontations between the two lawyers. . . . They fall into a vaudeville dance number that is hilariously done."

Donal Henahan "Musings on An Anthem, A Libretto and A Festival," *New York Times* (July 4, 1982), section 2, p. 15

"(Paulus) had to deal, however, with a lumpish, unsingable libretto by Colin Graham that emphasized the story's most pedestrian aspects."

Andrew Porter "American Verismo," *New Yorker* (August 2, 1982), pp. 80–82

"The words of the libretto are in large part drawn from those of the book. . . . The amplifications needed for songs, arias, and other set pieces are deftly written."

"He brings Act I to an effective climax. The scene is strong in itself. . . . Paulus's music makes the scene stronger still."

"The Cora-Frank duets of Act II, which should carry the emotional burden of the drama, don't really get off the ground. Their music is aspirant but thin. . . . But it's intelligently and carefully worked."

THE VILLAGE SINGER

Bittersweet short story. One act, five scenes (60 minutes). Prelude. Through-composed with dialogue, duets, ensembles, arias. Traditional hymns as well as traditional sounding melodies used to reflect culture and time frame. Tonal, melodious vocal lines as well as use of bitonality in juxtaposition of hymns.

Libretto by Michael Dennis Browne, based on a story by Mary Wilkins Freeman. Commissioned for the Opera Theatre of St. Louis by the New Music Circle of St. Louis. Premiere: Opera Theatre of St. Louis 6.9.79.

PLOT

Setting: a New England village, circa 1900.

The members of Candace Whitcomb's church choir, where she has been the paid soloist for forty years, surprise Candace with a party at her cottage next to the church. Amidst the festivities, Candace and William Emmons, who has been her choir director and suitor all these years, even sing a song together. After the bravos, William and the choir members gather up their things, seeming somewhat nervous, and discreetly leave a photo album on Candace's table. When Candace finds the album, she delightedly reminisces in her rocking chair. She finally finds a note in the back of the album from William, thanking her for her forty years of service and concluding that the young singer, Miss Alma Way, is now available, and that Candace's services will no longer be required. Candace is shocked, especially because Alma is her nephew Wilson's fiance.

On the Sunday morning following the party, the church windows are open as Reverend Pollard signals the nervous Alma to move forward for her solo. Suddenly, from the parlor organ in her cottage, Candace begins singing her own solo—a different hymn tune in another key. The choir members crane in disbelief toward the church windows that are next to Candace's cottage. After the service, Reverend Pollard goes to speak with Candace. He comes right to the point about the matter of her singing a bit loudly this morning while their church service was going on next door. But Candace's wounded pride makes her repeat her performance during the afternoon church service anyway. As the church fades from view, Candace's nephew, Wilson, is seen hurrying towards the cottage threatening to pitch her organ out the window. Candace angrily responds that Wilson will not get a cent of her money, and will not be able to marry that Alma Way without it. Candace suddenly feels very ill. After Wilson runs out, she drags herself off to bed. Three weeks later, Candace's sister, Nancy, tearfully moans that Candace lies there like a repentant soul just waiting. Candace finally agrees to see William and Reverend Pollard. Both Candace and William immediately apologize to each other; he for not being straight with her, she for her pride. Nancy brings in her son, Wilson, and Alma. Candace tells Wilson that she didn't change her will and asks Alma to sing for her. Alma tenderly sings, but Candace gets the last word by telling Alma she flatted a little on the last note, "soul." Resting peacefully at last, Candace hears a choir in the distance.

PRODUCTION REQUIREMENTS

Major Roles. Candace Whitcomb, a woman in her sixties (s): B2 to B4. Alma Way, engaged to Candace's nephew (s): D3 to C♯5. William Emmons, choir director in his sixties (bar): E♭2 to E♭3.

Supporting Roles. Wilson Ford, Candace's nephew (t): E♭2 to G♯3. The Reverend Pollard (t): D2 to A♭3.

Minor Roles. Choir members: Minnie Lansing (s); Jenny Carr (m-s); Nancy Ford, Candace's sister (m-s); Todd Wilkins (t); Brent Freeman (bs).

Chorus. SATB (made up of characters listed above).

Orchestra. 2 fls, ob, 2 cls in B♭, bsn, hrn in F, perc, timp, harp, piano (elec org), strings (5–4–3–2–1).

Material. FS–P and VS: European American Music. VS: American Music Center.

REVIEWS

Harold Blumenfeld "A Stunning Young Company," *Opera* (August 1979), pp. 764–765

> "Paulus's score is as conservative as it is well-crafted, and its general tone lies somewhere between Copland's *Tender Land* and the recent work of another Minneapolitan, his teacher and mentor, Dominick Argento (*The Last Voyage of Edgar Allan Poe,* 1977)."

> "Paulus's predilection for bitonal procedures is given full rein in his cacophonously Ivesian setting of Candace's first musical confrontation with the church choir. The young composer handles most of his tricky ensemble situations with skill and a strong sense of timing."

Andre Porter "Prima Donna," *New Yorker* (June 25, 1979), pp. 96–97

> "What was striking about *The Village Singer* (Paulus's first opera) is how little its composer still has to learn about dramatic timing, balancing musical forms and theatrical discourse, creating melodic curves that reveal character or convey emotion, and other specifically operatic skills. His score is at once fresh and masterly."

> "It is a good subject for musical treatment, since it can be vividly realized in musical terms, and a fine subject for an American opera with a universal theme and particularity of setting and local color."

> When the hymn tunes are juxtaposed, "one hymn is in 4/4 and the other in 3/4, but the quarter notes march at the same tempo, and the result is controlled (not by chance) cacophony. All Paulus' score is marked by command of harmonic tension that defines the dramatic tensions."

THE WOODLANDERS

Three acts. Libretto by Colin Graham based on Thomas Hardy's novel. Premiere; Saint Louis Opera Theatre 6.13.85.

Cole Porter (1891–1967)

KISS ME KATE

Comedy. Two acts, sixteen scenes (full evening). Musical theater with jazz and dance rhythms. Vocal parts require quasi-recitative sections, cadenzas for Kate.

Libretto by Sam and Bella Spewack after Shakespeare's "Taming of the Shrew." Premiere: New York 12.30.48. Recordings: Columbia OC, Capitol OC (1953); Chilton (1973).

PLOT

Setting: backstage and onstage, Ford's Theatre, Baltimore, during one evening's tryout of the musical version of "The Taming of the Shrew."

The egotistical producer, Fred Graham, and Lilli Kanessi, his firy ex-wife, act out scenes from the play onstage, but behind the scenes they fight, make up, and eventually show their lasting affection, just like the characters they play, Shakespeare's Kate and Petruchio. Lois Lane and Bill Calhoun also carry on a bit of backstage romance, complicated by Bill's gambling habits.

PRODUCTION REQUIREMENTS

Major Roles. FRED GRAHAM/PETRUCHIO (bar): B♭1 to F3. LILLI KANESSI/KATHERINE (m-s/s): C3 to B♭4 (strong low notes required, as well as operatic cadenzas). LOIS LANE/BIANCA (a): F♯2 to F4. HARRY TREVOR/BAPTISTA (actor, chorus). HATTIE (a): B♭2 to G4 [A4 opt].

Supporting Roles. HORTENSIO (t): C2 to A♭3. GREMIO (bar): C2 to F3. LUCENTIO (bar): C2 to F3. PAUL (bar): B1 to E3. BILL (bar): C2 to E3. TWO GANGSTERS (bars): B1 to E3.

Minor Roles. HABERDASHER, RALPH, STAGE DOORMAN, HARRISON HOWELL, SPECIALTY DANCERS.

Chorus. SATB (14).

Ballet. Dance ensemble (14).

Orchestra. ww #1: cl/alt sax/fl, ww #2: cl/alt sax/bs cl, ww #3: cl/t sax/

ob/Eng hrn, ww #4: cl/t sax/fl/picc, ww #5: cl/bar sax/bsn, fr hrn, 3 trps, trb, perc, harp, piano (cel), guitar (mand), strings.

Material. FS–P and VS: Tams-Witmark Music Library.

Jay Reise (1950–   )

RASPUTIN

Historical fiction. Two acts, eight scenes (full evening). Chromatic, often dissonant style. Voice parts rhythmically and chromatically difficult, some sprechstimme. Orchestra plays important role, often with more complex and demanding writing than vocal roles.

Libretto by the composer with collaboration by Frank Corsaro. Commission and premiere: The New York City Opera 9.17.88.

PLOT

Setting: dawn of the Russian revolution, 1917.

The monk, Rasputin, professed servant of Church and State, seethes with designs for power and conquest. He controls the minds of his devout followers, turning them against the Tsar's choice for head of churchly affairs, the monk Iliodor. Rasputin goes to Moscow himself, quickly winning the trust of Tsaritsa Alexandra. The weak Tsar Nicholas is wracked with indecision. But Rasputin calms an angry mob and magically stops the bleeding of the Tsar's hemopheliac infant son (when even Dr. Sokolsky's attempts fail). Thus, Tsar Nicholas succumbs to Rasputin's powers, much to the chagrin of his cousins and advisors, Prince Felix Yusupov and the Grand Duke Dmitry Pavlivich (homosexual lovers).

Russia, now devastated by World War I, tires of the Tsar's ineffectual rule, and turns to new leaders such as Lenin. More than ever, Nicholas and Alexandra look to Rasputin for help. But, following Yusupov's performance as drag queen at a cabaret, his friend Dr. Sokolsky commits suicide, having been recently fired and replaced by Rasputin. Yusupov swears vengeance for his friend's suicide. He goes to the monk's apartment only to find Rasputin with a harem of ladies—among them Irina, Yusupov's wife. Yusupov and his hired thug, Smerdsky, fall upon Rasputin and beat him, but Rasputin intimidates Smerdsky. Yusupov, too, succumbs to Rasputin's hypnotic powers.

Seeing the royal couple caught helplessly in these hypnotic powers, Yusupov tries again to murder the monk. Yet heavy doses of poison do not fell the powerful man. Yusupov finally pulls a revolver and shoots Rasputin point-blank. When his accomplices, Dmitry, Smerdsky and General Zhevadov enter from hiding, Rasputin rises again. But the four men throw Rasputin from the window to his death. Rasputin's final screams hail the coming of a new Russia, as mobs pass by bearing banners of revolution. Chaos overtakes the stage—a last flash of gunfire reveals the execution of the Imperial family.

PRODUCTION REQUIREMENTS

Major Roles. RASPUTIN (bs-bar): F1 to F♯3 (D3 to E♭4 fals). TSARITSA ALEXANDRA (s): B2 to C5. PRINCE FELIX YUSUPOV, cousin and advisor to the Tsar (t): C♯2 to B3 (G♯3 to D4 fals).

Supporting Roles. TSAR NICHOLAS II (t): D2 to B3. GRAND DUKE DMITRY PAVLOVICH, advisor to Tsar and Yusupov's lover (bar): D2 to E3.

Minor Roles. DR. SOKOLSKY, physician to the royal family (t). GENERAL ZHEVADOR (bs). ILIODOR, a monk/SMERDSKY, cowardly thug employed by Yusupov (buf t) (two may be same singer).

Speaking Roles. LENIN. STAGE MANAGER.

Bit Roles. PRINCESS IRINA YUSUPOV (c). 2 MESSENGERS (t,t).

Chorus. SATB with divisi, especially among women's voices (SSSSAATB at times). Men's chorus in drag (Act II).

Dance. Yusupov and men's chorus dance cabaret number.

Orchestra. 3 fls, 3 obs, 3 cls, 3 bsns, 4 hrns, 3 trps, 3 trbs, bs tuba, timp, perc, piano, harp, celeste, strings.

Material. FS–P and VS: T. Presser.

REVIEWS

Thor Eckert Jr. "New York City," *Opera News* (December 10, 1988), p. 48

> "Reise has concentrated on the extroverted aspects for his erratic score and flimsy libretto. One gets orgies, murder and mayhem but little characterization."

"There are effective moments, though puzzlingly, Rasputin's bizarre murder . . . is not among them. The seething maelstrom that closes the opera, with the orchestra rising to a hellish crescendo, is. Reise lavishes on Alexandra his finest melodic and characterizational efforts. Otherwise, the blending of pastiche-Russian idiom with an encroaching serialistic undercurrent does not jell into a gripping whole."

Herbert Kupferberg "New York," *Musical America* (January 1989), pp. 43–44

"The work has a strong historical background, plenty of dramatic confrontations, a couple of orgies, a bizarre transvestite scene, and some memorable, if not admirable, characters. In fact, it has just about everything, except music of inspiration and individuality."

"Nevertheless, Reise . . . is a composer of skill and resourcefulness. He knows how to knit together a score that ranges through romanticism, atonalism, and minimalism, not to mention jazz, ragtime, and a charming takeoff on a Tchaikovsky waltz. What's missing is any real creativity, originality, or musical character, although, thanks to the weird story and the many excellences of the cast . . . the dramatic impact of *Rasputin* is considerable."

George Rochberg (1918–   )

THE CONFIDENCE MAN

Moral drama. Prologue, two acts, and epilogue; sixteen scenes; one set (150 minutes). Mostly tonal music with occasional atonal passages. No overture, long recitatives join some set pieces: melodious arias and duets, ensembles, and choruses.

Libretto by Gene Rochberg, based on the novel by Herman Melville. Commissioned by Santa Fe Opera. Premiere: Santa Fe Opera 8.82.

PLOT

Setting: mid-nineteenth century, a riverboat town.

When the Confidence Man is unable to con a skeptical audience into buying his wares, he tells them the story of China Aster, the candlemaker. China and Annabella bemoan their lack of money, although they are happily in love. When Orchis generously offers China a thousand dollars of his newly won money, Annabella takes the offer as a joke. However, Orchis writes a check to China, which the candlemaker hesitantly agrees to repay in four years. Despite warnings from Annabella and other friends against accepting the money, The Angel of Bright Future seduces China with dreams of wealth and convinces him to cash the check.

A year later, Orchis returns to collect the money. When China confesses that he has no money, Orchis orders him to repay the loan in three days. China despondently sees death in his future. On the due date, a minstrel show is interrupted by China, chased by creditors. When he falls dead to the ground, Annabella cries that he was worthy of love rather than destruction. His epitaph reminds men that free indulgence of trust has destroyed him, in the form of a friendly loan. The Confidence Man is left to convince people to trust their fellowmen.

PRODUCTION REQUIREMENTS

Major Roles. THE CONFIDENCE MAN (bar): $A^{\flat}1$ to $F^{\sharp}3$ (A3 falsetto). CHINA ASTER (t): C2 to B3 (C3 opt). ORCHIS (t): B1 to $A^{\flat}3$. ANNABELLA, China Aster's wife (s): D3 to $C^{\sharp}5$. THE ANGEL OF BRIGHT FUTURE (s): $C^{\sharp}3$ to E5.

Supporting Roles. OLD PLAIN TALK (bs): B1 to $E^{\sharp}3$. OLD PRUDENCE (bs): E1 to E3. THE BARBER (t): $B^{\flat}1$ to $B^{\flat}3$.

Minor Roles. MRS. ORCHIS (m-s). A YOUNGER PEDDLER (t). THE MISSOURIAN (bs). A MINISTER (bs). AVATAR NO. 1 (t). AVATAR NO. 2 (bar). AVATAR NO. 3. (bs). MINSTREL SHOW PLAYERS: BLUEBEARD (bs), GRIPSACK (t), FATEEMA (t), MAFAIRY (bs), BEPPO (bar), GREPPO (bar).

Chorus. Townspeople and travelers.

Orchestra. 3 fls (picc), 3 obs (Eng hrn), 3 cls, 3 bsns (cont bsn), 4 hrns, 3 trps, 3 trbs, 1 tuba, harp, cel, perc, timp, strings.

Material. FS–P and VS: Theodore Presser. VS: American Music Center.

REVIEWS

Peter G. Davis "Lost in the desert," *New York* (August 23, 1982), pp. 79–80

"Rochberg is nothing if not a masterly technician — but, . . . no composer can help himself to so much borrowed goods and keep his identity and integrity intact."

Donal Henahan "Focusing on The Vexing Libretto Problem," *New York Times* (August 15, 1982), section 2, p. 15

"It takes away Melville's bleak vision and gives us nothing in its stead but cherry homily."

"There are many splendid musical ideas in the score that might be enhanced by pruning and grafting of the libretto . . . a tightening of the interminable recitatives might be the first step."

Donal Henahan "Opera: Melville's 'Confidence Man' in Santa Fe," *New York Times* (August 2, 1982), section 3, p. 14

"Mr. Rochberg's score . . . is for the most part tonal, though at times as vocally rigorous as the most serious modernist might demand."

"The major figure often evoked . . . is Verdi. The . . . score bounces and tumbles along in the manner of 'Falstaff,' . . . much of the lyric interest to be heard in the orchestra."

"The obsession with telling the story results in a boring kind of barked parlando, seldom relieved by anything like a lyrical episode."

Robert Jacobson "Santa Fe," *Opera News* (November 1982), p. 38

"Melville's vignette became stretched to interminable length. . . . but with a muddled basic philosophic overview and un-Melvillian moral that failed to satisfy the emotions or the brain."

"Characters have little sense of motivation . . . and cannot engage our interest or sympathies, no matter how hard the composer tries with his . . . lushly eclectic, highly tonal score . . . which offers skillful orchestration and some splendid vocal lines."

Andrew Porter "A Frail Bark," *New Yorker* (August 16, 1982), pp. 66–68

Discussion of Melville's book with references to critiques of that work.

"the opera is largely a reworking of ideas that other, better composers—Walton, Britten, Kurt Weill, Stephen Foster, Mozart, Menotti, Mahler, Sigmund Romberg, Pierre Boulez—have put to more effective and generally, more responsible use."

Patrick J. Smith "Rochberg's 'The Confidence Man'," *Musical America* (November 1982), pp. 30–31

"Although he now and then constructs acceptable set pieces, such as the . . . first act chorus (a la *Peter Grimes*) and uses short motifs as building blocks for effective moments, the heterogeneousness of the writing, and its inability to hold to a dramatic thread is everywhere evident."

Michael Walsh "In Santa Fe, a Worthy Failure," *Time* (August 16, 1982), p. 64

"The opera is filled with striking set pieces: a lyrical duet for China and his wife Annabella; an ominous interview between China and his moneyed friend, Orchis, whose threatening nature is underlined by a snap-pizzicato line in the low strings; a good-natured bibulous ensemble lauding the joys of wine. In his handling of choruses, Rochberg is especially skillful; indeed the final chorus . . . recalls the Falstaffian spirit of Verdi. . . . Ultimately, though, these isolated moments are not enough to make 'The Confidence Man' into a coherent operatic whole."

"The quality of Rochberg's lyric invention is high and the fast-moving sequences, such as the minstrel show, are handled with dashing technical assurance. . . . The two scenes with the angel . . . display a strong command of modern musical materials."

Richard Rodgers (1902–1979)

THE BOYS FROM SYRACUSE

Comedy. Two acts (full evening). Fanfares give pseudo Ancient Greek atmosphere, but music generally jazzy; i.e., "Andrews sisters" trio, burlesque dance. Extensive ballet music.

Lyrics by Lorenz Hart, book by George Abbott, based on "The Comedy of Errors" by Shakespeare. Premiere: Alvin Theatre, N.Y. 11.23.38. Performances: Off-Broadway revival 63. Recordings: Columbia SC, Capitol OC (1963).

PLOT

Setting: Ephesus, Ancient Asia Minor.

Antipholus and his servant, Dromio, arrive from Syracuse to find their long lost twins who have the same names. Aegeon, father of the Antipholus twins, is hunting for his sons as well. The wives of the Ephesians, Adriana and her servant, Luce, mistake the boys from Syracuse for their husbands, causing much confusion. But when Adriana's sister, Luciana, admits that she loves Antipholus, of Syracuse, that is, the confusion is eventually sorted out.

PRODUCTION REQUIREMENTS

Major Roles. ANTIPHOLUS OF SYRACUSE (bs-bar): A1 to F3. ANTIPHOLUS OF EPHESUS (bar): E^b2 to F3. ADRIANA, Antipholus of Ephesus' wife (s): B^b2 to B^b4. LUCIANA, Adriana's sister (m-s): B^b2 to G4. LUCE, Adriana's servant (a): A^b2 to E^b4. DROMIO OF SYRACUSE, Antipholus' servant (bar): A^b1 to E^b3. DROMIO OF EPHESUS, servant (bar): C2 to F3.

Supporting Roles. SERGEANT (bar): C2 to G3. AEGEON (bar): D2 to G3. COURTESAN (m-s): A2 to C4 (dances also).

Minor Roles. DUKE (bs-bar). ANGELO (bar/t). Other roles can be drawn from chorus.

Dance. 17 women, 11 men in original production. Extended ballets for courtesans, twins, in addition to shorter numbers.

Chorus. Full chorus divides into women's and men's.

Orchestra. fl (picc, cl opt), 2 cls (bs cl), 2 trps, trb, perc, 2 perc, harp, strings (2–0–1–1).

Material. FS–P and VS: Rodgers & Hammerstein.

CAROUSEL

Dramatic fantasy. Prelude, two acts, nine scenes (full evening). Musical theater. Extended recitatives and soliloquy arioso for Billy, extended ballet scene for his daughter. Orchestra plays large role: atmosphere, dances, commenting on action.

Libretto and book by Oscar Hammerstein, based on Ferenc Molnar's "Liliom." Premiere: Majestic Theatre, N.Y. 4.19.45. Performances: Music Theatre of Lincoln Center, N.Y. 65. Recordings: RCA OC (1965), MCA SC (1987), Ransom House (1945).

PLOT

Setting: the New England coast, 1873–1888.

Julie Jordan, a local factory worker, meets and falls in love with Billy Bigelow, the handsome barker at the carnival. While her friend, Carrie, decides to marry the stable fisherman, Mr. Snow, Julie makes the controversial decision to marry this traveling carnival barker. When Billy discovers that he will be a father, he becomes desperate for money, agrees to participate in a robbery with Jigger, but is killed in the attempt. Fifteen years later, Billy is able to return, unseen, to witness his daughter, Louise's, rejection by the righteous Snow children. He attends the lonely girl's graduation and encourages Louise and her mother, Julie, to listen to the words, "You'll Never Walk Alone."

PRODUCTION REQUIREMENTS

Major Roles. Billy Bigelow, Carnival barker (bar): $B^{b}1$ to G3. Julie Jordan, a local factory worker (s): C3 to G4. Carrie Pipperidge, Julie's friend, later Mrs. Snow (s): C3 to A4. Mr. Enoch Snow (t): B1 to A3.

Supporting Roles. Nettie Fowler, owner of the ocean front spa (m-s): C3 to G4. Jigger Craigin, Billy's cohort (bs): A1 to D3.

Minor Roles. Arminy (m-s).

Speaking Role. Mrs. Mullins.

Dance. Louise, Billy and Julie's daughter (dancer). Group dances for men (hornpipe) and women.

Chorus. Unison and multipart; men, women and mixed.

Orchestra. fls I–II (picc), ob (Fr hrn), cls I–II, bsn, hrns I–II, hrn III, trps I–II, trb I, trb II, tuba, perc, vlns A–B, vln C, vla, vcl, bs, harp, piano-cond.

Material. FS–P and VS: The Rodgers & Hammerstein Theatre Library.

FLOWER DRUM SONG

Comedy. Two acts, fourteen scenes (full evening). Musical theatre. Conservative, some songs with oriental flavor. Orchestra provides typical intros, interludes and several dance numbers.

Libretto by Oscar Hammerstein, based on the novel by C. Y. Lee. Book by Hammerstein and Joseph Fields. Premiere: St. James Theatre, N.Y. 12.1.58. Recording: Columbia (1959).

PLOT

Setting: Chinatown, San Francisco.

The traditional standards of Chinese parents conflict in a humorous way with the Americanized younger generation: Wang Ta, Mei Li, Linda Low, and matchmaker Sammy Fong. Though Mei Li and Wang Ta have never met, Sammy Fong attempts to arrange their marriage through their parents. But Mei Li's father still hopes to honor a former contract for Mei Li to marry Sammy himself. Further complications arise when Wang Ta proposes to Linda Low, the owner of a strip-tease joint in town. Sammy Fong has his eye on Linda as well. But all is resolved temporarily when Mei Li actually meets Wang Ta and falls in love at first sight. However, when Wang Ta hears that Mei Li has taken refuge from his parents at the apartment of the seamstress, Helen Chao, she believes he has been unfaithful, and the relationship is off again. The Three Family Association, a traditional tribunal, makes a ruling that Mei Li should marry Sammy Fong. The wedding occurs, but when the veil is lifted, the bride turns out to be Linda. Mei Li has decided to disclaim all contracts because she is in the country illegally, and she and Wang Ta are free to marry after all.

PRODUCTION REQUIREMENTS

Major Roles. WANG TA (t): C♯2 to G3. LINDA LOW, owner of a strip-tease joint (m-s): A♭2 to D4 (dancer also).

Supporting Roles. MEI LI (s): B♭2 to E♭4. MADAM LIANG (m-s): G2 to D4 (F2 opt). SAMMY FONG (bar): B♭1 to E3. HELEN CHAO, friend of Wang

Ta (s): D3 to A^{b}4. FRANKIE WING, strip joint performer (bar): B1 to D3.

Minor Roles. Many, can be drawn from chorus.

Dance. Linda Low, Sammy Fong, Frankie Wing, Wang Ta and ensemble dance.

Chorus. SATB, much unison.

Orchestra. 2 fls (picc), ob (Eng hrn), 2 cls (alt sax), bs cl (t sax), 2 hrns, 3 trps, 2 trbs, tuba, perc, strings (4–1–1–1), harp, guitar (banjo and mand).

Material. FS–P and VS: Rodgers & Hammerstein.

THE KING AND I

Musical theater. Two acts (full evening). Standard Rodgers format: medley overture, dialogue, songs, dance numbers, extended Uncle Tom's Cabin ballet scene. Requires large chorus of children.

Libretto and book by Oscar Hammerstein, based on Margaret Landon's novel, *Anna and the King*. Premiere: St. James Theatre, N.Y. 3.29.51. Performances: Music Theatre of Lincoln Center, N.Y. 64. Recordings: RCA OC (1964), RCA OC (1977), Random House (1951).

PLOT

Setting: the King's palace, Bangkok, Siam, early 1860s.

Anna, an Englishwoman, ventures to Siam with her son to become governess and teacher to King Mongkut's many children. She gradually exerts her influence with the semi-barbaric ruler and helps to democratize his country. Though the two headstrong individuals disagree often, when the King lays dying, Anna's visit reveals her true love and respect for the man. Anna remains on after his death to advise his successor, Crown Prince Chulalongkorn. The subplot concerns one of the King's wives, Tuptim, and her lover Lun Tha. Tuptim narrates the ballet story of *Uncle Tom's Cabin,* but the tale represents their own enslavement and, finally, the tragic death of her lover, Lun Tha.

PRODUCTION REQUIREMENTS

Major Roles. ANNA, English governess (m-s): B2 to E4. THE KING (bs-bar): C2 to E3. TUPTIM, one of the King's young wives (s): C3 to A#4. LUN THA, Tuptim's secret lover (bar/t): C2 to G3. LADY THIANG, wise older wife of the King (s): C#3 to G4.

Supporting Roles. LOUIS, Anna's son (boy s): G2 to B3. PRINCE CHULALONGKORN, the King's oldest son (boy s): G2 to A3.

Speaking Roles. Several speaking roles such as CAPTAIN ORTON, THE INTERPRETER, KRALAHOME, have no musical solos.

Minor Roles. Small adult and children's solos can be drawn from chorus.

Dance. Royal dancers (14 in original production).

Chorus. Full chorus divides into scenes for wives' chorus and children's chorus only.

Orchestra. 2 fls (picc), ob (Eng hrn), 3 cls (bs cl), bsn, 3 hrns, 3 trps, 2 trbs, tuba, harp, perc, strings (3–1–1–1).

Material. FS–P and VS: Rodgers & Hammerstein.

OKLAHOMA

Tragicomedy. Two acts, six scenes (full evening). Many choruses, lengthy dream ballet, dance scenes.

Libretto by Oscar Hammerstein. Premiere: St. James Theatre, New York 3.31.43. Performances: New York 12.13.79. Recordings: RCA OC (1979), Random House (1943).

PLOT

Setting: Indian Territory, just after the turn of the century.

A love story with a threatening twist: Laurey and Curly are falling in love, but Laurey's crude, jealous ranchhand, Jud, also fantasizes about Laurey's attention. Laurey and Curly are married at the end, as all celebrate Oklahoma's impending statehood. But Jud picks a fight and is accidently killed by Curly. Finally, Laurey and Curly ride off in the surrey with the fringe on top. The secondary comic love conflict involves Ado Annie, the local flirt; Will Parker, the cowboy; and a traveling salesman, Ali Hakim.

PRODUCTION REQUIREMENTS

Major Roles. CURLY (bar-t/bar): C♯2 to F♯3. LAUREY (legit s): C♯3 to A4. WILL PARKER (bar): D2 to F3. ADO ANNIE CARNES (m-s): C3 to F4. JUD FRY (bs-bar/bar): D2 to C♯3.

Supporting Roles. AUNT ELLER (a): F2 to F4. ANDREW CARNES (bar): E2 to F3.

Minor Roles. Several small solos can be drawn from chorus.

Chorus. SATB chorus in several scenes.

Ballet. Several dance scenes and long dream ballet.

Orchestra. fl (picc), ob (Eng hrn), cls I–II, bsn, hrns I–II, trps I–II, trb, perc, vlns A–B, vla, vcl, bs, guitar, harp, piano-cond. Bandstration available.

Material. FS–P and VS: Rodgers and Hammerstein.

THE SOUND OF MUSIC

Musical. Two acts, twenty-five scenes. Various styles include German and Austrian folk, sacred choral music, and traditional musical theater.

Lyrics by Oscar Hammerstein. Book by Howard Lindsay and Russell Crouse, as suggested by "The Trapp Family Singers" by Maria Augusta Trapp. Premiere: New York 11.6.59.

PLOT

Setting: Austria, early 1938.

Because of Maria's fondness for enjoying the sound of music in the hills, rather than her duties as a postulant, the Mother Abbess suggests that Maria become the governess for the children of the wealthy Captain Von Trapp. Maria wins the hearts of the children as she teaches them songs. The Captain also falls in love with her, breaks his engagement to the socialite, Elsa Schraeder, and marries Maria instead. After their wedding, the Captain is called to serve in the Nazi Army. The Von Trapp family decides to attempt an escape after singing at an amateur concert. While hiding from their pursuers, Liesl's Nazi boyfriend, Rolf, finds the family, but pretends not to see them, allowing the Von Trapps to escape to Switzerland.

PRODUCTION REQUIREMENTS

Major Roles. MARIA (s): D2 to B♭4. CAPTAIN VON TRAPP (bs-bar): F♯1 to G3. LIESL, Captain Von Trapp's oldest daughter (m-s): A2 to F♯4. ELSA SCHRAEDER (s): C3 to B4. MOTHER ABBESS (m-s): B2 to A♭4.

Supporting Roles. Von Trapp children: FRIEDRICH: G♯2 to G4; KURT: G♯2 to F♯4; LOUISA, BRIGITTA, MARTA and GRETL: A2 to F♯4. ROLF GRUBER, Liesl's boyfriend (t): D2 to E3. MAX DETWEILER (t): C2 to F3.

Minor Roles. SISTER MARGARETTA (s). SISTER SOPHIA (s). SISTER BERTHE (a). FESTIVAL CONTESTANTS.

Chorus. Neighbors of Captain Von Trapp; SSAA nuns, novices, and postulants; contestants in the Festival Concert.

Ballet. Brief Austrian ballroom style dancing.

Orchestra. Large orch: 2 fls (2 picc), 2 cls, bsn, 3 hrns in F, 3 trps, 2 trbs, tuba, perc, harp, strings (2–1–1–1–1), guitar-vln II. Small orch: fl (picc), ob (Eng hrn), 2 cls, hrn, 2 trps, trb, perc, strings (2–1–1–1), guitar.

Material. FS–P and VS: Rodgers & Hammerstein.

SOUTH PACIFIC

Romantic tragicomedy. Two acts (full evening). Musical theatre: love scenes and ballads contrast, use of lively men's and women's choruses. Orchestra provides overtures, interludes, dances, reprises, scene changes. Exotic harmonies reinforce Polynesian setting.

Lyrics by Oscar Hammerstein. Book by Hammerstein and Joshua Logan. Premiere: Majestic Theatre, N.Y. 4.7.49. Recording: Columbia OC (1967), CBS SC (1986), Random House (1949).

PLOT

Setting: two islands in the South Pacific, World War II.

Emile de Becque, a French planter, and Nellie Forbush, an American army nurse, fall in love while she is stationed on the island during the war. Though Nellie overcomes her initial hesitation about their differences in age, nationality and backgrounds, Nellie pulls away when she discovers that Emile lived with a native woman who bore him two children. Lt. Joseph Cable falls in love with Bloody Mary's beautiful daughter, Liat. Racial prejudice initially haunts Cable as well, but he decides that he will spend his life on Bali Hai with Liat. Emile, despondent over losing Nellie, agrees to accompany Lt. Cable on a dangerous mission behind Japanese lines. Though the mission is successful, only Emile escapes alive. When he returns home, he is surprised to find Nellie waiting for him, playing lovingly with his children.

PRODUCTION REQUIREMENTS

Major Roles. Nellie Forbush (m-s): $A^{b}2$ to F4. Emile de Becque (bar): A1 to E3.

Supporting Roles. Lt. Joseph Cable (high bar/ten): D2 to G3. Bloody Mary (a): G2 to $F^{\#}4$ (mostly below C4).

Minor Roles. Ngana and Jerome (child s). Luther Billis (bar). Other short solos drawn from chorus.

Mute Roles. Liat (little dialogue).

Chorus. Male and female choruses, mostly unison singing.

Ballet. Male and female choruses move; Nellie dances.

Orchestra. fl (picc), ob (Eng hrn), cls I–II, bsn, hrns I–II, hrn III, trps I–II, trp III, trb I, trb II, tuba, perc, vlns A–B–C–D, vla, vcl, bs, harp, piano-cond.

Material. FS–P and VS: Rodgers and Hammerstein.

Robert Xavier Rodriguez (1946–   )

THE OLD MAJESTIC

"Backstage comedy romance." Two acts, thirteen scenes, one set (90 minutes). Style varies from 12-tone, bel canto, opera buffa, to broadway and popular tunes of the 1930s. Much ensemble singing.

Libretto by Mary Duren. Commissioned by the San Antonio Festival. Concert premiere: University of Texas, San Antonio 5.28.88.

PLOT

Setting: Majestic Theatre, 1930.

During a matinee performance, vaudeville performers prepare for their acts: the magician Nelsoni is jeered offstage after his finale fails to work; he blames Nora, although she had been kind enough to assist on short notice. Fifi and her sisters invite Nora to join them for the evening, but Nora stays behind to dream of becoming a star. Ben joins her for a love scene. Finally, Fifi's dogs escape during her act, and a chase ensues.

Six months later, the group reconvenes at the theatre. Nelsoni amuses the showgirls by telling their fortunes, while the others discuss the growing popularity of films. The group playfully acts out the story of the Valentino film that will precede their show that evening. Meanwhile, Ben and Nora meet again. Ferren frets about how to tell his partner, Sammy May, that he has signed a movie contract; and Sammy and Fifi express their love, even though they don't know how they will manage when films replace their livelihood. A telegram arrives to inform Sammy that he has inherited a large sum of money, and their problems are solved.

PRODUCTION REQUIREMENTS

Major Roles. NORA KELLY, singer/dancer (s): B2 to C5 [D5 opt]. MADAME FIFI, glamorous show-biz veteran, passed her prime (m-s): $G^{b}2$ to A4. LOU FERREN, comedian, leading man type, (t): $D^{b}2$ to B3 (C4 opt). BEN PALMER, handsome son of the theatre owner (bar): $B^{b}1$ to G3. NELSONI, pompous magician (bs-bar): F1 to G3. SAMMY MAY, aging comedian (bs): E1 to G3.

Supporting Roles. Nora's sisters, part of the "sister" act: PLUM SISTER #1 (s): B2 to B4. PLUM SISTER #2 (m-s): G2 to G4.

Mute Roles. Male and female acrobats (3–4), jugglers (1–2), messenger boy (age 10–12), a lariat-twirling cowboy, tango dancers, plus additional optional vaudeville performers (all may be played by chorus members).

Chorus. Offstage mixed chorus.

Orchestra. fl (picc), ob, cl (sax), tr, bs trb, 2 perc, harp, accordian, piano, strings.

Material. FS–P and VS: Galaxy Music.

REVIEWS

David Anthony Richelieu "Brilliant opera must get on stage," *San Antonio Sunday Express-News* (May 29, 1988)

> "a sort of vaudeville-era 'A Chorus Line,' as the performers explore their lives and futures. . . . Well, the whole opera is just a romp, full of fun, wit, charm, drama, good music—heck, even tunes you can leave humming to yourself."

> "Despite all the borrowing from the past, 'The Old Majestic' is decidedly contemporary with atonalities, multiple meter and other devices giving proper tension, drama and believability to the fun and games."

THE RANSOM OF RED CHIEF

Comic opera. One act, five scenes (55 minutes). Conservative modern idiom with bluegrass flavor. Through-composed with melodic interest mainly in orchestra. Much spoken and sung dialogue. Mozartean fughetto finale.

Libretto by Daniel Dibbern, based on a story by O. Henry. Commissioned by the Mesquite Sesquicentennial Committee. Premiere: Lyric Opera of Dallas, Mesquite, Texas 10.10.86.

PLOT

Setting: town square and a campsite outside of a city on the plains of West Texas, mid 1890s.

Sam and Bill, two Yankee desperados, are counting their money in the town square, and scheming about ways to make money. After a passing conversation with Mr. Dorset and his rambunctious son, Johnny, they decide to kidnap the wealthy banker's son for the ransom money. Johnny is nabbed when he sneaks out of church. The ransom note is sent to Mr. Dorset, and the desperados await a reply.

But the victim proves to be too much for the kidnappers. Fancying himself to the wild Indian warrior, Red Chief, Johnny terrorizes the kidnapper's camp. When the reply to the ransom note finally arrives, the desperados fully expect to receive the money they demanded for Johnny's return. Instead, Mr. Dorset's response states that he will be glad to take little "Red Chief" off their hands if the desperados will pay him! Sam and Bill are more than willing to take the loss to get rid of the little pest. They pretend to take him on a bear hunt, but end up back in the town square. The opera ends as it began: Sam is counting the money, but this time, it is to pay Dorset.

PRODUCTION REQUIREMENTS

Major Roles. Two harmless desperados: SAM (t): C2 to C4, BILL (buffo bs/bar): D1 to G3 (falsetto to C♭4).

Supporting Roles. JOHNNY (boy s): B♭2 to B4.

Minor Roles. MR. DORSET, Johnny's father (bar).

Chorus. Short offstage SATB.

Orchestra. fl (picc), cl in B♭, trp in C, bs trb, perc, harmonica/banjo, accord, piano, vln, vcl.

Material. FS–P and VS: Galaxy Music.

REVIEWS

Wayne Lee Gay "Mesquite (TX): Lyric Opera of Dallas: Rodriguez 'The Ransom of Red Chief' (premiere)," *Musical America* (March 1987), p. 20

> "drawing on the materials of folk music, hymnody, ragtime, and Dixieland (as well as, according to the program book, Rossini, Puccini, Monteverdi, and the *Play of Herod*), Rodriguez produced a score that, on first hearing, was both sophisticated and accessible. The orchestration for chamber ensemble was unfailingly lucid and colorful; ditto the vocal writing."

> "(Though) the joke gets a little thin when stretched over an hour, Rodriguez's music keeps the interest level high."

SUOR ISABELLA

Comic opera. One act (70 minutes). Chromatic musical language, not wholly atonal, interspersed with medieval melodies, often in contrapuntal texture. Through-composed structure created by recitative style and rapid declamatory song; few arias.

Libretto by Daniel Dibbern, based on a tale from Giovanni Boccaccio's *The Decameron* (c. 1348). Commissioned by the National Endowment for the Arts. Premiere: Univ. of Texas, Dallas (piano) 7.7.82; Boston University (orch) 5.3.84.

PLOT

Setting: fourteenth-century Italian convent.

Sisters Sgridaretta and Ficcanaso gossip with the other nuns about Suor Isabella, whom they suspect has been sneaking a man into her cell each night. Their discussion is interrupted by the Abbess Usimbalda, who is directing the delivery of a heavy trunk, which arrives nightly to her quarters, to be removed each morning. After the evening prayers, Isabella contemplates her moral dilemma: whether physical and spiritual love can co-exist. Deciding that they can, indeed, Isabella goes to join her secret lover.

After spying through Suor Isabella's keyhole at the young nun's transgressions (and enjoying every minute!), Sgridaretta and Ficcanaso wake the rest of the convent for a blow-by-blow description of the action. Finally, they decide to summon the Abbess. Usimbalda is outwardly horrified at Isabella's sin, lecturing about the tortures of hell that await such sinners. In her haste, however, the Abbess has not donned her nun's veil on her head, but a pair of black pants, belonging to the priest who arrives in the heavy trunk each evening. Isabella, the first to notice, turns all to her advantage and the embarrassed Usimbalda quickly changes the point of her lecture, convincing the community that all must experience the joys of both spiritual and physical love. The nuns joyfully agree, except for the prudish Sgridaretta, who flees in disgust. When all have returned to their cells, Usimbalda and Isabella give thanks for their deliverance and rush back to their respective lovers.

PRODUCTION REQUIREMENTS

Major Roles. SISTER ISABELLA, a young and beautiful nun (s): B♭2 to C5 [D5 ossia]. ABBESS USIMBALDA, Mother Superior of the convent (m-s): G2 to A4. SISTER FICCANASO, a prying and meddlesome nun (s): A2 to B♭4. SISTER SGRIDARETTA, an old and punctilious nun (m-s): G2 to A4.

Mute Roles. ISABELLA'S LOVER, disguised.

Chorus. SSA nuns can be three solosits or chorus.

Orchestra. fl (picc), cl (bs cl), trp, bs trb, perc, piano, harp, vln, vcl.

Material. FS–P and VS: Galaxy Music. VS: American Music Center.

REVIEWS

Derrick Henry "Banned in Texas, Isabella's at BU," *Boston Globe.*

> "Daniel Dibbern's English libretto does considerable justice to the subtleties of Boccaccio's richly human tale, suggesting issues that go beyond blasphemy."

> "Medieval roots pervade 'Suor Isabella," A famous saltarello . . . appears as a recurring thread, distorted in all manner of ingenious ways. Protracted use is made as well of medieval sacred music and complex fourteenth-century rhythmic techniques. . . . Thus his 70-minute opera views the medieval world through twentieth century eyes and ears, and does so colorfully, engagingly, and not too harshly."

TANGO

Comic chamber opera. One act, three scenes, one set (22 minutes). Conservative modern idiom with cabaret flavor. Quotes famous compositions in tango rhythms. Vocal part contains much spoken dialogue, chant-like recitation, and arioso.

Libretto by the composer based on news clippings, letters and sermons from the tango craze. Commissioned by the National Endowment for the Arts for Voices of Change (Dallas), The Chicago Ensemble (Chicago), and The Twentieth-Century Consort (Washington, D.C.). Premiere: Dallas, Texas 1.29.86.

PLOT

Setting: orchestra on stage, 1913–1914.

In scene one, the tenor is an elegant tango dancer, quickly changing into a radio newscaster, reporting the worldwide reactions to the tango. In scene two, he becomes Cardinal Basilio Pompili, Vicar of Rome, denouncing the tango, but succumbing to its rhythms by the end of his sermon. In his final scene as newscaster, he reports on attempts to reform the tango into a more respectable dance. But, once again, he succumbs to the lure of the tango, exiting as the original tango dancer.

PRODUCTION REQUIREMENTS

Major Roles. A TANGO DANCER/RADIO NEWSCASTER/THE CARDINAL — VICAR OF ROME (t): C♯3 to A3 (D1 and A1 are suggested as ossia for vocal color).

Orchestra. Several options suggested by composer. Full instrumentation: fl, cl in A, accord, perc, piano, vln, vcl. Other options, piano reduction with: accord; accord and perc; accord and vln; or accord, vln, and perc.

Material. FS–P and VS: Galaxy Music.

REVIEWS

Wayne Lee Gay "Dallas: Voices of Change: Rodriguez 'Tango' [premiere]," *Musical America* (June 1986), pp. 40–41

> "as usual, composer Rodriguez has triumphed. His musical language . . . is both refined and colorful, displaying a remarkable command of timbre. Very few composers could use a typewriter and tango rhythms, as well as quotes from Beethoven, Bach, Schubert, Brahms, and Mozart all in one brief piece without sounding gimmicky. But in 'Tango,' Rodriguez can and does."

Lou Rogers

THE SPECIALIST

One act (35 minutes). Libretto by Stuart Michaels. Premiere: Golden Fleece, Ltd., New York 78.

Material. The composer (contact through AMC); American Music Center.

Willard Roosevelt (1918–)

AND THE WALLS CAME TUMBLING DOWN

Historical fiction. One act, four scenes (55 minutes). Each scene through-composed though a few set numbers exist. Chromatic accompaniments cloud tonal foundations. Vocal parts more conjunct with complex rhythms, some spoken dialogue. Much contrapuntal ensemble writing.

Libretto by Loften Mitchell. Premiere: Harlem School of the Arts, New York 3.76.

PLOT

Setting: Greenwich Village (New Amsterdam), 1664.

Joshua, a preacher and leader among the free black community established in the Dutch colony of New Amsterdam, attempts to settle a dispute between Pieter and Hermann, while dealing with the more serious threat that his colony is about to be beseiged by the British. The enemy's ships are already bombarding New Amsterdam from the sea, though the killing has not reached the black community north of the wall which separates them from the whites. Joshua decides to travel south of the wall to lend the Governor his support. News of the loss of Gretchen's innocent son to the British convinces Joshua's wife, Mary, as well as Gretchen, Pieter and Hermann to accompany Joshua. Hermann, afraid of being sold back into slavery, refuses to support Joshua's plan to rally the colonists, blacks and whites, together. The people follow Joshua into battle, a battle lost to the enemy. With the colony under enemy control, Hermann avenges himself by turning Joshua over as a traitorous rebel. Pieter, in turn, stabs Hermann and kills him. Joshua's words of hope, as he goes to his hanging, offer comfort to Mary, Pieter, and Gretchen, that the "walls" men build between themselves might one day come tumbling down.

PRODUCTION REQUIREMENTS

Major Roles. JOSHUA (bs): F1 to E3. MARY, Joshua's wife (c): G2 to E♭4. HERMANN (bar): A♭1 to F3.

Supporting Roles. GRETCHEN (s): C♯3 to B4. PIETER (t): B2 to A3.

Orchestra. fl (picc), ob, 2 cls in B^{b}, bsn, 2 hrns in F, 2 trps in B^{b}, trb, perc, piano, strings (1–1–1–1–1).

Material. FS–P: American Composers Alliance, NY. FS, VS and libretto: American Music Center.

REVIEWS

Robert Sherman "Music: Harlem Benefit," *New York Times* (March 18, 1976), p. 51

"The opera . . . has some effective dramatic moments, but the characterizations are murky, and the music stays for its full 55 minutes on a high-intensity plateau."

Drewry Wofford "New York," *Opera News* (June 1976), p. 39

"Originally conceived as a 'station-wagon opera' for touring (with). . . . a score relying heavily on a contemporary idiom that stems from Schoenberg."

"Mitchell's libretto tries to operate on three levels—plot, psychological and social—but is greatly hampered by an elementary use of language."

Ned Rorem (1923–)

HEARING

Fantasy. Five scenes (20 minutes). Each scene is a closed number, but scenes flow in continuous succession. Solos and duets are lyrical with some disjunct motion. Enriched by use of quartal chords and modal harmony. Orchestra's role varies from soloistic to accompaniment.

Libretto by James Holmes, based on poems by Kenneth Koch, Premiere: Gregg Smith Singers, St. Stephen's Church, N.Y. 3.15.77 (unstaged).

PLOT

Setting: a fantasy park: "yesterday and tomorrow."

A revision of a six-movement cycle of poems for mezzo-soprano and piano. The libretto was fashioned to create a scenario which utilizes five of these poems.

The words of the poems are assigned to the characters so as to create a trite drama in which an intense young man falls in love with a flighty girl, who becomes infatuated with a mature gentleman. The gentleman and the girl go off together, bringing unhappiness to the gentleman's lady and causing the young man to become jealous. However, when the lady confronts the girl and wins back her gentleman, the girl happily returns to the young man. The drama unfolds mainly through actions and implications rather than through the words: though the words do occasionally coincide with the actions, the poetry is often only vaguely related to the story.

PRODUCTION REQUIREMENTS

Major Roles. A Lady In Lilac (s): A2 to A4. A Jealous Gentleman (t): A1 to G♯3. A Poetic Lady (m-s): F♯2 to G4. A Young Man With A French Horn (bar): G1 to E3.

Orchestra. cl (E♭ alt sax), trp, perc, piano (harm), mandolin, vln, vla, bs.

Material. FS–P and VS: Boosey and Hawkes. VS: American Music Center.

REVIEWS

None located.

Michael Sahl (1934–)
Eric Salzman (1933–)

CIVILIZATION & ITS DISCONTENTS

Music-theater pop-opera comedy. One act, three scenes (45 minutes). Passages vary from contemporary disco and rock styles, conversational, conventional ensembles, to dissonant harmonic language. Vocal styles from pop and improvisational to coloratura operatic. Sections titled "voids" employ aleatory or chance music and explore psychological aspects of characters.

Libretto by the composers. Premiere: American Musical and Dramatic Academy 5.19.77. Performances: National Public Radio 80. Recordings: Nonesuch Records N-78009.

PLOT

Setting: Club Bide-a-Wee (a disco) and Jill's apartment, the present.

Although Club Bide-a-Wee is filled with chatter, music, and noise, there is still an underriding sense of emptiness. Jill and her boyfriend, Derek, have a fight. After they part ways, Jill meets Jeremy Jive and takes him back to her apartment. At the potential love nest, Jill persists in answering the phone at the most inopportune moments. Jeremy becomes so frustrated and angry that he rips the phone out of the wall. Just as Jeremy is about to leave, Derek appears. The confrontation between the two rivals is superseded by a business deal, when Derek learns that Jeremy is the talent agent that his advertising firm has been trying to land a deal with. Meanwhile, Jill becomes distressed that the two men have not considered her talents for the part of the "Singing Chicken" in the ad campaign. Thus, she threatens to commit suicide with an electric knife. Arachnid, guru of the Club Bide-a-Wee arrives, spouting his spiritual banter, and leaves with Jill. Back at the Club, all the characters join to espouse their modern ideal: "If it feels good, do it!"

PRODUCTION REQUIREMENTS

Major Roles. Jill Goodheart, an aspiring singer (s): A♭2 to G♭5 (G5 not absolutely required, ossia suggests higher notes, up to F6, if possible, lower range requires musical theater quality.) Jeremy Jive, a young theatrical agent (t): B♭1 to C4 (improvisational or pop ability desirable).

Supporting Roles. Carlos Arachnid, guru of Club Bide-a-Wee (operatic t): A♭1 to B♭3. Derek Dude, a media type (bar): F1 to F3 (ossia C4 falsetto, some pop style required).

Chorus. Enough dancing and singing patrons to suggest a crowded bar or club scene. Amateur, pop singing style for optional chorus passages.

Orchestra. Keyboard (piano, organ or synthesizer), drums and percussion, bass.

Material. FS–P and VS: G. Schirmer.

REVIEWS

Peter G. Davis "Quog Music Theatre Twin Bill Limns City Life Then and Now," *New York Times* (May 24, 1977), p. 31

"All this smacks of a latter-day Menotti libretto, with its self-conscious and occasionally embarrassing attempts to be psychologically up-to-the-minute. . . . But the score . . . is a brilliant amalgam of jazz, pop, blues and classical forms, cleverly developed and timed to make the satiric points stand out in the most vivid musical and theatrical terms."

"None of the performers had what might be called beautifully trained operatic voices, nor was that necessary."

STAUF

American Faust story. Two acts, eleven scenes (100 minutes). Music theater with pop elements: soft rock, jazz, and blues. Set numbers joined by spoken dialogue. Vocal parts require pop orientation with pop embellishments, especially for Margarita.

Libretto by the composers. Premiere: Cubiculo (Quog Music Theatre), N.Y. 5.76. Performances: American Music Theatre Festival, Philadelphia, Pa. 9.20.87.

PLOT

Setting: modern-day American city.

Henry Stauf, the idealistic inventor of a wind generator that he believes will solve the energy crisis, approaches Goodwerx, a company he hopes will financially back his machine for the benefit of humanity. There, he meets and falls in love with the receptionist, Margarita Morales. But, without his knowledge, Stauf becomes a trump card in a game being played in the heavens by the gods Jove and Kali. To win the trick, Jove becomes chairman of Goodwerx, and takes on Stauf as a member of the team. Stauf rises through the ranks, soon becoming an executive of the much larger Goodco, a corporation specializing in nuclear power. Caught up with his new power, Stauf remains faithful to his boss, Dr. Jove, even when Margarita is fired. Margarita joins a commune in the desert. Unfortunately, a Goodco nuclear reactor is nearby. Eventually, Margarita goes back to work for Goodco. In an attempt to force Jove's hand, Kali makes Margarita aware of problems with the nuclear generator, attempting to force the plant to be shut down. But Stauf seems helpless, and the plant remains open despite his command to close it. Frustrated, Stauf tries to convince Margarita to run away with him, but Margarita decides that she must inform the newspapers of the reactor's imminent breakdown. To avoid the scandal, Stauf finally orders

Margarita's death. As the story closes, Stauf has decided to enter politics, but is confronted by a reporter (Kali) probing Margarita's mysterious death in a car accident.

PRODUCTION REQUIREMENTS

Major Roles. HENRY STAUF (bs-bar): F1 to G3. MARGARITA MORALES (s): A2 to G♯4. JOVE, God of reason and control (t): A1 to B3. KALI, God of nature and passion (m-s): F2 to F♯4.

Chorus. SATB (4 min) should be dancer-singers.

Orchestra. 2 reeds, drums, perc, piano synthesizer, bs.

Material. VS: contact Eric Salzman, 29 Middagh St. Brooklyn, N.Y. 11201.

REVIEWS

Peter G. Davis "Fatal Flaw," *New York* (October 19, 1987), pp. 110–111

> Salzman and Sahl's "homemade theatre pieces gleefully romp through whatever genre happens to suit the occasion: pop, gospel, grand opera, country and western, blues, musical comedy—even serial dogma. . . . All the various elements fit smartly into place, each number has a precise musical function . . . to enhance the overall dramatic effect."

> "wimpy Henry Stauf and his ill-fated girl friend, come off as little more than pallid cliches. As usual in such morality tales, all the best scenes go to the Devil, divided into two squabbling deities: Dr. Jove . . . and Kali, a raunchy nature goddess . . . who can outbelt Ethel Merman."

Raymond Ericson "Stage: New Deal for Faust," *New York Times* (May 28, 1976), section 3, p. 14

> "the plot may not sound like much, but . . . it is a strong enough springboard for the songs, dances and dialogue scenes that spin out the evening. The overall tone of the work is satiric, although in a search for variety it becomes compassionate and melodramatic at times."

> "The lyrics, sometimes touching, sometimes amusing, are not quite as pungent or acid as might be expected. . . . but together

with the inventive and first-rate music, the songs make the evening worthwhile."

NOAH

Music theatre pageant. Two acts (105 minutes). Premiere: Pratt Institute, Brooklyn, NY 2.78. Performances: Washington Square Methodist Church, New York 78. Radio version: WBAI, New York 78/79.

Material. G. Schirmer.

PASSION OF SIMPLE SIMON

Music theatre. Three acts (90 minutes). Premiere: Theatre for the New City, New York 2.79. Performances: National Public Radio 79/80.

Material. Eric Salzman, 29 Middagh St., Brooklyn, NY 11201.

Gregory Sandow (1943–)

A CHRISTMAS CAROL

One act, several scene changes (75 minutes). Nineteenth-century musical style. Through-composed, containing arias and dialogue. Brief prelude to Act I and several orchestral interludes. Written to be performed by an ensemble company of eleven people, playing numerous roles.

Libretto by the composer, based on Dickens' tale. Commissioned by the Eastern Opera Theatre. Premiere: Eastern Opera Theatre, Stratford, Conn. 2.21.77.

PLOT

Setting: London, nineteenth century.

Scene i: Scrooge's counting house; ii: Fezziwig's warehouse; iii: A park bench; iv: A room with a fire; v: A room in Bob Cratchit's house; vi: Parlor of Scrooge's nephew's house; vii: A city at twilight; viii: A dark bedroom; ix: A room at Cratchit's house; x: Scrooge's counting house.

The classic Dickens' *A Christmas Carol* with a few adaptations: some scenes are cut; there are small changes in wording. Sandow expands certain scenes, using his own words and nineteenth-century British poems by Rossetti, Mackay, and Dickens himself. The opera opens in Scrooge's office on Christmas eve. Scrooge rejects all Christmas wishes from Cratchit (his clerk), his nephew, carolers and collectors for charity. He is then visited at home by the Ghost of his former partner, Marley, and the Ghosts of Christmas Past, Present, and Future. The Ghosts force him to see his disillusioned fiancee from his past; his nephew's and Cratchit's Christmas celebrations in the present, and his own death and Tiny Tim's (Cratchit's crippled child), which lurk in the future. Scrooge sees his folly and vows to become a changed man on Christmas Day.

PRODUCTION REQUIREMENTS

Major Roles. SCROOGE (actor). SOPRANO (Scrooge's fiancee, Martha Cratchit, etc.): C♯3 to B♭4. MEZZO I (Ghost of Christmas Past, Nephew's wife, etc.): G2 to F4. MEZZO II (Mrs. Fezziwig, Mrs. Cratchit, etc.): G2 to F4. TENOR I (Scrooge's nephew, etc.): D2 to B♭3. TENOR II (Bob Cratchit, etc.): C♯2 to A3. BARITONE (Ghost of Christmas Present, etc.): G♭3. BASS (Marley's Ghost, Ghost of Christmas Yet to Come, etc.): E1 to F3.

Minor Roles. BOY I (s). BOY II (s). GIRL (s).

Chorus. Optional adult and children's chorus may be added.

Orchestra. fl, ob, cl, hrn, bsn, 2 vlns, vla, 2 vcls, bs, perc.

Material. FS–P and VS: Theodore Presser. VS: American Music Center.

REVIEWS

Robert Sherman "An Old Favorite With A New Melody," *New York Times* (January 1, 1978), p. 4

> "Mr. Sandow has concocted a consistently attractive score: its full measure of tunefulness . . . (includes) several real live Christmas carols, and its many outbursts of folklike-rhythmic buoyancy reminded me of . . . Menotti's "Amahl and the Night Visitors."

FRANKENSTEIN

Libretto by Thomas M. Disch based on the Shelley novel. Premiere: C. W. Post Center, Brookville, N.Y. 6.23.82.

THE RICHEST GIRL IN THE WORLD FINDS HAPPINESS

Fantasy, comedy, a "pop" opera. One act, no sets required, but costumes should be elaborate. (20–25 minutes). Written in a pop idiom, but intended to be sung by operatic singers using "show biz" style. Linear, melodic vocal lines; simple harmonic accompaniment. Conversational, except for Singer's introduction and central song, homophonic ensemble finale. Frequent shifts in rhythmic mood (i.e., jazz, rock, tango, etc.) depict various settings. Orchestral intro.

Libretto by Robert Patrick, cleverly written in rhymed couplets. Commissioned by Michael Feinjold. Premiere: Theatre at Noon, New York 12.1.75.

PLOT

Setting: a 1200-room mansion in New Jersey, the present.

Madalayna eagerly directs Geoffrey to Geraldine, the richest girl in the world, knowing that the handsomest movie star plans to propose to her mistress. However, the maid soon finds a special delivery letter in the mail informing Geraldine that she is to be voted Miss America that evening. Realizing that a marriage proposal would invalidate the vote, the maid scurries off to find the couple. However, Geraldine has decided to take her suitor on a tour of her fantastic mansion to delay the proposal. As they walk through treasures brought from all over the world, Madalayna tries to find them. Finally, just as Geraldine accepts Geoffrey's proposal, Madalayna comes running in with the letter. Luckily, Geraldine realizes that they are in part of the house that is over the international date line; therefore, she will be able to accept the title which will not be awarded until that evening on the other side of the date line. In her happiness, the richest girl gives her wealth to the poor children of the world, but they return it as a wedding present. Thus, Geraldine achieves her richest dream of finding true happiness.

PRODUCTION REQUIREMENTS

Major Roles. THE RICHEST GIRL IN THE WORLD ("legit" s): B2 to A4. MADALAYNA, her maid (s or m-s, "needs belt and legit qualities"): B2 to A4. THE HANDSOMEST MOVIE STAR IN THE WORLD ("legit" t): C2 to A3. SINGER (t or high bar "legit not required"): C2 to A3.

Orchestra. piano.

Material. VS: Theodore Presser and American Music Center.

REVIEWS

None located.

Bruce Saylor (1946–)

MY KINSMAN, MAJOR MOLINEUX

Mystery/character study. One act, six scenes, four sets (50 minutes). Conservative twentieth-century idiom. Open harmonic structure with shifting tonal centers. Each scenic division through-composed with orchestra providing important bridges. Vocal parts generally lyrical, with some chromaticism and disjunct leaps often supported by cues from accompaniment.

Libretto by Cary Plotkin, based on a story by Nathaniel Hawthorne. Commissioned by Mrs. Albert F. Keister and the Opera Workshop, Inc. (Pittsburgh). Premiere: Opera Workshop, Pittsburgh, Pa. 8.28.76.

PLOT

Setting: a colonial town during the American Revolution.

Robin, a young English lad, has come to an American town expecting to be met and established socially by his wealthy kinsman, Major Molineux. Once he comes ashore, Robin is shocked to find himself alone, with no welcoming party. He wanders the darkened streets, meeting a lamplighter, a gravedigger, a Redcoat, a Harlot and some local townsmen, drinking and gambling at an inn. Despite his inquiries, no one will direct Robin to his relative's door. All brush him off, assuring him that he shall meet Molineux soon enough. Just as Robin concludes that the whole town must be mad, everything bursts into chaos. The townspeople flood the streets, raving and cursing the King, as they run Major Molineux (the King's appointed governor) out of town. Molineux cannot reason with the rebellious crowd, and spying Robin standing agape among them, he even thinks his own kinsman has betrayed him. Robin is once again left alone in the darkened streets as the Major is cast out to sea on the Old Ferryman's boat.

PRODUCTION REQUIREMENTS

Major Roles. Robin (t): D2 to A♭3.

Supporting Roles. MAJOR MOLINEUX, THE REDCOAT and SECOND TOWNSMAN (bar): C2 to F♯3. OLD FERRYMAN and MAN WITH MASK (bs-bar): C2 to E3. INNKEEPER (m-s): C3 to G4. LAMPLIGHTER and THIRD TOWNSMAN (t): C2 to A♭3. GRAVEDIGGER and FIRST TOWNSMAN (bar): C2 to E3. HARLOT (s): D3 to A4.*
*No roles doubled at premiere.

Chorus. SATB (made up of smaller roles, may be augmented).

Orchestra. fl (picc), B♭ cl (E♭ cl), bs cl (B♭ cl), hrn, trp, trb, perc, piano, strings (1–0–1–1–0).

Material. FS–P: contact composer through AMC. FS: American Music Center.

REVIEWS

Robert Croan "Pittsburgh," *Opera News* (November 1976), p. 92

> "for the most part [Saylor] has made it work in musical and theatrical terms. The libretto . . . is literate and singable, and Saylor's musical language emerges close to the meaning of the words and is grateful to the voices."

> "Saylor creates a macabre atmosphere in the opening scene. . . . and provides several big solo moments — Robin's soliloquy, the harlot's aria and a climactic arioso in which the Tory Molineux, tarred and feathered, still preaches the divine right of kings to a crazed mob."

Peter Schickele [P.D.Q. Bach] (1935–)

THE ABDUCTION OF FIGARO

Comic parody. Three acts, nine scenes (165 minutes). Mock-Mozart with references to musical theatre, cabaret, rock, country. Overture and set numbers with recitative and spoken dialogue.

Libretto by the composer. Premiere: Minnesota Opera 4.84. Performances: Stockholm, Sweden 7.89.

PLOT

Setting: a seacoast town "in Spain or Italy or somewhere," time of Mozart's "Figaro."

At the palace of Count Alma Mater, Figaro lies in bed, gravely ill, attended by his wife, Susanna Susannadanna, her servant, Pecadillo, and the doctor Al Donfonso. Donna Donna arrives in search of the infamous Donald Giovanni. Her servant, Blondie, and Pecadillo fall in love at first sight. Donald Giovanni and his supposedly mute servant, Schlepporello, arrive in the palace courtyard. Schlepporello complains that his mute role is underwritten: he wants to sing. But when Susanna appears on the balcony, Don turns on his charm and goes inside with her. Don is immediately recognized by Donna Donna, who threatens to kill him if he doesn't marry her. Captain Kadd emerges from one of Donna Donna's steamer trunks, brandishing a pistol and announcing that he is hijacking this "ship" to Cuba, in pursuit of treasure. When it becomes clear that he is not aboard a ship, Kadd realizes that, on land, he is a wanted man. He takes Figaro (and his bed) hostage and escapes.

Al Donfonso, Pecadillo and Schlepporello sail away, but their sinking ship is marooned in an unknown land. They soon encounter Opec, Pasha Shaboom's servant, picking fruit in front of the palace. The pasha arrives with a grand chorus. After a brief audience, he leaves Don and Pecadillo alone with two harem girls. The girls turn out to be Blondie and Donna Donna, who refuse to be wooed by the fickle men. Captain Kadd passes through, pushing Figaro's bed, and asking directions to Cuba. Don and his party go to the rescue in Opec's boat. On an unknown tropical island, Opec, Pecadillo, Don and Schlepporello discover a swineherd and his wife, Papa and Mama Geno. Captain Kadd arrives with Donna Donna, Blondie and Figaro. Papa Geno gives Kadd a treasure map which leads to the spot where Figaro's bed is located. Figaro has disappeared, but in his place is the Captain's prize, the jewel-filled Maltese Falcon. Pirates and Valkyries sing the Captain's praises. However, when the bird is opened, it is empty—Schlepporello has stolen the jewels. He negotiates with the opera manager, agreeing to exchange the jewels for the chance to sing (and tap dance) an aria. The finale resumes with all extolling the virtues of wealth.

PRODUCTION REQUIREMENTS

Major Roles. BLONDIE (s): C3 to C5 (D5 in final ensemble only). DONNA DONNA (s): B2 to C5 (D5 in final ensemble only). PECADILLO, Susanna Susannadanna's servant (t): D2 to A3. DONALD GIOVANNI (bar): G♯1 to F3. CAPTAIN KADD (bs-bar): F2 to F3 (to B3 falsetto). SCHLEPPORELLO, Donald Giovanni's servant (bar): G2 to E3 (vaudevillian acting role with one aria and tap dance).

Supporting Roles. *AL DONFONSO, Figaro's doctor (bar): G1 to F3. OPEC (ct): F2 to G4 (dances also). *SUSANNA SUSANNADANNA (m-s): B♭2 to G4.

Minor Roles. *PASHA SHABOOM (bar). *PAPA GENO (bar). *MAMA GENO (m-s).

Speaking Roles. *OPERA MANAGER. *FIGARO. NARRATOR (offstage, may be drawn from chorus).
*The above roles may be doubled as follows: Al Donfonso/Pasha Shaboom/Papa Geno; Susanna Susannadanna/Mama Geno; Opera Director/Figaro.

Chorus. SATB.

Ballet. Opec and Schlepporello dance.

Orchestra. 2 fls, 2 obs, 2 cls in B♭ and A, 2 bsns, 2 hrns in F, 2 trps in B♭, 3 trbs (3rd tenor/bs), timp, 2 perc, ukele, pedal steel guitar, elec guitar, piano or harpsi, strings.

Material. FS–P and VS: Theodore Presser.

REVIEWS

Michael Anthony "Minneapolis," *Musical America* (August 1984), pp. 23–24

"As expected, it is full of gags, both musical and visual. The musical ones work beautifully because of Schickele's deep understanding of the eighteenth-century musical idiom, specifically Mozart's. . . . The music isn't Mozart's, it's Schickele's, and it's quite lovely, except that as the scene progresses you notice that the strings have slipped momentarily into 'Ta-rara-boom-ti-ay.' "

"There is also the nagging suspicion, sacreligious as it is, that some of Schickele's characters are just a wee bit more interesting than Mozart's originals. Donna Donna and Blondie . . . sing a terrific duet in the second act during which they say things one imagines these characters have always wanted to say."

John Von Rhein "Hysteria in the making at 'Abduction' premiere," *Chicago Tribune* (April 30, 1984), section 5, p. 1+

"a manic, if overextended musical burlesque, the kind of Cuisinart concoction that might result if the Mozart operas were rewritten and staged all at once—by the Marx brothers."

"Most of the gags are, in fact, verbal, relying chiefly on '80s vernacular . . . The musical fun resides not just in the goofy misquotations and transformations of familiar classical tunes, but in the contemporary pop (tunes) that turn up in the middle of 'normal' arias and ensembles."

A LITTLE NIGHTMARE MUSIC

Spoof. One act, four numbers (20 minutes). Entire score is Mozart's "Eine Kleine Nachtmusic," with vocal melodies derived from the themes in comical, ingenious ways. One number for each movement of serenade.

Libretto by the composer. Premiere: Carnegie Hall, N.Y. 12.27.82. Recording: Vanguard.

PLOT

Setting: a Viennese palace, the eve of December 4, 1791.

Satirizing both the legend behind Mozart's death and the successful play about that story, "Amadeus," by Peter Shaffer, Salieri sits half asleep drinking in the beautiful music led by Mozart himself and drinking wine served by P.D.Q. Bach. When the vainglorious Schlafer enters, a row erupts between playwright and composer. Schlafer contends that Salieri seethes in jealousy regarding the young Mozart's capabilities; Salieri is disgusted at the writer's pomposity. Fed up with his guest, Salieri attempts to poison Schlafer's glass of wine, but through the clumsy interference of the servant, Bach, Mozart's drink is tainted by mistake. Mozart quenches his thirst, and the poison takes immediate effect. Salieri drops to the writhing Mozart's side as the oafish servant enters, this time spilling wine on Schlafer's favorite dinner jacket. As the curtain falls, the three surviving characters attack one another, hardly aware of Mozart's last gasps.

PRODUCTION REQUIREMENTS

Major Roles. ANTONIO SALIERI, a successful composer (bar): G1 to E3. PETER SCHLAFER, a mysterious writer (t): C2 to $B^{b}3$ (C5 to E5 fals).

Mute Roles. WOLFGANG AMADEUS MOZART, a not so successful composer (preferably a violinist, to lead string ensemble on stage). P.D.Q. BACH, a servant.

Orchestra. String ensemble (Mozart's original scoring).

Material. FS–P and VS: T. Presser.

OEDIPUS TEX

Spoof. One act, six numbers (30 minutes). In mock classical/baroque style. Originally an oratorio, later staged as an opera. Arias, duet, choruses, chorale, etc.

Libretto by composer. Premiere: Plymouth Music Series, Minneapolis, Minn. 3.15.88 (opera). Premiere: Jessie Jones Hall, Houston, Texas 4.1.86 (oratorio).

PLOT

Setting: Texas, in old Western days.

Oedipus Tex, the little known American cowboy brother of Oedipus Rex, shot some strangers and solved a riddle posed by Big Foot on his trip to town. He likes the town and resolves to give up the cowboy life, find a woman and settle down. The woman is Billie Jo Casta, Queen of the Rodeo. She forgives him for killing her husband on the way to town, but a plague descends on the town and Madam Peep, the fortune-teller and shepherdess, explains that Oedipus' actions are the source of the trouble. Billie Jo decides to hang herself and when Oedipus hears of her death, he puts his eyes out with her rhinestone barettes. The chorus laments: "the eyes of Texas are upon you" and the Narrator proclaims the moral: love your horse, not your mother.

PRODUCTION REQUIREMENTS

Major Roles. BILLIE JO CASTA (s): $B^{b}2$ to $B^{b}4$. MADAM PEEP (m-s): A2 to E4. NARRATOR (t): E2 to $A^{b}3$. OEDIPUS TEX (bar): C2 to F3.

Mute Roles. FRENCH HORN PLAYER (gradually assembles horn during opera). INSTRUMENT MAKER, supplier of french horn parts (opt).

Chorus. Mixed.

Orchestra. fl, ob, cl in B^{b}, bsn, solo hrn in F (see mute roles above), 2 trps in C, trb (t/bs), timp/perc, perc, keyboard harmonica or pump harmonium, strings (5–5–4–3–2).

Material. FS–P and VS: T. Presser.

REVIEWS

None located.

THE STONED GUEST

Satirical comedy. "A Half-Act Opera" (35 minutes). Humorous spoof on late Baroque and early Classical cliches. Brief overture. Set pieces: arias, duets, recitatives, trios, quartets.

Libretto by the composer. Premiere: Weber State College, Ogden, Utah 11.75. Recordings: Vanguard—VSD6536.

PLOT

Donna Ribalda bemoans that she is lost in a forest, having been abducted by an unknown assailant from whom she subsequently escaped. She is soon joined by Carmen Ghia. Hearing approaching footsteps, they quickly disguise Donna Ribalda as a man. Don Octave enters, bemoaning his life as a failure. When he removes his mask, Donna Ribalda recognizes him as her assailant. When she removes her disguise, he recognizes her as his sister and she berates him for having tried to abduct her. Competing for Don Octave's attention, Carmen bests Donna Ribalda in a competition of musical prowess. Donna Ribalda interrupts the others' amorous play, reminding them that they are still lost in the forest. However, help arrives in the form of a St. Bernard dog with an empty cask around its neck. Their curiosity about who emptied the cask is satisfied with the disconcerting arrival of the stoned guest, Il Commendatoreador, whom Carmen soon identifies as her father. Jealous of her brother's new-found love, Donna Ribalda attacks and strangles Carmen Ghia. Trying to avenge his lover's death, Don Octave lunges toward his sister, but ends up stabbing himself. Il Commendatoreador shoots Donna Ribalda and keels over, dead drunk. Nevertheless, the cast rouses itself for a happy finale.

PRODUCTION REQUIREMENTS

Major Roles. DONNA RIBALDA, a high-born lady of the lowlands (m-s): E2 to A^b4. CARMEN GHIA, a woman of ailing repute (s): B^b2 to B^b4 [opt C5]. DON OCTAVE, an itinerant nobleman (t): A1 to D4.

Minor Roles. IL COMMENDATOREADOR, the stoned guest (bs). DOG, a large, friendly St. Bernard dog.

Orchestra. fl, ob, bsn, hrn in F, trp in B^b, trb, strings, harpsichord.

Material. FS–P and VS: Theodore Presser.

REVIEWS

None located.

Harvey Schmidt (1929–)

THE FANTASTICKS

Bittersweet coming of age story. Two acts (full evening). Musical theater. Sparse sets, much miming of action. Intimate feeling with jazz, blues, Spanish influences. Some long structurally complex numbers with spoken dialogue interjections.

Book and lyrics by Tom Jones, suggested by the play "Les Romanesques" by Edmund Rostand. Premiere: Sullivan Street Playhouse, N.Y. 5.3.60. Recording: Polygram (1964).

PLOT

Setting: Then, Act I: "in the moonlight," Act II: "in the sun."

A story of love, parenthood, growing up, seasonal renewal. Matt and Luisa's fathers decide that the best way to insure that their children fall in love is to build a wall between them. Later, they hire the actor, El

Gallo, to stage a mock rape so that Matt may prove his love by rescuing Luisa. Once the children learn of their father's trick, they begin to quarrel and drift apart. Matt goes away to see the world, and Luisa runs away with El Gallo. Each of them is made wiser by their encounters with reality and return home to each other at last.

PRODUCTION REQUIREMENTS

Major Roles. El Gallo, the narrator (bar): A♭1 to G3. Luisa, the girl (s): B2 to C5. Matt, the boy (bar): A1 to F3.

Supporting Roles. Hucklebee, the boy's father (bar): A1 to G3. Bellomy, the girl's father (bar): A1 to F♯3.

Minor Roles. Ensemble singing only: Henry, the old actor; Mortimer, the man who dies; The Handyman.

Mute Roles. The Mute.

Chorus. Unison and two-part by minor characters.

Orchestra. harp, bs, drum, piano.

Material. FS–P and VS: Music Theatre International.

110 IN THE SHADE

Small town drama. Two acts, eleven scenes (full evening). Musical theater with simple, melodic vocal lines and orchestration.

Lyrics by Tom Jones. Book by N. Richard Nash. Premiere: Broadhurst Theatre, N.Y. 10.24.63. Recording: RCA OC/TW.

PLOT

Setting: a Western town in the U.S.

A brash rainmaker, Starbuck, makes great promises to the people of this Western drought-stricken town. Only Lizzie sees Starbuck as the fake that he really is. But Starbuck turns his charms on the plain, love-starved woman, and the two make love while the townsfolk enjoy the annual picnic. Starbuck promises to take Lizzie away with him, but Lizzie finally realizes that she prefers a simple life. She decides to remain with her hometown suitor, Sheriff File. Starbuck is driven off as a fake, but, lo and behold, the rain does comes.

PRODUCTION REQUIREMENTS

Major Roles. Lizzie Curry (s): G2 to G4. Bill Starbuck (bar-t): G1 to A♭3.

Supporting Roles. File, the sheriff (bar): B♭1 to F♯3. H. C. Curry, Lizzie's father (bar and speaking). Lizzie's brothers: Noah and Jimmie Curry (bars and speaking).

Minor Roles. Toby (bar). Snookie (a). Other minor roles sung and spoken by chorus members.

Chorus. SATB (much unison and two-part writing). Brief number for children's voices.

Ballet. Toby and Snookie dance.

Orchestra. Woodwind I: pic, fl; II: ob, Eng hrn, III: E♭cl, cl; IV: cl fl; V: cl, bs cl; VI: bsn, bar sax, cl; 2 hrns; 3 trps; trb; 2 perc; guitar; harp; 4 vlas (or vlns); 2 vcls; bs.

Material. FS–P and VS: Chappell Music Company.

William Schuman (1910–)

A QUESTION OF TASTE

Light romance. One act, one scene (55 minutes). Through-composed, tonal, moderately dissonant. Short prelude; arias, ensembles embedded in texture. Vocal style patterned after speech with textual clarity of utmost importance.

Libretto by J. D. McClatchy, based on a story by Roald Dahl. Commissioned for Glimmerglass Opera by a grant from The Eugene V. and Clare Thaw Charitable Trust. Premiere: Glimmerglass Opera, N.Y. 6.24.89.

PLOT

Setting: the dining room of an elegant New York brownstone, 1910.

The Schofield household prepares for dinner with a guest of honor, the noted gourmet and wine connoisseur, Phillisto Pratt. Louise's boyfriend, Tom, hopes to use the occasion to ask Mr. Schofield for his daughter's hand in marriage, despite parental objections to his lack of financial means. But the unassertive fellow does not get a chance to ask before the dinner with Mr. Pratt begins. Mr. Schofield immediately challenges the connoisseur to identify his choice of wine by taste alone. Mr. Pratt, clearly infatuated with Louise, proposes a wager. The over-confident Schofield allows Pratt to set the stakes. The bet is to be Louise's hand in marriage against a check made out to her in the amount of a half million dollars. Louise is outraged at being victim of a wager, but her father's assurances and prospect of financial independence for herself and Tom convinces her to go along. The tasting begins. Mr. Pratt artfully builds the suspense, but when he makes his guess, he is exactly right, much to the distress of his host. Just before the reluctant bride is given away, Mrs. Hudson, the housekeeper, enters with Mr. Pratt's eyeglasses which he left in the study on Mr. Schofield's wine cabinet! Pratt unmasked as a cheat, leaves in a huff, failing to retrieve his check. All toast to the young couple's change of fortune and bright future.

PRODUCTION REQUIREMENTS

Major Roles. LOUISE, the Schofield's daughter (s): D3 to C5. MR. SCHOFIELD (bar): B♭1 to F♯3. PHILLISTO PRATT (bs-bar): F1 to E♭3. MRS. HUDSON, the housekeeper (m-s): A2 to G♯4. TOM, Louise's boyfriend (t): D2 to C4.

Supporting Roles. MRS. SCHOFIELD (m-s): C♯3 to A♭4.

Mute Roles. SARAH, a servant (preferably comic).

Orchestra. 2 fls, 2 obs, 2 cls, 2 bsns, 2 hrns, 2 trps, 2 trbs, 2 perc, cel, strings.

Material. FS–P and VS: T. Presser.

REVIEWS

Bernard Holland "'Casey,' New Schuman Work, as Glimmerglass Opens," *New York Times* (June 26, 1989), p. 14

"Mr. Schuman's transformations of waltz time use a single dance form to pull us between hope, happiness and downright anguish."

"'A Question of Taste' is going to be the kind of period melodrama that these 1910 diners might have seen in the theatre the night before. There is villainy and virtue, love and contempt—but no people."

Charles Shere (1935–)

THE BOX OF 1914

Peformance art. Two acts, sixteen scenes (20 minutes). Avante-garde style. Largely aleatoric, chance music. Each short scenario based on formally given or suggested musical motives which could vary with each performance. Prerecorded tape sounds and unconventional notation employed. Vocal solos in short phrases not directly supported by orchestra.

Libretto by Marcel Duchamp, based on his work of the same name, as translated by the composer, and related to concepts in Duchamp's "The Bride Stripped Bare by Her Bachelors, Even." Premiere: New Music Ensemble, San Francisco Conservatory, Calif. 1.30.81.

PLOT

Setting: Paris, 1914.

A musical representation of Duchamp's Dada play, a loosely associated series of scenarios in a "cubist" musical patchwork: partly sung, partly narrated, partly mimed, and pulled together by pictures and designs projected on the backdrop. The composer lists the Duchampian methods and principles he has employed in his introduction: "found material (or 'readymades'), irony, obsession, arbitrary and random choices deliberately interfering with conscious decision, slight shifts of perspective, anachronism and so on." Seemingly plotless, the text is made up of questions about Art itself, taken from snatches of Duchamp's own writings.

PRODUCTION REQUIREMENTS

Major Roles. TENOR: C2 to $B^{\flat}3$ (ossia $B^{\flat}1$). SOPRANO: $B^{\flat}2$ to B4 ($^{\flat}$ indicates quarter tone).

Supporting Roles. NARRATOR (spoken role).

Chorus. Women's (opt).

Ballet. MIME-DANCER (mute).

Orchestra. fl (picc), ob (Eng hrn), cl (alt cl opt), bsn, hrn, trp, trb, 2 perc, harp, piano, strings (1–1–1–1), prerecorded tapes.

Material. Score: American Music Center or contact composer through AMC.

REVIEWS

Robert Commanday "Major Premieres at Conservatory," *San Francisco Chronicle* (February 2, 1981), p. 45

> "John Adams, guiding the critical timing and some open musical choices . . . and Jeanne Thomas who directed the production, had a major creative share. 'The Box' captures the Duchamp quality of eccentric play in the paintings and apparently random notes. It made a highly diverting music play."

> "The understated, unpushy style of the performance overall, avoiding the sassy tone of the iconoclast, enabled the ironies, puns and ambiguities of the piece to work at an unpretentious level."

Michael Walsh "An evening of new music," *San Francisco Examiner* (January 31, 1981), section A, p. 10

> " 'The Box' is, despite the array of contemporary compositional and instrumental procedures employed, immediately accessible; it could easily be done by even modestly talented college opera departments. Second, it is musically witty at times, and at others quite beautiful."

Elie Siegmeister (1909–   )

NIGHT OF THE MOONSPELL

Comedy. Three acts, nine scenes (full evening). Set arias, trios, quartets joined by recitative. Variety of styles from atonal, angular, chromatic to jazz. Cajuns have much spoken dialogue.

Libretto by Edward Mabley, based on Shakespeare's "A Midsummer Night's Dream." Commission: Shreveport Symphony Society. Premiere: Shreveport, Louisiana 11.14.76.

PLOT

Setting: forest and bayou country of Louisiana, turn of the century during Mardi Gras season.

A recasting of Shakespeare's play with the black King and Queen of the Mardi Gras replacing Oberon and Titania, and the Cajuns performing a masked opera within an opera (Pyramus and Thisby). The noble characters of the play's original (Theseus and Hippolyte) are here made wealthy plantation owners (the Colonel and Josephine). Shakespeare's guildhall tradesmen are cast now as Cajuns and the fairies are young black children. Robin (Shakespeare's Puck) is a young black fellow who dabbles in voodoo magic. His miscast spells bring calamity and hilarity to the two mismatched pairs of aristocratic lovers: Margaret and Anthony (Hermia and Lysander), and Holly and David (Helena and Demetrius). One of the Cajuns, Nic Mazette, plays the buffoon (Bottom). The libretto remains quite faithful to the original plot with the added color, colloquialisms, and dialects of the Cajun and southern black backwoods.

PRODUCTION REQUIREMENTS

Major Roles. MARGARET (s): C3 to B4. ANTHONY, a young man from the city (bar): F♯1 to G3. HOLLY (s): D♭3 to C5. DAVID, a local young man (t): C♯2 to B♭3. ROBIN (t): D2 to B♭3. KING OF THE MARDI GRAS (bar): G♯1 to G3. QUEEN OF THE MARDI GRAS (m-s): B2 to A4.

Supporting Roles. NIC MAZETTE, a weaver (buf bs-bar): F1 to G3 (A2 to B♭3 falsetto). THE COLONEL, owner of the plantation (bs-bar): G1 to F♯3. JOSEPHINE, the Colonel's wife (m-s): A2 to G4. MATTHEW, Margaret's father (bs): F♯1 to E3. CRICKET, a fairy (boy s): D3 to B4.

Minor Roles. The other fairies (mostly ensemble singing): WHISTLEBERRY (girl s): D3 to B4; MINOU (girl a): G2 to D4. BAMBOULA (boy s): G2 to D4. The Cajuns. FRANCOIS FLUTE, a harness maker (t): C2 to B♭3 (B♭2 to C4 falsetto); PIERRE MARTEAU, a carpenter (bs); THOM LEBEC, a tinker (t); JEAN BIENADROIT, a boatbuilder (bs); and ROBERT FAIMDELOUP, a tailor (bar).

Mute Roles. THE INDIAN BOY. THE CAJUN "ORCHESTRA." BUTLER.

Ballet. Attendants to the King and Queen.

Orchestra. 2 fls (2 piccs), 2 obs (2 Eng hrns), 2 B^b cls (2 bs cls), 2 bsns (2 cont bsns), 4 hrns, trp in C, 2 trps in B^b, 3 trbs, tuba, timp, 3 perc, piano, harp, strings.

Material. FS–P and VS: Carl Fischer. VS: American Music Center.

REVIEWS

Mark Melson "Siegmeister's 'Night of the Moonspell,' " *Musical America* (April 1977), pp. 19+

"The composer cleverly gave each social group its own musical language: atonal and aggressively 'modern' for the plantation owners, earthy and rough-hewn for the Cajuns, and jazzy (usually with an accent on the blues) for the blacks."

Highlights: "The first act is strong, with a fine love duet in the first scene, a stirring 'Exultate'-like entrance for the black Mardi Gras King and Queen. . . . The last act, . . . includes a lively reconciliation duet, . . . an almost vaudevillian opera-within-an-opera that quotes everything from *Eine Kleine Nachtmusik* . . . to . . . the *Tristan* Liebestod."

Harlan Snow "Shreveport," *Opera News* (February 12, 1977), p. 38

"Siegmeister's score is an ingenious composition of beautiful sonorities, powerful and illuminating effects and solid dramatic integrity. The composer possesses a Puccinian sense of the dramatic."

"The sounds of *Moonspell* are not tonal for the most part. There is not much for the singer to hang on to, but there are relationships that unfold with calculable logic. . . . and the singers are provided with soaring expressive melodies."

Carol Traub "Shreveport," *Music Journal* (January 1977), 35(1):34

"Siegmeister has invested his score with imagination and mature individual style, and the high-spirited writing is attractive for both the large cast and orchestra."

Stanley Silverman (1938–)

HOTEL FOR CRIMINALS

Stylized satire. Two acts, sixteen scenes, two sets (90 minutes). An opera/ music theater piece, avant-garde with Brecht-Weill influence. Short scenes with spoken dialogue, taped narration, one or two songs. Dissonant at times, but mostly lighter style. Generally conjunct, lyrical vocal lines.

Libretto by Richard Foreman, based on Louis Feulliade's silent crime-serial films. Commissioned by the National Opera Institute. Premiere: Lenox Arts Center, Mass. 8.14.74. Performances: Music-Theatre Performing Group, Exchange Theatre, Wesbeth, N.Y. 12.30.74.

PLOT

Setting: Paris, just before World War I.

A pastiche of surrealistic black and white film vignettes focus on the characters Feulliade portrayed in his films: Fantomas, the arch-villain and master criminal; Judex, the fanciful do-good detective; Irma Vep, the sexy yet dangerous vamp; the innocent lovers, Max and Helene; and the crafty gangsters (Gaston, Duchamp, L'Enjoleur, and Dr. LaCloche). In brief glimpses, we learn that Max has fallen in love with Fantomas' daughter, Helene. But the treacherous Fantomas holds Max captive in his hotel suite. Judex comes to the rescue disguised as a priest (to perform the wedding ceremony). But Judex cannot save Max from the conniving Irma Vep, who gains entrance to the hotel disguised as a chambermaid. All the while, Max is plagued by confused identities, he doesn't recognize Helene, and is temporarily blinded by Irma's sultry advances. But he remains true to Helene!

Helene is struck by Fantomas' cruising silver Rolls Royce. Or is it Max who's struck? As the gangsters marvel at the silver Rolls (which is now cruising through the hotel corridors), Fantomas dons a gas mask, as the car spews forth deadly gases which fell the whole crowd. The prerecorded tape asks all to return next week for further adventures of Fantomas, Irma Vep, and the mysteriously recovered Judex.

PRODUCTION REQUIREMENTS

Major Roles. MAX BEAUCHAMP (t): $E^{b}2$ to C4 (ossia $B^{b}1$). FANTOMAS (bar): G1 to E3. JUDEX (bs): C1 to F3. HELENE (spinto s): A2 to $B^{b}4$. IRMA VEP (m-s): $F^{\#}2$ to B4.

Minor Roles. Vampire Gang: M. GASTON (lyr t); ALAIN DUCHAMP (t); JULOT L'ENJOLEUR (bar); DR. LACLOCHE (bs).

Chorus. TTBarBs (sung by minor roles). SATB finale (sung by company).

Orchestra. fl (picc), cl in B^b (bs cl in B^b and alt sax in E^b), trp in B^b, trb, tuba, perc, classical guitar (banjo and mand), piano (optional: cel and elec piano), violin, auto horns.

Material. FS–P, VS and libretto: Belwin-Mills Pub. VS: American Music Center.

REVIEWS

Leighton Kerner "Lenox, Mass.," *Opera News* (November 1976), p. 52–53

> "Foreman's text and staging captured with amazing accuracy the visual style, sexual allusions and black poetry of the films, despite the constant and successfully carried out satirical overlay of the whole show."

> "Silverman's many-textured chamber score draws on many styles, from Satie through cafe-Parisian and Kurt Weill right into post-Webern vocal leaps. . . . The many infectious tunes sound endearingly familiar, but they are Silverman's own."

Leonard Marcus "Lenox Arts Center: 'Hotel for Criminals,' " *Musical America* (December 1974), pp. 25–26

> "All told, it's more fun than a lot of works being produced today, at least for the first hour. . . . Then the gimmick begins to pall, at least for the adults in the audience. The production is a delight, with Foreman's sets . . . absolutely ingenious."

MADAME ADARE

Satire. One act, six scenes, four or five sets (60 minutes). Musical theater style with jazz and blues elements, mixed meters, frequent tempo changes. Through-composed with orchestral prologues, introductions, and vamps. Alternates between conversational and aria-like sections, with brief recitatives.

Libretto by Richard Foreman. Commissioned by New York City Opera. Premiere: New York City Opera 10.9.80.

PLOT

Setting and time: turn of the century.

Dr. Hoffman refuses to give Miss Adare any more psychiatric treatments until she pays her bill. To force him to help her, she unsuccessfully tries to shoot him. Her agent encourages her to choose a profession: with her talents, she could be a film star or an opera singer. When the Devil tempts her, she leans toward film stardom. However, when Diaghilev offers her the glory of the opera stage and the opportunity to fight cultural decadence, she chooses opera. Despite her pure intentions, the Devil claims victory over her soul.

When the successful Madame Adare returns to pay Dr. Hoffman, his experience at her recent debut prevents him from accepting her money. He explains that in treating her, he tried to squelch the very force that enables her to sing with such beauty. He refuses payment since she is, happily, not cured. Enraged that he is mocking her, she again shoots him, this time with a true shot. In a publicity interview, she explains the shooting by describing her fundamental depravity, a trait she believes that she shares with all humans beings. No longer concerned with fighting cultural decay, she cites being openly trashy as the basis for her success—as a film star.

PRODUCTION REQUIREMENTS

Major Roles. MADAME ADARE (s): C3 (B^{b}2 opt) to C5. DR. HOFFMAN, her psychoanalyst (bs-bar): F1 to F3. BOOTH, her agent (t, med.-low): B1 to A^{b}3.

Supporting Roles. THE DEVIL (bs): $F^{\#}$1 to B2. DIAGHILEV (t, high): E2 to A3 (C4 opt).

Minor Roles. INTERVIEWER (bar). DIRECTOR (t). CAMERAMAN (bs).

Chorus. SATB, Seven nurses, seven men.

Orchestra. 2 fls (picc), 2 obs (Eng hrn), 2 cls (alt sax and bs cl), 2 bsns (cont bsn), 4 hrns, 2 trps, 2 trbs, tuba, timp, 2 perc, harp, piano (cel), mini–synthesizer, guitar (banjo).

Material. FS–P: G. Schirmer. FS: American Music Center.

REVIEWS

Donal Henahan "Opera: 'An American Trilogy,' 3 One-Act Works," *New York Times* (October 10, 1980), section 3, p. 14

> "This, in some ways, is a modern myth as theatrically viable as any that Euripides explored — well, perhaps that goes a little too far — but 'Madame Adare' represented the evening's most adventurous thrust. At least, it tried to depict the Janus-faced ambition of many contemporary artists. . . . However, the outcome here was rather lame, in spite of a few entertaining patches."

Patrick J. Smith "New York City Opera: An American Trilogy," *Musical America* (February 1981), pp. 20–21

> "a trivialization of Brecht and Weill, but it does have a certain show biz glitter about it, especially when tricked out with Silverman's music, which includes a torch song, a patter song, various bows to Hollywood 'movie music,' lots of ersatz Weill, and even the coronation scene from *Boris Godunov* . . . "

Julia Smith (1911–1989)

DAISY

Historical drama. Two acts (full evening). Overture, entr'acte for Act II and orchestral interludes throughout. Arias and vocal ensembles interspersed with dialogue. Tonally conservative light opera/musical theater style incorporating excerpts of famous melodies as well as traditional Girl Scout songs.

Libretto by Bertita Harding. Commissioned by The Opera Guild of Greater Miami and The Girl Scout Council of Tropical Florida. Premiere: Greater Miami Opera Association 11.3.73. Recording: Orchestra and Chorus of the Charlotte Opera Association for Orion Master Recordings Inc., 5840 Busch Drive, Malibu, California 90265. ORS 76248.

PLOT

Setting: chronicles the American Girl Scout movement, beginning in Warwickshire, England; to London; Lochs, Scotland; Savannah, Georgia; Washington D.C.; New York City; and Briarcliff, New York, 1899–1927.

The morning after giving a successful party in honor of the Prince of Wales, Daisy is crushed when her husband asks for a divorce. Twelve years later, she attends the opera in London with Sir Robert Baden-Powell, founder of the Boy Scouts and the English Girl Guides. He sparks her interest in the Girl Guides, and they discuss starting Guiding in America. Soon after, Daisy begins to teach Scottish girls how to spin and weave. Back home in Savannah, Georgia, she asks Nina Pape to help her start Girl Guiding in America. Nina provides a group of enthusiastic girls, and the first meeting takes place in 1912. Daisy soon changes the name of the organization to "Girl Scouts," and the movement quickly spreads to Washington, D.C. and New York City. In 1917, Girl Scouts from across the country meet in New York to discuss how they can contribute to the war effort. A small scout convinces Daisy and the Executive Board that by selling her mother's cookies, the Scouts can buy bonds to help their country.

In 1925, while working to spread the Girl Scout movement internationally, Daisy learns that she has an incurable illness. The next year, she persuades Jane Rippin to convene the Fourth International Conference in Briarcliff, N.Y. With this final great achievement, Daisy is content that she has helped hundreds of thousands of young girls "find their own way" through the inspiration of the Girl Scout movement.

PRODUCTION REQUIREMENTS

Major Roles. DAISY OR JULIETTE LOW (s): D3 to B4. TOM, the Low's gardener: A2 to F♯3. BILLOW, Daisy's husband (t): G3 to A3 (B♭ opt). SIR ROBERT BADEN-POWELL, founder of Boy Scouts (bar): B♭1 to F♯3.

Supporting Roles. BELLA, the Low's Scottish maid (m-s): G2 to F♯4. LADY WARWICK, the Low's neighbor (m-s or c): B♭2 to G4.

Minor Roles. MRS. BATEMAN (s). MOSIANNA (m-s or c). MISS JOHNTSON (m-s). SMALLEST SCOUT (child s). MR. GAMMON (t). DEAN RUSSEL (bs). JANE RIPPIN (s).

Chorus. SATB, a strong female chorus. Male quartet: TTBB (opt).

Ballet. Final sequence of international ballets could be performed by various groups of girls.

Orchestra. fl (picc), ob (Eng hrn), 2 cls in B♭ (bs cl), bsn, 2 hrns in F, 2 trps in B♭, trb, timp, 2 percs, harp and/or piano, cel, strings (4–4–3–2–2 minimum).

Material. FS–P and VS: Theodore Presser. VS: American Music Center.

REVIEWS

Martha F. Van Camp "Opera's good deed," *Christian Science Monitor* (November 7, 1973), p. B10

" 'Daisy' certainly should not be permitted to pass into musical limbo. . . . A suggestion might be to tighten up the story, prolong some of the lovely musical interludes, emphasize some of the heart-warming moments — such as the World War I decision to bake cookies as a bond-buying money source — and resolve it into a musical production which could be played throughout the country."

James Roos "Opera 'Daisy' Is a Spirited Charmer," *The Miami Herald* (November 5, 1973), p. 8-C

"this musical biography . . . is something of a charmer. . . . It turned out to be a vivid, colorful, spirited show, part opera, part Broadway musical, all pleasure."

"From the start it has glittering promise with a ballroom scene. . . . Daisy's husband . . . breaks the divorce news soap-opera style, and from then on it's all high aims and firm resolve with quick shifts in scenes."

"At its best the music has vitality and validity to set an audience applauding or to keep it in lethal silence, which is even a bigger tribute. There is at least a baker's dozen of lyric tunes."

Stephen Sondheim (1930–)

COMPANY

Contemporary concept musical. Two acts, fourteen scenes (full evening). Musical theater with pop rhythms, ballads, and wordy "patter songs." Many ensembles: small solos in dialogue style, unison, or two parts.

Lyrics by the composer. Book by George Furth. Premiere: Alvin Theatre, N.Y. 4.26.70. Recording: Columbia OS-3550.

PLOT

Setting: New York City, early 1970s.

Robert has just celebrated his thirty-fifth birthday, and still remains an eligible bachelor. His social life revolves around his married friends (who feel he should settle down) and the women he dates: April, the stewardess; Kathy, who marries someone else; and Marta, the oddball. Through these friendships and encounters, Bobby comes to see the pros and cons of married life in a big city, but concludes that having someone to share life with might not be such a bad idea.

PRODUCTION REQUIREMENTS

Major Roles. ROBERT [BOBBY] (bar/ten): A1 to A3.

Supporting Roles. JOANNE, middle-aged drinker (a): E2 to B♭3 (talky role for actress). MARTA (m-s): C2 to E♭4 (sings long-lined patter song). AMY (m-s): G2 to C♭4 (rapid chatty style in low tessitura). JENNY (legit s): C2 to A♭4.

Minor Roles. Women (comfortable pop s): SARAH, SUSAN, KATHY (also a dancer), APRIL [to A4]. Men (comfortable high bar): HARRY, PETER, DAVID, PAUL, LARRY.

Chorus. Comprised of roles listed above.

Orchestra. Reed I: alt sax, cl/E♭cl, fl/alt fl, picc; Reed II: cl, t sax, bs cl, picc or fl/alt fl; Reed III: t sax, bs cl, cl, fl; Reed IV: cl/Eng hrn/ob, bar sax; Reed V: bar sax, bsn, cl, bs cl; trps I & II (flugel hrn); trp III; hrns I & II; trb I; trb II; vlns ABC; vcls I & II; 4 female pit voices; elec keyboard—piano conductor; guitars I & II (acoustic, amplified, banjo plus bs guitar on II); bs; perc I & II.

Material. FS–P and VS: Music Theatre International.

FOLLIES

Concept musical. Originally one act, two acts optional (full evening). Contemporary conversational style with flashbacks to earlier vaudeville style solos, ensembles, dance numbers. Large role for orchestra: dance music, interludes, atmosphere settings, reprises, etc.

Lyrics by the composer. Book by James Goldman. Premiere: Winter Garden Theatre, N.Y. 4.4.71. Recording: Capitol-SO 761.

PLOT

Setting: reunion at the Weismann Theatre, the present.

Middle-aged performers from the Weismann Follies come together for a reunion before the old theater is torn down. The four main characters, Phyllis and Ben Stone, and Sally and Buddy Plummer, deal with the realities of their lives in contrast with the unreality of the theatre. They relive memories of their youth through their young counterparts, and Sally and Ben even attempt to rekindle their old romance. Solange, a French cabaret singer, and Stella, Carlotta, and Hattie (old American Vaudeville stars), also offer performances. The chorus numbers have an eerie quality as aging performers mingle with the ghosts of their youthful Follies counterparts. Finally, a real revival of a Follies show begins, focusing on the real follies of youth, love, and life. Each of the four main characters also performs, concluding that they cannot turn back, and must leave the dying theater.

PRODUCTION REQUIREMENTS

Major Roles. SALLY DURANT PLUMMER (m-s): F2 to G4. BENJAMIN STONE (bar): A1 to F3. BUDDY PLUMMER (high bar): C2 to F3. PHYLLIS ROGERS STONE (m-s): F♯2 to E4.

Supporting Roles. SOLANGE, a French cabaret singer (m-s): A2 to G4. STELLA, Vaudeville belter (a): E2 to A3. CARLOTTA, Vaudeville singer (a): E♭2 to B3. HATTIE, Vaudeville belter (a): G2 to B3.

Minor Roles. ROSCOE, master of ceremonies (t). MR. WHITMAN (bar). MRS. WHITMAN (m-s). YOUNG BEN (bar). YOUNG BUDDY (bar/ten). YOUNG SALLY (s). YOUNG PHYLLIS (m-s). YOUNG HATTIE (s). HEIDI (s): to G4. YOUNG HEIDI (s): to A♭4.

Chorus. SATB, showgirls, singers and dancers.

Ballet. Follies type line dancing for choruses; Hattie, Stella, Buddy, Phyllis and Ben dance solos; Young Ben, Phyllis, Buddy, Sally and "Old" Sally also move.

Orchestra. Reed I: alt sax, fl, picc, alt fl, cl, E♭ cl, s sax; Reed II: alt sax, fl, picc, cl; Reed III: t sax, fl, cl, bs cl; Reed IV: t sax, ob, Eng hrn, cl; Reed V: bar sax, bsn, cl, fl; hrn; trps I & II; trp III; trb I; trb II; trb III; vlns; vla; vcl; bass; harp; guitar; perc; piano–conductor.

Material. FS–P and VS: Music Theatre International.

INTO THE WOODS

Material. Score not published in time for inclusion.

A LITTLE NIGHT MUSIC

Witty, bittersweet romance. Two acts, fifteen scenes (full evening). Sophisticated musical theater mostly in 3/4 time. Vocal writing from declamatory to lyric, from patter song to madrigal style of the "liebeslieder" ensemble.

Lyrics by the composer. Book by Hugh Wheeler, as suggested by Ingmar Bergman's film, "Smiles of a Summer Night." Premiere: Shubert Theatre, N.Y. 2.25.73. Recording: Columbia JS 32265.

PLOT

Setting: turn-of-the-century Sweden.

People of all ages and social position become a part of this intertwined romantic tale: Fredrik Egerman, a middle-aged lawyer; his eighteen-year-old virgin bride, Anne; his son, Henrik, who is in love with Anne; his former mistress, the actress Desiree; Desiree's lover, the arrogant Count Carl Magnus Malcolm; the Count's depressed wife, Charlotte; and even the maid, Petra. After much struggle and suffering over mismatched relationships, Desiree's mother, a former mistress of several noble characters, invites them all to a weekend in the country, where the appropriate pairs are finally united.

PRODUCTION REQUIREMENTS

Major Roles. FREDRIK EGERMAN, a middle-aged lawyer (bar): A1 to F3. DESIREE ARMFELDT, a middle-aged actress (m-s): G^b2 to G4.

Supporting Roles. MADAME ARMFELDT, Desiree's mother (m-s): C3 to $F^\#4$. ANNE EGERMAN, Fredrik's child-bride (s): $G^\#2$ to A^b4. HENRIK EGERMAN, Fredrik's son (t): G1 to B3. PETRA, the Egerman's maid (a): F2 to D^b4. COUNT CARL-MAGNUS MALCOLM (bar): C2 to F3. COUNTESS CHARLOTTE MALCOLM (a): G2 to B3.

Minor Roles. THE "LIEBESLIEDERS:" MRS. NORDSTROM (s I) to sustained E5, MRS. ANDERSSEN (s II): to B^b4, MRS. SEGSTROM (m-s), MR. ERLANSON (t): to B^b4 (possible C4), MR. LINDQUIST (bs).

Bit Roles. FREDERIKA ARMFELDT (m-s). Non-singing: FRID, Madame Armfeldt's butler; MALLA, Madame Armfeldt's maid; BERTRAND, a page.

Chorus. None, except the "liebeslieder" ensemble.

Orchestra. Reed I: fl, picc, alt fl, bs fl, cl; Reed II: fl, picc, alt fl, cl; Reed III: cl, bs cl, fl; Reed IV: ob, Eng hrn; Reed V: bsn, cl; hrns I & II; hrn III; trp I & II; trb; perc; cel (piano); harp; vlns ABC; vla; vcl; bs; piano–conductor.

Material. FS–P: Music Theatre International. VS: widely available, Revelation Music Publishing & Rilting Music.

PACIFIC OVERTURES

Kabuki/musical theatre. Two acts, twelve numbers (full evening). Contemporary pop-rock style with oriental influences. Set numbers with spoken dialogue. Orchestra plays large role. All roles played by men; women change sets and appear in final chorus.

Lyrics by the composer, book by John Weidman with additional material by Hugh Wheeler. Premiere: Winter Garden, N.Y. 1.11.76. Performances: Off-Broadway revival 84. Recordings: RCA (1977).

PLOT

Setting: Japan, 1853–present.

Recounts the history of Japan, from the time of the Floating Kingdom, the isolated island empire, to its emergence in its present role, as leader of international commerce. Until 1853, when Commodore Matthew Perry and his American fleet arrived to open Japan to the West, Japan had lived in peace, undisturbed by intruders for centuries. We witness the many changes in social order, customs and dress that were part of the price Japan paid to move from isolation to world influence.

PRODUCTION REQUIREMENTS

Major Roles. RECITER (bs-bar): G1 to E3. KAYAMA (t): $E^{b}2$ to G3 (one G1). MANJIRO (t): D2 to F3. ABE, First Councillor (bar): C2 to D3.

Supporting Roles. THIEF/SOOTHSAYER/WARRIOR/RUSSIAN ADMIRAL (bs-bar): F1 to G3. SHOGUN'S MOTHER/AMERICAN ADMIRAL (bar/t): A1 to A3. OLD MAN/FRENCH ADMIRAL (bar/t): A1 to G3. MADAM/BRITISH ADMIRAL (t): C2 to $F^{\#}3$. FISHERMAN/WRESTLER (bar): $C^{\#}2$ to $G^{b}3$. BOY (boy s): A2 to F4. DUTCH ADMIRAL (bar): $B^{b}1$ to E3.

Speaking Roles. TAMATE, Kayama's wife.

Minor Roles. SHOGUN'S WIFE (t), 3 SAILORS (t,bar,bar).

Bit Roles. ADAMS, WILLIAMS, COMMODORE PERRY, SAMURAI, SERVANTS, OBSERVERS, PRIESTS, GIRLS, BOYS, NOBLES, ETC. all drawn from chorus.

Chorus. Unison or SATB, not a large role until final chorus.

Orchestra. Reed I (fl, picc, rec, alt fl); Reed II (B^b cl, E^b cl, fl); Reed III (cl, bs cl, fl); Reed IV (ob, Eng hrn); Reed V (bsn); hrns I & II; trps I & II; trb; harp; vlns AB; vla; vcl; bs; perc I & II; keyboard (RMI, cel); stage band I (shamisen); stage band II (perc). Off Broadway: fl, cl, piano, cel, synth, perc.

Material. FS–P and VS: Music Theatre International.

SUNDAY IN THE PARK WITH GEORGE

Study of the artistic process. Two acts, three scenes (full evening). Impressionistic use of color chords in spun-out set numbers. Contemporary musical theater vocal style from patter and parlando to broad lyricism. Vocal parts not directly supported by rhythmic accompaniment. Orchestra serves important unifying role.

Book by James Lapine with lyrics by the composer, suggested by the life of Georges Seurat and his painting, "A Sunday Afternoon on the Island of La Grand Jatte." Premiere: Booth Theatre, N.Y. 5.2.84. Recording: RCA HBC 15042; HBE15042 (cassette); RCD 15042 (CD).

PLOT

Setting: Act I: Outside Paris, Sundays from 1884–1886. Act II: American Art Museum, 1984; La Grande Jatte, present day.

George is diligently at work, painting Parisians, as they enjoy a Sunday afternoon on the Island of La Grand Jatte. From the now familiar painting, the characters spring to life and we get to know each of them and their various relationships. The most colorful of the characters is George's mistress and model, Dot. Due to George's obsession with his work, their relationship is doomed. When Dot realizes that she is pregnant, she finally accepts a marriage offer from Louis, the baker.

The second act leaps forward to 1984, where George's great-grandson, a multi-media sculptor named George, is unveiling his seventh "Chromolume." Though he can deal well with the politics of the situation, George struggles with his desire to break new artistic ground. His grandmother, Marie (Dot's daughter), is there to encourage him and relate tales of his great-grandfather. George visits La Grande Jatte and is reinspired by the ghost of his great-grandmother to "move ahead."

PRODUCTION REQUIREMENTS

Major Roles. GEORGE SEURAT/GEORGE, great-grandson (bar-t): G1 to A♭3 (flexible voice required, one song mostly falsetto). DOT, George Seurat's mistress/ MARIE, young George's grandmother, Dot's daughter (m-s): E2 to D4.

Minor Roles. OLD LADY/BLAIR DANIELS, art critic (c); NURSE and MRS. HARRIET PAWLING, patron of the arts (m-s); BOATMAN/ CHARLES REDMOND, visiting curator (bs-bar).

Chorus/Minor Roles. SATB made up of minor characters whose small solos are in comfortable ranges (S need strong soprano range, possible E5 in choral passages only): FRANZ, servant/DENNIS, technician; YOUNG MAN and FRIEDA/BETTY, an artist; MAN, LOUIS, the baker/BILLY WEBSTER, Harriet's friend; JULES, artist/BOB GREENBERG, museum director; YVONNE, Jule's wife/NAOMI EISEN, a composer; CELESTE #1/A WAITRESS; CELESTE #2/ELAINE; LOUISE, Jules and Yvonne's daughter, and BOY; SOLDIER/ALEX, an artist; MAN WITH BIKE/MUSEUM ASSISTANT; WOMAN WITH CARRIAGE/ PHOTOGRAPHER; MR. LEE RANDOLPH, museum publicist.

Orchestra. Reed I: fl, cl, bs cl, Eng hrn, picc, s sax; Reed II: fl, ob, cl, Eng hrn, picc, alt sax; hrn (B♭ and F); violins I and II; viola; cello; harp; perc; synth; piano/cel; piano–conductor.

Material. FS–P and VS: Music Theatre International. Note: optional laser package to create Cromolume avail for rental from MTI.

SWEENEY TODD
THE DEMON BARBER OF FLEET STREET

Musical theater that approaches opera. Two acts (full evening). Subtitled "a musical thriller." Organ prelude, orchestral transitions between scenes, but orchestra generally accompanies. Set pieces: arias, duets, full choruses. Vocal counterpoint in ensembles a highlight.

Lyrics by the composer. Book by Hugh Wheeler. Premiere: Uris Theatre, New York 3.1.79. Performances: New York City Opera 84; Houston Opera 84. Recording: Original broadway cast; RCA Red Seal CBL2-3379.

PLOT

Setting: Fleet Street and environs; Industrial Revolution, nineteenth century.

Having found Todd shipwrecked at sea, Anthony returns him to London. Todd goes to his old apartment and is recognized by Mrs. Lovett as the neighbor who had been unjustly sentenced by Judge Turpin. She informs Todd that after he left, the Judge raped his wife and adopted his daughter, Johanna. Todd vows revenge, but first must reestablish himself as a barber. He publicly bests the barber, Pirelli, and sets up business above Mrs. Lovett's pie shop. However, Pirelli has recognized him. When he demands hush money, Todd strangles him and hides the body. Meanwhile, Anthony falls in love with Johanna. Not knowing that she is Todd's daughter, he asks the barber for help to steal her from the Judge. The Judge also intends to marry Johanna and comes for a shave to make himself more attractive. Just as Todd is about to slit his throat, Anthony runs in to say that Johanna will marry him, alerting the Judge, who immediately leaves. When Mrs. Lovett rejoins the barber, they realize that Pirelli's body can be used as filling for meat pies, beginning their successful partnership. Business booms, their secret suspected only by a beggar woman. Mrs. Lovett's assistant, Tobias, also becomes suspicious, but he escapes after discovering the nature of the pie fillings. Meanwhile, Anthony has found Johanna in an asylum and plots to rescue her. Todd notifies the Judge of the plan as a means of luring him to the shop. When Anthony leaves Johanna there as planned, she hides and thus witnesses the murder of both the beggar woman and the Judge. Johanna escapes the barber's knife when Todd is distracted by screams from below. Mrs. Lovett is appalled that Todd has murdered the beggar woman, whom Todd now recognizes as his wife. He kills Mrs. Lovett, and is, in turn, killed by the now insane Tobias.

PRODUCTION REQUIREMENTS

Major Roles. SWEENEY TODD (bs-bar): $F^{\#}1$ to $G^{b}3$. MRS. LOVETT (c): F2 to E4. ANTHONY HOPE (t): $A^{b}1$ to $F^{\#}3$. JOHANNA (s): $B^{b}2$ to $B^{b}4$. TOBIAS RAGG (t): A1 to A3 (B3, C4 opt).

Supporting Roles. BEGGAR WOMAN (m-s): G2 to $F^{\#}4$. PIRELLI (high t): B1 to C4. BEADLE (high t): D2 to D4 (E4 opt.) JUDGE TURPIN (bs): E1 to F3.

Chorus. Full chorus with solos throughout.

Orchestra. Reed #1: fl (picc [alt and sop rec opt]); Reed #2: B^{b} and E^{b} cl, fl, picc; Reed #3: bs cl, B^{b} cl, [fl opt], Reed #4: ob, Eng hrn [B^{b} cl opt]; Reed #5: bsn [B^{b} cl opt]; 2 trps in C; 1 fr hrn; 3 trbs [2 t, 1 bs]; Yamaha ES organ; cel; harp; perc (large section); strings (6–2–2–1).

Material. FS–P: Music Theatre International. VS: widely available, Revelation Music Publishing & Rilting Music.

Robert Starer (1924–)

APOLLONIA

Melodrama. Two acts, six scenes, five sets (90 minutes). Conservative modern idiom is not wholly tonal. Generally conversational writing, but arias, duets, ensembles (including a Mozartian finale) do exist. Chromatic, though conjunct, motion in vocal lines. Short overture and orchestral preludes introduce scenes.

Libretto by Gail Godwin. Premiere: Minnesota Opera, St. Paul, Minn 5.22.79.

PLOT

Setting: a city, the present.

Act I, scene i: Mrs. Everett's apartment; ii: Flashback to Apollonia's high school stage, with flashbacks to Apollonia as a child with her uncle; iii: The Arcadia Sanatorium. Act II, i: Marius' apartment; ii: Mrs. Everett's apartment; iii: The tearoom.

With the help of childhood training from her uncle, Apollonia helps Mrs. Everett to recognize and become the person she dreams of being. Although she is pleased with her success, Apollonia has not forgotten how her powers had led a young man to his death. Appolonia remembers preparing for a play in which two lovers achieve such perfect love that they must die. Apollonia underestimated the power that her words would have on the actor who played her lover. At the end of the play, the boy shot himself with a real bullet. Still cautious, Apollonia decides to undertake more important work. Having offered her services at a sanatorium, she focuses her attention on Marius, an opera singer who refuses to sing because he does not believe he can change peoples' lives through his art. When he finally sings to her, she is so overcome that he regains confidence in his talents.

A year later, Marius is a rising opera star. As his lover, Apollonia has found the greatest happiness that she can imagine. Unfortunately, Marius decides that he requires solitude for his life. She is devastated by this, but offers to leave him. A few months later, Apollonia meets her uncle for tea. She tells him of her love for Marius and her unhappiness without him. As they talk, she is haunted by the spirit of the young man who killed himself and is tempted to commit suicide herself. Marius' voice comes on the radio and Apollonia overcomes her depression. She finally understands what she has taught others: she must live for herself.

PRODUCTION REQUIREMENTS

Major Roles. APOLLONIA (s): C3 to A4. MARIUS (bar): A1 to A3.

Supporting Roles. MRS. EVERETT (m-s): G2 to G♭4. UNCLE OF APOLLONIA (bs): E1 to E♭3. DOMINICK/SASHA (t): C2 to A3.

Minor Roles. CHANTAL/THESBIAN I (s). DOCTOR/THESPIAN III (bar). HOWARD/THE WAITER/THESBIAN II/ACCOMPANIST (high bar).

Mute Roles. APOLLONIA AS A CHILD (mime/dancer).

Orchestra. fl (picc), ob (Eng hrn), cl in B♭, hrn in F, trp in B♭, trb, vln, vla, vcl, guitar (acoustic and electric), electric organ, piano, perc.

Material. FS–P and VS: Theodore Presser.

REVIEWS

None located.

THE LAST LOVER

Morality play. One act (40 minutes). Duets patterned after spoken dialogue as well as arias. Texture broken by spoken dialogue. Short orchestral introduction. Atonal with some dissonance. Orchestra (quintet or piano) is situated on stage and participates in the drama.

Libretto by Gail Godwin, based on various legends about a woman called Pelagia. Premiere: Caramoor Festival, Katonah, N.Y. 8.2.75.

PLOT

Setting: Antioch, fourth century.

As Pelagia and her maid discuss the many lovers they have had, the holy man, Veronus, contemplates how he can give himself more fully to

God. Seeing Pelagia, Veronus is struck by her efforts to look beautiful for her earthly lovers. Attracted by Veronus' remoteness, Pelagia tries to seduce him, but is impressed by his devotion to his Lord. Pelagia begins to reexamine her life, rejecting the advances of the Seducer. She dons a monk's robe and becomes Brother Pelagius, vowing to devote her life to a worthy love. A nun seeks Pelagius' advice and returns to meditation after receiving it. However, when the Seducer dances off with the nun, Pelagius is dishonored and banished to a mountain cave. The Seducer, the devil, proclaims Pelagia's guilt, although she accepted her punishment without defending herself. Because the devil had the last word by winning the soul of the young Nun, Pelagia had lost. Nevertheless, each musician bows to Pelagia as he leaves the stage.

PRODUCTION REQUIREMENTS

Major Roles. PELAGIA (m-s): A♭2 to F4. BARITONE (Veronus, a Holy Man; The Seducer; Voice of a Judge): F1 to F3. SOPRANO (Pelagia's Maid, A Young Nun): C3 to A4.

Minor Roles. Members of the orchestra, pianist, or members of the audience needed to ask questions at end.

Orchestra. Woodwind Quintet: fl (picc), ob (Eng hrn), cl in B♭ (bs cl), hrn in F, bsn. (Piano may be used in place of woodwind quintet.)

Material. FS–P and VS: MCA Music (rent). VS: American Music Center.

REVIEWS

Peter G. Davies " 'Last Lover' Premier is Sung Zestfully," *New York Times* (August 4, 1975), p. 14, column 4

"Miss Godwin makes her points with a good deal of wittily ironic commentary. . . . [the libretto] is weighted with a strongly feminist viewpoint, but the moral, sexual and social implications of the legend are all lightly and subtly underscored."

"Mr. Starer's music is neat, expertly crafted and apt enough in gesture and mood, although its rather pallid Stravinskian neoclassicisms rarely hold the memory."

Frank Stewart

TO LET THE CAPTIVE GO

Premiere: Mannes College, New York 3.5.74.

Material. Seesaw Music Corporation.

William Grant Still (1895–1978)

A BAYOU LEGEND

Melodrama. Three acts (120 minutes). Through-composed, in a tonal, conservative modern idiom. Orchestral overture and minstrel's aria form the prologue. Conversational vocal writing, although arias exist; few choruses.

Libretto by Verna Arvey, based on a legend from Biloxi, Mississippi. Premiere: Opera/South, Jackson, Mississippi 11.15.74. Performances: Los Angeles Community College 2.13.76. PBS televised opera (Opera/South: 6.15.81.

PLOT

Setting: A primitive community near a Bayou, the present (can also be presented as a fairy tale).

Clothilde spurns her suitor, Leonce, and tries to persuade Bazile to marry her. Although Bazile protests that he does not love her, he agrees when she tells him that she will soon bear his child. Later, a beautiful spirit, Aurore, appears to Bazile and reminds him that they have been sweethearts throughout the ages. Aurore's assurance that Clothilde has lied to him strengthens Bazile's determination to resist Clothilde. Aurore vanishes as Clothilde enters with Leonce, jealously demanding to know the identity of Bazile's companion. When Bazile persistently rejects Clothilde's advances, she threatens to denounce him for consorting with spirits.

Clothilde gives a betrothal party, hoping that Bazile will relent. When he does not, she accuses him of witchcraft. Leonce, horrified that she would send the man she professes to love to his doom, tries to intercede in Bazile's behalf. However, the angry villagers hang Bazile from the tree offstage. When Bazile's spirit rises from his dead body to join Aurore, the Priest proclaims that a miracle has blessed the village. Leonce brings the news to Clothilde, who confesses that she lied about bearing Bazile's child. When she seductively suggests that she and Leonce marry, he rejects her, leaving her to her tears.

PRODUCTION INFORMATION

Major Roles. BAZILE (t): E2 to B3. CLOTHILDE (s): D3 to G4. AURORE (s): $E^{b}3$ to B4. FATHER LESTANT (bs): $G^{b}1$ to C2. LEONCE (bar): D2 to F3.

Supporting Roles. THREE GAY BLADES: No. 1 (t): F2 to $A^{\#}3$; No. 2 (t): $E^{b}2$ to F3; No. 3 (bar): C2 to $D^{b}3$. THE MINSTREL (t): $E^{b}2$ to $B^{b}3$.

Minor Roles. (To be sung by members of the chorus.) FIRST WOMAN (s). SECOND WOMAN (c). THIRD WOMAN (m-s). FOURTH WOMAN (s). FIRST MAN (bar). SECOND MAN (t). THIRD MAN (t). THE DEACON (t). THE WARDEN (bs).

Chorus. S,S,M-S,A,T,T,BAR,B.

Ballet. 6 dancers required.

Orchestra. 3 fls, 2 obs, 3 cls, 3 bsns, 3 hrns, 3 trps, 3 trbs, tuba, timp, perc, harp, strings.

Material. V-S: American Music Center. FS–P: William Grant Still Music.

REVIEWS

Martin Mayer "TV Opera Hits a High Note," *American Film Magazine* (January-February 1981), pp. 53–54

"Like Pizzetti, he has more melodic imagination than has been fashionable in the last generation, and huge skill at writing for chorus. The vocal writing is graceful, with few wide skips . . . and the orchestration is supportive throughout, though rarely striking."

"Though there is nothing in *A Bayou Legend* of the magical quality of 'A Real Slow Drag' in Joplin's *Treemonisha* . . . it's really a considerably better opera." "Opera in Mississippi," *Time* (November 25, 1974), p. 84

"In the case of Still, *A Bayou Legend* reveals him as a kind of American Grieg—a miniaturist gifted with melody, an unerring sense of color and a fondness for the folklore. Although the performers were all black, *Legend* is not especially a black opera."

Richard F. Shepard "TV: 'A Bayou Legend,' Still's Opera of South," *New York Times* (June 15, 1981), p. 24

"musically it reflects the romantic tradition rather than the story's own roots in the bayou country, where one would expect to hear more in the Afro-American beat."

"Still's music often soars with the spirit of his legend, particularly in the love-song duets. He injects small-town humor in the persons of the Three Blades, a trio of happy-go-lucky ne'er-do-wells who mean trouble but are lighthearted relief from the heavy romance."

HIGHWAY 1, U.S.A.

Melodrama. One act, two scenes (60 minutes). Through-composed in a tonal but chromatic style. Vocal lines vary from conversational on repeated pitches to lyrical with disjunct vocal lines. Little independent use of orchestra.

Libretto by Verna Arvey. Premiere: University of Miami 5.11.63. Performances: West Virginia State College 4.30.67.

PLOT

Setting: a small southern town, the present.

Bob and Mary have worked hard and sacrificed much in order to put Nate through college, fulfilling a promise made to Bob's mother on her deathbed. Mary dreams of the new life they will have now that Nate's education is completed. However, Bob explains that they must continue to support Nate until he is established. Friends take Bob to the station, leaving Mary to tell Aunt Lou of her hatred for Nate. She vows to convince Bob of the futility of their efforts by forcing Nate to reveal his true character. After a year of laziness, Nate has not found an outlet for his talents. He lives with Bob and Mary, contributing nothing for his upkeep. One morning, Bob expresses doubts concerning Nate's intentions. When Nate comes in for breakfast, he egotistically mistakes Mary's sarcasm for flattery. He tries to make love to her, inciting her laughter and a reaffirmation of her love for Bob. Enraged, Nate stabs her. Mary's screams bring Bob to her side, while Aunt Lou runs for help. Believing that Mary is dead and that he has nothing to live for, Bob takes the blame in order to shield his brother. However, Mary regains consciousness and identifies Nate as her assailant. As he is led away, Nate begs Bob to save him. Ignoring his pleas, Bob kneels by Mary's side and promises that, together, they will share a brighter future.

PRODUCTION REQUIREMENTS

Major Roles. MARY (s): D3 to B♭4. BOB (bar): C♯2 to F3. NATE (t): E♭2 to B♭3.

Supporting Roles. AUNT LOU (m-s or s): D3 to F♯4.

Minor Roles. SHERIFF (bar).

Chorus. Small SATB (m-s, a, t, bar solos required from chorus).

Orchestra. 2 fls (picc), 2 obs (Eng hrn), 2 B♭ cls (bs cl in B♭), 2 bsns, 4 hrns in F, 2 trps in B♭, 2 trbs, 2 timp, perc, harp, strings.

Material. FS–P: William Grant Still Music.

REVIEWS

George Armstrong "Locally Produced Opera Impressive," *Charleston Daily* (May 1, 1967), p. 17

"The opera is unmistakably modern, but its dissonances are mild and largely confined to the brief orchstral interludes. It is very singable."

"Two of the choruses are excellent. In the first, the townspeople and church committee extol the friendly qualities of Bob and Mary with toe-tapping, folksy rhythms, and, in the second, they express indignation at the actions of Nate with exciting musical shouts, and extend melodic sympathy and best wishes for the young couple."

Mark O. Polo "Opera Premiere Scores Sweet Success," *Miami Hurricane* (May 17, 1963), p. 15

"On the surface, the work sounds like a Bernstein Broadway musical, but it is much deeper and more complex. Interesting interplay of melodies depict moods of the personalities characterized."

Doris Reno "Premiere Enthralls Audience," *The Miami Herald* (May 12, 1963), p. 22-A

"One of the hardest things to do in all art is to write about 'ordinary' people. . . . yet [Still and Arvey] . . . have achieved an artistic work that is fresh and deeply sincere, and that evokes a genuine emotion."

"The music is highly original, yet fits the 'ordinary' material for which it is intended. It is lively, free in spirit, and with a touch of nobility about it. The arias, ensembles, and choral sections were expertly handled."

MINETTE FONTAINE

Melodrama. Three acts, five scenes (120 minutes). Set pieces, traditional harmonies, straightforward rhythms and meters. Conversational duets, arias, brief recitatives and small ensemble work throughout.

Libretto by Verna Arvey. Premiere: Baton Rouge Opera 10.24.84.

PLOT

Setting: New Orleans, 1880.

As Minette, the guest diva, finishes a concert at Madame de Noyan's school, Diron, the wealthy planter arrives. When they meet, they are quickly separated by Madame de Noyan, who reunites Diron with her daughter, Clarice. Minette fumes at the snobbery of the Creole gentry. Though she knows that Diron and Clarice are to be married, she vows to wed Diron herself. In the French market, Minette sees Diron again, but he refuses her invitation to call at her home. Determined to win him, Minette visits Marie, the voodoo priestess. After Minette agrees that she'll take Diron at any price, Marie instructs Minette on how to achieve her goal.

Diron suddenly falls madly in love with the singer, and they plan to marry the next day. His former friends confront him, but Diron refuses to listen to their entreaties. After the wedding, Minette's cousin, Lucien, shows Diron evidence of Minette's consultation with Marie. Diron angrily realizes that what he took for love was merely Minette's vanity and selfishness. In the midst of confronting Minette, Diron suffers an incapacitating stroke. Horrified by what she has done, Minette vows to end her career and spend the rest of her life caring for him. (The ending was changed for the premiere production: the angry Diron threatens Minette with a pistol, but is himself shot by Lucien. The horrified Minette still vows to spend the rest of her life on Diron's estate.)

PRODUCTION REQUIREMENTS

Major Roles. Minette Fontaine, a visiting diva (s): $E^{b}3$ to $B^{b}4$. Diron Hachard, a planter (t): (D2 opt) $E^{b}2$ to A3.

Supporting Roles. Madame de Noyan (m-s): D3 to E4. Clarice de Noyan, Madame's daughter (s): E3 to B4. Lucien Fontaine, Minette's accompanist and cousin (bs-bar): B1 to E3. Claude Dupre, a physician (bar): D2 to F3. Felice, Minette's servant (m-s): C3 to C4. Marie Laveau (c): G2 to C♯3.

Minor Roles. Vendors (t,t,bar,bs). Shoppers (s,m-s,m-s,s,c). Lame Beggar (t). Two Marchands (t,bs). Cleon (bar).

Orchestra. 3 fls (picc), 2 obs, Eng hrn, 2 cls in B^{b}, bs cl in B^{b}, 2 bsns (cont bsn), 3 hrns in F, 2 trps in B^{b}, 3 trbs, tuba, timp, perc, harp, strings.

Material. FS–P and VS: William Grant Still Music.

REVIEWS

Cynthia V. Campbell "Baton Rouge Opera: Still 'Minette Fontaine' [premiere]," *Musical America* (February 1985), pp. 19–20

> "*Minette Fontaine* falls into the musical genre of Gershwin and his contemporaries. . . . Still, who is recognized as perhaps the major black composer of his generation, combined his love of Puccini and his interest in the avant-garde to create an opera that is recognizably a product of the 1930s and 40s, tinged throughout by a coloration of jazz and the blues."

> "Among the highlights of the opera was a romantic duet, 'My Beloved,' sung by . . . [Diron] and . . . the jilted financee."

Helen Deermont " 'Minette Fontaine' meets audience's expectations," *State Times* (October 25, 1984), p. 3-D

> Still's "understanding and sympathy for the traditions and haunting moods of New Orleans comes through in almost every

passage in the opera. The libretto, written by his wife, Verna Arvey, ties in with the score and rounds out the imagery with skillful detail."

"The voodoo dance that highlights the opera's first act is an interesting combination of African rhythm and 1940s swing—and it works."

Charles Strouse (1928–)

THE FUTURE OF THE AMERICAN MUSICAL THEATRE

One act opera (60 min). Libretto by the composer. Premiere: Midland Music Society, Mich. 6.6.85.

NIGHTINGALE

Fairy tale. One act (70 minutes). Contemporary, pop musical theater idiom with oriental flavor, intended to appeal to audiences of all ages. May be performed by adults or children. Continuous texture of dialogue, arias, duets, and choral sections. Overture. Melodic vocal lines contrast with recitative sections.

Libretto by the composer, based on the Hans Christian Anderson story. Premiere: First All Children's Theater, New York City 3.80. Performances: Wolf Trap Barns 82.

PLOT

Setting: ancient China.

The discontented Emperor requests that the Maid bring the Nightingale to the palace to give him pleasure. The Nightingale soon becomes the people's "superstar." When the Emperor appears to have died, the Nightingale's song brings him back to life. Life in the palace now seems ideal for everyone, except the unhappy Nightingale, who longs to be free. When the people's interest turns to a new superstar, the Mechanical Bird, the real Nightingale flies away. But the peasants tire of the Mechanical Bird, which is not repaired when it breaks down. The unhappy Emperor throws himself into his work, yet the Maid realizes that she loves him. Death comes again to visit the Emperor. The Nightingale returns and is again victorious over death. The Emperor asks the Nightingale to give him the greatest gift, to teach him the song of life. The Nightingale responds that the Maid has already given him the greatest gift . . . her love. The Nightingale teaches the song to both of them and all join in.

PRODUCTION REQUIREMENTS

Major Roles. Story Teller (bar): $B^{\flat}1$ to $E^{\flat}3$. Emperor (bar/bs-bar): G1 to $F^{\#}3$. Nightingale (s): G2 to A4. Maid (s): $B^{\flat}2$ to G4.

Minor Roles and Chorus. A Minister, Sculptor, Banker, Mechanical Bird, Peacocks, various animals, etc. (Solos, duets, and choral parts.)

Orchestra. Piano only.

Material. VS: G. Schirmer.

REVIEWS

Irving Lowens "Wolf Trap Barns: Strouse 'Nightingale,' " *Musical America* (August 1982), 32:20–21

> "The composer/librettist is Charles Strouse, who wrote the music for *Bye Bye Birdie,* . . . *Applause,* and *Annie* . . . Strouse calls his piece an opera, and I suppose it qualifies as such even though there is a strong flavor of Broadway musical in it."

> "His solid background in serious music—he studied with Copland, Boulanger, Berger, and Diamond—is quite evident . . . Regrettably, Strouse's music is not especially distinguished, and the weakness of the score is most evident in those moments which are supposed to touch the heart."

John Wilson "Opera: Children's Theatre Gives 'Nightingale'," *New York Times* (May 9, 1982), p. 44, column 1

> "Much of the music stays close to a recitative level . . . but this level simply accents the contrasts of the Emperor and his court to the Nightingale, whose floating songs are the key to the development of the tale."

"The range and balance of the dazzling colors (of the production) hold one's attention while the situation of the plot is being established. It takes a little while to get this done, and this may be heavy going for a very young audience. But once some of the youngest members . . . come pouring on as a congregation of . . . barnyard animals, the spirit of the tale lightens and . . . moves it smoothly through a steady flow of sentiment, crisis and humor."

Conrad Susa (1936–)

TRANSFORMATIONS

Fantasy, psychological drama. Two parts, ten scenes (120 minutes w/intermission). Employs various styles of American popular music of the 40s and 50s. Requires singing actors who can play several roles and sing in popular and classical styles. Much ensemble singing with all participating in each scene.

Conceived by H. Wesley Balk (with detailed stage directions included), based on Anne Sexton's book of the same name. Commissioned by the Minnesota Opera Company. Premiere: Minnesota Opera 5.5.73. Performances: Manhattan Theatre Club 5.76; Amsterdam 4.2.77; Wolf Trap Opera 85.

PLOT

Setting: a ward in a hospital or an institution.

A succession of Grimm's fairytales are told, illustrating not only the stories and their morals, but deeper psychological relationships as seen through the eyes of the narrator, Anne Sexton. The introduction to the score describes them as follows: *Snow White and the Seven Dwarfs* deals with the relationship between mother and daughter; *The White Snake* considers the madness of the artist; *Iron Hans* questions society's treatment of the insane; *Rumplestiltskin* explores the Doppelganger inside us all; *Rapunzel* reveals need of women for each other; *Godfather Death* considers the fear and desire for death; *The Wonderful Musician* illustrates the power of music; *Hansel and Gretel* depicts mother love and cannibalism; and *Sleeping Beauty* explores the relationship between daughter and father.

PRODUCTION REQUIREMENTS

Major Roles. Ensemble consists of eight singers who play various roles. #1, PRINCESS (s): G♯2 to C5. #2, ANNE SEXTON, WITCH (s): A♭2 to B4. #3, GOOD FAIRY (m-s): F2 to G4. #4, WIZARD (t): B1 to A♭3. #5, MAGIC OBJECT (t): B1 to C4. #6, PRINCE (t): B1 to B♭3. #7, KING (high bar): B1 to B♭3. #8, NEIGHBORING KING (bs-bar): F1 to F3.

Chorus. Consists of eight cast members.

Orchestra. cl/sax, trp, trb, cb, piano/elec harpsi/elec piano/elec cel, elec org, perc.

Material. FS–P and VS: E. C. Schirmer.

REVIEWS

Rodney M. Bennett "Young Vic: *Transformations,*" *Music and Musicians* (November 1978), 27(3):58–59

> "The light scoring for the small orchestra of eight players never gave the singers any problems in being heard, and they had pleasant easy vocal lines, which made no excessive demands on their vocal techniques. The musical vocabulary was limited, and by contemporary standards tonal and melodic."

M. A. Feldman "Minneapolis," *Opera News* (July 1973), p. 23

> "an opera about Woman that is poignant, funny and frightening all at once."

> "Conrad Susa has provided a modest but effective score in which motifs are subtly transformed for dramatic purposes. The music spans rhythmically nuanced recitative, pop idioms of recent decades and full-blown lyricism."

John H. Harvey "Minnesota Opera premieres work of Conrad Susa," *Musical America* (September 1973), pp. 20, 26

> "The writing for voice, which also includes a men's quartet and other set pieces and a good deal of supple recitative, is eminently vocal and is distinguished by skillful English prosody."

Robert Jacobson "New York," *Opera News* (August 1976), p. 38

"This is a fascinating piece primarily because of Anne Sexton's text, which reexamines several of Grimm's Fairy Tales in a modern sophisticated manner, relating to her own fantasies and fears, a mingling of narrative and action. . . . The trouble with *Transformations* is that the words are far more satisfying than Susa's setting . . . which too often seems to intrude rather than illuminate."

Bruce Taub (1948–)

PASSION, POISON, AND PETRIFACTION

Farce. One act (35 minutes). Freely atonal and highly chromatic writing contrasts use of the tune "Bill Bailey" as a recurrent motive. Very chromatic vocal lines are often doubled in orchestra. Singing and spoken parts intertwine—only three roles are sung, others are spoken with rhythmic indications.

Libretto by the composer, based on the play by George Bernard Shaw. Commission: written for the Composers Ensemble with support from the National Endowment for the Arts. Premiere: Composers Ensemble, N.Y. 76.

PLOT

Setting: a fashionable London apartment, turn of the century.

George Fitztollemache plots to murder his wife, Lady Magnesia, who is carrying on with a lover, the young dandy, Adolphus Bastable. Armed with a dagger, George sneaks into the Lady's bedchamber. As he hides behind her couch, Lady Magnesia is awakened by a knock at the door. Adolphus has arrived to show off his new clothes. Though surprised to find her husband present, Lady Magnesia invites Adolphus in anyway, and George prepares some gazogene as a nightcap for everyone. Altering his original plan, George poisons Adolphus' seltzer. As the young man writhes with stomach cramps, George explains that he has poisoned Adolphus in order to regain his wife's love and attention. Magnesia offers to become her own husband's "lover," which means, however, that she will no longer serve him as a wife (preparing his meals, darning his socks, cleaning up after him, etc.). Faced with this new situation, George attempts to revive the poisoned victim before it is too late. The only antidote being lime, the couple begin to force-feed Adolphus bits of plaster from the ceiling and even the bust of Lady Magnesia herself.

The commotion brings forth the landlord, a police officer and a doctor. Nothing can save the poor, young lover. As the plaster begins to harden inside him, Adolphus is turned into a human statue. With this, a lightning bolt passes through the bedroom window, reducing the landlord, police officer and doctor to ashes. As Phyllis, the maid, sweeps them out of the room, Lady Magnesia and George reunite in love and consolation as they stand Adolphus nobly in the corner.

PRODUCTION REQUIREMENTS

Major Roles. LADY MAGNESIA (s): A2 to C5. GEORGE FITZTOLLEMACHE (bs): E1 to F3 (G3 in sprechstimme). ADOLPHUS BASTABLE (t): B1 to C♯4 (A♭3 to D4 falsetto).

Speaking Roles. PHYLLIS, the maid. THE LANDLORD. POLICE CONSTABLE. DOCTOR.

Orchestra. fl (picc), cl, bsn, guitar (amplified), vib, bs drum, susp cym, piano, vln, vcl.

Material. FS–P and VS: C. F. Peters. VS: American Music Center.

REVIEWS

John Rockwell "Opera: 'Passion' of Shaw," *New York Times* (April 3, 1976), p. 20

> "It was good-humored, to be sure . . . but the rambunctious farciality seemed more jejune than witty. Mr. Taub's music . . . is full of energy, noise, and quotations, and punctuates the obvious pictorial moments with innocent decisiveness. More power to him if he perseveres in musical theatre; one assumes this will eventually be consigned to the category of student work."

Edward Thomas (1924–)

DESIRE UNDER THE ELMS

"American folk opera." Three acts, eight scenes (120 minutes). Conservative twentieth-century idiom. Though set numbers exist, generally through-composed. Vocal parts, occasionally chromatic, mostly conjunct and lyrical.

Libretto by Joe Masteroff, based on the play by Eugene O'Neill. Premiere: New York Opera Repertory Theatre, City Center, N.Y. 1.13.89. Workshop development: Eugene O'Neill Theatre Center 78. Recording: audio tape through publisher.

PLOT

Setting: summertime, the Cabot farm.

Hate, distrust and division wrack the Cabot family when all vie to claim the well-kept family farm. Eben Cabot would seem to have the most rightful claim, as the farm had belonged solely to his mother before she died. But since then, his father, Ephraim Cabot, and two stepbrothers, Peter and Simeon, have taken it over. Eben buys out his brothers' shares, so that they might pursue promise of gold in California. But Eben's position is threatened again when his father brings home a new wife, Abbie, a conniving young woman who has her own designs on the farm. Abbie convinces Cabot that they should have a son of their own, so that he might have a legitimate heir. But she also wins Eben's attention—Eben delighting in the revenge of sleeping with his father's wife. Cabot is overjoyed when Abbie finally gives birth to a son. But in his drunken revelry, he confronts Eben with his knowledge of the relationship between him and Abbie, threatening to oust Eben as soon as the baby is old enough to take over the work. After the men come to blows, Eben confronts Abbie in all his hatred and resentment. Distraught over losing Eben's love, Abbie smothers the child to remove the obstacle that stands between them. But when she confesses that the child is actually Eben's, Eben moves to have her arrested for murder. By the time the sheriff arrives, Eben confesses that he still loves Abbie, and demands to be arrested as an accomplice to the murder. Drained and alone, Cabot turns to the farm work, as the sheriff remarks that he wished that he owned such a beautiful farm.

PRODUCTION REQUIREMENTS

Major Roles. EBEN CABOT, Ephraim Cabot's son (t): C2 to B3. ABBIE, Ephraim's new wife (s): $B^{b}2$ to B4. EPHRAIM CABOT, aging patriarch (bs-bar): G1 to F3.

Supporting Roles. Eben's step-brothers: PETER (t): C2 to $F^{\#}3$; SIMEON (bar): $B^{b}1$ to $F^{b}3$.

Speaking Roles. SHERIFF.

Mute Roles. DEPUTY.

Orchestra. fl (picc), ob (Eng hrn), cl (bs cl), bsn, 2 hrns, trp, trb, harp, perc (timp), guitar, harmonica, piano (cel), strings (6–5–4–3–2).

Material. FS–P and VS: Somat Publishing Ltd., Suite 602, 157 W. 57th St. New York, N.Y. 10019.

REVIEWS

Allan Kozinn "Premiere of 'Desire' Based on O'Neill," *New York Times* (January 13, 1989)

> "Apart from a few lovely set pieces for Abbie—particularly a simple but sweetly melodic lullabye in the last act—much of the work was put forth in moderately paced declamation."

> "the work's musical language is genial enough. . . . the work is built of melodies that are simple and constrained, and there is only the mildest hint of dissonance in the harmonization. There are also a few overtly folksy touches."

Tom Pniewski "N.Y. Opera Repertory Presents Strong 'Desire Under the Elms,' " *New York City Tribune* (January 17, 1989)

> "His handling of the orchestra is particularly noteworthy; numerous small touches and accents highlight the score and make it sparkle with some of the glitter of Broadway."

> "The melodies are smooth and. . . . tend to be stately, slow of delivery and with many sustained notes. This helps the audience grasp the text, of course, but it also slows down dramatic progress."

Bill Zakariasen "An Opera That's All You Could 'Desire,' " *Daily News* (January 13, 1989)

> "This new opera is a first-rate piece of musical theatre. In fact, it's one of those works . . . that actually improves upon its source. Masteroff's canny, concise libretto eschews hortatory breast-beating for completely believable and often heartbreaking realism, and Thomas' flavorful score . . . really gets under the surface of the characters."

Virgil Thomson (1896–1989)

LORD BYRON

Historical fiction. Three acts (99 minutes). Conservative modern style with tonal harmonies and stepwise vocal lines. Much ensemble work. Orchestral interludes and intros to acts. Extensive use of percussion.

Libretto by Jack Larson. Premiere: Juilliard American Opera Theatre: 4.20.72. Performances: New York Opera Repertory Theatre: 12.7.85.

PLOT

Setting: London, 1824.

Act I: Inside Westminster Abbey. Act II, scene i: the same; ii: Lady Melbourne's house, spring of 1812; iii: Burlington House, summer of 1814; iv: Lady Melbourne's house and Byron's club, New Year's Eve, 1814 (a scene on two levels). Act III, i: Mrs. Leigh's country house, August 1915; ii: Westminster Abbey, as before.

While the people of London lament Lord Byron's death and shades of the great poets mourn in the Poet's Corner of Westminster Abbey, Byron's friends and relatives gather there to discuss petitioning for an Abbey burial. Byron's good friend, Hobhouse, urges the Contessa Guiccioli and her brother to present a statue to the Abbey to ensure Byron's burial there. Moore reveals that Byron had given him a manuscript of memoirs, as yet unread. The others beg him to destroy it, fearing that its publication would ruin Byron's reputation. The memoir's contents are revealed in a series of flashbacks: the disillusioned, pessimistic poet meets and marries Annabella, who dedicates herself to reforming his immoral lifestyle, even after she discovers Byron in a compromising situation with his sister, Augusta. After reading the memoirs, Moore gives the work to Augusta who decides to destroy them. The Dean of the Abbey enters as the memoirs are burned, refusing to honor a poet whose life story must be destroyed. The Contessa reclaims the statue, vowing to take it where Byron will be truly appreciated. After Byron's friends leave, the shades of the great poets reconvene. Despite his official rejection by the Dean, they welcome Byron as their peer.

PRODUCTION REQUIREMENTS

Major Roles. LORD BYRON (t): E♭2 to C4. LADY BYRON, nee Anabella Millbank (m-s): B♭2 to A♭4. AUGUSTA LEIGH, Lord Byron's sister (s): D3 to C5. THOMAS MOORE, the poet (bar): B♭1 to G3.

Supporting Roles. JOHN HOBHOUSE, Byron's good friend (bs-bar): G♭1 to F3. JOHN MURRAY, Byron's publisher (t): D2 to B3. COUNT GAMBA, Byron's companion in the Greek War (bar): C2 to G3. CONTESSA GUICCIOLI, Byron's last mistress (s): D3 to B4. LADY MELBOURNE, a former mistress (s): D3 to A♭4. JOHN IRELAND, Dean of Westminster Abbey (bs): F♯1 to D♯3. SHELLEY (bar): F2 to G3.

Minor Roles. TWO ENGLISH NOBLEMEN (bars). ABBEY POETS: GRAY AND THOMPSON (ts), SPENSER AND DRYDEN (bars), MILTON AND JOHNSON (bss). LADY CHARLOTTE (s). LADY JANE (m-s). YOUNG LADY (c-a).

Chorus. People of London (opera chorus), Abbey Choir (church choir at premiere), and Sailors.

Orchestra. 2 fls (picc), 2 obs (Eng hrn), 2 B♭ cls (bs cl), 2 bsns, 4 hrns in F, 2 trps, 3 trbs, tuba, timp, harp, organ (offstage), strings.

Material. FS–P and VS: Southern Music Publishing.

REVIEWS

Frank Merkling "New York," *Opera News* (June 1972) pp. 23–24

> "The prevailing freshness of melody and rhythm, if not the supple texture of arioso blossoming into ensemble, brings to mind *The Beggar's Opera* and lends *Lord Byron* a real 'English' flavor."

> "There is beautiful writing for the voice and instruments; there are few concessions to theatricality. . . . Characters are differentiated by vocal line as well as by the quality of their words."

Harlow Robinson "N.Y. Opera Repertory Theatre: Thomson 'Lord Byron'," *Musical America* (April 1986), p. 19

"the libretto, in two acts and six scenes, is really a series of tableaux, lacking any central dramatic interest or movement."

"Musically, *Lord Byron* has many attractive moments, but the style is eclectic and lacking in personality."

Winthrop Sargeant "Rake's Egress," *New Yorker* (April 29, 1972), p. 106

"Mr. Thomson, always an eclectic composer, has used several techniques—the sort of pseudo eighteenth-century style that Stravinsky taught to the Ecole de Paris, the sort of American hymn-tune style employed in Thomson's earlier operas, passages in the whole-tone scale, and a small dash of dissonance here and there. The result is not unpleasant, but in the end the work is boring. And nowhere, except in the love scene between Byron and his sister, does it approach anything in the nature of lyricism."

Harold C. Schonberg "The Opera: 'Lord Byron,' " *New York Times* (April 22, 1972), p. 38

"[Mr. Thomson] has used some heavier dissonance than is to be found in his two previous operas, but there is a good deal of the 'white key' music that is basic to his style. What is missing is the charm and sophistication of 'Four Saints in Three Acts' or 'The Mother of Us All.' "

"It is hard to imagine Mr. Thomson writing a conventional opera, but with 'Lord Byron' he has nobly succeeded."

Hiram Titus

ROSINA

Libretto by Barbara Field in her own sequel to *The Barber of Seville* and *The Marriage of Figaro.* Premiere: Minnesota Opera, Minneapolis 4.26.80.

Stewart Wallace

WHERE'S DICK

Premiere: Texas Opera Theatre 6.1.89.

Robert Ward (1917–   )

ABELARD AND HELOISE

Historical fiction. Prologue and three acts, eleven scenes, eight sets (full evening). Conservative modern idiom, utilizing structure of late romantic opera: recitative, arias, ensembles, etc. Gregorian chant and quartal harmonies add to the medieval ambience.

Libretto by Jan Hartman. Commissioned by Charlotte Opera Association. Premiere: Charlotte Opera, N.C. 2.19.82.

PLOT

Setting: twelfth-century France.

Prologue: November 1142, France, the courtyard of the Paraclete. Act I, scene i: Paris, 1116, on the steps of Notre Dame; ii: Deny's rooms; iii: Upstairs in Fulbert's house; iv: Deny's rooms. Act II, i: The street in front of Fulbert's house; ii: Fulbert's parlor; iii: Deny's rooms. Act III, i: Spring 1140, the street in front of Deny's door; ii: Summer 1140, the courtyard of the Paraclete; iii: June 1140, the cathedral at Sens; iv: same as Prologue.

As Peter Abelard's coffin is brought to the Paraclete, his controversial and turbulent past is remembered by his wife, Heloise, and his faithful friend, Peter the Venerable. Years before, the famous teacher and scholar came to teach Heloise at Heloise's uncle, Fulbert's, request. Fulbert's joy at having Abelard within his household blinded him to the obvious attraction that grew between teacher and pupil. When Heloise became pregnant, the couple left Paris and Fulbert went mad. After secretly marrying Heloise, Abelard sent her to a distant convent for safety and to still the rumors of their marriage. When Abelard himself was attacked by Fulbert's men, the scholar refused to seek revenge, believing that his castration was just punishment for his betrayal of Heloise.

Years later, Abelard's following had grown, as had his rivalry with Bernard, the Abbot of Clairvaux. Thibault warned Abelard that the upcoming debate at Sens would actually be a trial by Bernard. Nevertheless, at Sens, Abelard refused to recognize the authority of the Council and vowed to go to Rome for judgment. However, he never made it to Rome. The night before he died, he wrote Heloise a letter, which Peter the Venerable delivers to her with the coffin. Although Heloise is now an Abbess, she has remained devoted to her husband. And in Abelard's final letter, he admits that he led her to the veil so she could belong to no other man.

PRODUCTION REQUIREMENTS

Major Roles. ABELARD (t): C♯2 to C4. HELOISE (s): C♯3 to B4.

Supporting Roles. DENYS, a Canon of Notre Dame, Abelard's mentor (bar): A1 to G3. BERNARD, Abbot of Clairvaux (bs): A1 to G♭3. FULBERT, a Canon of Notre Dame, Heloise's uncle (t): C♯2 to B♭3. THIBAULT, protege of Abelard (bs-bar): B♯1 to F♯3.

Minor Roles. PETER, THE VENERABLE/ZOPHAR (bs). JOB'S WIFE/BERTHE/SISTER SIMONE (m-s). JOB/ALBERIC (bar). ELIPHAZ/LOTULF (t). BILDAD (c).

Chorus. SSAATTBB

Orchestra. trp, organ, perc, harp, strings.

Material. FS–P and VS: Highgate Press/Galaxy Music.

REVIEWS

Terrell Cofield "Abelard and Heloise by Robert Ward: A Viewpoint," *Opera Journal* (1982), 25(3):29–33

"There were some moments in the opera that needed heightened tension. . . . But there were many more moments of absorbing music drama, rewarding to the audience."

"The ensemble writing is some of the best music of this opera. . . . Scene 2 of Act III displays a fine balance of choral and orchestral sound."

"Mr. Hartman's fine text was sometimes obscured and unintelligible, perhaps because of occasional thick orchestral writing. . . . But Ward's music is melodic, romantic, and appealing."

Harold F. Farwell "Charlotte," *Opera News* (September 1982), 47:46

> "The music is lush and lyrical, while Jan Hartman's libretto, though episodic and too distracted by the politics of Abelard's career, offers a reasonable exposition of the strange history of the lovers."

> "Ward's score proved most impressive in lyric moments. When the lovers first confess their love in Act I, the music builds in long, arching melodic lines. . . . The opera closes with equally ecstatic music celebrating another kind of love — that which transcends the lover's separation."

James Shertzer "Charlotte," *Musical America* (June 1982), 32:20–21

> "the opera is an immediately accessible work conceived largely in the musical language and theatrical style of the late nineteenth and early twentieth centuries. The score is deftly orchestrated, and the music again displays Ward's ability to write warm vocal lines that are touching in their directness. What the opera is short of are big, convincing arias and the complexities that invite repeated hearings."

> "Hartman's libretto does little to explore the characters, leaves much of the excitement of the story offstage, and treats sex and violence with Victorian reticence."

CLAUDIA LEGARE

Tragedy. Three acts, one set (120 minutes). Contains set numbers: overture, arias, and ensembles. Conservative, romantic music. Melodious vocal lines.

Libretto by Bernard Stambler, based on "Hedda Gabler" by Henrik Ibsen. Commissioned by the New York City Opera. Premiere: St. Paul, Minn. 4.14.78. Revised June, 1978.

PLOT

Setting: Charleston, South Carolina, after the Civil War.

George and his new bride, Claudia, arrive home with a plan to rebuild the war-devastated South. Aunt Julia and Jenny, Claudia's maid, try to remember Claudia's strength as General Legare's child, even though the strife has made her bitter and sullen. An old acquaintance, Daphne Grayson, calls on Claudia after returning from the North. Claudia reproaches Daphne for leaving her husband in order to pursue Orlando Beaumont, who has come to Charleston with the plan that he and Daphne had written for saving the South. Daphne speaks of her devotion to Orlando, even though he seems haunted by his memory of another woman. Meanwhile, Colonel Bladgen arranges a meeting at which George and Orlando will present their rebuilding plans. George is discouraged with Blagden's enthusiasm for Orlando's plan, which would build industry in the South instead of plantations, but would leave him and Claudia with no income. When Claudia vents her frustration by firing a pistol into the garden, Blagden admonishes her, and she angrily accuses him of trying to control her life. Claudia proclaims that he shall never have her, but Blagden is merely amused and even more self-assured. Alone again, at last, Claudia and Orlando trade accusations about the past. Although Orlando still loves Claudia, Claudia feels only bitterness that Orlando could not be as great and pure as her father, General LeGare. When Daphne interrupts them, Claudia nastily tempts Orlando with drink, which the reformed alcoholic spitefully accepts before departing for the meeting.

While the women await the men's return, Daphne dreams that Orlando's child is cast into a fire. George returns with the news that although Orlando's plan was ingenious, Orlando left the meeting in a drunken state. George found the plan laying in the road — Claudia seizes the opportunity, declaring that George must leave it with her. When Orlando excitedly enters, Daphne wakes and accuses him of killing "their child," the plan they had formulated together. After Daphne leaves, Claudia gives Orlando a pistol, suggesting that he end his misery. When George returns, Claudia confesses not only that she burned Orlando's plan, but that she will bear George's child. George is overjoyed about the baby, but warns that no one should know she burned the plan. When Blagden announces that Orlando has shot himself and is dying, George and Daphne vow to rewrite Orlando's plan. Blagden reveals to Claudia that he has recognized the fatal pistol as hers, giving him the power to control her. As George and Daphne begin to reconstruct the plan, a shot is heard in the next room. This time, Claudia has fatally shot herself.

PRODUCTION REQUIREMENTS

Major Roles. George Lowndes (t): E2 to B♭3 (C4 opt). Claudia Legare Lowndes (dram s): C3 to B♭4. Orlando Beaumont/Voice of General Legare (bar): C2 to G♭3 (G♯ opt). Daphne Grayson (s): C♯3 to C5. Colonel Blagden (bs-bar): C2 to G♯3.

Supporting Roles. Aunt Julia Lowndes (s): E3 to B4.

Minor Roles. JENNY (m-s).

Orchestra. 2 fls (picc), 2 obs (Eng hrn), 2 cls (bs cl), 2 bsns (cont bsn), 4 hrns, 2 trps, 2 trbs, perc, timp, harp, strings.

Material. FS–P and VS: Galaxy Music Corp. VS: American Music Center.

REVIEWS

John H. Harvey "Minnesota Opera Company: Robert Ward's 'Claudia Legare,' " *Musical America* (August 1978), pp. 17–18

"Ward and his librettist transplanted (the story) to Charleston, South Carolina, in the period just after the Civil War. . . . Such changes as have been made benefit the work as opera, clarify the central character's motivations, and present the story in terms to which a modern American audience can more readily respond. . . . Ward has been able to write in a more expansive and romantic style than in his well-known opera, *The Crucible.*"

"Ward's prosody is skillful as usual, and the vocal lines are comfortably and effectively singable. . . . The orchestral writing is successful in creating moods and atmospheres."

Harold C. Schonberg "Premiere of 'Claudia Legare,' " *New York Times* (April 17, 1978), pp. 22–23

" . . . the tensions and motivations remain the same (as Ibsen's)—old vs. new thought; imagination as opposed to pedantism; the New Woman with her sharp intelligence, frustrations, boredom, romanticism. . . . It is a good, tight libretto."

" . . . the musical idiom is of the nineteenth century. . . . the approach misses the strength of the libretto by astronomical units. Mr. Ward is a short-winded composer who does not think in terms of the long line. Nor does he have the lyric invention to create melodies of any personality."

THE LADY FROM COLORADO

Light opera. Two acts. Libretto by Bernard Stambler. Premiere: Central City Opera 7.17.64.

Material. Galaxy Highgate.

MINUTES TILL MIDNIGHT

Melodrama. Three acts, nine scenes, five sets (full evening). Harmonically tonal with dissonant added notes. Through-composed with prominent orchestral interludes, etc. Vocal writing ranges from syllabic, conversational to arias, ensembles.

Libretto by Daniel Lang. Commissioned by Greater Miami Opera. Premiere: Greater Miami Opera, Florida 6.5.82.

PLOT

Setting: United States, end of the twentieth century.

Act I, scene i: Laboratory in a university research center; ii: Roszak apartment; iii: Laboratory. Act II, i: Roszak apartment; ii: Outside the research center; iii: White House conference room. Act III, i: Laboratory; ii: Laboratory; iii: Hospital room.

Although Emil played an important role in the development of nuclear energy, the aftermath of the atomic bomb made him reject defense research. He and his protege, Chris, are working to develop cosmic energy, which they hope will improve the world. When a dictator threatens the security of the U.S.A.'s nearest ally, Amory, the Secretary of Science, tries to persuade Emil that a cosmic bomb is essential to national security. At the White House, Emil tries to convince the Cabinet of the unknown and potentially dangerous effects of cosmic energy. Later, Emil discovers the final part of the cosmic energy formula, but collapses at the realization that he will contribute again to mortal destruction. Meanwhile, unrest grows among peace supporters. Chris becomes disillusioned and resigns from the project. However, as he gives an antiwar speech, he is shot. Emil receives the news of his death while Amory begs, once again, for the cosmic formula. But Emil decides to send the formula to the editor of an international science journal so that all the scientists and national leaders will be responsible for the world's fate.

PRODUCTION REQUIREMENTS

Major Roles. EMIL, scientist (bar): A1 to A♭3. CHRIS, Emil's protege (t): D2 to C4. JULIE, Emil's assistant and Chris' girl friend (s): C3 to D5. MARGO, Emil's wife (m-s): A2 to C5. AMORY (bass-bar): A1 to F3.

Mute Roles. President.

Chorus. Minor roles (students, cabinet ministers, etc.) played by mixed chorus members.

Ballet. Small group, modern dancers.

Orchestra. 2 fls (picc), 2 obs (Eng hrn), 2 cls (bs cl), 2 bsns (cont bsn), 4 hrns, 2 trps, 2 trbs, timp, 2 perc, harp, strings.

Material. FS–P and VS: Highgate Press/Galaxy Music.

REVIEWS

Donal Henahan "Opera: Ward's 'Midnight' Opens Miami Festival," *New York Times* (June 7, 1982), section 3, p. 12

"its operatic potential is real, even if Mr. Ward and his librettist, the late Daniel Lang, do not seem to have any clear notion of how didacticism differs from drama. What they produced is not musical theatre so much as an earnest, well-meaning tract whose rhetoric smacks of advertising copy."

"The score . . . emerged as a restless mixture of traditional idioms. But, at least, it did not sound melodically jagged and emotionally flat in the reigning style of contemporary opera. It actually flapped its wings in lyrically tonal flights now and then, and even flirted with a pop style. Most often, however, it slipped into prosaic declamation and was never able to get far off the ground for long."

Smith "Minutes Till Midnight," *Variety* (June 9, 1982), p. 72

"Pseudo-Broadway tunes take the place of arias and duets . . . while the orchestra provides a minimum of harmonic novelty and instrumental color."

Richard Wargo (1957–   )

THE MUSIC SHOP

Farce. One act (42 minutes). Conservative modern idiom. Vocal lines chromatic, angular at times, not always doubled by accompaniment. Borrows melodies from many musical classics.

Libretto by the composer, based on Anton Chekhov's short story, "Forgot." Can be performed alone or as part of "A Chekhov Trilogy," which includes *Seduction of a Lady* (1985) and *A Visit to the Country* (Anticipated premiere 7.90). Commissioned by Midwest Opera Theater and the Jerome Foundation. Premiere: Midwest Opera Theater, St. Paul, Minn. 10.85 (piano only). Anticipated premiere: Chautauqua Opera, N.Y. 7.90 (full orchestra). Performances: Greater Miami Opera 9.86 (reduced six-piece orchestra); Wolf Trap Opera Company 7.87; Ithaca Opera Association 2.88.

PLOT

Setting: a music shop in czarist Russia, nineteenth century.

Ivan goes to the music shop to purchase a song for his wife to perform at the Prince's wedding. Unfortunately, he cannot remember the title. To jog his memory, the shop-owner and his assistant proceed to sing through every piece of music in their large stock. Calamities mount in the midst of this musical guessing game, when Ivan is plagued by hallucinations of his wife as Brunnhilde, chastising him for his forgetfulness. The series of farcical twists of the plot continue to the end.

PRODUCTION REQUIREMENTS

Major Roles. MASHA (lyr s): C3 to C5. DIMITRI PETROVSKY (bar): F1 to G♯3. IVAN STEPANOVICH (t): B1 to B3.

Supporting Roles. WIFE (m-s): E2 to B♭4.

Minor Roles. Masha, Dimitri and Wife portray minor roles in Ivan's hallucinations.

Orchestra. fl (picc), ob (Eng hrn), cl (E♭ cl), cl (bs cl), bsn, hrn, trp, trb, 2 perc, harp, piano, strings.

Material. FS–P and VS: Richard Wargo, 107 S. Irving Ave., Scranton, Pa. 18505.

REVIEWS

Joseph McLennan "For Kids, a Sweet 'Shop,' " *Washington Post* (July 18, 1987), p. G4

"a funny, unpretentious, tuneful little confection."

"the most spectacular number comes when Dimitri and his assistant, Masha, try to jog Ivan's memory by singing every tune they have in stock: Mozart's 'Allelulia,' 'The Volga Boatman,' . . . and many more. Could a child have a more vivid or wide-ranging introduction to the delights of opera? Could an adult opera-lover find a funnier variation on 'Name That Tune?' "

THE SEDUCTION OF A LADY

Comic opera. Prologue, one act, epilogue (42 minutes). Traditional harmonies and mixed meters. Conversational ensemble work throughout, arias, some a cappella vocal lines. Employs various musical forms: theme and variations, waltz/polka, cadenza, scherzo, etc.

Libretto by the composer, based on "The Seduction" from Neil Simon's THE GOOD DOCTOR, after a story by Anton Chekhov. Can be performed separately or as part one of "A Chekhov Trilogy" (see *The Music Shop*). Professional premiere: Lake George Opera Festival 8.10.85. Performances: The National Institute for Music Theatre 5.11.84 (workshop).

PLOT

Setting: Russia, the late nineteenth century.

Peter offers to give the audience a demonstration of his never-fail technique for seducing married women. He begins the step-by-step process of luring Irena to him, using her unsuspecting husband, Nicky, as his spokesman. When they are introduced, he pointedly ignores Irena, persuading her and Nicky that he is interested in another woman. Over the following weeks, he confides his longing and admiration for this mysterious woman to Nicky in such a way that when Nicky repeats the conversations to his wife, she understands that the words are meant for her. The combined effect of Nicky's blase attitude toward her and Peter's messages encourage Irena's interest in her admirer. Finally, Peter's venture nears success when Irena secretly meets him in the park. However, when she puts her fate in his hands, transferring to him the responsibility for destroying her happy marriage, Peter is unable to complete his plan. Profoundly moved, he resolves never to seduce another married woman—until a rather attractive couple happen to walk by, and the process begins again.

PRODUCTION REQUIREMENTS

Major Roles. PETER SEMYONYCH (t): C2 to B3. NICKY, the Husband (bar): A♭1 to F3. IRENA, the Wife (s): C♯3 to D5.

Orchestra. vln, vcl, piano.

Material. FS–P and VS: Richard Wargo, 107 S. Irving Ave., Scranton, PA 18505.

REVIEWS

Doug De Lisle "Lake George, NY. Tenors to the fore," *Opera* 36 (November 1985), pp. 1314–1315

> "The lines are clever, making this chamber opera a laugh-out-loud affair."

> "The music is mainstream-melodic but never trite, and uses the device of having Peter ask the on-stage ensemble . . . for the musical mood called for by a scene. This allows great diversity without awkward transitions or bumpy patches. *Lady* is not a substantial work, but it is a bon-bon of the first order and a natural for regional companies."

Andrew Porter "Musical Events," *New Yorker* (September 2, 1985)

> "The opera is a light, beguiling piece. . . . Wargo sets words deftly and melodiously. His score is formally dapper and neatly composed; the jokes are trimly made."

Kurt Weill (1900–1950)

LOST IN THE STARS

"Musical tragedy." Two acts, twenty scenes (full evening). Harmonies and rhythmic passages lend an ethnic quality as does heavy use of chorus answering responsorially to leader. Set numbers include operatically conceived solo ariosos.

Libretto by Maxwell Anderson, based on Alan Paton's novel on South Africa, *Cry, the Beloved Country*. Premiere: Music Box Theatre, N.Y. 10.30.49. Performances: New York City Opera 58. Broadway: 74. Film: 74. Recording: MCA (1976).

PLOT

Setting: South Africa, the present (1949).

Stephen Kumalo, a Negro preacher from the village of Ndotsheni and his wife anxiously await word from their son, Absalom, who has gone to Johannesberg to earn money for his education. When Stephen goes to find his son, he learns that when Absalom's girl friend, Irina, became pregnant, Absalom took part in a gang robbery which ended with the murder of a white man. Absalom honestly confessed and was sentenced to death, even though the other gang members lied about their innocence and were freed. Stephen visits his son in prison, but cannot ask him to lie even to save his life. The preacher returns heartbroken to his village and is visited by Alex, the father of the white man Absalom murdered. Though of different races, they find solace in each other's words, united by their shared tragedy.

PRODUCTION REQUIREMENTS

Major Roles. STEPHEN KUMALO, preacher from a small village (bs-bar): G1 to F3. LEADER (t): C2 to A♭3.

Supporting Roles. IRINA, Absalom's girl friend (s): C2 to F4. LINDA, honky-tonk entertainer (m-s): B♭2 to D4. ALEX, Stephen's nephew (bar): B♭1 to C3.

Speaking Roles. ABSALOM, Stephen's son. FATHER OF THE SLAIN MAN.

Chorus. SSAATTBB plays large role with minor solos.

Orchestra. Reed I: fl, cl, alt sax; Reed II: ob, Eng hrn, cl, t sax; Reed III: cl, bs cl, alt sax; trp; perc; harp; strings (0–2–2–1).

Material. FS–P and VS: Rodgers & Hammerstein.

STREET SCENE

Domestic tragedy. Two acts. Operatically conceived musical theater with set pieces: arias, duets, many ensembles. Spoken dialogue as well as recitative. Recitative style employed in several ensembles involving minor characters.

Book by Elmer Rice and lyrics by Langston Hughes. Adelphi Theatre, N.Y. 1.9.47. Performances: New York City Opera 59.

PLOT

Setting: the front stoop of a tenement building in New York, 1940s.

The comings and goings and the conversations of crowded neighbors set the stage for this domestic tragedy. Ladies of many ethnic backgrounds sit on the front stoop and gossip about Anna Maurrant, whose loveless marriage has driven her to an affair with the milkman, Mr. Sankey. Her daughter, Rose, shares a dream with her neighbor, Sam Kaplan, of finding a life for themselves beyond the ghetto. On the other hand, Harry Easter, a married man tries to convince her that he can make her a star. But Rose's concerns are closer to home, as she tries to deal with her parent's problems. Her father, Frank, drunk and obsessed by the local gossip, ultimately catches his wife and her lover, shooting them both and killing them. After her father is taken off to jail, Rose realizes that she cannot escape with Sam, but must leave New York on her own to find a new life for herself and her younger brother, Willie.

PRODUCTION REQUIREMENTS

Major Roles. ROSE MAURRANT (lyr s): C3 to A4. SAM KAPLAN (t): E♭2 to B♭3. MRS. ANNA MAURRANT (dram s): D3 to A4. MR. FRANK MAURRANT (bs-bar): A1 to F3.

Supporting Roles. GRETA FIORENTINO (high s) to D♭5. EMMA JONES (m-s). OLGA OLSON (c). CARL OLSEN (bs). HENRY DAVIS (high bar). DANIEL BUCHANAN (buf ten). LIPPO FIORENTINO (t). HARRY EASTER (lt bar). MAE JONES (singing dancer). DICK MCGANN (singing dancer).

Minor Roles. JENNIE HILDEBRAND (m-s). ABRAHAM KAPLAN (t). GEORGE JONES (bar). WILLIE MAURRANT (boy s). MRS. HILDEBRAND (m-s). TWO NURSEMAIDS (s and m-s). TWO GRADUATES (s and m-s). Children: CHARLIE AND MARY HILDEBRAND, GRACE DAVIS.

Speaking Roles. SHIRLEY KAPLAN. STEVE SANKEY. VINCENT JONES. DR. WILSON, OFFICER MURPHY. CITY MARSHALL. FRED CULLEN.

Chorus. Minor roles sing ensemble and chorus parts.

Ballet. Couple sings and dances one number.

Orchestra. fl, ob, 2 cls, bs cl, bsn, 2 hrns, 2 trps, 2 trbs, harp, piano, perc, strings.

Material. FS–P and VS: Chappell/Intersong Music Group—USA.

Larry Weiner

CHIPITA RODRIGUEZ

Premiere: Corpus Christi Symphony, Tex. 4.3.82.

Hugo Weisgall (1912–)

JENNY, OR THE HUNDRED NIGHTS

A contemporized fable. One act, three scenes (85 minutes). Chromatic vocal lines and harmonies, complex rhythmic structures. Opens with brief orchestral interlude. Through-composed with arias, recitative-like sections, and complex ensembles.

Libretto by John Hollander, based on a noh play translated by Yukio Mishima. Commissioned by the Juilliard School, New York. Premiere: Juillard American Opera Center, New York 4.22.76. Recording: (Tape) American Music Center.

PLOT

Setting: the Albert Memorial in Kensington Gardens, London, 1899.

While scavenging for discarded items in a park, the old hag, Jenny, encounters George, a photographer, who wants to photograph lovers in the park but doesn't feel that Jenny fits in. This surprises her, since her 99 years have taught her that to live is to endure: beauty outlives youth, and everyone who recognizes her beauty dies when they tell her of it. Intrigued, the photographer asks about her youth. She tells him that 80 years before, she promised a suitor that if he courted her for one hundred nights, she would be his. While Jenny describes the hundredth night, George enters into the story, entranced by the young woman. When he begins to tell her of her beauty, Jenny interrupts, warning that he will die. Returning to his senses, he reminds himself that Jenny is an old hag. Nonetheless, he eventually succumbs to the image in his mind and tells her of her beauty. As he dies, he prophesies that they will meet in a hundred years. Exhausted, Jenny bemoans the fact that she must wait another century.

PRODUCTION REQUIREMENTS

Major Roles. JENNY (s): C3 to C4. GEORGE, young man and photographer (bar): $A^{\flat}1$ to A3.

Supporting Roles. WOMAN C or 3 (col s): $G^{\sharp}3$ to $F^{\sharp}5$. SOLO TENOR (t): D2 to A3.

Minor Roles. WOMEN A AND B, or 1 and 2 (s,m-s). MEN A,B,C or 1,2,3 (bar,bar,t). TWO BOBBIES (t,bs-bar).

Chorus. SATB, TTB men's chorus also.

Orchestra. 6 fls, 4 obs, 5 cls, 3 bsns, 4 hrns, 4 trps, 4 trbs, tuba, timp, perc, harp, strings, wind machine.

Material. FS–P and VS: Theodore Presser. VS: American Music Center.

REVIEWS

Andrew Porter "Earthbound," *New Yorker* (May 10, 1976), pp. 131–133

> "I heard lots of notes; much would-be lyrical song along chromatic phrases of wandering, unmemorable line; declamation that proceeded with unnatural slowness, in which short English syllables were unhappily prolonged; dance metres . . . that were lively enough in themselves but were clad in harmonies and melodies of hessian. Things perked up when two London bobbies came on."

Alan Rich "Shadow Play," *New York* (May 10, 1976), p. 79

> "Weisgall's musical style is not immediately ingratiating to the operatic crowd. Alban Berg is the composer his music brings first to mind, especially Berg's haunting way of compounding harmonic densities. What appeals in Weisgall's music is, first of all, that he works in his chosen idiom with great skill, and also, that he has the gift . . . of making voices serve drama."

> "It is an atmosphere piece, but it is built on beautifully realized characters whom Weisgall's music fleshes out with a sweeping lyricism and a skillfully managed leavening of wit. I think the opera is a work of considerable emotional power."

NINE RIVERS FROM JORDAN

Surreal, allegorical drama. Prologue and three acts, eight scenes (full evening). Atonal, through-composed with clear arias, duets, quartets and ensembles. Chromatic, disjunct vocal lines aided by accompaniment.

Libretto by Denis Johnston, based on Johnston's novel. Premiere: New York City Opera 10.9.68.

PLOT

Setting: a battlefield in Italy during World War II.

It is May 1945; World War II has just ended. The American Sergeant, Abe Goldberg, and a grave-identification team come upon a dirty figure sitting on the grave of "Hanwell, D. R." Abe recognizes the figure as Don Hanwell, a British soldier and comrade. Is Don alive or in the grave? The four-member team moves off, while Abe experiences Don's spiritual journey from cynicism to commitment, through a series of flashbacks. At the Dead Sea, the advice of a Salt Woman (who represents the biblical Lot's wife) causes him to renounce his weapons. On Christmas Eve, Don joins Copperhead Kelly and a group of boisterous soldiers with his German prisoner, Otto Suder. Don callously allows Suder to escape, since he has no gun to prevent it. In Rome, Michelangelo's Pieta comes to life to chastise Don for his cynical ways and false sense of right and wrong. The Pieta leads Don to the gates of a concentration camp, Todenwald, where Suder is the guard. Confronted by the horrors of the camp, Don is convinced that justice will be served only through the trial and death of Suder. A surreal mock trial takes place, but Suder escapes. This time, Don is blamed because he had let the prisoner, Suder, go once before. Armed with a grenade, Don finally finds Suder. Suder is killed when Don's grenade goes off in his hands. But a part of Don also dies, thus the grave from the Prologue is marked with Don's name. When he shouts to heaven for understanding, a vision of Copperhead Kelly appears, in the guise of Judas. Don sits atop the grave awaiting a sign of his true release—a dove. The dove arrives as part of some Italian graffiti read by the grave-identification team on a nearby wall. "Sia sacra agli Italiani, la via *dove* passarano i fanti," ("Let Italians hold sacred this road where their infantry passed.") The Italian word "dove" symbolically offers that release because a "dove" in English symbolizes peace.

PRODUCTION REQUIREMENTS

Major Roles. DON HANWELL (bar): $B^{\flat}1$ to G3 (A3 ossia). ABE GOLDBERG (bar): $F^{\#}1$ to F3. SALT WOMAN, PIETA, WOMAN (s): $A^{\flat}2$ to $B^{\flat}4$.

Supporting Roles. COPPERHEAD KELLY, an Irishman (high bar/t): C2 to A3. OTTO SUDER, a soldier in the Afrika Korps (t): $D^{b}2$ to B3. LIEUTENANT JEAN L'AIGLON (t): D2 to B3. MAJOR MARK LYON (t): $D^{b}2$ to B3. CAPTAIN FATHER MATTEO ANGELINO (bar): $B^{b}1$ to G3. CAPTAIN REVEREND LUCIUS BULL (bs): F1 to E3.

Minor Roles. ANDREW, the Highlander/Andy (t). TOSSER, the tea-maker (t). PETE, the Sergeant (bar). THE DEAD MAN (t). PHIL, the Signalman (t/bar). MUEZZIN (t). Several other small baritone roles can be played by chorus members.

Chorus. Large men's, women's and mixed.

Orchestra. 2 fls (picc), 2 obs (Eng hrn), 2 B^{b} cls (bs cl), 2 bsns (cont bsn), 4 hrns, 3 trps, 3 trbs, tuba, 6 perc/timp, piano (cel), harp, strings.

Material. FS–P and VS: Theodore Presser.

REVIEWS

Irving Kolodin "Talvela and Ghiaurov; Weisgall's 'Nine Rivers,' " *Saturday Review* (October 26, 1968), p. 57

> "The mixture of symbolism and soldier talk in the libretto does not have a true parallel in Weisgall's setting. . . . There was, most regrettably, rarely a fusion of values to define an underlying attitude or relate the auditor's emotions to what he was watching and hearing."

Frank M. Merkling, "New York," *Opera News* (November 23, 1968), p. 22

> "Weisgall writes cerebral rather than theatrical music. What interests him is the counterpoint and development of themes which . . . steer clear of sentimental associations. . . . As a result, his new opera often had the effect of a cantata or oratorio, which suited much of the libretto."

> "This whole scherzo scene, in fact, made one wonder if Hugo Weisgall isn't repressing a real gift as a comic composer."

Winthrop Sargeant "Muddy Water," *New Yorker* (October 19, 1968), p. 218

> "the libretto, though its philosophy is ambiguous and its symbolism often imcomprehensible, has a certain amount of theatrical flair."

"This libretto . . . was written in five different languages, but with Mr. Weisgall's music clouding every phrase, it might as well have been in Bantu."

"The high points of the evening, musically, were 'Lili Marlene,' which was sung over a radio set, and Mr. Weisgall's own setting of the 'Song of the Afrika Korps,' which was, surprisingly, not atonal at all, and quite likeable."

WILL YOU MARRY ME?

Romantic drama. One act (23 minutes). Through-composed, conversational style, disjunct vocal lines, nontraditional harmonies.

Libretto by Charles Kondek based on the play, "A Marriage Has Been Arranged," by Alfred Sutro. Intended to combined with "The Stronger" (1952) and "Purgatory" (1961) to form a triptich entitled "Martinis, Murder and a Marriage." Premiere: Opera Ensemble of New York 3.8.89.

PLOT

Setting: Long Island, early 1920s.

A man and a woman self-consciously meet during a party, knowing that her parents expect them to become engaged. He blatantly flaunts his fortune and his boorish manner. She explains that her only love was a poor lieutenant and that she could never love a man who would make such a crude proposal. He is moved by her honesty and offers to help the lieutenant become rich. Although she refuses the offer, her opinion of him begins to change. When he asks for her recommendation of whom he can marry, she describes a "friend" who is not attractive, but is not flighty; someone who once loved deeply but was betrayed by her lover. Before they go back to the party, they propose to each other and happily accept.

PRODUCTION REQUIREMENTS

Major Roles. She (s): D♭3 to C5. He (bar): B♭1 to G3.

Orchestra. cl in B♭ (E♭ cl, sop sax), cl in B♭ (bs cl, alt sax), bsn, hrn, trp in C, piano, perc, strings (2–1–1–1).

Material. FS–P and VS: Theodore Presser.

REVIEWS

Andrew Porter "Musical Events: Tragical-Comical-Historical-Pastoral," *New Yorker* (April 17, 1989), pp. 117–119

"Weisgall is an urbane, sensitive, and thorough composer. . . . Offstage in 'Will You marry Me?' a dance is in progress; popular dance forms, cunningly and expressively distorted, underpin the couple's conversation. Both of these mordant, intelligent comedies ['The Stronger' was also performed] depend on attention at once to words and music."

" 'Will You marry Me?' demands little in the way of staging. . . . The piece lives not in action but in the lively interplay of two personalities, their lines, and the instrumental lines."

Barrymore Laurence Sherer "New York City," *Opera News* (May 1989), pp. 45–46

"It's a very New York kind of work, requiring a consistency of style poised between cynicism and genuine emotion—exactly what is received."

"The music is evocative and canny. . . . his handling of text (and ensuring audibility for crucial passages through thinned orchestration) is exemplary. What a pleasure it is to hear a master at work! The sly use of the saxaphone and dance rhythms intimated what was going on at the party inside the hotel while also subtly sketching the world in which these two are condemned to live."

Dan Welcher (1948–   )

DELLA'S GIFT

Drama. Prologue and two acts (75 minutes). A conservative modern work with romantic lyricism. Orchestra plays important role especially in instrumental prologue, pantomimed by actors. Scenes rather than set numbers form structure; vocal lines approximate speech accents and rhythms.

Libretto by Paul Woodruff, based on O. Henry's short story "The Gifts of the Magi." Premiere: Univ. of Texas Opera Theatre, Austin, Texas 2.26.87. Recording: tape available through Theodore Presser.

PLOT

Setting: New York City at Christmas time, 1905.

Jim and Della Young, a poor young couple, cannot afford to buy each other gifts for the coming holiday. They can't even afford to pay rent to their landlord, Mrs. Purdy, or to reimburse the butcher, Mr. McCool, for their modest holiday meal. Their most valuable possessions are Jim's gold pocket-watch and Della's beautifully cascading hair. Even rich people, such as Sheba and Solomon, envy these. After much soul-searching, Della decides to cut off and sell her hair to a wigmaker. Thus, she earns enough money to buy a gold chain for Jim's watch. Jim, in the meantime, has sold the watch to a jeweler in order to afford a set of tortoise shell combs for Della's lovely hair. As the gifts are exchanged, the sad irony is revealed, but Jim and Della realize that their most valued possession is the love they share for each other. Having found the true spirit of Christmas, Della and Jim take to the streets to embrace and sing carols as they pass Sheba and Solomon (the jaded new owners of a gold watch and a fanciful wig).

PRODUCTION REQUIREMENTS

Major Roles. DELLA YOUNG (s): C3 to C5 (A♭4 ossia). JIM YOUNG (bar): A1 to G3 (falsetto: C3 to A3).

Supporting Roles. MRS. PURDY, the landlady (m-s): C3 to G4; MADAME SOPHRONIE, owner of a coiffure shop (m-s): C3 to E4; QUEEN OF SHEBA, a rich lady (m-s): A2 to F4.* MR. MCCOOL, the butcher (t): G2 to A3; THE JEWELER (t): E♭2 to G♯3; KING SOLOMON, a rich man (t): E2 to G3.*

*The above roles can be combined and played by one m-s and one t.

Orchestra. fl, ob, 2 cls, bsn, 2 hrns, 2 trps, trb, perc, piano, harp, strings (4–4–3–2–1 min).

Material. FS–P, VS and tape: Theodore Presser.

REVIEWS

John Ardoin " 'Della's Gift' is charming fun," *Dallas Morning News* (March 3, 1987), pp. 5C–6C

"The music is disarming in its charm and eminently singable. And as theatre, *Della's Gift* is uncomplicated and affecting."

Welcher "has constructed a musical aura that evokes a bygone American era in a gentle, loving way . . . Turn-of-the-century tunes . . . are transformed in a highly personal way and cleverly scored to recall the theatre bands and popular musical idioms of the day. Welcher has also included several musical puns that are guaranteed to bring a smile to the face of discerning listeners."

Jerry Young " 'Hin und Zuruck' retains humor; 'Della's' is a gift." *Austin American-Statesman* (February 28, 1987), p. 13

"The music does what an opera should. It conveys emotions, supports the action and gives the characters some charming music to sing."

"familiar tunes . . . become essential to the story and serve to help the audience overcome making *Della's Gift* 'modern opera anxiety.' In trade-off, one walks away humming those melodies rather than Welcher's."

Claude White (1949–)

LOVE, DEATH, AND HIGH NOTES

Comedy. One act, one scene (36 minutes). Conservative twentieth-century idiom. Vocal parts not difficult. One solo scene for each character with duets and quartets.

Libretto by Linda Brovsky. Commissioned by the Opera Theatre of St. Louis. Premiere: Parkway Central Senior High School, St. Louis, Mo. 10.1.88.

PLOT

Setting: a rehearsal stage, the present.

The young singers, Paula and David, cast in the roles of "Maria" and "Carlo," join Lynn, the stage director, Jeffrey, the set designer, and the Opera Coach to rehearse a new opera. They are thrilled to find that the final act of the score has just arrived. The reading progresses quite smoothly under Lynn's direction, although Jeffrey is distraught at the scene changes called for in this newly written act. Suddenly, all comes to a halt when the final page is discovered missing. David and Paula offer their own improvised conclusions, drawing upon standard opera cliches. Finally, the last page arrives and the rehearsal is completed.

PRODUCTION REQUIREMENTS

Major Roles. PAULA, cast in the role of "Maria" (s): $C^{\#}3$ to $B^{b}4$. LYNN, the stage director (m-s): $B^{b}2$ to F4. DAVID, cast in the role of "Carlo" (t): C2 to $B^{b}3$. JEFFREY, set and lighting designer (bar): $A^{b}1$ to E3.

Speaking Roles. OPERA COACH (also serves as accompanist at piano).

Minor Roles. FEDERAL EXPRESS MESSENGER (non-singing walk-on role for local celebrity: principal, teacher, etc.).

Orchestra. piano.

Material. VS: contact Opera Theatre of Saint Louis.

REVIEWS

James Wierzbicki "One-Act Performance Bringing Opera To Schools," *St. Louis Post Dispatch* (October 3, 1988), p. 6D

> "the older kids—and also their parents—paid close attention, not because they were forced to but because, one presumes, what was happening on stage struck them as well worth their while."

> "its eclectic musical elements are clearly illustrative of a good many bits of operatic information. The libretto does not blatantly declare that the opening dialogue mimics the brightly conversational first act of Puccini's 'La Boheme,' . . . that the tenor's exaggerated 'death aria' is a takeoff on the Baroque *opera seria* style or that the soprano's proposed finale parodies the 'mad scene' from Donizetti's 'Lucia di Lammermoor.' But that is indeed what happens."

Jack Eric Williams

MRS. FARMER'S DAUGHTER

Premiere: Pepsico Summerfare, Purchase, N.Y. 7.83. Revised performances: American Music Theatre Festival 84.

Material. Jack Eric Williams, 162 W. 54th St., New York, NY 10019.

Meredith Willson (1902–   )

THE MUSIC MAN

Romantic comedy. Two acts, sixteen scenes (full evening). Musical theater with set numbers in a spoken play. Orchestral overture, several interludes and dance sections. Large role for chorus with ensembles juxtaposing one song over another. Rhythmic speech frequently employed by chorus and Harold Hill.

Lyrics and book by the composer. Story by the composer and Franklin Lacey. Premiere: Majestic Theatre, New York 12.19.57. Recording: Capital W-990; SW-990 (S).

PLOT

Setting: River City, Iowa, 1912.

On the Fourth of July, Harold Hill, the salesman who always gets his sale, descends on River City, convincing the townsfolk to spend their money to create a marching band for their children, with Harold himself as director. Only Marian, the local librarian and piano teacher, is skeptical. But as she gets to know him, even Marian is won over by his charm. When the time comes to take the money and skip town, Marian convinces Harold to stay. At the moment of truth, the town's children can barely play a note, but the parents burst with pride to see them trying, as Harold and Marian lead them through the streets in a triumphal parade.

PRODUCTION REQUIREMENTS

Major Roles. HAROLD HILL, sly salesman turned music director (bar): A♭1 to F3. MARIAN PAROO, librarian (s): G2 to F♯4 (A♭4 ossia).

Supporting Roles. MRS. PAROO, Marian's mother (m-s): A♭2 to E♭4. EULALIE MACKECKNIE SHINN, the Mayor's wife (m-s): E3 to E4. WINTHROP PAROO, Marian's brother (boy s): C3 to E4. MARCELLUS WASHBURN (t): G2 to A3.

Minor Roles. BARBERSHOP QUARTET: JACEY SQUIRES (t I), EWART DUNLOP (t II), OLIVER HIX (bar), OLIN BRITT (bs). ALMA HIX, MAUD DUNLOP, MRS. SQUIRES, ETHEL TOFFELMIER (all comfortable female range). AMARYLLIS, Marian's piano student (girl s).

Speaking Roles. MAYOR SHINN.

Chorus. SATB and divisi (fairly large forces).

Ballet. Several orchestrated dance sections.

Orchestra. Reed I: fl, picc; Reed II: B♭ cl, ob, Eng hrn; Reed III: B♭ cl, E♭ cl, s sax; Reed IV: B♭ cl, fl, bs cl; Reed V: bs sax, B♭ cl, bsn; trp I & II; trb I; trb II; trb III; vlns ABC; vcl; bs; perc; piano–conductor.

Material. FS–P and VS: Music Theatre International.

Charles Wuorinen

THE W. OF BABYLON

"Baroque burlesque." Two acts. Libretto by R. C. Bruce. Premiere: San Francisco Symphony's New and Unusual Music Series 1.20.89 (concert version).

Eugene Zador (1894–1977)

YEHU

"A Christmas legend." One act, one scene (30 minutes). Through-composed in conservative modern idiom. Vocal writing in lyrical arioso, recitative style, some sprechstimme required.

Libretto by Anna Egyud, based on a Christmas legend. Premiere: Los Angeles Bureau of Music, Calif. 12.21.74.

PLOT

Setting: Bethlehem, the first Christmas.

When Rachel hears of King Herod's call for a census to be taken, she is overjoyed because her son, Yehu, a soldier in Herod's army, will have to return home to Bethlehem. Her husband, Simon, mocks her happiness in disbelief, while their mute niece helps prepare for Yehu's homecoming. A knock at the door reveals a poor young couple, expecting a child, who seek lodging for the night. Rachel and Simon can offer only the warmth and comfort of their stable. As Simon shows the weary travelers to their quarters, Sharah, the neighborhood gossip visits Rachel, exclaiming that Herod's soldiers are digging a large communal grave—Herod has ordered that all infants of Bethlehem should be murdered. Yehu finally arrives: drunk, toughened by war, plagued with leprosy and in a belligerent state. He shuns the open arms of his cousin, Zura, and his mother, Rachel. Sharah bursts in to report that child has just been born in Simon and Rachel's stable. But Rachel's cries of protest don't stop Yehu from leaving the house, armed to do his duty and slay the newborn. But Yehu returns transfixed—a new man. He could not do the evil deed, and, furthermore, would gladly give his life in place of the child's. As he lifts his cup to pour wine on his leperous body, Yehu realizes that his affliction has vanished. With this miracle, Yehu can be touched; he can love again. To everyone's amazement, the beautiful, yet silent Zura sings forth "Hosanna," and a prayer for peace and love. All join her hymn of praise.

PRODUCTION REQUIREMENTS

Major Roles. Yehu, Herod's soldier (t): D2 to B♭3 [ossia B♭1]. Rachel, Yehu's mother (a): G♯2 to G4.

Supporting Roles. Simon, Yehu's father (bs): F1 to F3. Sharah, the neighbor (s): C♯3 to A4.

Minor Roles. Zura, the mute girl (s): G3 to B♭4. The Herald (bar).

Chorus. SSA (offstage or in orchestra pit).

Orchestra. piano, drums.

Material. FS–P and VS: C. Fischer, New York and American Music Center.

REVIEWS

Henry Reese "Yehu by Eugene Zador," *The Opera Journal* (1975), 8(2):19–20

"Anna Egyud's libretto has the brilliance of simplicity. . . . It is a straightforward, unpretentious libretto, not distinguished for lyricism, but thoroughly dramatic."

"Zador's music supports, elevates, and intensifies it, which is what operatic music should do. . . . it is a relief to hear Zador's music sung in an extension of human speech. It could well sing more — longer than its present half hour."

Willard Hyatt "Los Angeles," *Music Journal* (February 1975), 33(2):47

"the work is marked by a rapidly changing lyric line. One minute it is dissonant and angular, the next passionate with mounting emotional intensity to fit the excitement and dramatic content of the libretto. Here was a skillful blending of atmosphere and tonal color."

PUBLISHERS AND OTHER SOURCES

American Composer's Alliance
c/o American Composers Edition, Inc.
170 W. 74 St.
New York, NY 10023
(212) 362-8900

American Music Center
Suite 1001
30 W. 26th St.
New York, NY 10010-2011
(212) 366-5260

Associated Music Publishers, Inc.
(Division of G. Schirmer)
24 E. 22 St.
New York, NY 10010
(212) 254-2100
(Distributed exclusively by Hal Leonard)

Belwin-Mills Publishing Corp.
15800 N.W. 48 Ave.
Miami, FL 33014
(305) 620-1500 (rental only)
(See Theodore Presser Co.)

Boosey & Hawkes, Inc.
24 W. 57 St.
New York, NY 10019
(212) 757-3332

Bote & Bock, Berlin
(See Associated Music Publishers and Hal Leonard)

Carl Fischer, Inc.
62 Cooper Square
New York, NY 10003
(212) 777-0900

C. F. Peters
373 Park Ave. S
New York, NY 10016
(212) 868-4147

Chappell/Intersong Music Group — USA
810 Seventh Ave.
New York, NY 10019
(212) 399-6910
(Distributed by Hal Leonard)

Cherry Lane Music Co., Inc.
110 Midland Ave.
Port Chester, NY 10573
(914) 937-8601

E. C. Kerby, Ltd.
198 Davenport Rd.
Toronto 5, Ontario
Canada

E. C. Schirmer Music Co.
138 Ipswich St.
Boston, MA 02215
(617) 236-1935

European American Music Distributors Corp.
P.O. Box 850
Valley Forge, PA 19482
(215) 648-0506

Frank Music Corp.
39 W. 54th St.
New York, NY
(212) 246-5757

Galaxy Music Corp.
131 W. 86 St.
New York, NY 10024
(212) 874-2100

G. Schirmer Rental Department
P.O. Box 572
Chester, NY 10918
(914) 469-2271

Hal Leonard Publishing Corp.
P.O. Box 13819, 8112 W. Bluemound Rd.
Milwaukee, WI 53213
(414) 774-3630

Jerona Music Corp.
81 Trinity Pl.
Hackensack, NJ 07601-4299
(201) 488-0550

MCA Music
(See Hal Leonard Publishing Corp.; rental: see Theodore Presser Co.)

Music Associates of America
224 King St.
Englewood, NJ 07631
(201) 569-9527

Music Theatre International
545 8th Ave.
New York, NY 10018
(212) 868-6668

Novello & Co., England
(See Theodore Presser Co.)

Oxford University Press
200 Madison Ave.
New York, NY 10016
(212) 679-7300

Peer-Southern Organization
1740 Broadway
New York, NY 10019
(212) 265-3910

Revelation Music Publishing and Rilting Music, Inc.
Suite 2110
1270 Avenue of the Americas
New York, NY 10020

The Rodgers & Hammerstein Theatre Library
598 Madison Ave.
New York, NY 10022
(212) 486-0643

Seesaw Music Corp.
2067 Broadway
New York, NY 10023
(212) 874-1200

Shawnee Press Inc.
(Subsidiary of Waring Enterprises, Inc.)
Waring Dr.
Delaware Gap, PA 18327
(717) 476-0550

Southern Music Publishing
(See Peer-Southern Organization)

Tams-Witmark Music Library
560 Lexington Ave.
New York, NY 10022
(212) 688-2525

Theodore Presser Co.
Presser Pl.
Bryn Mawr, PA 19010
(215) 525-3636

William Grant Still Music
c/o Judith Anne Headlee
Suite 422
22 San Francisco St.
Flagstaff, AZ 86001-5737
(602) 526-9355

TITLE INDEX

DURATION INDEX FOR OPERAS UNDER 90 MINUTES

PUBLISHERS INDEX